# CITIZEN SCIENCE FOR COASTAL AND MARINE CONSERVATION

In recent years, citizen science has emerged as a powerful new approach to enable the general public, students, and volunteers to become involved in scientific research. A prime example is in biodiversity conservation, where data collection and monitoring can be greatly enhanced through citizen participation. This is the first book to provide much needed guidance and case studies from coastal and marine conservation.

The novelty and rapid expansion of the field has created a demand for the discussion of key issues and the development of best practices. This book demonstrates the utility and feasibility, as well as limitations, of using coastal and marine citizen science for conservation, by providing critical considerations (i.e. which questions and systems are best suited for citizen science) and presenting recommendations for best practices for successful coastal and marine citizen science projects.

A range of case studies, for example, on monitoring seabird populations, invasive species, plastics pollution, and the impacts of climate change, from different parts of the world, is included. Also included are discussions on engaging youth, indigenous communities, and divers and snorkelers as citizen scientists, as well as best practices on communication within citizen science, building trust with stakeholders, and informing marine policy as part of this exciting and empowering way of improving coastal and marine conservation.

**John A. Cigliano** is Professor of Biology and Director of Environmental Conservation in the Department of Biological Sciences, Cedar Crest College, Allentown, Pennsylvania, USA; adjunct faculty at the Schoodic Institute at Acadia National Park, Winter Harbor, Maine, USA; and an Earthwatch Institute Principal Investigator. He collaborates with citizen scientists to study the effects of ocean acidification and warming on temperate rocky-intertidal organisms and communities. John is currently the Past President of the Marine Section, the Vice President of the Participatory and Citizen Science Working Group, both of the Society for Conservation Biology, and a founding member of the Citizen Science Association.

**Heidi L. Ballard** is Associate Professor of Environmental Science Education and Faculty Director of the Center for Community and Citizen Science at the University of California, Davis, USA. She leads research on what and how adults and youth learn about science, the environment, and their communities through participation in citizen science and community science. She is on the Editorial Board of *Citizen Science: Theory and Practice*, and a member of several professional societies' working groups focused on citizen science. She has collaborated with numerous citizen science and community science projects internationally to help improve design and evaluation of their programs.

## Earthscan Oceans

For further details please visit the series page on the Routledge website: www.routledge.com/books/series/ECOCE

**Citizen Science for Coastal and Marine Conservation**
*Edited by John A. Cigliano and Heidi L. Ballard*

**Marine and Coastal Resource Management**
Principles and Practice
*Edited by David R. Green and Jeffrey Payne*

**Marine Transboundary Conservation and Protected Areas**
*Edited by Peter Mackelworth*

**Transboundary Marine Spatial Planning and International Law**
*Edited by S.M. Daud Hassan, Tuomas Kuokkanen, Niko Soininen*

**Marine Biodiversity, Climatic Variability and Global Change**
*By Grégory Beaugrand*

**Marine Biodiversity Conservation**
A Practical Approach
*By Keith Hiscock*

**The Great Barrier Reef**
An Environmental History
*By Ben Daley*

# CITIZEN SCIENCE FOR COASTAL AND MARINE CONSERVATION

*Edited by John A. Cigliano and Heidi L. Ballard*

LONDON AND NEW YORK

from Routledge

First published 2018
by Routledge
2 Park Square, Milton Park, Abingdon, Oxon OX14 4RN

and by Routledge
711 Third Avenue, New York, NY 10017

*Routledge is an imprint of the Taylor & Francis Group, an informa business*

*British Library Cataloguing-in-Publication Data*
A catalogue record for this book is available from the British Library

*Library of Congress Cataloging-in-Publication Data*
Names: Cigliano, John A., editor. | Ballard, Heidi L., editor.
Title: Citizen science for coastal and marine conservation / edited by John
    A. Cigliano and Heidi L. Ballard.
Description: Abingdon, Oxon : Routledge, 2017. | Series: Earthscan oceans |
    Includes bibliographical references and index.
Identifiers: LCCN 2017021352 | ISBN 9781138193192 (hardback) |
    ISBN 9781138193222 (pbk.) | ISBN 9781315638966 (ebook)
Subjects: LCSH: Coastal ecology—Citizen participation. | Marine resources
    conservation—Citizen participation. | Marine habitat conservation—
    Citizen participation. | Science—Social aspects.
Classification: LCC QH541.5.C65 C48 2017 | DDC 577.5/1—dc23
LC record available at https://lccn.loc.gov/2017021352

ISBN: 978-1-138-19319-2 (hbk)
ISBN: 978-1-138-19322-2 (pbk)
ISBN: 978-1-315-63896-6 (ebk)

Typeset in Bembo
by Apex CoVantage, LLC

# CONTENTS

# CONTRIBUTORS

**Duncan Bailey** is the Systems Developer at MDI Biological Laboratory. In this capacity he builds and manages websites, creates data management systems, and consults with departments on technology needs. He is the creator of Anecdata.org and project lead on the crowdsourcing initiative called "Eelgrass in Maine."

**Heidi L. Ballard** is an Associate Professor of Environmental Science Education in the School of Education, and founding Faculty Director of the Center for Community and Citizen Science, at University of California, Davis, USA. She has a background in conservation biology, natural resource social sciences, and science education, and studies how and what people learn through participation in citizen science and other participatory approaches to environmental science.

**Giacomo Bernardi** is a Professor of Ecology and Evolutionary Biology at the University of California, Santa Cruz. He specializes in the ecology and genomics of temperate and tropical reef fishes, with a particular emphasis on fishes that lack a pelagic larval stage.

**Hillary K. Burgess** is the Science Coordinator for COASST, responsible for project development, participant training, and data management and delivery to users. She has spent the better part of a decade managing and studying citizen science in conservation contexts, including graduate work on home gardens as pollinator habitat. Her current focus is on furthering scientific applications of citizen science while facilitating meaningful experiences for participants.

**John A. Cigliano** is Professor of Biology and Director of Environmental Conservation at Cedar Crest College in Pennsylvania, USA; adjunct faculty at Schoodic Institute at Acadia National Park, Maine, USA; and an Earthwatch Institute Principal

Investigator. He has a background in behavioral ecology, marine conservation ecology, and marine conservation education. His current research interests include the effects of ocean acidification and warming on temperate rocky intertidal organisms and communities. John has involved citizen scientists in all his research projects since the late 1990s.

**Jenny A. Cousins** is Regional Manager for East Africa at WWF in Surrey, UK. She has a background in conservation science, social science, and citizen science. She leads on conservation programs in the Mau Mara Serengeti landscape. Previously she was Earthwatch Institute's (Europe) Senior Research Manager leading on project development and delivery.

**Nicole L. Crane** is a Professor in the Biology Department at Cabrillo College in Aptos, California, and Senior Conservation Scientist with the Oceanic Society. Crane has more than 20 years of experience working with communities and conducting ecological assessments of reefs. She is dedicated to linking rigorous science with cultural knowledge and community leadership in conservation. Her background includes developing and implementing science education programs, with a focus on enhancing diversity in the sciences.

**Jane E. Disney** is a Senior Staff Scientist and Director of the Community Environmental Health Laboratory at MDI Biological Laboratory. She works with community members on a number of research and education projects that span environmental and public health boundaries. In addition, she leads eelgrass restoration research and restoration efforts in Maine. She is co-developer of the citizen science online data portal, Anecdata.org, which provides data management and sharing capabilities for citizen science projects throughout the world.

**Jane Dolliver** served as a Program Assistant, then Program Coordinator for COASST from 2002 to 2015. She is currently a graduate student in the Department of Fisheries and Wildlife at Oregon State University.

**Anna Farrell** is the Program Coordinator at the Community Environmental Health Laboratory at MDI Biological Laboratory. She served two terms of service as an AmeriCorps Environmental Steward at the laboratory prior to settling into her current position. She plans and coordinates all research and restoration efforts with citizen scientists, as well as follow-up monitoring and reporting.

**Emma L. Fox** is a PhD student in the Ecology and Environmental Science Program at the University of Maine in Orono. Her work as an AmeriCorps Environmental Educator with the Maine Conservation Corps brought her to the MDI Biological Laboratory to work with citizen scientists and community volunteers on eelgrass habitat restoration in Frenchman Bay. While Emma's background is in coastal ecology, she now studies decision-making around natural resource use.

**Amy Freitag** has a passion for figuring out how knowledge is created and how different forms of knowledge production might bring innovation to environmental management. During her time in California, she worked with the citizen science groups of the Central Coast to learn from their experiences informing management. Learn more about her at www.amyfreitag.org.

**Erika Frost** is the Participant Engagement Manager for COASST, responsible for the recruitment and retention of coastal citizens and undergraduate interns. Her background is in wildlife biology and communications, and she has spent the past nine years engaging people of all ages in science through positions with zoos, aquariums, environmental non-profits, and university programs.

**Magdalena Gatta** is a Marine Biologist working within the citizen science program *Científicos de la Basura* in Coquimbo, Chile. She is interested in marine science education and develops tools (for example the videogame *Acuáticos.org*) to bring schoolchildren closer to the marine environment.

**Todd Hass** is the Executive Liaison for Washington State's Puget Sound Partnership, where he links people and leverages resources that unite and accelerate ecosystem recovery efforts across the Salish Sea. He is also an Affiliate Curator of Ornithology at the Burke Museum and Affiliate Assistant Professor in the School of Marine and Environmental Affairs at the University of Washington.

**Edward J. Hind-Ozan** is a Research Associate in the Sustainable Places Research Institute at Cardiff University, UK. He has a strong interest in participatory research approaches, with the main body of his work focusing on facilitating the inclusion of stakeholder knowledge in fisheries science and management. He is currently trialing approaches where citizen scientists lead interviews aimed at discovering local climate change adaptation strategies.

**Sunwook (Sunny) Hong** is a Research Scientist and President of Our Sea of East Asia Network (OSEAN), which is a non-profit organization in South Korea dedicated to research, education, policy development, and international cooperation to protect the marine environment from marine debris. OSEAN is a network hub for cooperation of scientists, governments, citizens, and private sectors in Asia Pacific region. She had served as a country coordinator of International Coastal Cleanup for 13 years since 2002.

**Daniela Honorato** is a Marine Biologist with a Diploma in Natural Resources Management. Her main interests focus on the environmental sustainability and rational use of marine/coastal ecosystems, and she has always believed that environmental and scientific education is a critical instrument to achieve this goal. She is currently working in the citizen science program *Científicos de la Basura*, coordinating the Chilean-German project "Following the Pathways of Plastic Litter" in Chile.

**Mark Huxham** is Professor of Research and Teaching in Environmental Biology at Edinburgh Napier University. He works on coastal ecology and conservation with a particular interest in mangrove ecosystems. He is a founding Director of the Association for Coastal Ecosystem Services and helps to run Mikoko Pamoja, the world's first community-based mangrove conservation project to be funded through the sale of carbon credits.

**Kieran Hyder** is a Fisheries Scientist at the Centre for Environment, Fisheries and Aquaculture Science (Cefas) in the UK. His work focuses on social, economic, and biological impacts of recreational fisheries and, as part of the UK government, provides evidence and advice for policy making and marine management. He is interested in how citizen science can be used to support marine policy and management, including the opportunities provided by new technologies to support the collection, collation, and analysis of data.

**Jenna R. Jambeck** is an Associate Professor of Environmental Engineering in the College of Engineering at the University of Georgia, USA. She has a background in solid waste management and marine litter, often interweaving social context with technical aspects. She is co-developer of the mobile app Marine Debris Tracker, a tool that continues to facilitate a growing global citizen science initiative.

**Timothy Jones** is a Postdoctoral Researcher within the School of Aquatic and Fishery Sciences at the University of Washington. He has a background in quantitative ecology and studies how models can be applied to natural science datasets to understand ecological patterns and how they are affected by large-scale forcing.

**Tim Kiessling** holds a degree in Marine Conservation and works at the Universidad Católica del Norte in Coquimbo, Chile. He is investigating ocean and river pollution by plastic litter with the help of citizen science data, and is also interested in social aspects of waste generation and management.

**Katrin Knickmeier** is the Coordinator of the Kieler Forschungswerkstatt, a school lab of the University of Kiel, and the Leibniz Institute for Science and Mathematics Education (IPN), Kiel, Germany. She has a background as a marine biologist, and has worked on plankton in the Arctic Ocean and in Chile. Since 2000 she has gained extensive experience in science communication and school programs, teacher trainings, and the development of course materials. In the ocean:lab students and trainee teachers have the opportunity to get involved in marine sciences, with citizen science projects.

**Katrin Kruse** is a teacher (Biology and Chemistry) and PhD candidate at the Leibniz Institute for Science and Mathematics Education (IPN), Kiel, Germany, partly working in a school in Ahrensburg and in the ocean:lab of the Kieler Forschungswerkstatt. She is working in the field of citizen science and plastic in the ocean. In her PhD she studies how schoolchildren learn through participation in citizen science projects and if this has an influence on their self-efficacy in cases of environmental behavior.

**Carrie LeDuc** came to the laboratory in the capacity of citizen scientist, contributing to restoration efforts and research on restoration outcomes. In this capacity, she helped to map the extent of eelgrass re-growth over multiple years and conduct research on possible contributors to eelgrass loss. She was trained in marine biology and genetics and has worked as a biologist and manager in related fields ever since. She worked with friends and colleagues to start two biotech companies, and is now working with Hydro-Photon in bringing safe drinking water to everyone. She sees great value in community involvement in science and is an active participant in citizen science at every opportunity.

**Kate Litle** is the Assistant Director for Programs at Washington Sea Grant. With a background in biology and marine policy, she has spent the past 16 years working on coastal issues in Washington State, with a particular interest in connecting science, management, and volunteers.

**Erin Meyer** is a Senior Scientist with California Ocean Science Trust where she directs the monitoring program and leads its data and technology initiatives. She has traveled around the world pursuing her passion for connecting science to governance in Alaska, the Caribbean, and Thailand. Erin holds a PhD in Integrative Biology from the University of California, Berkeley.

**Ryan Meyer** is Executive Director of the Center for Community and Citizen Science at the University of California, Davis, and former Program Director at the California Ocean Science Trust. His career has focused on complex interactions between science and society, through topics such as climate change, coastal and ocean resource management, and public participation in science.

**Peter A. Nelson** is a Senior Fish Ecologist at H.T. Harvey & Associates and a Research Associate with the Institute of Marine Sciences at the University of California, Santa Cruz. His scientific background is in animal behavior and marine ecology; his current work is focused primarily on collaborative fisheries research and fisheries science.

**Michelle J. Paddack** is an Assistant Professor of Biology at Santa Barbara City College, and a Research Scientist/Expedition Leader with Oceanic Society and *One People One Reef*. Along with her scientific work in marine ecology, conservation biology, and marine resource management, she has extensive experience creating and leading citizen science trips globally.

**Jon Parr** is Deputy Director at the Marine Biological Association (MBA) in the UK. Awarded a Royal Charter in 2013, the MBA has been involved in awareness raising and citizen science in some form since 1888, including a public aquarium and early marine faunas. Building on this tradition, Jon has led modern citizen science at the MBA and remains an interested citizen who wants to make a difference.

**Julia K. Parrish** is the Lowell A. and Frankie L. Wakefield Professor of Ocean Fishery Sciences in the College of the Environment at the University of Washington, and the Executive Director of the Coastal Observation and Seabird Survey Team (COASST). She has spent the last 30 years studying natural and anthropogenic impacts on Pacific Northwest coastal ecosystems, with a focus on marine birds.

**Gretta T. Pecl** is an Associate Professor of Marine Ecology at the Institute for Marine and Antarctic Studies and the Centre for Marine Socioecology in Hobart, Tasmania, Australia. She has broad interdisciplinary research interests and a passion for science engagement and communication with the public. Much of her current research centers on understanding climate change impacts in marine systems, and how our marine industries and communities may best adapt to these changes. She developed and leads the national citizen science project Redmap Australia, the Range Extension Database and mapping project, which invites fishers and divers to help monitor ecological changes in Australian seas.

**April D. Ridlon** is a PhD candidate at the University of California, Santa Barbara, USA, with a professional background in marine research, conservation, and education. She has directed citizen scientists in research projects for various non-profit organizations since 2000, including as Team Scientist for Reef Check in the Sapodilla Cayes Marine Reserve, BZ, and as a research assistant for the Earthwatch Institute. April is broadly interested in human impacts to predator-prey dynamics; her current research interests include the indirect effects of recreational divers and spear fishers on marine fish, and the roles of predators in marine invasions.

**John B. Rulmal Jr.** is the Finance Director for the Ulithi Falalop Community Action Program, and a Community Liaison/Project Manager for *One People One Reef*. His work includes liaising with government and international aid agencies and with Micronesian Outer Islands communities through community outreach and youth education to support sustainable development. His work focuses on the preservation and revival of indigenous conservation techniques and integrating these with Western science.

**Jack Sewell** is Senior Science Interpreter at the Marine Biological Association (MBA) in the UK. He has been involved in developing and leading coastal citizen science projects for more than 15 years. Several of these projects have supported research into non-native species distributions, linking to his work on non-native marine species on a Great Britain and wider European level. Jack is a part-time illustrator, producing works to share his passion for the ocean and in particular marine science.

**Leila Sievanen** is an Environmental Social Scientist at California Ocean Science Trust, a non-profit in Oakland focused on integrating science into ocean policy. With a PhD in Environmental Anthropology from the University of Washington, she is working to increase social and ecological resilience on the West Coast to changing ocean conditions through interdisciplinary research collaborations and participatory approaches.

**Lei Lani Stelle** is a Professor of Biology at University of Redlands in California, USA. She has studied marine mammals for over 25 years, and her current research investigates the impacts of human impacts on a variety of species. She has involved citizen scientists in projects in British Columbia (Canada), Baja (Mexico), and California (USA).

**Martin Thiel** is Professor of Marine Biology at Universidad Católica del Norte in Coquimbo, Chile, and Associate Researcher at the Center for Advanced Studies in Arid System and the Millennium Nucleus Ecology and Sustainable Management of Oceanic Islands. He has a background in general biology, ethology, ecology, and oceanography, and he directs the Citizen Science Program Científicos de la Basura (litter scientists; www.cientificosdelabasura.cl), where K-12 students examine the problem of marine litter in collaboration with professional scientists.

**Bryony L. Townhill** is a Marine Climate Change Scientist at the Centre for Environment, Fisheries and Aquaculture Science (Cefas) in the UK. Her work focuses on the effects of climate change on marine ecosystems, industries, and coastal communities, and on the use of citizen science methodologies to monitor the recreational fishing impacts.

**Christine A. Ward-Paige** is a Postdoctoral Fellow at Dalhousie University, and founder and principal scientist at eOceans. She has a background in marine ecology, environmental science, and conservation biology, and studies marine ecosystems and human use patterns to inform policy and management using citizen science observations.

**Ann Wasser** is the Director of Education for the Severson Dells Nature Center and the Forest Preserves of Winnebago County in Rockford, Illinois, USA. Her background is in a wide range of informal science education – aquariums, outdoor schools, on-board boats, and in science centers. She was formerly the Director of Education for the Pacific Grove Museum of Natural History in Pacific Grove, California, where she managed the LiMPETS program for the California Central Coast.

**Debbie Winton** is a Programme Manager at Earthwatch Institute (Europe) in Oxford, UK. She has worked on marine conservation projects internationally, particularly the Indo-Pacific and Caribbean, and is currently involved in a number of citizen science projects including UK-based Capturing Our Coast. Previously she worked as a Programme Manager for Oman and the Middle East.

**Charlie W. Wright** is a Citizen Science Data Verification Specialist with COASST. He has a background in avian field biology, is versed in the natural history of Pacific Coast birds, and is interested in shaping and guiding citizen science with rigorous end uses in mind.

# PREFACE

This book came about as a natural outgrowth of the global and explosive expansion of citizen science and other forms of public participation in scientific research. While scientists and non-scientists have been collaborating to better understand coastal and marine environments for many years, we've recently seen a perfect storm of available technologies, open source hardware and software, cultural and social awakening, social justice and community-based movements, and government need and interest resulting in what we see now as a firmly established field of citizen science. While many people associate this field with bird watching and stargazing, the fact is that one of the most crucial contexts in need of broad spatial and temporal data sets for environmental and conservation science is coastal and marine systems; and marine scientists and members of the public have responded with hundreds of citizen science projects around the world. Therefore, when the 2014 International Marine Conservation Congress in Glasgow, Scotland, called for symposia, several of us knew a citizen science–focused symposium could help to push this under-discussed field forward. That original symposium included scientists and citizen science project leaders from a wide range of project areas: Tina Phillips, Ann Wasser, Ryan Meyer, Jake Levenson, Amy Freitag, Jason Holmberg, and the two of us, many of whom have authored chapters in this book.

We particularly appreciate that at that conference Tim Hardwick at Earthscan suggested this might make a good focus for a book. Since then we have discovered dozens and dozens of projects around the world working on nearly every coastal and marine ecosystem, at varying stages of development and maturity as programs. This book represents a small fraction of the coastal and marine citizen science projects that exist and continue to emerge, and we selected those that seemed to offer representative cases for the variety of technologies, contexts, audiences, and conservation goals that have been up and running long enough to offer lessons for the fields of citizen science and conservation more broadly. We regret that many exemplary projects with amazing successes and/or thoughtfully designed programmatic structures could not be included in the book, but we tried to ensure that each author discussed many of those programs to provide the broader context for their work.

Heidi would like to thank her team of amazing graduate students and collaborators at UC Davis and beyond who have discussed big-picture thinking about coastal and marine citizen science. At UC Davis, that's been Ryan Meyer and Jen Metes in particular, and Emily Harris, Colin Dixon, Erin Bird, Sinead Brien, Lina Yamashita, Sally Neas, and Karen Bush. Alison Young and Rebecca Johnson at the California Academy of Sciences have pushed my thinking about what coastal citizen science can do (Snapshot Cal Coast!), and Julia Parrish at the University of Washington and COASST have pushed my thinking about what it can do well and how. My THAW colleagues who have provided support and guidance in both scholarly and work-life balance conundrums: Gail Patricelli, Kari Cooper, Amber Boydstun, and Magali Billen. Finally, I want to thank my family for supporting me unwaveringly in all my work with warmth and constructive criticism: Jill, Gary, Matt, Jeff and Marny.

John would like to thank all the citizen scientists who have collaborated with him on his citizen science projects for their enthusiasm, hard work, and inspiration. Earthwatch Institute not only provided funding for my projects but also invaluable guidance and support over the years that turned an interest into a passion. A special thanks goes to Mark Chandler. I would also like to thank colleagues that helped me think deeply and broadly not only about the process of citizen science but also about the nature of citizen science, especially Abe Miller-Rushing at the National Park Service, Hannah Webber at Schoodic Institute, and Tina Phillips at Cornell University. And to Rich Kliman for his good cheer and hard work. No one could ask for a better collaborator. A very, very special thanks, of course, goes to my family, Karen, Marisa, Olivia, and Darwin, whose unconditional and unwavering support over the years has allowed me to pursue my passion for coastal and marine citizen science.

We particularly want to acknowledge all the hard work of the authors of chapters in this book, and their thousands of volunteers and participants in the projects they write about. Without the passion, expertise, experience, enthusiasm, time, and energy of the people who make up these citizen science projects around the world, we would already be far behind in our understanding and application of coastal and marine conservation, and in our understanding of the ways the human communities and individuals can positively impact our ecosystems as stewards and scientists. If anything, the expansion of citizen science for coastal and marine conservation has provided a whole new arena for people to enact their conservation values, and we are so honored to be able to highlight some of the ways that can be effectively, rigorously, ethically done by scientists and members of the public alike.

# PART I
# Introduction

# 1

# THE PROMISE OF AND THE NEED FOR CITIZEN SCIENCE FOR COASTAL AND MARINE CONSERVATION

*John A. Cigliano and Heidi L. Ballard*

The dramatic expansion in recent years of the approach to scientific research that involves members of the public in one or more stages of the scientific process, typically called citizen science, immediately raises a wide range of questions. How reliable are the data that come from volunteer data collectors? Who are the participants in these projects, where do they come from, why do they volunteer to do this work, and what do they get out of it? Can these data be used for real natural resource management and conservation decisions? Can citizen science project findings be used to inform conservation policy? Can indigenous knowledge be a part of citizen science, and what are the ethical issues around data ownership and real collaboration? Where in the world is citizen science really happening? Is this just a fad, or a significant transformation of the way science can be conducted, who can do science, and how science can contribute to conservation?

In no context are these questions being asked and answered more clearly than in coastal and marine conservation. Coastal and marine social-ecological systems have a rich history of collaborative natural resource management, local and traditional ecological knowledge holders partnering with scientists, and monitoring to inform decision-making. These systems also have a history of conflict and tensions between science and management, between livelihoods and recreational use, and between locals and tourists, and difficulty in getting quality data across broad spatial and temporal scales. Perhaps most urgent, coastal and marine systems are ground zero for the impacts of climate change, species loss, habitat destruction, sea-level rise, ocean acidification, and myriad other conservation threats. All of these threats, and our responses in the form of adaptation and mitigation, require new kinds of data and data collection, and new kinds of engagement with stakeholders, including scientists, managers, businesses and non-profits, people who live on the coast, people who fish and depend on natural resources, and people who recreate and care deeply about our oceans.

We offer this book as a partial answer to the question of whether and how citizen science contributes to coastal and marine conservation. We think it is not a fad, but a new way of doing science for conservation that is more inclusive and can mean more conservation impacts on the ground. However, the rapid expansion of the use of citizen science for coastal and marine conservation does not necessarily mean that these projects are always appropriate, effective, efficient, or ethical. Many projects develop and fail without significantly impacting conservation, providing quality data to scientific research, or engaging members of the public in sustainable ways. Our goal is to provide examples of coastal and marine citizen science projects that have contributed to conservation through research, education, management, and/or policy, and illustrate how they are structured to do so, from volunteer recruitment and retention to data quality control and assurance. Citizen science is not the only effective approach to coastal and marine conservation science, but it can be a powerful one if designed and implemented well, drawing on the lessons of the many projects working on similar goals and in similar contexts.

## What is citizen science?

Citizen science, or as it is also referred to, public participation in scientific research (Shirk et al., 2012), has several definitions. The *Oxford English Dictionary* defines citizen science as "the collection and analysis of data relating to the natural world by members of the public typically as part of a collaborative project with professional scientists." However, Bonney et al. (2016) correctly points out that this definition does not include the fact that citizen scientists often go beyond collecting and analyzing data, that they often work as individuals often without directly collaborating with scientists, and that many projects are community-driven (see "Typologies of Citizen Science").

Here we distinguish between the public collecting and sharing data for their own or even their community's education and awareness, and the public collecting data that are used, reviewed, and acted upon by other scientists and/or resource managers for basic science or natural resource management. In this book, we follow and apply the definition that citizen science is scientific research and monitoring projects for which members of the public collaborate with professional scientists to collect, categorize, transcribe, or analyze scientific data, and may also help define the research questions and design, as well as communicate and act on the project's findings, a definition consistent with Bonney et al. (2014). That is, the public contributes to and participates in one or more steps of the scientific process. However, it should be noted that while citizen science projects have scientific goals and objectives at their core, they may also have social and educational objectives and outcomes (Bonney et al., 2014); for example, in Chapter 11 Ann Wasser discusses the educational benefits of involving middle-school students in monitoring, and in Chapter 8 Jane Disney and colleagues discuss the community benefits of their restoration project. This book will focus on evidence and processes for how citizen science has been used to advance coastal and marine conservation, and most importantly, how this might inform future use of this approach.

## The growth and promise of citizen science for coastal and marine conservation

The use of citizen science has dramatically increased in recent years (Conrad and Hilchey, 2011; Follett and Strezov, 2015; Kullenberg and Kasperowski, 2016) and has had positive impacts on conservation research in general (Theobald et al., 2015). However, the use of citizen science in coastal and marine contexts is underrepresented compared to its use in terrestrial and freshwater research and monitoring (Roy et al., 2012). Even so, coastal and marine citizen science has shown significant growth in the last several years as evidenced by the growth in citizen-science related presentations and organized sessions at the International Marine Conservation Congress (IMCC), which has become one of the largest professional meetings solely devoted to coastal and marine conservation (Figure 1.1), and an increase in the number of publications of marine-related studies that used citizen science (Thiel et al., 2014). Further evidence for the potential for continued growth in coastal and marine citizen science is provided by Martin et al. (2016), who found in a study of potential marine citizen scientists that there is significant interest in citizen science among marine users (primarily SCUBA divers).

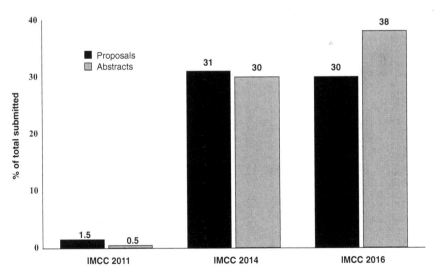

FIGURE 1.1    Percentage of proposals and abstracts submitted under the citizen science theme (*Participation in Marine Conservation Science*). Proposals include workshops, focus groups, and symposia. Abstracts include oral, speed, and poster presentations. IMCC 2011 did not have a citizen science theme and the number of proposals and abstracts represent the number of each that had "citizen science" in the title or abstract.

## Why use citizen science for coastal and marine conservation?

There has been a significant amount of discussion on the utility of citizen science for ecological and conservation-related research, and these reasons are applicable to coastal and marine conservation. Many of the reasons given for the value of citizen science are based on the fact that using volunteers can lead to a large increase in the number of researchers (professional and volunteer) working on a project. The greatest strength of citizen science is often suggested to be that it allows for the collection of fine-grained information over greater spatial and temporal scales than conventional research projects and that it allows for the processing of large amounts of data (Miller-Rushing et al., 2012; McKinley et al., 2015). The increase in the number of researchers can also increase the likelihood of detecting environmental perturbations and changes, lead to better monitoring of the effectiveness of management practices as part of an adaptive management program, and fill in data gaps. Citizen scientists can also represent a source of free labor and a possible source of financing (Silvertown, 2009). Jenny Cousins and co-authors in Chapter 3 discuss a mangrove project that employs Earthwatch volunteers who pay a fee to join the project. A portion of this fee goes to researchers to support their research, thus providing both funding and enthusiastic citizen scientists.

But the value of citizen science goes beyond just numbers. Citizen science can also allow for projects to operate at times when professional scientists are not collecting data (Miller-Rushing et al., 2012). Citizen scientists can also help refine research questions because for many projects the citizen scientists are locally connected to and affected by the issue being addressed by the project; citizen scientists can also assist researchers in understanding the social dimensions of the project among the stakeholders (McKinley et al., 2015). Miller-Rushing et al. (2012) also suggest that citizen science allows for projects to be conducted that would not be done by professional scientists, for example, because the question is too narrow in scope to appeal to a large audience of professional scientists or to be widely cited in scientific publications. And McKinley et al. (2015) suggest that citizen science can lead to broader public participation in policy decisions (see also Cigliano et al., 2015), foster environmental stewardship, and promote the spread of knowledge about the conservation issue and project through the social networks of the citizen scientists.

We would also add that conducting citizen science projects can be enjoyable and rewarding for professional scientists because of the enthusiasm and curiosity that the citizen scientists bring to projects. And working with an excited and engaged public who are so willing to give their time, effort, and sometimes money to help conserve and manage biodiversity can provide real hope for the future (#OceanOptimism) to professional scientists who have seen environmental degradation and species extinction up close and too often.

## Typologies of citizen science

While all citizen science projects (as defined here) share the goal of producing quality scientific data, several citizen science typologies have been developed to describe the degree (Shirk et al., 2012; Haklay, 2013) and quality (Shirk et al., 2012) of participation by citizen scientists, the organizational and macrostructural properties of the projects (Wiggins and Crowston, 2011), and project outcomes (Cigliano et al., 2015). Other typologies have been proposed, but we will limit our review to these because of their usefulness for describing and categorizing coastal and marine conservation citizen science projects. Understanding the various typologies is useful when planning such projects because it can help define the goals and expected outcomes of the project and help in designing project methodology including how best to utilize citizen scientists (Shirk et al., 2012). However, we don't see these typologies as set in stone or mutually exclusive; they are a useful way to disaggregate the factors, processes, goals, and outcomes of coastal and marine citizen science projects to analyze their outcomes and design better programs and projects in the future.

### Degree and quality of citizen scientist participation (Shirk et al., 2012)

Why develop a typology based on the degree and quality of participation by citizen scientists? Shirk et al. (2012) found that the degree and quality of a citizen scientist's participation are closely related to the range and types of project outcomes, and that having a framework based on participation can inform project design. Shirk et al. (2012) defined degree of participation as the extent to which citizen scientists are involved in the scientific process (i.e. from formulating questions to analyzing data and dissemination of results). Quality of participation describes how well the project's goals and activities "align with, respond to, and are relevant to the needs and interests" of the citizen scientists. By considering the degree and quality of participation, Shirk et al. (2012) developed models of citizen science based projects (degree of participation) and a framework that can be used for project development (quality of participation).

Five models based on degree of participation were developed. Three of them include contributions from citizen scientists in collaboration with scientists. They are:

*Contributory projects*: designed by professional scientists; citizen scientists primarily contribute data; these are often projects that need to collect data on a large geographic or temporal scale;

*Collaborative projects*: projects that are also designed by professional scientists; citizen scientists primarily contribute data but may also help to refine project design, analyze data, and/or disseminate findings;

*Co-created projects*: designed by professional scientists *and* the public, where at least some of the public participants are actively involved in most or all aspects of the research process; these projects are often initiated by the public, and collaborating with scientists is done to ensure that the project is conducted in a scientifically rigorous manner.

Quality is central to design and implementation of citizen science projects, because it reflects whose interests can and should be considered and negotiated, and how the project's goals or outcomes are defined. The fundamental question of this framework is "whose interests are being served?" The elements of the framework include *inputs* (hopes, desires, goals, and expectations of the professional scientists and citizen scientists); *activities* (tasks necessary to design, establish, and manage a project); *outputs* (initial products or results of activities); *outcomes* (measurable elements such as skills, abilities, and knowledge that result from the specific outputs of a project; measured within 1–3 years of project start); and *impacts* (long-term and sustained changes; occurs 4–6+ years after project starts). Shirk et al. (2012) identified three categories of outcomes: (1) for science, (2) for citizen scientists, and (3) for socioecological systems, and suggests that for a project to be sustainable, it must yield outcomes in all three categories.

### Level of participation and engagement in citizen science activity (Haklay, 2013)

Haklay (2013) also developed a typology based on participation but focused on the level of participation and engagement by the citizen scientists. This typology focuses on the level of participation because it is indicative of the power relationships that occur within social processes, such as planning or decision-making. This is particularly relevant to conservation-related citizen science because ultimately these projects are collecting information for use in management and planning.

The typology proposed by Haklay (2013) from most passive to most active includes the following categories:

*Crowdsourcing*: a process of obtaining data by soliciting contributions from a large group of people, especially from an online community;[1] participation by citizen scientists is limited to providing data with limited cognitive engagement; citizen scientists act as "sensors," and engagement between citizen scientists and professional scientists is indirect.

*Distributed intelligence*: citizen scientists provide their the cognitive abilities to the project; after some basic training, citizen scientists conduct simple interpretation activities; engagement between citizen scientists and professional scientists is indirect.

*Participatory science*: the research question is determined by the citizen scientists with professional scientists acting as consultants to develop data collection and analysis methods, thus the citizen and professional scientists are directly engaged; citizen scientists collect data, but require the assistance of the professional scientists in data analysis and interpretation, but can suggest new research questions based on the data analysis; this type of citizen science is particularly relevant to "community science."

*Extreme citizen science*: there is direct engagement between professional and citizen scientists, and citizen scientists are assumed to be in comparison to professional scientists equally capable in the production of scientific knowledge;

these projects are truly collaborative, with the citizen scientist contributing to problem definition, data collection, and analysis; the professional scientist acts not only as an expert but also a facilitator.

## Organizational and macrostructural properties of citizen science projects (Wiggins and Crowston, 2011)

Wiggins and Crowston (2011) developed a typology based on project characteristics that they suggest are important for successful project design and management, as a complement to typologies based on degree and/or quality of participation like Shirk et al.'s (2012) and Haklay's (2013). The categories of this typology are defined by the primary goals of the project and the importance of a physical component to participation, that is, the degree of virtuality. Five mutually exclusive types of projects were identified. However, here we do not discuss the *Education* category as it does not fit with our definition of citizen science. Thus we confine our discussion to the science-based components of the typology developed by Wiggins and Crowston (2011).

*Action*: projects conceived by citizen scientists to address "local environmental concerns for which science-oriented activities are intimately linked to the physical world." Research using minimal technology is done to support civic agendas, and professional scientists act as collaborators or consultants rather than initiators; the results from the projects tend not to be published in the peer-reviewed literature; because the projects are organized through grassroots efforts, the projects are generally successful only at a local level, and long-term sustainability can be an issue.

*Conservation*: the primary goal of these projects is to generate information for natural resource management decision-making; many projects also include educational goals or content to promote environmental stewardship and awareness in the citizen scientists; citizen scientists are engaged in data collection and outreach, and the projects are regional in scope and are likely to have affiliations with state or federal agencies; the projects are most often organized by academics and consist of long-term monitoring efforts; there is strong emphasis on data quality control to ensure that the results are valid; these projects include both top-down (researcher-initiated) and middle-out (management-initiated) organizing structures, and projects employ a wide range of technologies from very simple to very complex.

*Investigation*: focused on scientific research with education often an unstated goal – citizen scientists are often given educational materials or tasks to encourage continued learning; scale of projects range from regional to international, often with large numbers of citizen scientists; similar to *conservation* projects, there is strong emphasis on data quality control to ensure that the results are valid and a wide range of technologies is used in data collection and analysis; top-down organizational structure is a defining characteristic of these projects.

*Virtual*: these projects share similar scientific and data quality goals with *investigation* projects, but differ in that these projects do not have a physical component to participation and are conducted entirely through online participation; the lack of a physical component differentiates these projects from all of the other science-based components of this typology; virtual projects also have a top-down organizational structure and as expected take advantage of advanced technologies for data collection and analysis.

While the typologies described here can be used to describe a range of citizen science activities and projects, we agree with Haklay (2013) that no project should be classified by any single category. For example, depending on the level to which a citizen scientist wishes to be engaged, as well as the level of expertise and knowledge, various citizen scientists on a project may be engaged in different levels of participation with different levels of quality. And as citizen scientists become more experienced, they may be assigned tasks with ever-increasing complexity and perhaps eventually become a co-lead of the project. Furthermore, projects might span more than one component of a typology – a *conservation* project (sensu Wiggins and Crowston, 2011) could also be classified as an *investigation* project (Wiggins and Crowston, 2011) – or may be described using multiple typologies – a *conservation project* (Wiggins and Crowston, 2011) could also be a *co-created project* (Shirk et al., 2012) or *extreme citizen science project* (Haklay, 2013).

## Why use typologies?

All of this could be seen as mere "stamp collecting," but we agree with Shirk et al. (2012) that considering the quality of participation is critical during project development, as is the primary goal and the degree of virtuality (e.g. the degree to which there is a physical or virtual component to participation in a project). Understanding the fundamental components and goals of a project allows for a clearer understanding of the appropriate level and mechanisms of citizen scientist engagement – should they be deeply engaged in place and brought in during the creation of a project, or is a *distributive intelligence model* more appropriate? It is also critical for the long-term sustainability of projects that project managers be open to modifying how citizen scientists participate as a project matures.

Furthermore, having clear outcomes is critical for ensuring success for conservation projects (Kapos et al., 2009), including citizen science projects as described earlier (Wiggins and Crowston, 2011). With the goal of developing a framework for the effective and rigorous use of citizen science for coastal and marine conservation, Cigliano et al. (2015) developed a typology based on conservation-related outcomes that can be addressed using citizen science along with "toolkits" for each outcome to guide new and existing citizen science projects that aim to support management and conservation of coastal and marine resources for one or more of the outcomes. The outcomes, based on Kapos et al. (2009), include policy, education, community capacity building, site management, species management, and research.

This framework included recommendations for developing successful coastal and marine citizen science projects that address particular outcomes. For example, for projects with the goal of affecting policy, Cigliano et al. (2015) identified three modes by which coastal and marine citizen science may lead to positive policy change: (1) informed advocacy, (2) co-created/cooperative policy change, and (3) policy evaluation. The three modes share several potential outcomes that can be grouped into three general categories: (1) inspiring effective advocacy, (2) increasing public awareness of the issue, and (3) increasing the likelihood of policy change. To fulfill these outcomes, Cigliano et al. (2015) suggested that it is critical to understand the policy needs, process, and policy context. This will likely involve developing partnerships and effective communication. It is also critical that the project is conducted at the temporal and spatial scale that is relevant to the policy issue. However, the most significant concern for projects that are designed to affect positive policy change is a lack of trust by policy makers in the process and data. To overcome this, it is recommended that relevant partners and stakeholders are included in all aspects of the project, whether the project is initiated by the citizen scientists (informed advocacy) or policy makers or managers (co-created/cooperative projects), or whether the project's goal is to inform policy development (informed advocacy or co-created/cooperative projects) or to evaluate an existing policy (policy evaluation).

We've reviewed here only just a few of the typologies developed for citizen science projects. While the sheer number of possible typologies might seem daunting and even counterproductive, using a typology or a combination of typologies will allow one to think deeply about the design of the project and will lead to a project design that is appropriate for the goals and outcomes of the project, and one that appropriately integrates the involvement of citizen scientists, which will not only positively affect project effectiveness but also project sustainability.

## Challenges and opportunities that are unique to coastal and marine citizen science

While the value of using citizen science for coastal and marine conservation is similar to using it for conservation research in general, there are issues and challenges of employing citizen science in coastal and marine ecosystems not faced in terrestrial systems. Cigliano et al. (2015) suggested that these are primarily logistical, especially the significant challenges in gaining access to and collecting and recording data in marine habitats. For example, conducting marine research often requires expensive gear, such as boats, and specialized expertise, such as the ability to snorkel or dive. Such requirements will also limit the size of the pool of potential volunteers. However, there are also larger social challenges, such as competing interests in fisheries and coastal land use or in using mangroves as a carbon sink or a source for fuel (see Chapter 3). And, of course, there are safety issues with working on, under, or near the ocean.

The context and challenges of working in coastal and marine environments and communities also presents opportunities. To overcome the logistical challenges of conducting coastal and marine research, scientists can reach out to and enlist passionate audiences such as divers and snorkelers (Chapter 12), beach walkers

(Chapter 2), and youth (Chapter 11). To overcome the social challenges, scientists can conduct collaborative or co-created citizen science projects to help overcome conflicts and build a stronger project from the ground up. Furthermore, coastal communities with key livelihoods of fisheries and/or tourism provide a particularly rich source of local and traditional ecological knowledge often with a strong tradition of collaborative fisheries management (Chapter 10).

## Scope and aim of the book

The aim of this book is to demonstrate the range, utility, feasibility, challenges, and affordances of doing coastal and marine citizen science for conservation. We will do this by providing critical considerations (i.e. which questions and systems are best suited for citizen science?) and recommendations for best practices for the design and implementation of effective (and safe) citizen science projects for coastal and marine conservation from a range of authors working in a variety of contexts with a diversity of audiences. This range of experiences provides a rich set of examples and lessons of when, how, where, and why citizen science can be an effective approach to conservation in coastal and marine systems.

Part II of the book offers a range of perspectives on the *practice* of coastal and marine citizen science for conservation. We delve into specific issues that citizen science has addressed for coastal and marine conservation, and the methods and strategies used by different scientists and organizations. We do this by presenting case studies of successful projects that have been conducted by scientists and practitioners who are experienced in using citizen science for coastal and marine conservation on one or more project. Each chapter in this part not only summarizes the projects but also discusses key issues and challenges and lessons learned. The issues addressed in these chapters begin with Parrish and colleagues using citizen science to establish baseline information for tracking seabird populations (Chapter 2). In Chapter 3, Jenny Cousins and colleagues discuss using citizen science to study the effects of climate change on coastal (mangrove) systems and describe Africa's first community-based blue carbon project, which has engaged a wide range of citizen scientists in data collection and restoration activities with a focus on climate change mitigation. Next, Jack Sewell and Jon Parr (Chapter 4) explain the impact and spread of invasive species and how citizen science can act as "sentinels" to increase the probability of early detection and ultimately the control or management of invasive species. In Chapter 5, Lei Lani Stelle explores how citizen science can be used to monitor marine mammal populations to study the effect of human activity, including whale watching, on these populations. In Chapter 6 Martin Thiel and colleagues discuss the effects of plastic debris on coastal and marine ecosystems and how citizen scientists can be powerful allies in generating large-scale data and raising awareness about this global environmental problem. While all chapters include case studies of successful projects, Part II ends with three chapters that focus on solutions: Ryan Meyer and colleagues discuss the evidence and potential of citizen science as a source of rigorous and cost-effective long-term monitoring data to inform ocean and coastal resource management in California (Chapter 7); Jane Disney and colleagues show how citizen science can be used to effectively and efficiently restore temperate eelgrass beds in Maine (Chapter 8); and Bryony L. Townhill and Kieran Hyder discuss how citizen science can be used to effectively and efficiently inform and affect positive decision-making and policy change (Chapter 9). After all, the goal of all marine conservation projects is to effect positive change that will lead to the maintenance and restoration of biodiversity.

Part III takes a closer look at some of the citizen scientists that are unique or especially critical to coastal and marine conservation. We start with Crane and colleagues' discussion of how indigenous peoples and communities can use citizen science to address local issues (Chapter 10). This is especially critical to coastal and marine conservation because of the social challenges that come from conflict over common-pool resources, which are resources from which it is costly to exclude potential users and which can be reduced from use (i.e. anything one user takes reduces what is available for other users; Ostrom, 1990; see also Kittinger et al., 2014). Fisheries, of course, are a common-pool resource. Common-pool resources are at risk of being over-exploited because often there is a divergence between individual and group interests leading to a "tragedy of the commons" (Hardin, 1968). Ostrom (1990) developed key institutional design principles that are associated with successful management of common-pool resources (see Kittinger et al., 2014 for a full discussion). Two of these are relevant to citizen science and specifically indigenous people acting as the citizen scientists: (1) clearly defined boundaries and membership so that both the boundaries of the resource system and the individuals (or households) who have rights to use the resource are clearly defined, and (2) active monitoring of the resource by individuals who are accountable to the users or are the users themselves. Such a system is described by Crane and colleagues in Chapter 10, where they describe the *One People One Reef* program which operates in the Federated States of Micronesia. The project's primary goal is to strengthen community capacity to manage marine resources using input from both Western and local science teams. People from local communities do more than collaborate with Western scientists as citizen scientists. Their knowledge of the system (i.e. Traditional Ecological Knowledge, or TEK) is integral to and has guided the research. This case study is an excellent example of a true collaborative approach that has included a two-way exchange of knowledge and has led to successful management of a common-pool resource. Next in Chapter 11, Ann Wasser discusses how schoolchildren can contribute to sandy beach and intertidal monitoring in California, and explains the educational benefits they receive from participating. One of the more unique aspects of marine citizen science is the involvement of recreational divers and snorkelers as citizen scientists. In Chapter 12, John Cigliano and April Ridlon discuss the unique challenges and opportunities that involving these audiences present, and discuss how to effectively include them in citizen science for coastal and marine research and monitoring.

In Part IV of the book, we discuss some of the best practices for coastal and marine conservation citizen science. Hind and colleagues (Chapter 13) in this section discuss citizen science communication to the broader public and trust-building. Communication is of course critically important for conservation. And when citizen scientists participate in research it promotes trust, which is critical for stakeholder buy-in for management and policy. But what is the best way to communicate to citizen scientists and other stakeholders? Finally, Heidi Ballard and John Cigliano conclude with a chapter synthesizing key themes, questions, and lessons drawn from the previous chapters to provide the main considerations for scientists, conservationists, educators, and anyone working on coastal and marine conservation that might involve citizen science. We will also synthesize the current evidence and big thinking about potential for the future of coastal and marine citizen science: what might the future hold? Conducting citizen science projects and collecting data in coastal and marine environments can be challenging, but these challenges can be overcome. Citizen science holds great promise for coastal and marine conservation, and we hope the evidence from the authors in this book provides lessons for building and enriching the field into the future.

## Note

1 www.digitalgov.gov/communities/federal-crowdsourcing-and-citizen-science/.

## Literature cited

Bonney, R., Cooper, C., Dickinson, J., Kelling, S., Phillips, T., Rosenberg, K., and Shirk, J. (2009). Citizen science: A developing tool for expanding science knowledge and scientific literacy. *BioScience*, 59(11), 977–984.

Bonney, R., Shirk, J., Phillips, T., Wiggins, A., Ballard, H., Miller-Rushing, A., and Parrish, J. (2014). Next steps for citizen science. *Science*, 343(6178), 1436–1437.

Bonney, R., Cooper, C. and Ballard, H. (2016). The theory and practice of citizen science: launching a new journal. *Citizen Science: Theory and Practice*, 1(1), 1. http://doi.org/10.5334/cstp.65.

Cigliano, J.A., Meyer, R., Ballard, H.L., Freitag, A., Phillips, T.B., and Wasser, A. (2015). Making marine and coastal citizen science matter. *Ocean & Coastal Management*, 115, 77–87. http://doi.org/10.1016/j.ocecoaman.2015.06.012.

Conrad, C., and Hilchey, K. (2011). A review of citizen science and community-based environmental monitoring: issues and opportunities. *Environmental Monitoring and Assessment*, 176(1–4), 273–291.

Follett, R., and Strezov, V. (2015). An analysis of citizen science based research: Usage and publication patterns. *PLOS One*, 10(11), p.e0143687.

Haklay, M. (2013). Citizen science and volunteered geographic information: Overview and typology of participation. In Sui, D.Z., Elwood, S., Goodchild, M. (Eds.) *Crowdsourcing Geographic Knowledge: Volunteered Geographic Information (VGI) in Theory and Practice*, 105–122. Berlin: Springer.

Harding, G. (1968). The tragedy of the commons. *Science*, 162(3859), 1243–1248.

Kapos, V., Balmford, A., Aveling, R., Bubb, P., Carey, P., Entwistle, A., Hopkins, J., Mulliken, T., Safford, R., Stattersfield, A., and Walpole, M. (2009). Outcomes, not implementation, predict conservation success. *Ory*, 43(3), 336–342.

Kittinger, J.N., Cinner, J.E., Aswani, S., and White, A.T. (2014). Back to the future: Integrating customary practices and institutions into comanagement of small-scale fisheries. In *Marine Historical Ecology in Conservation: Applying the Past to Manage for the Future*, ed. J.N. Kittinger, L. McClenachan, K.B. Gedan, and L.K. Blight, 135–160. Berkley, CA: University of California Press.

Kullenberg, C., and Kasperowski, D. (2016). What is citizen science? – A scientometric meta-analysis. *PloS One*, 11(1), e0147152.

Martin, V.Y., Christidis, L., and Pecl, G.T. (2016). Public interest in marine citizen science: Is there potential for growth? *BioScience*, 66(8), 683–692.

McKinley, D.C., Miller-Rushing, A.J., Ballard, H.L., Bonney, R., Brown, H., Evans, D.M., French, R.A., Parrish, J.K., Phillips, T.B., Ryan, S.F., and Shanley, L.A. (2015). Investing in citizen science can improve natural resource management and environmental protection. *Issues in Ecology*, *19*, 1–27.

Miller-Rushing, A., Primack, R., and Bonney, R. (2012). The history of public participation in ecological research. *Frontiers in Ecology and the Environment*, 10(6), 285–290. http://doi.org/10.1890/110278.

Ostrom, E. (1990). *Governing the Commons: The Evolution of Institutions for Collective Action.* Cambridge: Cambridge University Press.

Roy, H.E., Pocock, M.J.O., Preston, C.D., Roy, D.B., Savage, J., Tweddle, J.C., and Robinson, L.D. (2012). *Understanding citizen science and environmental monitoring.* Final report on behalf of UK Environmental Observation Framework.

Shirk, J., Ballard, H., Wilderman, C., Phillips, T., Wiggins, A., Jordan, R., McCallie, E., Minarchek, M., Lewenstein, B., Krasny, M., and Bonney, R. (2012). Public participation in scientific research: A framework for deliberate design. *Ecology and Society*, 17(2).

Silvertown, J. (2009). A new dawn for citizen science. *Trends in Ecology & Evolution*, 24(9), 467–471.

Theobald, E., Ettinger, A., Burgess, H., DeBey, L., Schmidt, N., Froehlich, H., Wagner, C., HilleRisLambers, J., Tewksbury, J., Harsch, M., and Parrish, J. (2015). Global change and local solutions: Tapping the unrealized potential of citizen science for biodiversity research. *Biological Conservation*, 181, 236–244.

Thiel, M., Penna-Díaz, M.A., Luna-Jorquera, G., Salas, S., Sellanes, J., and Stotz, W. (2014). Citizen scientists and marine research: Volunteer participants, their contributions, and projection for the future. *Oceanography and Marine Biology: An Annual Review*, 52, 257–314.

Wiggins, A., and Crowston, K. (2011). From conservation to crowdsourcing: A typology of citizen science. In *Proceedings of the 44th Hawaii International Conference on System Sciences (HICSS), Koloa, Hawaii*, 1–10.

# PART II
# The practice of coastal and marine citizen science for conservation

# 2

# DEFINING THE BASELINE AND TRACKING CHANGE IN SEABIRD POPULATIONS

## The Coastal Observation and Seabird Survey Team (COASST)

*Julia K. Parrish, Kate Litle, Jane Dolliver, Todd Hass, Hillary K. Burgess, Erika Frost, Charlie W. Wright, and Timothy Jones*

## Introduction

Birds are highly attractive mega-fauna, and the natural history of birds is the basis for many citizen science programs worldwide (Dickinson et al., 2010). Nationally, avian citizen science programs collect baseline information on population size, range, habitat use, migratory timing and reproductive success at local to continental scales (e.g. Audubon Christmas Bird Count, eBird, Bird Atlases). Larger-scale programs have produced data that underpin many avian conservation efforts, simply because of the breadth of data across space and time (Cooper et al., 2014). Within the marine realm, this approach is more difficult, as the surface of the ocean is, with rare exceptions, uninhabited by people. However, the beach, at the interface between land and ocean, is a recognizable and attractive destination for many people (Haywood, 2016), which affords a wealth of data collection possibilities that speak to the health of the coastal marine ecosystem. Citizen science programs involving members of the public collecting data on marine bird stranding has a long tradition. Programs in Europe (Germany – Averbeck, 1991; Netherlands – Camphuysen, 1989; Shetland Islands – Heubeck, 2006; Belgium – Seys et al., 2002), New Zealand (Powlesland and Imber, 1988), Canada (e.g. British Columbia Beached Bird Survey – Stephens and Burger, 1994) and the United States (East Coast: SEANet; West Coast: BeachCOMBERS, BeachWatch) have been in existence for more than half a century. Collectively, these programs have allowed the local (defined as the geographic extent of the program) creation of indices of taxon-specific stranding (or encounter rate, in carcasses per lineal kilometer of beach searched) as a function of geography and time (usually months, or season). With respect to conservation, beached bird programs have been used to document anomalous mortality events (Camphuysen et al., 1999), assess the impact of oil spills (Stenzel et al., 1988; OSPAR, 1996; Newman et al., 2006) and fishery bycatch (Forney et al., 2001; Julian and Beeson, 1998; Hamel et al., 2009; Moore et al., 2009), and document and project the impacts of a changing climate (Parrish et al., 2007).

The focus of this chapter is one beached bird program, the Coastal Observation and Seabird Survey Team (COASST). Housed at the University of Washington, and currently operating in Alaska, Washington, Oregon and northern California, COASST is one of the youngest beached bird programs (17 years), although it is geographically the largest. By collaborating with our participants, the scientific community and natural resource management agencies, COASST works to translate long-term monitoring into actionable science. Within the realm of conservation, we define actionable science as generating knowledge about the degree to which the coastal system is changing as a function of human activities, and causal mechanisms of that change. With a statistically credible annualized (monthly) baseline in place, COASST becomes a program that documents departures from the mean, including catastrophic departures (unusual and mass mortality events), chronic (low signal to noise) shifts and the appearance of new modes in the baseline. In examining specific mortality events, COASST works with other experts, as relevant, to determine the mechanism(s) of elevated mortality and/or beaching, usually as a function of either lower trophic level and/or physical forcing, anthropogenic activity or both. In summary, COASST science focuses on three interlocking phases:

- Documentation of the baseline and statistical departures from it
- Determination of the mechanism(s) resulting in documented mortality events
- Exploration of the degree to which mortality events may be predictable as a function of the underlying forcing factors.

The program does not adopt advocacy positions, that is we do not lobby for a particular outcome within resource management or political realms based on our data. However, we do engage in the natural resource decision-making process by sharing and explaining COASST data relevant to management action.

COASST produces highly accurate and precise data at scales of space and time that are relevant to questions and issues within science and resource management. Our program depends on highly motivated and highly accurate data collectors who remain with the program for at least one year, ideally many years. To those ends, we have developed a strategy that simultaneously produces high quality data and secures long-term participation, and includes the following elements:

1   A *data collection design* that includes primary data (the "evidence") as well as deductions from that evidence allowing *independent verification* of all deductive data (e.g. species identification);
2   *Hands-on learning* in which disciplinary experts (scientists) with a high degree of training in informal settings work intensively with participants;

3    *Multi-channel* (print, web, phone, email, lecture, training/refresher, social) *and multi-touch communication* between program and participant including data feedback and communications centered around skill-building;

4    *Fine grain, broad extent* data at time and space scales appropriate to issues or questions of interest;

5    Scaling up of participant data into *analyzed patterns useful in science, society and resource management*;

6    *Follow-through* on connecting all participants to pattern information, with an ultimate goal of allowing citizens to also participate in its use.

While many versions of citizen science create large, credible datasets that are well-used in both scientific and conservation endeavors, COASST adopts a "court of law" standard – essentially, the ability to prove the deductive data returned by participants is true. This model of citizen science also allows the participant to (1) experience scientific data (evidence) collection leading to deductive scientific reasoning, (2) indirectly experience data analysis, (3) "see" the data through to use in scientific and resource management contexts and (4) make an individual decision about whether to use scientific program outcomes for further personal action.

## Overview of COASST as a case study

Starting from a small program of 12 participants on the south coast of Washington in 1999, COASST has steadily grown to almost 900 participants collecting data on more than 480 beaches from Mendocino along the northern coast of California north to Cape Lisburne in the Chukchi Sea, Alaska, and west to Adak in the western Aleutian Islands (Figure 2.1). The program is decentralized: participants collect beached bird data on beaches local to them, and send data to the COASST office at the University of Washington via a website, email and/or snail mail. The program is designed to be longitudinal: participants collect monthly data over years, contributing to decades of program data.

Participants are trained in an intensive five- to six-hour session run by an experienced professional with assistance from COASST staff and/or experienced COASST participants, as needed, to maintain a low instructor to participant ratio (1:10 max) during the hands-on portions of the training. All trainings are conducted in-community at approximately 50 different coastal locations, advertised according to local customs and contain information on issues of regional interest linked to COASST data (e.g. oil spills along the California-Washington outer coast; climate change impacts in northern Alaska). Attendance at trainings ranges from 3 to 40 (e.g. Alaskan villages versus larger urban communities). After training (training does not imply commitment), those who wish to sign up for COASST fill out a participant form; pay a deposit for a tool kit, protocol and field guide; and sign a contract identifying a date on which they will begin surveying at least monthly.

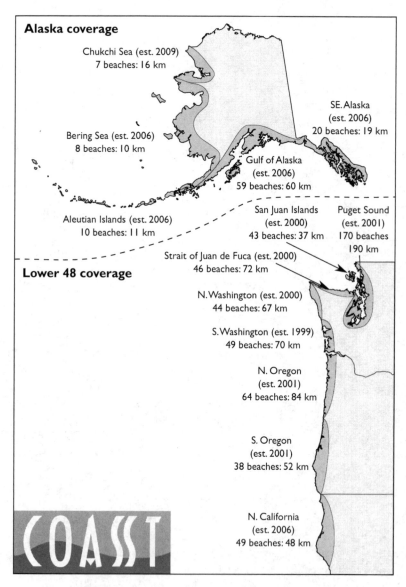

**Alaska coverage**

Chukchi Sea (est. 2009)
7 beaches: 16 km

SE. Alaska
(est. 2006)
20 beaches: 19 km

Bering Sea (est. 2006)
8 beaches: 10 km

Gulf of Alaska
(est. 2006)
59 beaches: 60 km

San Juan Islands
(est. 2000)
43 beaches: 37 km

Puget Sound
(est. 2001)
170 beaches
190 km

Aleutian Islands (est. 2006)
10 beaches: 11 km

Strait of Juan de Fuca (est. 2000)
46 beaches: 72 km

**Lower 48 coverage**

N. Washington (est. 2000)
44 beaches: 67 km

S. Washington (est. 1999)
49 beaches: 70 km

N. Oregon
(est. 2001)
64 beaches: 84 km

S. Oregon
(est. 2001)
38 beaches: 52 km

N. California
(est. 2006)
49 beaches: 48 km

COASST

**FIGURE 2.1**  Map of the COASST program, where shading indicates geographic
regions defined by political (i.e. state lines), oceanographic and/or
geomorphological boundaries. For each region, year of first beach
survey, number of survey beaches and cumulative beach length (as
of 2016) is shown.

## Connections to conservation

With respect to specific forcing factors of marine conservation import, COASST data have been used in three basic ways:

1   As a supplement to an existing study or report: for example, status reports for species of concern, for threatened or endangered species, or for impact categories monitored by a state or federal agency;
2   To examine a specific, often localized impact associated with a spike in beached carcasses, and assumed to be related to human activities;
3   To examine large-scale, even global, environmental forcing, most often associated with a changing climate.

### Conservation – fishery issues

Fishery bycatch is a global concern threatening several species of marine birds (Gianuca et al., 2017). Within coastal environments, gillnet fisheries have been shown to entangle diving seabirds (Hall et al., 2000; Davoren, 2007). In the Pacific Northwest, gillnet fisheries for salmon (*Onchorhynchus* spp.) inadvertently capture a range of non-target species, including diving piscivores, principally common murres (*Uria aalge*). In the late summer to early fall, salmon returning to the Fraser River are typically fished just as post-breeding murres and their fledglings are entering the Salish Sea after having dispersed from coastal colonies along the Oregon and Washington coastlines (Hamel et al., 2009).

In the fall of 2007, COASST participants documented 48 murres per kilometer on a single beach on Bainbridge Island in central Puget Sound, Washington State. As the baseline encounter rate for this region (Puget Sound) and season is essentially zero, this event was untoward. Several subsequent surveys in the area documented significant increases in murre beaching, and non-COASSTer reports of floating carcasses, including from captains of the regional ferry system transiting the area, were reported in the local press. An example of a "fishery-associated stranding," the Bainbridge event is periodically repeated throughout the Salish Sea during the salmon gillnet fishing season in August–November.

Hamel et al. (2009) used COASST data as well as data from a Canadian sister program – the British Columbia Beached Bird Survey (BCBBS) – to construct a baseline against which known fishery bycatch within the Salish Sea could be assessed. This work contrasted species diversity and carcass encounter rates of COASST/BCBBS baseline data against (1) known "fishery-associated strandings," or unusual mortality events associated with specific fishery openings and (2) data on carcasses recovered from the active Puget Sound gillnet fishery. Across all species, divers (including alcids, loons, grebes, cormorants and scoters) constituted 100% of the gillnet bycatch sample, 93% of the fishery-associated stranding sample, but only 44% of the baseline sample (restricted to only fishery-active months). Common murres (*Uria aalge*) were the major species reported in fishery bycatch and in fishery-associated strandings, whereas large gulls (*Larus* spp.) were the major taxon in the beached bird baseline data.

When compared with the baseline rate, fishery-associated strandings were acute and occasionally catastrophic (baseline: mean = 0.14 carcasses per kilometer; fishery-associated strandings: mean = 16.4 carcasses per kilometer); however, they were also sparse in both space and time (2,576 carcasses over 39 years). By contrast, baseline rates calculated from COASST/BCBBS data and applied throughout the Salish Sea coastline scaled to more than 10,000 carcasses annually. Thus, a cumulative comparison of fishery-associated strandings versus baseline beaching effectively flipped the relationship, and suggests caution when interpreting bycatch data.

Following publication of Hamel et al. (2009), COASST was approached about the possibility of stratifying beach sampling in high-fishery regions. This presented the program with a conundrum: should COASST preserve positive relationships with all geographic and ethnographic communities and communities of practice, or should COASST essentially endorse a policing function? In the end, COASST declined this request; however, the experience has brought both our program goals and our data use policies into sharper focus. COASST supports both broad extent, fine grain, high quality data and science literacy through experiential learning. We attempt to produce the very best data possible given the constraints of a geographically broad, long-term citizen-based data collection program, and then make those data widely available to scientists, resource managers, the media and – importantly – the participants and their communities.

## Conservation – climate forcing

In recent years, warming signals in the world's oceans have included the appearance of marine heat waves, that is large-scale persistent sea surface temperature anomalies of one to several degrees (Hobday et al., 2016). Documenting marine ecosystem responses is an essential first step to understanding immediate threats, as well as to predicting longer-term ecosystem shifts given climate model forecasts of future warming. COASST has been involved in documenting a series of marine bird mass-mortality events, which we define as beaching for one or more months at a rate at least an order of magnitude above the long-term mean (normal) signal and occurring over multiple beach sites such that the regional signal is also significantly elevated (Figure 2.2). Between 2013 and 2017, a total of five such events were recorded by COASST, totaling more than 15,000 carcasses found on beaches from northern California to Alaska. Models of total deposition, and/or total mortality, suggest that these events accounted for over one million birds. In the case of Cassin's auklets in 2014–2015, estimated total mortality exceeded 10% of the world breeding population (Jones et al., in review). While that number is not unexpected relative to the baseline modes of post-breeding mortality and winterkill, the pattern in space, time and biodiversity is pointedly different.

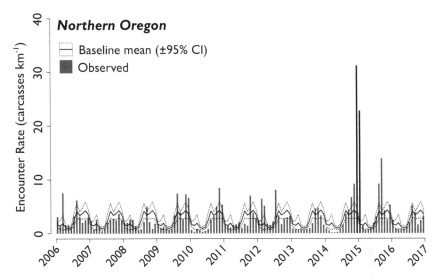

**FIGURE 2.2**   A sample baseline graphic (here the northern coast of Oregon) of encounter rate (mean carcasses per kilometer averaged over all surveyed sites monthly within a region). Gray bars – actual monthly (observed) average; black bars – unusual mortality events defined as five times baseline mean; solid and dashed lines – long-term baseline and 95% confidence intervals, exclusive of all unusual mortality events.

COASST data suggest that the Alcid family, including murres, puffins, auklets and murrelets, appear to be at higher risk of heatwave-induced mortality than other major marine families (e.g. Larids, Procellariids). All five recent events have entirely featured Alcids, as opposed to previous mass mortality events that were less frequent, relatively smaller in magnitude, and more diverse taxonomically (Figure 2.3). Alternatively, Alcids may be altering their distribution towards nearshore environments in response to ocean warming and "bottom-up" shifts in the marine food web, such that the chance of beaching given mortality is greatly increased (Jones et al., in review). In either case, COASST data have provided a unique window into the impacts of severe warming, which might otherwise go unreported or uncalculated. That is, broad extent, fine grain data collection programs like COASST are uniquely suited for this type of population monitoring.

Because the root causes of warming and associated ecosystem shifts are complex and beyond the ability of any one program, agency or government to control, positive conservation outcomes are few. Steps toward conservation outcomes at least include documentation of impact, in service of petitioning for increased threat or endangerment status at federal levels which then trigger a potential range of protections and mitigations.

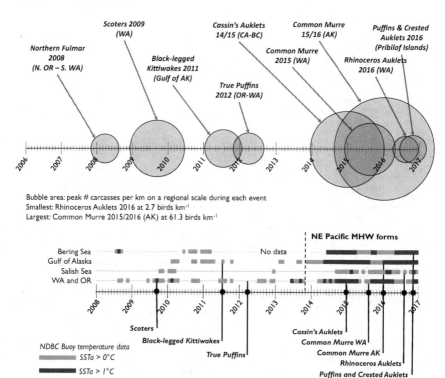

Bubble area: peak # carcasses per km on a regional scale during each event
Smallest: Rhinoceros Auklets 2016 at 2.7 birds km⁻¹
Largest: Common Murre 2015/2016 (AK) at 61.3 birds km⁻¹

**FIGURE 2.3** Top panel: Incidence of mass mortality events, defined as encounter rates (carcasses per lineal kilometer of beach) exceeding an order of magnitude above the long-term mean. Circles are sized relative to the region-wide peak in encounter rate of each incident, allowing comparisons across all events. Bottom panel: Timelines of region-specific sea surface temperature anomalies, measured relative to the long-term climatology, where light bars indicates a positive anomaly and dark bars indicates a positive anomaly of greater than one degree (C). Prior to the onset of the Northeast Pacific marine heatwave, there is no association between warmer than normal conditions and mortality events.

## Guidelines and lessons learned from COASST

### Materials

*Simple, straightforward, jargon-free materials* allowing participants to collect evidence and arrive at the correct deduction are essential. All COASST participants are given (1) an identification key specific to beached birds (Hass and Parrish, 2006, 2013; Parrish, 2009) and require no birding or science expertise to use, (2) a protocol that explains in text and graphic forms how all elements of the program work, (3) data sheets and (4) a tool kit with equipment for making necessary measurements, tagging carcasses and taking photographs.

Although only five species constitute 65% of all carcass finds within the COASST program (Figure 2.4), more than 170 species have been identified. Therefore, *teaching people not to guess* is fundamental to an accurate assessment of species richness and of rarity. COASST guides start with the body parts that last the longest on the beach – feet and wings – guiding users through a simple series of dichotomous and trichotomous questions to a greatly abbreviated set of choices – a "Foot-type Family" or a small selection of morphologically similar wings that cross phylogenetic lineages (e.g. the similarly sized and dark-plumaged: coot, American crow and tufted puffin). Because beached birds are often missing body parts due to predation and/or subsequent scavenging, even experts can be fooled. Therefore, all identification proceeds from basic evidence collection, first, to deduction based on that evidence, second. This simple procedure allows participants to prove to themselves that they are correct, with subsequent verification by marine bird professionals. Evidence followed by deduction is inherent in our keys, and is reinforced in our data sheets, our protocol and our website data entry system.

A second aspect of our approach is to *target materials to what participants will actually see* (i.e. photographs of dead, disheveled birds, or parts thereof) instead of a perfectly framed and sanitized version of the same (e.g. the photographs or drawings in most field guides), as most participants will not carry around any particular image of what a "type specimen" might look like.

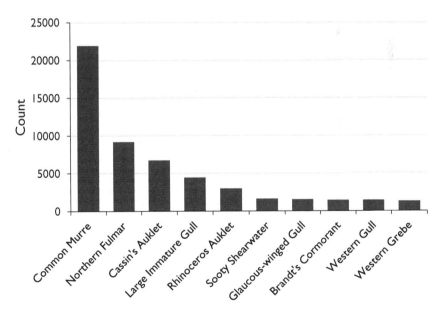

**FIGURE 2.4**    The 10 most abundant species in the COASST dataset, cumulatively across space and time.

A third aspect of our approach is *obvious language* even if it is "not as correct" in the mind of the scientist. For example, the beached bird key reads, "Wingpit," not axillaries; "bill," not culmen. In developing the key, our team literally sent it to our grandmothers to identify words and phrases that didn't make sense (aka jargon) so that we could replace it with more operational, common-sense phrasing, which proved – embarrassingly – effective. What we learned is that forcing people to learn extensive new terminology to participate sends the wrong message, that is that science is difficult, and that non-experts can't do it.

COASST keys proceed from these principles: (1) routes to correct identification should ideally be multiple and foolproof; (2) there are multiple ways of knowing – some people prefer text whereas others rely primarily on visuals (photographs, diagrams); (3) avoid subtle differences that non-experts won't be able to consistently assess correctly (i.e. literal shades of gray) and lump across categories if necessary (e.g. large immature gulls); and (4) redundancy is good, it can be used to reinforce learning.

To help remember each step that individuals learn in a day of training, COASST provides all participants with a protocol that details sampling, identification and data entry in written and graphic form. A living document, the protocol is updated as elements of the program are improved (often at the suggestion of participants) and/or new tools replace old ones (e.g. digital cameras and file sharing websites replace Polaroid cameras and snail mail). COASST datasheets are designed to be visually appealing (e.g. uncrowded, larger format type attentive to "old eyes"), move left-to-right from common to rare data types, always require evidence fields before deductive fields, and reinforce the fact that zeroes (i.e. no birds) are as important as finding something.

Finally, rather than high-cost, specialized and/or complicated tools (e.g. dial calipers, wing rulers) that break easily or intimidate new learners, COASST provides participants with simple tools needed to measure standard body parts accurately (dividers, ruler, measuring tape), mark carcasses (10 colors of cable ties) and record photographs accurately (photo ruler, photo slate, chalk, digital camera – if not already possessed by the participant).

## Training

In COASST, all trainings are conducted within coastal communities where we have established a connection to a local community organization (e.g. Sea Grant extension office, Audubon chapter, Sound and Bay Keepers chapter) or school, and/or an individual community member has contacted us to ask that we come give a training. In five to six hours, attendees without any prior knowledge of science or of birds can learn to reliably identify about 60 species, how to conduct a standardized beach survey, how to fill in the COASST datasheet and how to transmit their data to the COASST office at the University of Washington via web and snail-mail channels.

Many adult informal science education programs focus on lectures; by contrast, adults have positive impressions of programs exposing them to new perspectives or insights (Sachatello-Sawyer et al., 2002). In COASST, trainings focus on data-specific content and skills, moving participants gradually through *passive learning* (lecture format is used for the introduction to the program); to *participatory learning* (call and response is used for a live bird, dead bird quiz highlighting why knowing the former doesn't confer expertise in identifying the latter); to *experiential learning* (pair-share based problem-solving is used to guide attendees through use of the key, how to survey the beach, and how to fill in data sheets).

Because the latter portions of the training involve hands-on learning, we keep the trainer to trainee ratio low so that pairs of attendees working on mastering an element of the program do not have to wait long to interact with an expert. To accomplish this goal, COASST uses key staff who are well-versed in seabird identification and the COASST approach as the main trainers, and COASST undergraduate interns and local COASSTers as training assistants.

Finally, all COASST trainers are exuberant and non-judgmental teachers, and they are content experts. Detailed knowledge about the natural history and life history of marine birds is key to engaging public participation, as is general knowledge of marine biology, ecology and conservation. Positive affirmation of participant success (a foot well measured, a test carcass correctly identified) and patient guidance through the process when participants stumble (as opposed to simple identification of the correct answer) are also essential to allowing attendees to realize that they can do it, separate from their understanding that we know the answer. Yet when attendees ask a question, trainers absolutely need to know the answer.

## Follow-through and follow-up

Adults, and especially retirees, want to participate in activities that are meaningful to them, and do not want to waste their time. Knowing from the outset that a citizen science program is a serious endeavor and may require hours of steady, often tedious, work in a single session is a key message to give any potential participant. In COASST, we end all training sessions with a serious discussion of the time involved, the physical condition needed to survey (not stroll along) beaches, and the necessity of committing to monthly surveys. Attendees are invited to decide whether they wish to join – that is, attending a training program is not synonymous with joining COASST – and this step allows individuals who are not serious, or not able to fully participate, to step away gracefully. We also require all new participants to sign a contract pledging that they will survey monthly, and pay COASST a deposit for program materials (waived in remote, economically depressed communities). Instead of turning people away, these elements are taken as signs of a serious program, and that commitment is returned in kind, as the majority of attendees sign up.

Once participants have initiated data collection, we make sure to respond to questions immediately through multiple channels (phone, email). COASST staff contact new participants within five days of a training, and again after they submit their first survey data. After their first year of surveying, participants will have been contacted by COASST at least 10 times either directly or through program publications such as our website (www.COASST.org); our e-newsletter, blog, Facebook, Twitter, Science Updates and holiday cards; or through opportunities to engage in refresher sessions, assist others in local trainings and attend natural history talks and COASST socials. This level of attention to participant engagement, needs, communication and satisfaction is costly in terms of staffing, but we have found it is essential to maintaining a large group of committed and knowledgeable participants year after year (see Chapter 13).

## The data

The core component of any citizen science program are the data generated by the participants. Identification accuracy is at the heart of COASST, but so is uniform effort. When originally developing the COASST protocols, COASST pilot-participants helped us determine what we could ask surveyors to do: set specific start and turnaround locations, require survey partners to use a non-overlapping sine wave search pattern, and mark carcasses, for example. We also learned what we couldn't expect them to do: collect extensive body measurements, cut open carcasses and survey beaches much more than a kilometer in length. To combat potential differences in survey effort, COASST also assesses whether beaches with similar geomorphological (e.g. substrate, inclination) and orientation (e.g. compass direction, bay versus peninsula) features in the same bio-physical region (e.g. south outer coast of Washington State) have similar beached bird patterns, as assessed by our participants. Finally, we check the refind rate among beaches (possible because of individual marking) as a secondary clue to effort differences. Standardizing effort such that data are comparable with other programs remains the most difficult aspect of our program.

In COASST, we invite participants to enter their data online in a password-protected portion of our website. Data entry proceeds in the same sequence that field data collection does: evidence first, deduction second. Because participants must enter foot type and/or measurements first, automatic database filtering restricts subsequent choices. This enforced sequence combined with automatic feedback simultaneously helps the participant learn and acts as a first filter for data quality.

A key aspect of COASST's data is our independent verification. The scientific reputation of a citizen science program is based in large part on the quality and use of its data. Non-scientist, non-student collected data have an added burden of proof (Burgess et al., 2016). Without independent verification, citizen science data may not be used, other than cursorily, even if it is of high quality. In COASST, every single carcass identification is verified by staff experts using the evidence (foot type, measurements, photographs) collected by the participants. Verification allows us to do three things: identify participants who have recurring difficulty with identification, calculate participant accuracy program-wide and improve data quality. Most COASST participants are receptive when they learn that they made an incorrect identification, or – more often the case – that they could have taken the identification to a higher and more specific level (e.g. species instead of foot type family; sex or breeding status within species), and are eager to find out what character(s) they should have noted. Program-wide, COASSTers are accurate to species 83% of the time. This statistic is impressive, as less than half of the carcasses are intact (e.g. victims of predation, scavenging or severely decomposed). The process of verification not only allows staff to catch misidentifications, but to increase the number of identifications to species level, further improving data quality. Post check, identification rate to species is increased to 92%.

Constructing a data collection scheme that matches the space-time scales of the system, process and/or question is a basic component of study design. In field sampling, accounting for spatial variability, including patchiness and gradients, is also an important issue. However, in longitudinal citizen science programs requiring participants to return to "their" study site again and again, optimal sampling design is difficult, if not impossible. People have strong attachments to particular places – a specific park, beach or trail – and often will not volunteer to sample another site, even if it is geographically convenient to them. People are not uniformly arrayed on the landscape – over-sampling will occur nearer to settlement centers, and will be a function of community size. In COASST, early attempts to match new participants to particular beaches – chosen according to substrate representation within larger biophysical regions and arrayed to create uniform inter-site distances – was an utter failure. When we switched to allowing people to select their own sites, participation rates jumped up, as did retention rates. Practically, this means that (1) we may not be able to use data from a region we have recently "colonized" until site numbers have climbed to the point where coverage begins to approach a statistically meaningful sample, and (2) we will oversample as a function of human density.

## User engagement

*Participants*: A significant element of any longitudinal citizen science program is giving the analyzed data back to the participants at scales larger than the individual collector, and in forms they find attractive (the latter only rarely includes peer-reviewed papers). Committed participants are usually quite observant about the place they love – their study site – and notice changes that may, or may not, resolve to higher geographic or temporal scales. At the same time, participants may be aware of larger-scale forcing (e.g. coastal development, climate warming, ocean acidification) or even vaguely threatening factors (e.g. marine debris, avian influenza, radiation following the Japanese tsunami), and wonder to what degree these things may be connected to their local experience.

Compiling program data into simple, straightforward tabular (e.g. list of species and species counts) and graphic (e.g. annual phenology of occurrence, baseline versus mortality event) patterns can be a powerful way to show participants what is happening. Pulling out particular highlights in story fashion and connecting these data to life history, natural history and conservation resonates with many participants because it allows them to put their own personal observations in context. For instance, in 2015–2016 a massive die-off of common murres struck parts of the Pacific Northwest coastline, as well as the Gulf of Alaska (Figure 2.5). While Lower 48 COASSTers routinely experience elevated murre deposition during post-breeding months and thus were not seriously alarmed, Alaskan COASSTers had never experienced either the peak magnitude or the duration (up to 11 months in some location) of the event. Putting this very large spatiotemporal story into a

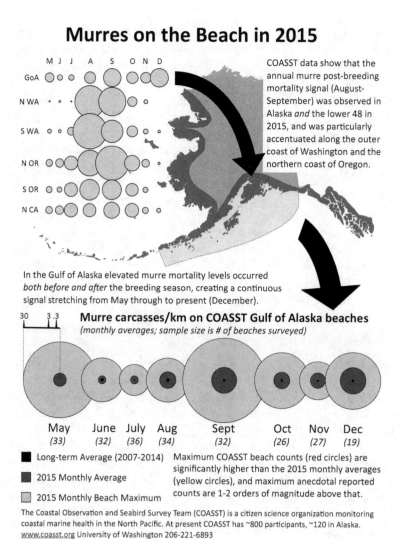

# Murres on the Beach in 2015

COASST data show that the annual murre post-breeding mortality signal (August-September) was observed in Alaska *and* the lower 48 in 2015, and was particularly accentuated along the outer coast of Washington and the northern coast of Oregon.

In the Gulf of Alaska elevated murre mortality levels occurred *both before and after* the breeding season, creating a continuous signal stretching from May through to present (December).

## Murre carcasses/km on COASST Gulf of Alaska beaches
*(monthly averages; sample size is # of beaches surveyed)*

| May | June | July | Aug | Sept | Oct | Nov | Dec |
|-----|------|------|-----|------|-----|-----|-----|
| *(33)* | *(32)* | *(36)* | *(34)* | *(32)* | *(26)* | *(27)* | *(19)* |

■ Long-term Average (2007-2014)

■ 2015 Monthly Average

□ 2015 Monthly Beach Maximum

Maximum COASST beach counts (red circles) are significantly higher than the 2015 monthly averages (yellow circles), and maximum anecdotal reported counts are 1-2 orders of magnitude above that.

The Coastal Observation and Seabird Survey Team (COASST) is a citizen science organization monitoring coastal marine health in the North Pacific. At present COASST has ~800 participants, ~120 in Alaska. www.coasst.org University of Washington 206-221-6893

FIGURE 2.5  Example of a COASST info-graphic distributed to COASST participants and partnering organizations, and placed on the COASST website, allowing individual participants within the affected geographic range to understand the extent of the die-off in space and time beyond their own experience. Originally in color: red outer circles (2015 monthly maximum) now dark gray; yellow circles (2015 monthly average) are light gray.

local context was an important part of helping participants see the larger picture. Placing such infographics on the COASST website and making them available to organizational and agency partners also helps convey the basic elements of emerging stories, well before causality is known or a peer-reviewed paper can be assembled and published.

*Other data users:* In an average year, COASST receives 15–20 requests for some/ all of our raw (e.g. beach-specific counts) and/or post-processed (e.g. encounter rates) data. If the data requests are legitimate, and the request does not involve excessive staff time to process and analyze raw data, then requesters must agree to sign a COASST data use agreement. COASST releases data to a wide range of users: from students conducting class projects (e.g. mapping the "true puffin" die-off of 2012 in a geographic information systems class); to academic researchers seeking to extend their work with COASST data (e.g. using species-specific data on body parts found to infer what indigenous coastal peoples in southern Washington may have been able to glean from the beach: Bovy et al., 2016); and resource managers at state, regional and national levels asking to include COASST findings in larger status reports (e.g. annual report to Congress on the national seabird plan-of-action including species threatened or endangered by fishery activities).

A nontrivial fraction of the information requests COASST receives is from media sources seeking information about a particular mass mortality event. For instance, COASST staff provided 20+ newspaper, website/blog, radio and TV interviews during and following a large die-off of Cassin's auklets in 2014–2015. As a rule, COASST engages all media, providing information and interviews with staff upon request, and contact information for COASST participants only after checking with each individual about their willingness to talk with the media. Since 2005, nine such massive mortality events (Figure 2.3) have resulted in dozens of interviews and subsequent translation of the COASST story into the news media. Although this coverage may not directly translate into conservation action, it does make tens of thousands of readers aware of what is happening along the Pacific coast, what COASST is and what we are doing.

## Program challenges

In designing a rigorous and intensive citizen science program, COASST has faced a series of challenges, including those we anticipated, largely arising from data quality and data use, and those that became apparent to us after we started, arising from the motivations of and constraints of our participants.

### The challenge of data quality

With respect to identification, COASST tackles the challenge of data quality in two ways. First, by ensuring that data collection is simple: collect evidence (foot morphology; foot, wing, and bill measurements; plumage characters), deduce species identification, document with dorsal and ventral photographs, and individually tag each carcass. Second, by creating a data collection scheme allowing experts to verify participant identifications using the same combination of evidence, photographs, and tag number in the case of re-found carcasses.

The second component of data quality – sampling accuracy – is harder to assess. COASST teaches participants to use a sinusoidal search pattern. To equalize search effort, narrow beaches are surveyed from set start to set turnaround point; wide beaches are surveyed both coming (low beach) and going (high beach). Mark-recapture studies, using a subset of COASST participants who collected data daily for 5–10 contiguous days monthly for up to two years suggests that the recapture rate was 75%–80%. However, this statistic conflates carcasses that are missed and those that are buried in wind-blown sand, becoming invisible on one or more subsequent surveys before becoming unburied. Without a targeted study of sampling accuracy, it is difficult to assess the degree to which participants truly miss carcasses. Despite this shortcoming, COASST data at regional scales do produce replicable (year-over-year) patterns of encounter rate with relatively small inter-beach variability, suggesting that participant sampling error does not overwhelm the underlying signal.

## The challenge of scale

COASST was originally designed to create a local baseline against which catastrophic mortality as a consequence of a local oil spill could be measured. With growth in the geographic extent of the program, other environmental issues can now be addressed, including problems local to an area of expansion (e.g. fisheries bycatch in Puget Sound, Washington; Hamel et al., 2009) as well as regional-scale forcing (e.g. response to anomalies in annual upwelling strength and timing; Parrish et al., 2007). However, COASST has occasionally struggled with matching the scale of an issue of interest to the scale of data collection, in both space and time. For instance, data collection in Alaska is severely hampered by the absence of human settlement, resulting in sparse coverage that returns a more variable monthly signal. Because many conservation issues are basin-wide, if not global, and marine birds are often long-distance migrants that may breed and overwinter thousands of kilometers apart, encompassing these larger spatial scales is simply not possible, at least for all species.

## The challenges of retention and demographic representation

Annual retention rate in COASST is approximately 80% program-wide, and the "half-life" of the average participant is about 4.5 years. Post-training, most new attendees (that is, excluding seasoned COASSTers attending training to refresh their skills, or visitors from partnering agencies) elect to sign up for the program; however, only 78% of those individuals go on to complete their first survey (Figure 2.6). This population of data collectors is relatively stable, with 90% completing more than one survey, an indication that the pattern of high fall-off rates after initial

# COASST Retention (Beached Birds)
*Classroom Trainings: Nov 2010 – Dec 2016*

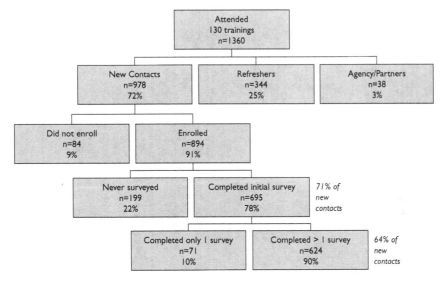

FIGURE 2.6    A flow diagram of participant recruitment (defined as signing up following training) and retention through to multiple surveys. Data are cumulative over all regions for 130 trainings conducted over a six-year period.

contact experienced by some volunteer programs does not appear to be indicative of COASST. Nevertheless, cumulative retention from novice attendees through completion of more than one survey is 64%, requiring continued trainings to maintain program size. In places where environmental extremes preclude surveying for some portion of the winter (e.g. Bering Sea), and/or the number of carcasses washing in is extremely low (e.g. Southeast Alaska, Puget Sound), attrition is higher. Although COASSTers living in regions where carcass deposition is regular and weather is not forbidding do tend to remain in the program longer, mass mortality events overwhelm and burn-out participants, as single surveys stretch to more than 10 hours at a time. As the frequency of these events has increased as a function of sea surface warming, the opposing stresses of scientific and resource management need to document and bound these events with participant burn-out during these events becomes a conservation cataclysm.

Average COASSTer age is 58 ($N = 385$ respondents), with a distinct difference between Alaska residents (average age = 47), relatively urban residents in locations like Puget Sound (average = 56), and smaller community outer coast residents of Oregon and Washington (average = 62). Females outnumber males across all regions (60%:40%, $N = 535$). Both patterns reflect a preponderance of retirees in the program (52%, $N = 339$ respondents). Appealing to a wider age range is difficult, as working individuals have less free time. COASST does not actively market to minors, in part because of issues of liability, and in part because working with school programs often means that beaches go unsurveyed during summer months.

At present, COASST does not collect information on the ethnicity of participants, but anecdotal information collected by trainers suggests that an overwhelming preponderance of participants are white. Under-represented minorities are largely under-represented in COASST, with the exception of Native Americans. Tribal participation includes four to six tribes throughout coastal Washington and a similar number of tribal corporations in Alaska. Although this is impressive, it also reflects the fact that tribal science and natural resource employees – whether they are Native American or not – participate. Participation by community members who are not directly affiliated with tribal government in a science or education capacity is much smaller. Engaging local coastal community members, and especially in communities with a strong non-Western culture, remains extremely difficult. This may well be because COASST is top-down, and built on a Western science way of knowing.

## Conclusions

The COASST program is one model of rigorous citizen science, producing high quality data of a grain and extent that are immediately useful in tracking marine bird populations. Because marine birds are subject to a wide range of impacts of human activities, beached bird programs like COASST have great potential to document mortality events stemming from a wide range of human actions. The impacts of fisheries, and of climate warming, are examples of the conservation issues COASST data can speak to at local and global scales, respectively. In both cases, program data has been used to document impact as statistically different from the long-term mean, or baseline.

In COASST, citizen science is a contract between scientists and participants, where neither party can truly exist without the other. Citizens need scientists to help design data collection protocols that can produce standardized, rigorous information at scales relevant to both individual data collectors and the underlying questions at issue. Scientists need well-trained participants to make the millions of observations that professionals alone will never achieve. Citizens need scientists to amalgamate those observations into larger space and time scales of pattern that can speak to causation and impact. And while some scientists may be content to stop at the production of a scientific product, this same knowledge set can empower citizens to take extra steps. We imagine tens of millions of people participating in rigorous citizen science programs each directly linked to resource management agencies and scientific experts. We imagine each geographic community filled with participants collecting multiple data streams that braid together to form a comprehensive picture of the environment and of environmental change.

Beyond work on any one conservation issue, perhaps the most positive conservation impact of COASST is on the knowledge base, and tendency to action, of participants. Haywood et al. (2016) examined the degree to which learning by COASST participants translated into conservation action. They found that our participants were more accurately knowledgeable about human activities and stressors on the nearshore marine environment, and particularly with respect to seabird mortality factors, than new recruits, a tendency they labelled as "informed concern." At the same time, they noted that participants strongly endorsed the program data, and specifically the power of a large, rigorous dataset. Finally, they documented that participants regularly communicate findings from the program to others, from friends and family to decision-makers (politicians, resource managers and members of the media). Thus, the collective reach of COASST, and "COASST stories," carries far beyond the publications and presentations of program scientists.

## Acknowledgements

This chapter was a collective effort of many generations of COASST staff and associated scientists, and was made possible through the collective effort of thousands of participants cumulatively over the lifetime of the program. Tim Jones created the maps and data figures. Work on this chapter was supported by NSF DRL 1114734 and 1322820 to JKP and Washington Sea Grant R/OLWD-1 to JKP.

## Literature cited

Averbeck, C. (1991). Ergebnisse des "Beached Bird Survey" der Bundesrepublik Deutschland im Februar 1990. *Mitteilungen Nord-deutsche Naturschutz Akademie*, 2, 50–52.

Bovy, K.M., Watson, J.E., Dolliver, J., and Parrish, J.K. (2016). Distinguishing offshore bird hunting from beach scavenging in archaeological contexts: The value of modern beach surveys. *Journal of Archaeological Science*, 70, 35–47.

Burgess, H., DeBey, L.B., Froehlich, H., Schmidt, N., Theobald, E.J., Ettinger, A.K., Hille-RisLambers, J., Tewksbury, J., and Parrish, J.K. (2016). The science of citizen science: Exploring barriers to use as a primary research tool. *Biological Conservation*, 208, 113–120. http://dx.doi.org/10.1016/j.biocon.2016.05.014.

Camphuysen, C.J. (1989). *Beached bird surveys in the Netherlands 1915–1988: Seabird mortality in the southern North Sea since the early days of oil pollution*. Technisch Rapport Vogelbescherming 1. Amsterdam: Werkgroep Noordzee.

Camphuysen, K.C.J., Wright, P.J., Leopold, M., Hüppop, O., and Reid, J.B. (1999). A review of the causes, and consequences at the population level, of mass mortalities of seabirds. *ICES Coop Res Rep*, 232, 51–62.

Cooper, C., Shirk, J., and Zuckerberg, B. (2014). The invisible prevalence of citizen science in global research: Migratory birds and climate change. *PLoS One*, 9(9), e106508.

Davoren, G.K. (2007) Effects of gill-net fishing on marine birds in a biological hotspot in the northwest Atlantic. *Conservation Biology*, 21, 1032–1045.

Dickinson, J.L., Zuckerberg, B., and Bonter, D.N. (2010). Citizen science as an ecological research tool: Challenges and Benefits. *Annual Review of Ecology and Evolutionary Systematics*, 41, 149–172.

Forney, K.A., Benson, S.R., and Cameron, G.A. (2001). Central California gillnet effort and bycatch of sensitive species, 1990–1998. In *Proc Seabird Bycatch: Trends, Roadblocks, and Solutions*, 141–160. University of Alaska Sea Grant, AK-SG-01–01.

Gianuca, D., Phillips, R.A., Townley, S., and Votier, S.C. (2017). Global patterns of sex-and age-specific variation in seabird bycatch. *Biological Conservation*, 205, 60–76.

Hamel, N.J., Burger, A.E., Charleton, K., Davidson, P., Lee, S., Bertram, D.F., and Parrish, J.K. (2009). Bycatch and beached birds: Assessing mortality impacts in coastal net fisheries using marine bird strandings. *Marine Ornithology*, 37, 41–60.

Hall, M., Alverson, D.L., and Metuzals, K.I. (2000) By-catch: problems and solutions. *Marine Pollution Bulletin*, 41, 204–219.

Hass, T., and Parrish, J.K. (2006). *Beached Birds: A COASST Field Guide to the North Atlantic.* Wavefall Press: University of Washington.

Hass, T., and Parrish, J.K. (2013). *Beached Birds: A COASST Field Guide, Fourth Edition.* Wavefall Press: University of Washington.

Haywood, B. (2016). Beyond data points and research contributions: The personal meaning and value associated with public participation in scientific research. *International Journal of Science Education, Part B*, 6(3), 239–262.

Haywood, B., Parrish, J.K., and Dolliver, J. (2016). Place-based, data-rich citizen science as a precursor for conservation action. *Conservation Biology*, 30(3), 476–486.

Heubeck, M. (2006). The Shetland beached bird survey, 1979–2004. *Marine Ornithology*, 34, 123–127.

Hobday, A., Alexander, L., Perkins, S., Smale, D., Straub, S., Oliver, E., . . . Wernberg, T. (2016). A hierarchical approach to defining marine heatwaves. *Progress in Oceanography*, 141, 227–238.

Julian, F., and Beeson, M. (1998). Estimates of marine mammal, turtle, and seabird mortality for two California gillnet fisheries: 1990–1995. *Fishery Bulletin*, 96, 271–284.

Moore, E., Lyday, S., Roletto, J., Litle, K., Parrish, J.K., Nevins, H., Harvey, J., Mortenson, J., Greig, D., Pianna, M., Hermance, A., Lee, D., Adams, D., Allen, A., and Kell, S. (2009). Entanglements of marine mammals and seabirds in central California and the north-west coast of the United States 2001–2005. *Marine Pollution Bulletin*, 58, 1045–1051.

Newman, S.H., Harris, R.J., and Tseng, F.S. (2006). Beach surveys past, present, and future: Toward a global surveillance network of stranded seabirds. *Marine Ornithology*, 34, 87–90.

OSPAR. (1996). *Joint Assessment Monitoring Program (JAMP) guidelines on standard methodology for the use of oiled beached birds as indicators of marine oil pollution.* Reference No. 1995–1996. London: OSPAR Commission.

Parrish, J .K., Bond, N., Nevins, H., Mantua, N., Loeffel, R., Peterson, W.T., and Harvey, J.T. (2007). Beached birds and physical forcing in the California current system. *Marine Ecology Progress Series*, 352, 275–288.

Parrish, J.K. (2009). *Beached Birds: A COASST Field Guide to Alaska.* Wavefall Press: University of Washington.

Powlesland, D.R.G., and Imber, M.J. (1988). OSNZ beach patrol scheme: Information and instructions. *Notornis*, 35, 143–153.

Sachatello-Sawyer, B., Fellenz, R.A., Burton, H., Gittings-Carlson, L., Lewis-Mahony, J., and Woolbaugh, W. (2002). *Adult museum programs.* Walnut Creek: Altamira.

Seys, J., Offringa, H., Meire, P., Van Waeyenberge, J., and Kuijken, E. (2002). Long-term changes in oil pollution off the Belgian coast: Evidence from beached bird monitoring. *Belgian Journal of Zoology*, 132, 111–118.

Stenzel, L.E., Page, G.W., Carter, H.R., and Ainley, D.G. (1988). *Seabird mortality in California as witnessed through 14 years of beached bird censuses.* Unpublished report, Point Reyes Bird Observatory, Stinson Beach, CA.

Stephens, C., and Burger, A.E. (1994). A comparison of two methods for surveying mortality of beached birds in British Columbia. *Canadian Veterinary Journal*, 35, 631–635.

# 3

# USING CITIZEN SCIENCE TO ADDRESS CONSERVATION ISSUES RELATED TO CLIMATE CHANGE AND COASTAL SYSTEMS

*Jenny A. Cousins, Mark Huxham, and Debbie Winton*

## Introduction

Coastal ecosystems are regions of remarkable biological productivity and have essential economic and cultural functions (Agardy and Alder, 2005). The degradation of these ecosystems and loss of their biodiversity threatens to have profound implications for ecosystem function and human health and well-being. Given their global importance, coastal marine environments are a major focus of concern regarding climate change impacts (Harley et al., 2006), but are also of growing interest because of their role in mitigating climate impacts. For example "blue carbon" ecosystems, such as mangroves, seagrasses and tidal marshes, are some of the most carbon-rich habitats on the planet, removing and storing carbon from the atmosphere and oceans. The growing need for scientific knowledge to underpin conservation and policy actions offers the potential to engage citizen scientists in studies related to coastal ecosystems and climate change.

Of the small proportion of citizen science projects focused on marine and coastal environments (around 14%, Roy et al., 2012), it appears that only a minority of these address climate change (Winton, pers. obs.). The projects that do address climate change tend to fit into three broad categories: (1) those that were not originally established with climate change in mind, but are now retrospectively looking at trends; (2) those that were set up specifically to understand more about climate change impacts; and (3) those that focus on climate change mitigation. The following text will look at these three project types in turn.

### Retrospective studies

There are a number of examples of long-standing citizen science projects in the marine environment generating data for climate change research, but which were not initially set up for that purpose. Marine citizen science is dominated by biodiversity monitoring and studies that have the goal of influencing marine protected area establishment (Hyder et al., 2015). However, such studies now have pre-perturbation baseline data and long-term datasets that can be used to demonstrate biodiversity shifts, particularly changes in numbers, types and distribution of species on local, regional and global scales. These studies are now providing an evidence base for climate change impacts (Theobald et al., 2015). Notable areas are coral reef monitoring (*Reef Check*,[1] *REEF*,[2] *CoralWatch*,[3] *Coral Cay Conservation*[4]), seagrass and mangrove monitoring (*SeagrassWatch*[5] and *MangroveWatch*,[6]) and population trends in fish (Wolfe and Pattengill-Semmen, 2013), manta rays (Jaine et al., 2012) and other elasmobranchs (Ward-Paige and Lotz, 2011; Ward-Paige et al., 2010). For example, data from *Reef Check* are frequently used to study the impacts of and recovery from coral bleaching events (Eakin et al., 2010; Chavanich et al., 2012). *Coral Cay Conservation* has also published a number of papers applying citizen science–generated coral-reef monitoring data to assess coral bleaching events (Beger al., 2001; Harding et al., 2003; Solandt et al., 2003).

## Climate change projects

In recent years, programs have been initiated with climate change questions as their founding objective. For example, in the UK, projects focusing on the rocky shore, such as *The Shore Thing*[7] (led by the Marine Biological Association) and the *Big Sea Survey* (led by Newcastle University), developed into a new initiative called *Capturing Our Coast*[8] (led by Newcastle University with seven main UK partners) to study the impacts of climate change on biodiversity patterns, including how climate change affects spread of invasive species. "Twinned" with the *Big Sea Survey* through the initiative *Oceans Connected*[9] is Earthwatch Australia's *ClimateWatch Marine*,[10] a project in association with the Bureau of Meteorology and the University of Melbourne. As the first continental phenology project in the Southern Hemisphere, *ClimateWatch* asks citizen scientists to collect and record data on presence, absence and abundance of marine plants and animals, providing the basis for a national monitoring program with the goal of helping shape the country's scientific response to climate change. The aim of linking these two projects was to remotely connect citizen scientists involved in similar projects across the globe. In the United States, the Earthwatch project *Climate Change: Seas to Trees at Acadia National Park*[11] is using citizen science to study the effects of climate change and ocean acidification on several key ecosystems of Acadia National Park (Maine, USA), including the rocky intertidal zone. In addition to coastal projects, scientists are also harnessing the skills of those who can snorkel and dive, such as the Earthwatch project *Coral Communities in the Seychelles*,[12] which looks at resilience, recovery and restoration of coral species in relation to environmental stress caused by climate change and other local factors. On a global scale, through *Dive Into Science*,[13] SCUBA divers are recording temperature using their dive computers, and thus filling a gap in global sea temperature data to inform ocean models and studies on the impacts of climate change.

Contributing to these two types of project are a number of internet-based crowdsourcing initiatives in which citizens can contribute from their homes, opening up the opportunity to get involved in marine research even for those who live far from the sea. For example, *Old Weather*[14] asks users to transcribe data from historical ships' logs, for scientists to understand historical weather variability and contribute to climate model projections. Their host site, *Zooniverse*,[15] features a number of climate change–focused projects, including one marine example, *Floating Forests*.[16] For this project, citizen scientists analyze LANDSAT images of kelp forests over a 30-year time series to determine how they are responding to climate change and identify hotspots of change. So far, over 600,000 images have been analyzed by 6,400 users, according to the *Zooniverse* website.

## Climate change mitigation projects

Another avenue of research that lends itself well to citizen science in coastal environments is climate change mitigation, specifically the carbon storage properties of ecosystems such as mangroves and seagrass beds. The recent growth of such "blue carbon" projects provides opportunities for contributions from citizen scientists, and an example of a project in which citizen scientists have been an integral part is detailed in the following case study.

## Case study: managing mangroves and capturing carbon in Kenyan communities

### Project rationale and background

For many coastal communities, such as those living around Gazi Bay on the coast of Kenya, mangrove ecosystems provide key services such as firewood and building poles, nursery provision for fish, coastal protection and opportunities for tourism. While mangrove forests have long been recognized as important, the scale of their contribution has only become apparent in the past 15 years. One of the most important functions associated with mangroves is their exceptional ability to trap and store significant amounts of carbon from the atmosphere, and as such they are recognized for their global role in mitigating climate change. They are exceptionally efficient carbon sinks because of their high productivity and the long-term stability of below-ground carbon stores. Their carbon storing powers are thought to be on average five times that of terrestrial tropical rainforests (Mcleod et al., 2011; Gress et al., 2016).

While mangroves provide an exceptional range of services, they have one of the highest rates of degradation of any global habitat and are one of the world's most threatened natural ecosystems (Giri et al., 2010). The unsustainable use of their provisioning services (such as firewood) and the undervaluation of regulating services (such as carbon storage) has contributed to the rapid removal of mangroves in recent decades. Globally, it is estimated that 30%–50% of mangroves have been destroyed since the 1960s (Valiela et al., 2001), and losses continue at about 2% per year (Giri et al., 2010; FAO, 2007). When mangroves are destroyed, usually for building materials or for fuel, the carbon that has been stored in the forest soil and in biomass, built up over thousands of years, is released into the atmosphere, contributing to climate change.

The mangroves of Gazi Bay (Figure 3.1) have supported people for millennia; however, current patterns of use are unsustainable, with projections based on business as usual suggesting that more than 40% of mangrove forests in southern Kenya will be lost in the next 20 years (Huxham et al., 2015). The degradation of these mangroves has resulted in shortages of building poles and firewood, decreased fishery resources and increased coastal erosion. The recognition of the importance of the

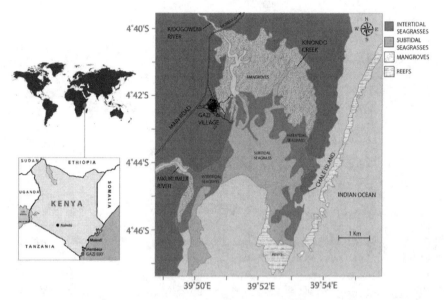

FIGURE 3.1    Gazi Bay is located 55 km (34 miles) south of Mombasa, along the southern coast of Kenya. It's an area of natural beauty with significant marine biodiversity including coral reefs, mangroves and seagrass meadows. The bay is 18 km² in size, and sheltered from strong sea waves by the presence of Chale Peninsula to the east and a fringing coral reef to the south. Livelihoods for the approximately 3,000 residents of the bay are provided predominantly by fishing, farming and tourism. The reef supports a local subsistence and commercial fishery, and the 5.9 km² of mangrove forests that border the bay are used by local people as a fishing ground and source of wood for building and fuel. Other local employment is provided by titanium mining and sugar cane farming. Local tourist attractions include a reserve for the black and white colobus monkey, the Shimba Hills National Park, the tourist resort of Diani Beach and the Kisite-Mpunguti Marine National Park.

*Source:* Taken (with permission) from Githaiga, M.N. (2017) *The role of seagrass meadows in Gazi Bay, Kenya as carbon sinks.* PhD thesis, Edinburgh Napier University.

ecological services mangroves provide to humanity, both globally (i.e. climate change mitigation) and locally, provides powerful arguments for their conservation and an opportunity to engage citizens directly in their scientific research and conservation.

## The Gazi Bay citizen science project

Since 2003, the authors have collaborated with James Kairo of the Kenya Marine and Fisheries Research Institute and Dr. Martin Skov of Bangor University and the Kenya Forest Service to engage citizen scientists in research and conservation activities towards the development of the first community-led blue carbon project.[17]

The project combines protection of existing natural mangrove habitat with long-term and large-scale experiments with the goal of informing restoration of mangrove habitat.

The project objectives are:

1   To test how the diversity of mangrove species in replanted stands affects a range of ecosystem functions, including primary and secondary productivity.
2   To collect data of direct relevance to practical restoration projects (such as the role of intercropping in enhancing productivity, and reducing disease), thus helping to inform future restoration efforts.
3   To use controlled experiments to test the effects of replanted mangroves on sediment dynamics (in both low and high energy areas), and to measure how these effects change as the trees mature.
4   To explore the potential for mangroves to act as carbon sinks and protect against the effects of sea level rise.
5   To develop a large scale demonstration project of sustainable mangrove utilization, and to use this to influence the management of mangrove habitats in Kenya and beyond.

Since 2003, 295 Earthwatch citizen scientists from 42 countries have joined the project, for up to two weeks at a time, in an intensive and immersive program of education, data collection and mangrove restoration, with opportunities to engage with and work alongside the local community. The Earthwatch Institute model is somewhat unique. Citizen scientists pay to participate in projects, either on their own or through sponsors, allowing Earthwatch to provide citizen scientist *and* financial support for research projects. The citizen scientists on the project have included self-funded volunteers (120), corporate employees from major international companies (130) and local stakeholders, students and early career scientists from Africa and Asia (45) (whose placements were funded).

Citizen scientists contribute to four main activities:

1   Planting trees as part of experimental studies and/or for general conservation and restoration purposes (over 20,000 mangrove trees have been planted and measured).

2 Monitoring the experimental stands already established to measure how the trees are growing and surviving and which species combinations are best suited for restoration; measurements include faunal surveys and measurements of the fluxes of greenhouse gases from the sediment surface.

3 Conducting a range of related experiments; for example, measuring the amounts of carbon accumulated above and below ground by different species of trees.

4 Working on aspects of the project related to social development and community involvement, for example helping with the design and facilitation of mangrove education days for local schoolchildren.

Citizen scientists joining the project receive a thorough program of lectures and onsite training by the project leaders including an introduction to the field of biodiversity research, how biodiversity may be linked with ecosystem function and how it is being lost; a guided tour around the village, including discussion of the ancient slave trading remains; an introduction to mangrove ecology, including the species found at the site; training on how to measure physical and chemical variables such as sediment size and greenhouse gas fluxes; a practical session on mangrove reforestation and nursery establishment; an introduction to mangrove species, their specific adaptations and their influence on mangrove ecosystem function; and an overview of the carbon cycle, climate change and the potential of mangroves in carbon sequestration. Days are structured around a mix of fieldwork (timing depending on the tides) and laboratory work, with lectures by project staff or invited speakers on subjects ranging from scientific research to life in the village. Typically, each team will participate in at least one social event involving the village, and volunteers are invited to share their own experiences and expertise with their teams through presentations and discussions. This intensive and immersive experience allows for rapid mutual learning, with team members sharing skills and experiences among themselves and with project staff.

Formal and informal evaluations are conducted with participants on each team, including feedback on the final day of the project and a post-project online questionnaire to gather feedback on the participant experience and information on personal learning (such as knowledge gained, increased understanding of science and environmental issues, increased sense of connection and motivation towards the environment, and changes in attitudes or behaviors toward the environment). This survey provides instantaneous participant feedback allowing for project adjustments, if necessary. In 2015 an additional online questionnaire was emailed to all 253 project participants fielded over the nine years of the project, with a 29% overall response rate (73 participants). This questionnaire was aimed at understanding participant outcomes over a longer time frame – and some of the results are detailed later in the chapter.

### Data quality assurance/quality control procedures

The involvement of hundreds of different people from a wide range of backgrounds and cultures inevitably raises challenges with data management. The

**FIGURE 3.2**   A volunteer from the primary school helps to plant a *Sonneratia alba* seed-
ling. These trees are grown in protected nursery sites and then transplanted
to exposed and eroding areas of the shoreline.

*Source:* Martin W. Skov.

approaches taken to address these evolved during the work and included the
following:

*   *Careful allocation of tasks.* All volunteers engage in authentic scientific and con-
    servation work. However some tasks – such as measuring gas fluxes, inter-
    viewing in Swahili and identifying fauna – require much more expertise than

others. These tasks are either kept for longer-term volunteers, PhD students or staff, or are closely supervised by them.

- *Careful scheduling of data entry.* On days which involve voluminous data collection, the project team are disciplined in ensuring there is sufficient time and resource to enter data on spreadsheets as quickly as possible and by the same teams of people who collected the data. This helps ensure data are not lost and obvious anomalies can be identified.
- *Standardized data spreadsheets with automated quality controls.* Using standard spreadsheets helps ensure all data are comparable and allows automatic checks of quality (such as formulas to prevent entry of negative numbers or percentages failing to sum to 100).
- *Checks on inter-recorder variability.* The data collected by different groups of people (volunteers, staff, students) were compared over three years to establish if there were consistent differences between them (no such differences were found).

## Did the project fulfill its conservation goals?

The scientific data collected by the citizen scientists has led to a greater understanding of mangrove forests and their management, including effective restoration. The work has helped to clarify the role of mangroves in storing carbon and has used experiments to measure carbon losses arising from deforestation. In 2009, The Mikoko Pamoja ('Mangroves Together' in Kiswahili) initiative was launched to apply the scientific research findings of the project, to use payments for ecosystem services (specifically payments for carbon credits) to safeguard the mangrove forests, improve the quality of life of the local community (by linking mangrove management with direct community benefit) and mitigate climate change. A first of its kind, it gained formal accreditation to sell carbon credits to people and institutions that are concerned with carbon offset – through the charity Plan Vivo.[18]

Outcomes of the project can be categorized as knowledge generation and climate change mitigation; managing sites, habitats and ecosystems; enhancing and/or providing alternative livelihoods; training and capacity building; and education and awareness raising (framework adapted from Kapos et al., 2008).

### Knowledge generation and climate change mitigation

- The generation of new scientific knowledge in the form of 19 peer-reviewed publications (for example, Huxham et al., 2010; Huxham et al., 2015).
- Carbon benefits of 2,500 tonnes $CO_2$ $yr^{-1}$ are derived from avoided deforestation, prevented forest degradation and new planting.
- Strengthening of national policy (such as REDD+) through provision of data to the Kenyan Ministry of Forestry and Wildlife. The project has been showcased by the Kenyan Government and the International Union for Conservation of Nature (IUCN) as an example of local responses to climate change.
- Establishment of a regional expert network to disseminate knowledge and help support similar initiatives (www.eafpes.org).

- Links with the United Nations Environment Programme (UNEP) Blue Carbon Initiative allow learning to be shared with similar projects.

## Managing sites, habitats, and ecosystems

- Enriched mangrove ecosystems (and their associated biodiversity) through ongoing restoration of degraded mangrove ecosystems – over 20,000 mangrove trees have been planted and measured, continuing with 4,000 trees annually over the next 20 years.
- Protection of 107 hectares of natural mangrove forest and 10 hectares of plantation through community policing of illegal harvesting.

## Enhancing and/or providing alternative livelihoods

- Income from the sale of carbon credits (which is about $12,000 every year) funds the planting of mangrove trees, and also supports a community fund that is spent on local priorities as determined by local people. These have included school buildings, books, water wells, beekeeping, and ecotourism developments.
- Seven members of the community are employed part-time on the project.
- Improved sustainability of local fuel and timber sources through the planting of woodlots for use by local people.

## Training and capacity building

- Increased community capacity to sustainably manage local mangrove forests (through, for example, the training of nursery teams, forest guards and local organizers).
- Increased technical skills and income to local people employed to assist with carrying out project functions.
- Enriched opportunities for women through their representation within the village and Mikoko Pamoja committees (minimum of 40% representation).
- Training to 30 local school students and four Kenyan master's students each year.
- Investment in 12 future conservation leaders from developing countries each year through immersive training programs and mentoring.

## Education and awareness raising

The immediate post-fieldwork evaluations of the program completed by volunteers consistently showed very high levels of engagement, enjoyment and learning. Volunteers emphasized the importance of working together as a team, being situated in a Kenyan village, working with the villagers and seeing how the field work contributed to global efforts to conserve habitats and tackle climate change as key features of the experience. The long-term follow-up questionnaire, sent to all volunteers including those who came nine years previously, demonstrated lasting effects on knowledge and attitudes, including some volunteers who had changed careers as a result of their experience. Participants reported that the project:[19]

- Changed their understanding of climate change (92%; 47 out of 51 respondents);
- Changed their perspective or opinion about climate change (71%; 35 out of 49 respondents);
- Changed their perspective about local community involvement in conservation (76%; 38 out of 50 respondents);
- Changed their understanding of science, the science process or scientists (75%; 38 out of 51 respondents);
- Changed how they felt about their role in environmental issues (84%; 42 out of 50 respondents);
- Influenced the way they live their everyday life (80%; 40 out of 50 respondents);
- Influenced the way they make decisions at work (63%; 31 out of 49 respondents);
- Inspired a number of actions to be taken after the project: talked to friends and colleagues about the experiences (98%; 49 out of 50 respondents); became more involved in their own local community (50%; 25 out of 50 respondents); gave presentations to schools or community groups (62%; 31 out of 50 respondents); went on to do further study (52%; 26 out of 50 respondents); became involved in other climate change or environmental projects (56%; 28 out of 50 respondents); changed jobs (16%; 8 out of 50 respondents);
- Has been useful to their professional development (76%; 37 out of 49 respondents);
- Has increased their connectedness with the scientific or environmental community (64%; 32 out of 50 respondents).

**FIGURE 3.3**   Secondary school children learn about mangrove ecosystems during a field trip to the site, with the help of an "eco-balloon."

*Source:* Martin W. Skov.

## BOX 3.1 JULIA GROLLMAN – PUBLIC PROGRAM VOLUNTEER

It showed me that really imaginative approaches, such as planting other sources of wood (*Casuarina*) to prevent mangrove depletion, and empowering a community to gain value from this via carbon credits, can be effective in fighting climate change. It was inspirational and gives me strength to continue being part of a community involved with nature conservation at home and to campaign against loss of habitat. I was impressed by the close engagement between the overseas scientists and the Kenyan scientists. Although I was aware that scientists of different nations collaborated, this was an example of it happening in practice. I saw how a lot of practical problem-solving goes into this project in order both to get scientific data and to keep the local community involved.

It makes me determined in general to keep involved in environmental issues. I am likely to be doing some citizen science in retirement. It keeps me aware of looking after the environment I live in, in particular not wasting food and recycling and using public transport. It provides further background to my personal interest in wet environments and provides a strong inspiration about what can be achieved: I expect to continue this involvement in retirement with the waterway charity Thames 21 with whom I already have close links.

FIGURE 3.4   Julia Grollman – public program volunteer.

*Source:* John Grollman.

## BOX 3.2 ARIEL HENDRICKSON – TEACHING FELLOW

Most of the volunteers I was with had little scientific study background, but we were able to help with instructions and contribute to a larger study of the mangroves. While I had been aware of climate change and its importance, seeing its effect firsthand was eye-opening. Seeing the lengths that scientists have to go to complete projects, get help, get funding, it's both impressive and depressing. These are such important projects that need to be focused on, yet the obstacles continue to grow.

I continue to do what I can in my personal life to make smart decisions that will affect the environment, but I also try harder to have conversations with people and try to help them understand small changes they can make that will have lasting effects on the world. Honestly, I never knew how horrible clothes dryers were until Mark made a comment about them. I now try to limit how often I use mine. It also encouraged me to read more and learn more about my personal impact, like reducing how often I fly, or using more renewable resources, even down to cloth wipes instead of disposable. Knowing that these small decisions, like composting, can have lasting importance encourages me. I try to gently harass my coworkers when I see them throwing away recyclable items, or encourage them to bring in their own utensils instead of always relying on the plastic forks available. I also try my best to remember to do all these things. Yes, it has made me more aware of the environmental opportunities in my local community.

**FIGURE 3.5**  Ariel Henderson – teaching fellow.

*Source:* Patrick Dickerson.

## Benefits, limitations and challenges

There have been numerous benefits from this citizen science model. These include some predictable ones, such as the contribution of time and funding by volunteers, and the development of a large network of alumni and friends who have helped disseminate and promote the project work. Some advantages, however, were not anticipated and came as a surprise to those working on the project. For example, the energy and enthusiasm of volunteers has helped sustain project staff and students: "sometimes one can forget the excitement and privilege of working on applied science in such a wonderful environment, and the citizen scientists help remind the project team of that" (Mark Huxham, project scientist). While scientific objectives were stated clearly from the outset, the emerging social impact of this project was partly driven by volunteer perspectives and feedback; working with people not as immersed in science, and sometimes more open to opportunities to help local development, has helped guide the evolution of the project into a practical exercise as well as a scientific one. This collective gathering and sharing of knowledge by local, regional and international stakeholders has increased the capacity of the project to find innovative solutions, and has also supported individual learning outcomes for the citizen scientists involved.

However, there are limitations and challenges in applying the citizen science model as well; some of these have been overcome while others remain significant constraints and may suggest contexts in which citizen science is unlikely to be helpful. Among these are:

- *Political instability.* Citizen scientists (particularly from Western countries) may be easily deterred from visiting a site if there is political violence, terrorism or other threats in the area; this is the case even if the risks at the field site have not changed. This can make long-term work vulnerable to sudden cancellation.
- *Infrequent sampling.* The model of visiting volunteers from overseas is an intensive one. There are typically three fieldwork teams per year; the resources and infrastructure to support more than this do not exist at this site or among the staff. Hence these volunteers cannot be relied upon for frequent monitoring or sampling; such tasks need to be supported in other ways.
- *Highly technical and specialized work.* Conducting experiments or measurements that requires specialized training or experience is not possible under this model of short but intensive involvement. However, longer-term volunteers have been involved in such work.
- *Higher risk activities.* There are health and safety constraints in using citizen scientists for some tasks in marine and coastal-related work – such as snorkel surveying or sampling from canoes. Focusing on work that can be safely done by people with a range of backgrounds and levels of fitness does determine some of the limits and objectives of the work.

In addition to the challenges we have identified, there are a number of other specific challenges for using citizen scientists for coastal and marine climate change research. These occur broadly under three themes: motivation, critical mass of data and data quality.

## Motivation

Motivation is critical to maintaining enthusiasm and retaining volunteers to ensure surveys are completed for the duration of the project. This can be particularly challenging for long-term projects. Part of the solution lies around three critical components: feedback, reward and progression (Geoghegan et al., 2016; Alender, 2016).

- *Feedback*: Project managers should communicate the importance and relevance of the work undertaken by the citizen scientists, and feedback should include how their data will be used and what outcomes are achieved. Feedback should begin at the start of the volunteer journey (providing instant gratification when the individual first begins to contribute to the project) and offered throughout the lifetime of the project. For example, Earthwatch Institute[20] project scientists provide direct feedback to participants while they are participating in Earthwatch field projects. After each field season, field reports detailing project activities, outputs and outcomes are made available to participants. These reports help to set the context of an individual's contribution within the wider project and provide up-to-date project news encouraging both new and repeat participation.
- *Reward*: Social networking sites such as Twitter and Facebook offer a forum for volunteers to share their experiences and findings or congratulate each other on achievements. These platforms also offer the opportunity for the project team to congratulate individuals or groups, or the community as a whole, for example when an unusual finding is made or a milestone is reached. Organizing events and group surveys also offer opportunities to reward volunteers and provide direct access to the project scientists. Enabling volunteers to contribute to project newsletters also demonstrates appreciation and recognition. *Capturing Our Coast*[21] is a relatively new project (2015–2018) which aims to train 3,000 citizen scientists to conduct rocky shore surveys around the UK coastline, identifying and quantifying the abundance and distribution of marine species to address key ecological questions to inform policy, conservation and science. Wide volunteer coverage and volunteer retention will be key to achieving the baseline coverage needed within the limitations of budget for training and providing equipment to volunteers. Use of newsletters (regional and national), volunteer reward schemes and multiple avenues of communication (Twitter, Facebook groups, social events) are all being employed to maintain enthusiasm and encourage continuing participation among volunteers.
- *Progression*: Building in opportunities for participants to progress from straightforward tasks to more complex tasks and responsibilities can be important for motivation. Training is a common method of ensuring skills progression and

builds people's confidence in taking part. Online resources and courses are frequently used (Roy et al., 2012). *Seasearch UK*[22] offers 50 courses a year which can take people from being raw beginners to experts. They have a training program at three levels, with a qualification process including tests at the higher level for the keenest volunteers. *Seasearch* receives about 2,000 forms each year and currently has over 300,000 records from 7,301 sites and more than 2,500 species (latest data 2011).

## Critical mass of data

Studies of climate change impacts often need repetition at a known location, in order to enable monitoring of change over time. Making use of freely available GPS tools can make it easy for volunteers with limited technical know-how to record their survey location. Volunteers can easily be taught how to use technology such as Google Earth, iPhone and Android apps, or GPS units to geo-reference their survey location. For those citizen scientists who are less technically minded, alternatives such as using grid references on a map should be available.

An example of a marine citizen science project that is collecting large amounts of data is *Dive Into Science*,[23] which is an initiative led by the Centre for Environment, Fisheries and Aquaculture Science (Cefas) in the U.K. *Dive Into Science* is attempting to collect data from about 10% of the estimated 20–30 million certified worldwide SCUBA divers. The majority of divers use dive computers which provide the ability to record temperatures, and thereby the opportunity to gather several million data points of global sub-surface sea temperature each year. The project requires latitude and longitude coordinates for the dives, which for those with GPS-enabled dive computers is very simple.

Data quantity issues are not unique to citizen science, and as with any study, larger sample sizes increase precision. In order to achieve high quantities of data, large numbers of citizen scientists need to be engaged. The more data points that are needed, the more restrictions this places on what can be achieved. Data collection protocols can't be overly complicated as complex protocols can deter participants, and greater consideration needs to be paid to the aspects of feedback, reward and progression, as mentioned earlier (Hochachka et al., 2012).

## Data quality

This is linked to critical mass of data mentioned earlier, in that if a critical mass of survey data is reached, overall the results are more robust for statistical analysis. However, although high volumes of data can help to offset any variance caused by surveyor bias, it cannot necessarily do the same for wildly inaccurate or poorly collected data (as any basic biological statistics textbook will confirm! [Dytham, 2011]). If data are received with anomalies, some are obvious, such as impossibly high counts in timed surveys, but others, such as confusion with species identification, may remain hidden unless proactively checked.

Data need to be quality checked and verified by experts, and there are many ways this can be done, at various stages in the process, ranging from verifying each data point for each individual submission as it comes in, to complex statistical analysis of large datasets collected by numerous surveyors over long periods of time. Many online databases feed into networks, such as *iRecord*[24] or the *NBN Gateway*[25] (Bonter and Cooper, 2012), and have their own data verification processes in place whereby experts double check data entered by a volunteer or organization.

Some projects also choose to check their participants' level of competence prior to any data collection. This means they can be aware of each individual's level of accuracy and include that information in statistical analyses, or to enable them to prevent anyone with a below-acceptable level of accuracy from having their data accepted. This requires structured and reinforced training, and re-testing, in order to work. Such high quality training programs, with multiple levels tailored to volunteer capacity, utilizing educational and supportive resources, are resource-intensive to set up and maintain, but can ensure the robustness of the data being submitted and increase the chance of policy makers utilizing the data. For example, *Seasearch*, which employs such a training program, was able to become an important contributor to the process in England for identifying Marine Conservation Zones. Their data have also been used by other policy makers in the UK, including Countryside Council for Wales (now Natural Resources Wales), for the Special Areas of Conservation program and towards the designation of the trawling ban in Lyme Bay (Baker et al., 2012).

Another example is *REEF* (Reef Environmental Education Foundation), which conducted a study on whether their volunteer-collected data were accurate and useful. For over two years, a team of marine ecologists and fisheries managers monitored and evaluated *REEF's* field methods and reporting procedures. The study confirmed that the collected data are of high value to the scientific community (Schmitt and Sullivan, 1996).

## Lessons learned

A small but growing number of research projects are usefully utilizing citizen scientists to study coastal systems in the face of climate change. Collectively, these projects not only contribute to our understanding of climate change impacts but also to new approaches to mitigating and adapting to climate change in coastal systems. Citizen science in this context is particularly useful for a number of key reasons. First, our knowledge of marine ecosystems lags behind that of terrestrial ecosystems (Parsons et al., 2014), and so citizen science offers the opportunity to gather much-needed data. Second, citizen science lends itself well to the broad spatial scales and long periods of time that data is typically required to study the influence of climate change, in marine as well as terrestrial systems. It would be difficult (if not impossible) for professional scientists to collect data over the spatiotemporal scales needed and to secure funding over the time frame required (McKinley et al., 2015).

While some citizen science projects are largely focused on utilizing citizen scientists as data collectors, others are also engaging citizens for the broader societal impacts they can foster, such as increased scientific and environmental knowledge and stewardship. For example, while the retrospective studies described earlier were not originally set up to study the effects of climate change (and therefore were not designed to foster engagement on the subject), more recently established projects have the opportunity to engage their participants in some of the complexities of climate change research and society's role in fostering solutions.

In the case of Mikoko Pamoja, a striking feature of the evaluation data collected from participants is the positive response to this daunting and often overwhelming problem of climate change impacts. Participants of the project often want to do something positive, even if it is small, and positive action can unleash energy, optimism and change. Hence citizen science in this area can help address the problems of fatalism and defeatism that are common in the face of climate change, and can connect the public to the realities of science, a vital task in the face of powerful climate change denial. The pressures to publish fast and move on, and the trends towards increasing specialization and technical expertise, can lead scientists to forget the importance of directly engaging with the wider public about climate change solutions. Citizen scientists joining projects with enthusiasm, new perspectives, experience, energy and time, and leaving inspired to make a difference, help to ensure that the wider public is part of the solution to climate change. We are reminded of the African saying – "If you want to go fast, go alone. If you want to go far, go together" – as this encapsulates citizen science, and in particular the approach taken by Mikoko Pamoja. Working directly with people on climate change science in coastal environments can provide a strong reminder for scientists of the need to make their work about people as much or more than it is about theory, and of the need to focus on questions of relevance to communities, climate adaptation and coastal sustainability.

Although the opportunities and benefits of using citizen science for marine and coastal conservation projects related to climate change are clear, there are a number of limitations to this approach. Coastal and marine environments have inherent risks associated with them that are not always suited to engaging the general public at large. There are health and safety constraints in using citizen scientists for some tasks in marine and coastal-related work – such as snorkel surveying or sampling from canoes. Focusing on work that can be safely done by people with a range of backgrounds and levels of fitness does determine some of the limits and objectives of the work that can be undertaken. Further, a certain level of pre-existing skills and swimming ability are required for snorkeling and dive work. Finally, accessibility can limit the number of people who can engage in these types of projects – not everyone has easy access to the coast – and it may be challenging to reach audiences who are not already engaged with the marine environment. As we develop new technologies and online citizen science portals (such as Zooniverse), there are growing opportunities to reach wider audiences, and to inspire more people to take positive action towards the long-term sustainability of our coastal and marine ecosystems.

## Web resources

1 www.reefcheck.org.
2 www.reef.org.
3 www.coralwatch.org.
4 www.coralcay.org.
5 www.seagrasswatch.org/.
6 www.mangrovewatch.org.au/.
7 www.marlin.ac.uk/shore_thing.
8 www.capturingourcoast.co.uk.
9 www.marinecitizenscience.com.
10 www.climatewatch.org.au/get-involved/marine.
11 http://earthwatch.org/expeditions/climate-change-sea-to-trees-at-acadia-national-park.
12 http://earthwatch.org/expeditions/coral-communities-in-the-seychelles.
13 www.diveintoscience.org.
14 www.oldweather.org.
15 www.zooniverse.org.
16 www.floatingforests.org.
17 http://earthwatch.org/expeditions/managing-mangroves-and-capturing-carbon-in-kenyan-communities.
18 www.aces-org.co.uk.
19 Percentages are of individuals that answered the question; not everyone answered all of the questions; 73 individuals responded to the survey.
20 http://eu.earthwatch.org/expeditions.
21 www.capturingourcoast.co.uk.
22 www.seasearch.org.uk.
23 www.diveintoscience.org.
24 www.brc.ac.uk/irecord/about.
25 https://nbn.org.uk/record-share-explore-data/verifying-data/.

## Literature cited

Agardy, T., and Alder, J. (2005). Coastal systems. In R. Hassan, R. Scholes, and N. Ash, ed. *Ecosystems and Human Well-Being: Current State and Trends, Volume 1*, 513–549. Washington, DC: Island Press.

Alender, B. (2016). Understanding volunteer motivations to participate in citizen science projects: A deeper look at water quality monitoring. *Journal of Science Communication*, 15(03), A04.

Baker, G.J., Parr, J., and Sewell, J. (2012). *Citizen Science: Engaging With Change in the Marine Environment*. Plymouth: Marine Biological Association.

Beger, M., Solandt, J-L., and Dacles, T. (2001). *Coral Reef bleaching at Danjugan Island, Negros occidental, Philippines: A two year monitoring programme*. Danjugan Island Survey Summary Report 2 to the Philippines Reef and Rainforest Conservation Foundation Inc.

Bonter, D., and Cooper, C. (2012). Data validation in citizen science: A case study from Project FeederWatch. *Frontiers in Ecology and the Environment*, 10(6), 305–307.

Chavanich, S., Viyakarn, V., Adams, P., Klammer, J., and Cook, N. (2012). Reef communities after the 2010 mass coral bleaching at Racha Yai Island in the Andaman Sea and Koh Tao in the Gulf of Thailand. *Phuket Marine Biological Center Research Bulletin*, 71, 103–110.

Dytham, C. (2011). *Choosing and using statistics: A biologist's guide, 3rd Ed.* Hoboken: Wiley-Blackwell.

Eakin, C.M., Morgan, J.A., Heron, S.F., Smith, T.B., Liu, G., et al. (2010). Caribbean corals in crisis: Record thermal stress, bleaching, and mortality in 2005. *PLoS One*, 5(11). www. plosone.org/article/info%3Adoi%2F10.1371%2Fjournal.pone.0013969.

FAO. (2007). *The World's Mangroves 1980–2005. A thematic study prepared in the framework of the Global Forest Resources Assessment 2005.* FAO Forestry Paper-153. Rome: Food and Agriculture Organization of the United Nations.

Geoghegan, H., Dyke, A., Pateman, R., West, S., and Everett, G. (2016). *Understanding motivations for citizen science.* Final report on behalf of UKEOF, University of Reading, Stockholm Environment Institute (University of York) and University of the West of England.

Giri, C., Ochieng, E., Tieszen, L., Zhu, Z., Singh, A., Loveland, T., Masek, J., and Duke, N. (2010). Status and distribution of mangrove forests of the world using earth observation satellite data. *Global Ecology and Biogeography*, 20(1), 154–159.

Gress, S., Huxham, M., Kairo, J., Mugi, L., and Briers, R. (2016). Evaluating, predicting and mapping belowground carbon stores in Kenyan mangroves. *Global Change Biology*, 23(1), 224–234.

Harding, S.P., Solandt, J-L., Walker, R.C.J., Walker, D., Taylor, J., Haycock, S., Davis, M., and Raines, P.S. (2003). Reef check data reveals rapid recovery from coral bleaching in the Mamanucas, Fiji. *Silliman Journal*, 44(2), 81–99.

Harley, C., Randall Hughes, A., Hultgren, K., Miner, B., Sorte, C., Thornber, C., Rodriguez, L., Tomanek, L., and Williams, S. (2006). The impacts of climate change in coastal marine systems. *Ecology Letters*, 9(2), 228–241.

Hochachka, W., Fink, D., Hutchinson, R., Sheldon, D., Wong, W., and Kelling, S. (2012). Data-intensive science applied to broad-scale citizen science. *Trends in Ecology & Evolution*, 27(2), 130–137.

Huxham, M., Emerton, L., Kairo, J., Munyi, F., Abdirizak, H., Muriuki, T., Nunan, F., and Briers, R. (2015). Applying climate compatible development and economic valuation to coastal management: A case study of Kenya's mangrove forests. *Journal of Environmental Management*, 157, 168–181.

Huxham, M., Kumara, M., Jayatissa, L., Krauss, K., Kairo, J., Langat, J., Mencuccini, M., Skov, M., and Kirui, B. (2010). Intra- and interspecific facilitation in mangroves may increase resilience to climate change threats. *Philosophical Transactions of the Royal Society B: Biological Sciences*, 365(1549), 2127–2135.

Hyder, K., Townhill, B., Anderson, L., Delany, J., and Pinnegar, J. (2015). Can citizen science contribute to the evidence-base that underpins marine policy? *Marine Policy*, 59, 112–120.

Jaine, F., Couturier, L., Weeks, S., Townsend, K., Bennett, M., Fiora, K., and Richardson, A. (2012). When giants turn up: Sighting trends, environmental influences and habitat use of the manta ray *Manta alfredi* at a Coral Reef. *PLoS One*, 7. http://dx.doi.org/10.1371/journal.pone.0046170.

Kapos, V., Balmford, A., Aveling, R., Bubb, P., Carey, P., Entwistle, A., Hopkins, J., Mulliken, T., Safford, R., Stattersfield, A., Walpole, M., and Manica, A. (2008). Calibrating conservation: New tools for measuring success. *Conservation Letters*, 1(4), 155–164.

McKinley, D.C., Miller-Rushing, A.J., Ballard, H.L., Bonney, R., Brown, H., Evans, D.M., French, R.A., Parrish, J.K., Phillips, T.B., Ryan, S.F., and Shanley, L.A. (2015). Investing in citizen science can improve natural resource management and environmental protection. *Issues in Ecology*, 19, 1–27.

Mcleod, E., Chmura, G., Bouillon, S., Salm, R., Björk, M., Duarte, C., Lovelock, C., Schlesinger, W., and Silliman, B. (2011). A blueprint for blue carbon: Toward an improved understanding of the role of vegetated coastal habitats in sequestering $CO_2$. *Frontiers in Ecology and the Environment*, 9(10), 552–560.

Parsons, E.C.M., Favaro, B., Aguirre, A.A., Bauer, A.L., Blight, L.K., Cigliano, J.A., Coleman, M.A., Cote, I.M., Draheim, M., Fletcher, S., and Foley, M.M. (2014). Seventy-one important questions for the conservation of marine biodiversity. *Conservation Biology*, 28(5), 1206–1214.

Roy, H.E., Pocock, M.J.O., Preston, C.D., Roy, D.B., Savage, J., Tweddle, J.C., and Robinson, L.D. (2012). *Understanding citizen science and environmental monitoring*. Final report on behalf of UK Environmental Observation Framework.

Schmitt, E.F., and Sullivan, K.M. (1996). Analysis of a volunteer method for collecting fish presence and abundance data in the Florida Keys. *Bulletin of Marine Science*, 59(2), 404–416.

Solandt, J.L., Harding, S.P., Dacles, T.P., Ledesma, G.L., and Raines, P.S. (2003). Effects of the 1998 bleaching event on a large *Pavona clavus* colony in a Philippine marine protected area. *Silliman Journal*, 44(2), 19–33.

Theobald, E.J., Ettinger, A.K., Burgess, H.K., DeBey, L.B., Schmidt, N.R., Froehlich, H.E., Wagner, C., HilleRisLambers, J., Tewksbury, J., Harsch, M.A., and Parrish, J.K. 2015. Global change and local solutions: Tapping the unrealized potential of citizen science for biodiversity research. *Biological Conservation*, 181, 236–244.

Valiela, I., Bowen, J.L., and York, J.K. (2001). Mangrove Forests: One of the world's threatened major tropical environments. *BioScience*, 51(10), 807–815.

Ward-Paige, C.A., and Lotze, H.K. (2011). Assessing the value of recreational divers for censusing elasmobranchs. *PLoS One*, 6, e25609. http://dx.doi.org/10.1371/journal.pone.0025609.

Ward-Paige, C.A., Pattengill-Semmens, C., Myers, R., and Lotze, H. (2010). Spatial and temporal trends in yellow stingray abundance: Evidence from diver surveys. *Environmental Biology of Fishes*, 90(3), 263–276.

Wolfe, J.R., and Pattengill-Semmens, C.V. (2013). Fish population fluctuation estimates based on fifteen years of reef volunteer diver data for the Monterey Peninsula, California. *California Cooperative Oceanic Fisheries Investigations Report*, 54, 141–154.

# 4

# CITIZEN SENTINELS

The role of citizen scientists in reporting and
monitoring invasive non-native species

*Jack Sewell and Jon Parr*

## Introduction

Non-native[1] species (NNS) are organisms which have been introduced by humans
outside their natural range (CBD,[2] 2015). Many such species live with no detectable
environmental economic or social consequences. There are a few, however, which
have identifiable negative impacts on the environment, the economy and the way
we live. These organisms are commonly referred to as "invasive non-native species"
(INNS) (NISC, 2006; DEFRA, 2015; CBD, 2015) and are the focus of many of the
case studies discussed in this chapter.

The potential for citizen science to benefit INNS research is clear. Observations
of species distribution is often required on a large scale, and people will often take an
interest in anything new which changes the appearance or amenity value of their own
local area. If harnessed appropriately, this interest can be utilized to engage non-expert
volunteers. Throughout the world citizen scientists have played and continue to play
increasingly important roles in research and management of INNS. The ways in which
citizen science is utilized in the process varies greatly. They include projects that:

- Target individual species of concern; for example, the Washington Sea Grant
  "Crab Team" initiative[3] targets the invasive European green crab (*Carcinus maenas*);
  and lionfish (Figure 4.1) detection and response in Alabama (Scyphers et al., 2015).
- Focus on surveying wider taxonomic groups or habitats, but specifically
  include NNS recording; for example the Big Seaweed Search[4] in the UK
  encourages participants to survey and record all the seaweeds that are found
  during a survey, several of which are INNS.
- Don't focus on INNS but have the potential to collect data on INNS. For
  example, the Tropical Reef Check program[5] includes on its Caribbean recording form a "lionfish" field despite INNS not being included in the project's
  information resources.

**FIGURE 4.1** The lionfish *Pterois volitans* and *P. miles* have been the focus of several targeted citizen science initiatives aiming to gather information about distribution and engage participants in the management and control of invasive populations. Their conspicuous nature and easily communicable risks they pose to human health and the environment make it relatively easy to encourage support and participation from the public.

*Image:* Jack Sewell.

In preparing this chapter, the authors reviewed a selection of 27 marine citizen science projects/schemes known to generate NNS data (Table 4.1). The projects were identified through an English language web search, and the list is by no means exhaustive. The list represents projects and schemes operating on a range of spatial and temporal scales. Of the 27 schemes reviewed, 14 focused exclusively on collecting records of NNS, 11 targeted NNS alongside native species research, and two focused primarily on native species but also generated information about NNS. The pattern perhaps reflects a perennial challenge for those trying to engage members of the public in the collection of NNS data. That is, the difficulty of engaging participants in a project where they might not encounter their quarry. The importance of a "not found" record is valuable particularly if combined with a record of effort and surveyor competence (Pocock et al., 2016), but this value can often be difficult to communicate to project participants. The addition of native species to a survey protocol where target species may not have arrived can add interest and may provide "pre-invasion" information should a native species be impacted in any way by the arrival spread or establishment of an INNS.

**TABLE 4.1** Summary of marine and coastal citizen science projects and schemes that collect information about non-native species (NNS) reviewed for this chapter. Information received by conducting a general Internet search.

| Project/Scheme Title | URL | Lead Organisation | Region | Run Time (years)★ | Scale |
|---|---|---|---|---|---|
| Alaska Alien BioBlitz | http://platewatch.nisbase.org/page/akpublications | Various | USA | <1 (F) | Regional |
| Big Seaweed Search | http://www.nhm.ac.uk/take-part/citizen-science/big-seaweed-search.html | Natural History Museum | UK | 7 (O) | National |
| Biolit | http://www.biolit.fr/?language=en | Planète Mer | France | ? (O) | National |
| C-Ocean | https://mote.org/research/program/coral-reef-science-monitoring/community-based-observations-coastal-ecosystems-assessment-network | Mote Marine Lab | USA | 16 (O) | Regional |
| Capturing our Coast | http://www.capturingourcoast.co.uk/ | Newcastle University | UK | 2 (O) | National |
| Chesapeake Bay Parasite Project | https://serc.si.edu/projects/get-involved/get-involved-0 | Smithsonian Environmental Research Centre | USA | ? (O) | Regional |
| CoastWatch | https://oregonshores.org/coastwatch/citizen-science-projects | Oregon State | USA | 49 (O) | Regional |
| ELNAIS | http://elnais.hcmr.gr/ | HCMR | Greece | 7 (O) | National |
| Invasive Tracers | http://www.mikedelaney.org/user/ | CSI MISMO | USA | >5 (O) | Regional |
| iTunicate | http://platewatch.nisbase.org/ | Various | USA | 6 (O) | Regional |
| Japanese Swimming Crab recording | http://www.reabic.net/journals/mbi/2015/3/MBI_2015_Hourston_etal.pdf | Department of Fisheries Western Australia | Australia | <1 (F) | Local |
| Kachemak Bay Citizen Science Program | https://www.uaf.edu/files/ces/pests/cnipm/annual_invasive_species_c/15th_annual_meeting_ancho/Bursch-Catie.pdf | Kachemak Bay Research Reserve | USA | >10 (O) | Regional |
| LIMPETS | http://limpets.org/ | Various | USA | 14 (O) | Regional |
| Marina Science Project | https://erccis.org.uk/NNS/MarineScienceProject | ERCCIS & MBA | UK | 4 (F) | Regional |
| Marine Invader Tracking & Information System (MITIS) | https://mit.sea-grant.net/mitis/ | The Massachusetts Office of Coastal Zone Management | USA | 9 (O) | Regional |

*(Continued)*

**TABLE 4.1** (Continued)

| Project/ Scheme Title | URL | Lead Organisation | Region | Run Time (years)★ | Scale |
|---|---|---|---|---|---|
| Mitten Crab recording | http://mittencrabs.org.uk/ | Natural History Museum/ Marine Biological Association | UK | 10 (O) | National |
| Observadores del mar | http://www.observadoresdelmar.es/projecte-9.php | Institut de Ciències del Mar and Consejo Superior de Investigaciones Científicas | Mediterranean | ? (O) | International |
| Recording Invasive Species Counts (RISC) | http://www.nonnativespecies.org/index.cfm?pageid=234 | CEH | UK | 6 (O) | National |
| Reef Lionfish project | http://www.reef.org/lionfish | Reef (www.reef.org) | USA | 24 (O) | Regional |
| ReefCheck – California | http://reefcheck.org/california/monitoring-protocol/ | Reef Check Worldwide | USA | 20 (O) | Regional |
| Reefcheck Tropical Program | http://reefcheck.org/tropical/overview | ReefCheck Worldwide | Multiple | 20 (O) | International |
| Seasearch | http://www.seasearch.org.uk/ | Marine Conservation Society | UK | 30 (O) | National |
| Shore Thing Project | www.mba.ac.uk/shore_thing | Marine Biological Association | UK | 10 (O) | National |
| Vectors – Watch for Jellies | http://www.marine-vectors.eu/deliverables/D2_1_2.pdf | VECTORS consortium | Mediterranean | 4 (O) | International |
| Virtue | http://www.virtuedata.se/en | University of Gothenburg & Maritime Museum & Aquarium in Gothenburg | Sweden | >3 (O) | International |
| Wakame Watch | http://wakamewatch.org.uk/ | Marine Biological Association | UK | 3 (O) | National |
| WSG Crab Team | https://wsg.washington.edu/community-outreach/environmental-threats/invasive-green-crab–volunteer-monitoring/ | Washington Sea Grant | USA | 0 (O) | Regional |

★ O = Ongoing, F = Finished

## Citizen scientists as sentinels

One of the most important roles for citizen scientists is acting as *sentinels* and reporting ad hoc encounters with a targeted species (e.g. the mitten crab[6] recording project and Wakame Watch[7]). These projects do not require a survey protocol to be followed, but require anyone finding the species to record their sighting along with basic biological geographical and environmental data. Such records provide vital information to help scientists map the distribution and rate of spread as well as providing information about the life history of target species. These data often contribute to applied research and allow science to inform environmental policy and practical management (e.g. Hourston et al., 2015; Zenetos et al., 2013). Where the positive identification of a target species is not possible from a photograph alone, the collection of specimens may also be incorporated into survey protocols. This, however, is only possible when adequate resources and/or training are provided to prevent the accidental removal of native species. In some cases, a citizen science project can be more effective at intercepting invasive species than professional survey work. For example, in 2010 following the detection of an individual Japanese swimming crab (*Charybdis japonica*) in the Swan River Estuary in Western Australia, local recreational crab fishers were successfully engaged in a program to collect records of the species (Hourston et al., 2015) resulting in the capture and removal of three individual specimens. Recreational fishers made these records in direct response to the public engagement campaign, while professional surveyors undertaking potting surveys at the same time did not record any specimens. The project clearly highlighted the value of public engagement in this type of survey. Knowledge of recreational crab fishing effort in the area allowed the authors to estimate search effort. The authors calculated that 8,874 fisher days resulted in three specimens. This very low catch per unit effort combined with a lack of specimens caught by the survey team enabled the authors to conclude that the population of *C. japonica* was likely very small in the survey area. Studies of this kind highlight the value of carefully targeting and engaging specialist groups – in this case the fishing community. The provision of clear identification materials – including photographs of native species likely to be confused with the target species – was cited by the authors as a key factor in enabling accurate recording and avoiding the unnecessary retention of native species which may otherwise have been kept for expert identification.

## Citizen scientists and INNS management

Simberloff et al. (2013) determined the cost and benefits associated with attempting to manage invasive non-native species at different stages of the invasion process (Figure 4.2). Targeting potential vectors of new non-native species and intercepting and swiftly eradicating species as soon as possible are the most effective ways of avoiding impacts. As the invasion continues eradication becomes prohibitively

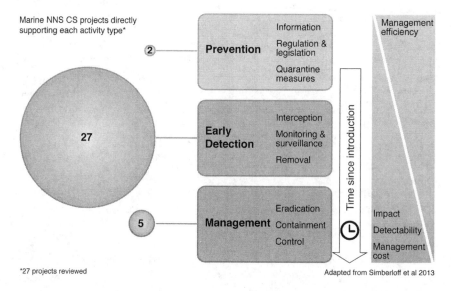

Marine NNS CS projects directly supporting each activity type*

Management efficiency

27

② — **Prevention**
- Information
- Regulation & legislation
- Quarantine measures

**Early Detection**
- Interception
- Monitoring & surveillance
- Removal

5 — **Management**
- Eradication
- Containment
- Control

Time since introduction

Impact

Detectability

Management cost

*27 projects reviewed

Adapted from Simberloff et al 2013

**FIGURE 4.2** How the 27 marine citizen science initiatives studied by the authors relate to the different stages of INNS management and their corresponding levels of management efficiency, cost, impact and detectability of populations, as described by Simberloff et al. (2013). Note that some programs addressed more than one stage.

expensive and less likely to succeed. So at what point in the invasion process do most citizen science programs operate? The most cost-effective and efficient point to address an invasion is through *Prevention* (Figure 4.2). Despite this, only a small number of programs reviewed explicitly include information about prevention. *Early Detection*, which includes interception monitoring and removal (Figure 4.2), can be costlier and less efficient than *Prevention* but has the greater potential for citizen science projects to be of benefit. All of the 27 programs reviewed focused on this area. Five of the programs studied included some degree of control and eradication. However, evidence suggests that in most cases once established this type of control is likely to be ineffective and economically unviable (Simberloff et al., 2013). As sentinels, citizen scientists have the potential to contribute to *Early Detection* provided effective links are developed between citizen scientists and those able to intercept and remove problem species or the citizens themselves are provided with the information and training to enable them to undertake this role (for example, McKnight and Chudleigh, 2015).

Miralles et al. (2016) detailed the successful use of citizen scientists in the identification and eradication of the invasive pygmy mussel (*Xenostrobus securis*) in a Spanish estuary. Citizen scientist observations were combined with the use of eDNA studies to locate populations. Once populations were located, teams including citizen scientists were trained and deployed to remove mussels from selected sites. Although eradication was not 100% successful, populations were sufficiently removed to (at least temporarily) prevent recolonization in some areas. The study highlights how citizen scientists can be of value scientifically and for managing populations of INNS. These and other studies (e.g. Hourston et al., 2015; Scyphers et al., 2015; McKnight and Chudleigh, 2015) illustrate that the inclusion of unpaid volunteers in detection eradication and control can reduce potentially inhibitive management costs described by Simberloff et al. (2013) and has the potential to increase the cost-effectiveness of any efforts. In a small number of cases this may mean that addressing management of INNS at the later stages of an invasion becomes a more realistic prospect than a scenario where volunteers were not included.

## Citizen science INNS management and public awareness

Involving people – in particular those who use the marine environment commercially or recreationally – in citizen science has potential benefits additional to simply collecting scientific data (see also Chapters 3, 7–9 and 11). High profile projects can help raise public awareness of the issue of INNS and raise support for active conservation and management. Although a relatively understudied area, there is evidence to suggest that involving people in citizen science can increase their intention to undertake pro-environmental activities (Crall et al., 2012). It is therefore possible that raising awareness of the problem and suggesting methods for reducing spread, such as improved biosecurity, could encourage positive behavior and reduce the potential for species to spread. If this is the case, then it could be argued that all projects have the potential to act at the *Prevention* stage of the invasion process (Figure 4.2). To date there has been very little study into how participation in INNS citizen science projects leads to changes in attitude and behavior.

## Management/control vs. citizen science

It is important to clarify the difference between citizen science and management/control. Management/control does not in itself always include the collection of data. For example, a fisher removing and killing any invasive crabs caught could be contributing to the control of the species. However, unless they share details about what they have been doing their actions have no scientific value. The most effective projects can combine these two elements. Investigations and data collection are often incorporated into practical management activity and are essential to monitoring the effectiveness of management measures. The CoastBusters project[8] on the southeast coast of England utilized teams of volunteers to undertake removal of the invasive Pacific oyster *Crassostrea gigas* from protected chalk reef habitat. The team also studied control sites to collect data to scientifically identify the impact of removal on the oyster populations. The resulting study and its findings have been published in a peer-reviewed journal (McKnight and Chudleigh, 2015) and provide a valuable contribution to conservation science. The authors acknowledged the project's participants and present the project as a relatively cost-effective method of survey and management. A secondary benefit identified by the project leads was the value of the project in terms of public outreach and communication. Through their presence on the shore and engagement with volunteers it was possible to raise awareness of non–native species as well as biosecurity in a wider sense.

Some projects, though, might involve citizen scientists at a stage in the invasion process where management may no longer be a viable option. Such studies might be undertaken to answer questions about how species spread and interact with native organisms. Such information can be useful in justifying future measures to prevent the introduction of the species into new uninfected regions. There is potential for frustration among participants if these motives are not properly communicated. It is therefore important to clearly explain the desired outcomes of the work and be realistic about what all parties can expect as a result of their contribution.

---

## BOX 4.1   THE VALUE OF LOCAL KNOWLEDGE

Most of the citizen science projects described involve people observing and reporting from their own local area. This is extremely valuable as those people will be familiar with the area prior to the arrival of a new species, may visit an area regularly and will be ideally placed to notice and report on any changes which may occur – including new or unusual species. Additionally, they will have a vested interest in protecting their local environment, as they will be the most likely to directly benefit economically and socially from the resources it provides and which may be jeopardized by the establishment of a harmful INNS. Once engaged, local communities are best placed to report on their own patches and may be able to identify smaller, less obvious pockets of NNS. They will also be best placed to monitor change over a range of timescales and may be able to provide information about the site prior to the invasion (including photographs, old species records or anecdotal information). Such information could prove very valuable when exploring potential impacts of INNS.

---

## Case study: mitten crab recording project (MittenCrabs.org.uk)

The Chinese mitten crab (*Eriocheir sinensis*) is a large species with a maximum carapace width of approximately 8 cm. It is currently the only diadromous brachyuran crab species in the UK and the only crab found in fully freshwater in the UK. It was first recorded in the UK after capture on the intake screens of Lots Road Power Station Chelsea in 1935. Following an apparently stable period with relatively low level populations in a small number of UK river systems it was noticed in 1992 that populations were increasing in range and density (Clark et al., 1998). Between 1992 and 1996 the population of *E. sinensis* in the Thames increased at a rate that was considered alarming by Clark et al. (1998). Scientists were keen to encourage the public to contribute records of the species from around the UK, the Thames region in particular, to increase scientific understanding of the rate of spread and level of establishment of the crab in the UK. To do this, an online recording page was set up by the Natural History Museum (London) and accompanied by an awareness raising campaign as part of the Marine Aliens Project[9] funded by the Esmée Fairbairn Foundation. The page was utilized by citizen scientists and professionals working in the estuary and river catchment to submit records for a number of selected marine NNS including mitten crabs. Upon completion of the Marine Aliens Project the Mitten Crab Recording Scheme[10] was formed to include a consortium comprising the Natural History Museum Marine Biological Association Royal Holloway University of London Countryside Council for Wales (now Natural Resources Wales) and Newcastle University. The project is UK-wide and targets professionals and naturalist groups most likely to encounter *E. sinensis*. The system can accept records from around Europe, and a small number of non-UK records have been received. After an initial input of funding for the project from the Welsh government, the Environment Agency Fishmongers' Company and the Great Britain Non-Native Species Secretariat, the scheme has not received any additional funding but continues to operate online.

Participation in the project requires no training other than familiarization with online identification resources. The website includes a printable identification guide (several guides were initially printed and distributed at promotional events); a Web page showing key identification features and species that might be confused for the mitten crab; an instructional video; and all information required to help users submit their records. The site also incorporates a map which displays records submitted by users alongside distribution data from other published sources.

Once records are received, feedback is provided to participants through email by expert volunteers, which can be a useful training opportunity for participants if misidentifications are made. For confirmed records the correspondence provides an opportunity to obtain additional useful information about and evidence to support the record including testimony images and occasionally video.

An additional form of feedback to participants is that records are shown on a live map before being passed on to the National Biodiversity Network and DASSH (the national archive for marine life data)[11] where they are publicly available. Data quality is maintained through an online validation system where experts examine verify and validate all records entered using the data storage and verification facility Indicia.[12] The site includes promotional and identification resources (Figure 4.3) and an online recording form with image upload facility. The scheme has generated around 300 new records of mitten crabs for the UK, adding significantly to the known distribution of the species. In 2016, this has included two new records from the Severn Estuary/Bristol Channel. These records are significant because they are the first sightings from this large environmentally important estuary system.

An exciting and unexpected benefit of the scheme has been the first two UK records of the invasive Asian shore crab (*Hemigrapsus sanguineus*) (Figure 4.4). Both records were made after members of the public found and photographed the specimens. On seeking information online, they decided that the mitten crab scheme

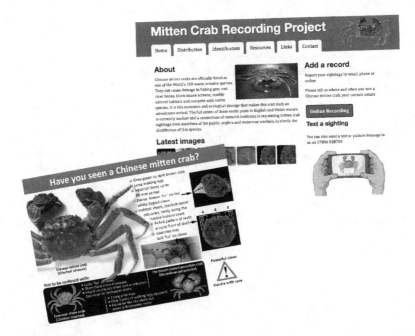

**FIGURE 4.3** The homepage (right) of the Mitten Crab Recording Project (www. MittenCrabs.org.uk) and the identification card (left) available digitally and in hard copy printed on waterproof paper and laminated to allow use in the field in all weather. Both tools have proved essential in ensuring participation in the project.

**FIGURE 4.4** The Asian shore crab *Hemigrapsus sanguineus* recorded for the first time in the UK through the Mitten Crab Recording scheme. Although not the intended focus of the project, its discovery demonstrates the potential wider value of schemes such as this.

*Image:* Jack Sewell.

would be the most appropriate place to submit their records, and these resulted in a published paper (Seeley et al., 2015) describing the records and crediting the Mitten Crab Recording Project as playing a key role in the process.

## Lessons learned

### Challenges

While the project has been very successful, there were a few challenges in working with citizen scientists. Some records were received without photographic evidence. However in some cases it has been possible through dialogue with recorders to establish whether or not records were genuine. A few records have been rejected. This is a common problem with collecting species data for citizen science projects and relies greatly on emphasizing the importance of providing evidence to support records. In some projects (such as the Marine Biological Association–led Shore Thing Project[13]), experts accompany citizen scientists in person to verify data on site. This is expensive and time-consuming, and given current technology and availability of smartphone technology is not always necessary (see also Chapter 13 for examples of how to work successfully with citizen scientists in crowdsourcing projects; sensu Haklay, 2013).

The Mitten Crab Recording scheme does not request absence/not-detected data from recorders, nor does it collect any information about search effort from the recorder. While the record on its own is valuable, the lack of additional data makes it difficult to precisely map distribution and will make the scheme unsuitable for recording the results of successful eradication or natural population declines.

Schemes aimed at recording individual species sightings or ad hoc records of species often do not collect information about searcher effort, nor do they easily provide data to indicate non-detection. There are many possible reasons for this, but the collection of extra data and imposition of protocols creates an additional burden on the recorder which may deter some from submitting a record. Of the 27 projects and schemes reviewed in preparation for this chapter (Table 4.1), only 14 explicitly included a record of searcher effort and "not-found" records. Pocock et al. (2016) provide a clear argument for the collection of searcher effort and "not-found" data in projects aiming to map the distribution (especially changing distribution over time) of INNS. Specifically, that an absence of records is not a record of absence, and unless absence records (preferably with a record of searcher effort) are recorded it is not possible to say whether records collected give a true indication of the range of a species. The Shore Thing Project[14] has collected effort-based survey data on 22 climate-change indicators and NNS from rocky shores around the British Isles since 2006. The survey protocols include standardized timed search and transect survey protocols. The data includes "not detected" data as well as a very simplified abundance scale. Training supervision detailed identification guides and search cards (Figure 4.5) are provided to all participants to ensure accurate identification of finds and standardized search effort. The project has produced new area records for several NNS including the first records of *Crassostrea gigas* (a Pacific oyster) in

**FIGURE 4.5** Using species identification cards to undertake timed (effort-based) searches for selected non-native and climate change indicator species in Scotland. Participants are asked to spend 20 minutes searching for two to three species each depending on their experience and ability. Collection of effort-based data is essential when attempting to gather information about range extensions, and population status.

*Image:* Jack Sewell.

Scotland, which led to further professional surveys (Cook et al., 2014) and the development of a management plan by the local management partnership (Solway Firth Partnership, 2015). The inclusion of "not detected" data can in some cases be used to approximate new arrival dates for species where repeat surveys take place adding scientific value to the data collected.

## Successes

The success and continued use of the project highlights the value of (1) investing in an easy-to-use data collection system, (2) providing effective instructional resources, (3) utilizing existing data collection verification and validation products and (4) working with enthusiastic individuals who are keen to continue to promote the project and interact with recorders.

The mitten crab is a large, charismatic and easily recognizable species. It is also known to "invade" people's personal space by occasionally venturing into gardens. Other features make encounters with humans likely too; they are known to take fishing bait and are caught in traps and nets intended for fish and other crustaceans and on power station screens. During their annual autumnal migration, they move downstream in large numbers through shallow water, bypassing obstacles such as weirs and waterfalls by walking over land, making them stand out dramatically and cross paths with humans. They are also the only crab species currently found in freshwater in the UK where there is an active angling community. These features facilitate participation and interest in the project.

The project has made use of clear, easy-to-use identification resources, and a website to encourage participants with no training or supervision by the project team (Figure 4.3). Without these key elements, the project would not have worked. The site also includes a mapping tool which provides rapid feedback to participants as to how their record fits the current known distribution of the species. Participants in marine and coastal citizen science projects place a very high value on feedback from scientists (Martin et al., 2016; Roy et al., 2012; Chapter 13) and, as such, this was seen as a very important element of the project. Roy et al. (2012) discussed a variety of methods of feedback and engagement with participants including feedback on species identification, sharing results and findings, and providing access to data. These methods of feedback are all utilized in the Mitten Crab Recording Project.

As well as a direct scientific use of data collected by recorders, the project team has direct links with the UK government–funded bodies responsible for the management and control of invasive species. An alert system associated with the recording scheme developed as part of the Great Britain Non-Native Species Information Portal (detailed in Roy et al., 2015) ensures records are passed to the appropriate authorities within one working day of the record submission. This has resulted in rapid response and more detailed professional-led surveys for the crab following records in Scotland and Wales. Additionally, data from the project have been used by mussel growers when selecting suitable areas for the collection of mussel seed for introduction to Menai Strait mussel-growing beds (Sewell et al., 2008). Accurate distribution data allows the collection of spat to be undertaken in "clean" sites reducing the risk of introducing *Eriocheir sinensis* into the commercially and environmentally important site. Such prevention activities depend on accurate and thorough information such as that provided by the scheme described.

## Conclusions

Despite the potential value of citizen science in the study and management of INNS, in a 2014 review of 27 published scientific marine papers in which citizen science was mentioned (Thiel et al., 2014), only two focused on INNS. The authors of the study acknowledge that the contribution of citizen science to NNS research may not be fully reflected in their review due to the variety of terms used within papers to acknowledge citizen scientists. However, the findings do suggest that there is potential for citizen science to be used more often.

There is a growing body of evidence discussed here which highlights the potential value of citizen science in the study and management of INNS. If developed carefully, initiatives have the potential to engage ordinary citizens in the interception of new arrivals, monitoring of existing populations and in some cases management or eradication of INNS populations. Although not currently widely prioritized, engaging people in INNS projects has the potential to raise awareness of the subject and develop increased vigilance and compliance with biosecurity measures. Further study should be undertaken to investigate the extent to which such impacts may occur.

## To use citizen science or not?

The important role that citizen science projects can play in the management of INNS is beginning to be better recognized; for example the Great Britain Invasive Non-Native Species Strategy (Defra, 2015) explicitly acknowledges the important role data from citizen science projects has on INNS management in Great Britain. The report identifies that continuing to "work with existing recording networks and citizen science initiatives to improve surveillance for non-native species" is a key action to help fulfil the aim of maintaining an early detection surveillance and monitoring mechanism that facilitates management responses including rapid response. There are many cases when mobilizing citizen scientists to support the study of INNS is the most appropriate and cost-effective option. For example, when a species is easily identifiable and safely accessible, and when study by experts at an appropriate scale would be financially inhibitive.

However, it is important to keep in mind that there are some species and scenarios when use of citizen scientists might *not* be appropriate or present significant challenges.

- *Identification of target species requires high level of technical expertise or specialist equipment:* The invasive colonial sea squirt (*Didemnum vexillum*) is a problem species in the United States and Europe. The first Alaskan records were identified by a citizen scientist participating in a BioBlitz event (Cohen et al., 2011). The event was supervised and attended by scientists who could collect specimens and send for laboratory analysis in order to confirm the identification. In the UK the RISC (Recording Invasive Species Counts) project includes *D. vexillum*. The project does not include expert support in the field but rather depends on the submission of photographs via a web-based system. To date, confirmation of species identification from photographs has proven very difficult, suggesting that the species may not be suitable for this type of citizen science approach.
- *Target species requires a high level of technical expertise or specialist equipment to survey or species may occur in a hazardous or inaccessible area:* Some groups of species, for example subtidal sediment dwelling infaunal species, are very difficult to sample without the use of specialist survey equipment and research vessels. While engaging divers and fishermen in projects may help alleviate some issues, citizen science projects may not be the most appropriate way to survey these species.
- *Interference with target species or habitat might increase dispersal of problem species:* Some species, including the invasive seaweed *Sargassum muticum* and the

invasive starfish *Asterias amurensis*, are able to reproduce and multiply following fragmentation. Inappropriate sampling or removal can therefore result in population increase and spread.

- *Access to key survey sites may be difficult to access or restricted*: Some of the key hubs for NNS arrival and establishment are among those not traditionally visited or explored by the public. For example, marinas, docks and ports are rarely visited and explored by divers for safety reasons, but also because these sites are often considered dangerous or are physically off-limits. Aquaculture facilities also known to be areas where new NNS might arrive are likewise often inaccessible to the public and in areas where access is difficult or dangerous. In these situations, engaging specialists who may be accessing and maintaining these sites can be essential.

When the study or management of an INNS is being planned, it is important to consider these issues, as a citizen science approach may not be the most appropriate option.

Some species are a more suitable subject of a citizen science initiative than others. Species which are easy to identify are charismatic or have an obvious impact on human health and wellbeing are particularly suitable. Those which occur in easily accessible locations such as the intertidal zone or on man-made structures are also particularly suitable. The specific biology and behavior of species and the nature of different marine habitats mean that the approach taken will need to be adjusted to suit the target species. The exploration of the marine environment may require specialist training. In this case, citizen science projects may not be open to all, but those with the required skills (i.e. divers, sailors, fishers) may need to be engaged in the process.

## Supporting resources

Production of good quality resources to support citizen scientists is essential. Examples of these can include printable or hard-copy identification cards or guidebooks; smartphone apps; training videos; instructional packs; or training workshops and events. However, simply providing clear simple instructions and a means to easily submit data can also be sufficient. Even where a single species is targeted, identification guides should still include native species likely to be confused with the target species to reduce misidentifications (Hourston et al., 2015). Misidentifications and misreporting can result in the death of native species and unnecessary burden on the time of record verifiers.

## Managing expectations and celebrating achievements

Whatever the focus of a project, it is very important to manage the expectations of participants. Citizen scientists react well to and participate in projects where action is required or where threat is perceived as imminent but avoidable. However, it is not always the case that the project will lead to direct management action. A project may aim to collect data that will be used to reduce spread into other locations or simply to collect information that will add to our knowledge of invasion biology. If this is the case, such information should be shared with participants. Likewise, any management action which does take place because of their participation should be widely shared and celebrated.

As discussed, it is difficult to engage people in looking for species that have not yet "arrived" in a scientifically useful way. However, it is essential to do so to maintain a network for early warning and intervention at the most appropriate point. This can be done by encouraging surveys of whole habitats or broad species groups reporting on non-target species alongside the absence of target species. Alternatively schemes that encourage ongoing vigilance and reporting of more recognizable INNS can also be effective (e.g. Zenetos et al., 2013). Of the examples reviewed, the level of information and data requested of citizen scientists varies from simple ad hoc records of individual species to regular detailed surveys of set areas. In most cases the level of information requested corresponds with the level of input required from the project lead in terms of training supervision and equipment provision and therefore cost. Schemes such as the Mitten Crab Recording Project include little training and any support is provided remotely. Effective targeted promotion allows participation.

## Acknowledgements

The authors wish to express their gratitude to Paul Clark of the Natural History Museum for his review and helpful comments. We also wish to thank all of those who have shared information about their projects and schemes online and in person and the citizen scientists who have given many hours to the projects discussed in this chapter.

## Web resources

1 Alien non-indigenous exotic or introduced.
2 Convention on Biological Diversity.
3 https://goo.gl/eb8OZM.
4 https://goo.gl/0AlWzD.
5 www.reefcheck.org/tropical.
6 www.mittencrabs.org.uk.
7 www.wakamewatch.org.uk.
8 www.oceannetworks.ca/learning/get-involved/citizen-science/coastbuster.
9 www.marlin.ac.uk/marine_aliens; www.sams.ac.uk/elizabeth-cook/aliens.
10 www.mittencrabs.org.uk.
11 www.dassh.ac.uk/.
12 www.indicia.org.uk.
13 www.mba.ac.uk/shore_thing.
14 www.mba.ac.uk/shore_thing.

## Literature cited

Clark, P., Rainbow, P., Robbins, R., Smith, B., Yeomans, W., Thomas, M., and Dobson, G. (1998). The Alien Chinese Mitten Crab, *Eriocheir Sinensis* (Crustacea: Decapoda: Brachyura), in the Thames Catchment. *Journal of the Marine Biological Association of the United Kingdom*, 78(4), 1215.

Cohen, C., McCann, L., Davis, T., Shaw, L., and Ruiz, G. (2011). Discovery and significance of the colonial tunicate *Didemnum vexillum* in Alaska. *Aquatic Invasions*, 6(3), 263–271.

CBD. (2017). *What are invasive Alien species?* [Online] www.cbd.int/invasive/WhatareIAS. shtml [Accessed March 4, 2017].

Cook, E.J., Beveridge, C.M., Lamont, P., O'Higgins, T., and Wilding, T. (2014). *Survey of wild pacific oyster Crassostrea gigas in Scotland*. Scottish Aquaculture Research Forum Report SARF099. Oban: Scotland.

Crall, A., Jordan, R., Holfelder, K., Newman, G., Graham, J., and Waller, D. (2012). The impacts of an invasive species citizen science training program on participant attitudes, behavior, and science literacy. *Public Understanding of Science*, 22(6), 745–764.

Defra. 2015. *The Great Britain invasive non-native species strategy*. York: U.K. Department for Environment Food & Rural Affairs. www.gov.uk/government/uploads/system/uploads/ attachment_data/file/454638/gb-non-native-species-strategy-pb14324.pdf.

Haklay, M. (2013). Citizen science and volunteered geographic information: Overview and typology of participation. In *Crowdsourcing Geographic Knowledge: Volunteered Geographic Information (VGI) in Theory and Practice*, 105–122. Berlin: Springer.

Hourston, M., McDonald, J., and Hewitt, M. (2015). Public engagement for the detection of the introduced marine species *Charybdis japonica* in Western Australia. *Management of Biological Invasions*, 6(3), 243–252.

Martin, V., Christidis, L., and Pecl, G. (2016). Public interest in marine citizen science: Is there potential for growth? *BioScience*, 66(8), 683–692.

McKnight, W., and Chudleigh, I.J. (2015). Pacific oyster *Crassostrea gigas* control within the inter-tidal zone of the North East Kent Marine Protected Areas, UK. *Conservation Evidence*, 12, 28–32.

Miralles, L., Dopico, E., Devlo-Delva, F., and Garcia-Vazquez, E. (2016). Controlling populations of invasive pygmy mussel (*Xenostrobus securis*) through citizen science and environmental DNA. *Marine Pollution Bulletin*, 110(1), 127–132.

NISC. (2006). *Invasive Species Definition Clarification and Guidance White Paper Submitted by the Definitions Subcommittee of the Invasive Species Advisory Committee*. Washington DC: National Invasive Species Council US Department of the Interior. www.invasivespecies-info.gov/docs/council/isacdef.pdf.

Pocock, M., Roy, H., Fox, R., Ellis, W., and Botham, M. (2016). Citizen science and invasive alien species: Predicting the detection of the oak processionary moth *Thaumetopoea processionea* by moth recorders. *Biological Conservation*, 208, 146–154.

Roy, H.E., Pocock, M.J.O., Preston, C.D., Roy, D.B., Savage, J., Tweddle, J.C., and Robinson, L.D. (2012). *Understanding citizen science and environmental monitoring*. Final report on behalf of UK Environmental Observation Framework.

Roy, H., Rorke, S., Beckmann, B., Booy, O., Botham, M., Brown, P., Harrower, C., Noble, D., Sewell, J., and Walker, K. (2015). The contribution of volunteer recorders to our understanding of biological invasions. *Biological Journal of the Linnean Society*, 115(3), 678–689.

Seeley, B., Sewell, J. and Clark, P. (2015). First GB records of the invasive Asian shore crab, *Hemigrapsus sanguineus* from Glamorgan, Wales and Kent, England. *Marine Biodiversity Records*, 8, e102.

Scyphers, S., Powers, S., Akins, J., Drymon, J., Martin, C., Schobernd, Z., Schofield, P., Shipp, R., and Switzer, T. (2015). The role of citizens in detecting and responding to a rapid marine invasion. *Conservation Letters*, 8(4), 242–250.

Sewell J., Pearce S., Bishop J., and Evans, J.L. (2008). Investigations to determine the potential risk for certain not-native species to be introduced to North Wales with mussel seed dredged from wild seed beds. *CCW Policy Research Report No. 06/3*, p. 82.

Simberloff, D., Martin, J., Genovesi, P., Maris, V., Wardle, D., Aronson, J., Courchamp, F., Galil, B., García-Berthou, E., Pascal, M., Pyšek, P., Sousa, R., Tabacchi, E., and Vilà, M. (2013). Impacts of biological invasions: What's what and the way forward. *Trends in Ecology & Evolution*, 28(1), 58–66.

Solway Firth Partnership. (2015). *Marine invasive non-native species in the Solway – plan 2015–2018*. www.solwayfirthpartnership.co.uk/uploads/Marine%20Invasive%20Non-native%20Species/Marine%20INNS%20in%20Solway%202015-2018.pdf.

Thiel, M., Penna-Díaz, M.A., Luna-Jorquera, G., Salas, S., Sellanes, J., and Stotz, W. (2014). Citizen scientists and marine research: Volunteer participants, their contributions, and projection for the future. *Oceanography and Marine Biology: An Annual Review*, 52, 257–314.

Zenetos, A., Koutsogiannopoulos, D., Ovalis, P., and Poursanidis, D. (2013). The role played by citizen scientists in monitoring marine alien species in Greece. *Cahiers de Biologie Marine*, 54(3), 419–426.

# 5

# USING CITIZEN SCIENCE TO STUDY THE IMPACT OF VESSEL TRAFFIC ON MARINE MAMMAL POPULATIONS

*Lei Lani Stelle*

## Introduction

People throughout history have been fascinated by marine mammals. These animals can therefore serve as umbrella species to encourage the public to learn more about marine life and value conservation. Unfortunately, many marine mammal species are endangered or threatened, and baseline data are lacking for most of the populations. Many populations were decimated by whaling, but even after gaining protection with the 1986 International Whaling Commission moratorium on commercial hunts, populations of most species remain a fraction of their historical size (Roman and Palumbi, 2003). Major threats today include incidental mortality from fisheries bycatch and vessel strikes, pollution (toxins and marine debris), noise, and climate change (Schipper et al., 2008; Reynolds et al., 2009).

Conservation efforts are hindered by the lack of reliable data on many marine mammal populations (Taylor et al., 2007); it is difficult to determine the exact number of many of these species because of the challenges associated with surveying animals that spend most of their time out of view and are distributed over a large geographic area (Schipper et al., 2008). Gathering data on species distribution and abundance is time-consuming and resource intensive. An analysis of monitoring data on stocks within the United States by Taylor et al. (2007) revealed that, based on current efforts, most precipitous declines of marine mammals would go undetected and a substantial increase in funding would be needed to increase survey extents and frequency to improve our detection ability. Researchers have begun to recognize the opportunity to greatly expand monitoring efforts by involving the public as "citizen scientists" (e.g. Embling et al., 2015; Tonachella et al., 2012).

Citizen science, the involvement of the public in collecting and analyzing data to contribute to research (Bonney et al., 2014), is not a recent phenomenon. Numerous examples are found in the field of ornithology, illustrated by the annual Christmas Bird Count, which began in 1900. The field is growing dramatically; it was barely visible in the published literature until the mid-1990s and has significantly increased as a percentage of the total articles within the Web of Science since 2010 (Kullenberg and Kasperowski, 2016). Ecological monitoring benefits from citizen science as traditional methods can't cover such broad geographic scales, especially with limits on funding (Dickinson et al., 2010). New technologies have the potential to expand the user base, motivate citizen scientists, and improve data quality, collection, and results (Newman et al., 2012); eBird, a tool for birders to record species online, exemplifies this approach, receiving millions of observations every month (Bonney et al., 2014).

Marine mammal research is ideal for citizen science efforts since most studies require extensive data collection and the animals have an inherent appeal that can attract motivated participants. Embling et al. (2015) quantified the effort required by citizen scientists to detect trends in the occurrence of bottlenose dolphins in Scotland and found that five watches per day was necessary; this would be nearly impossible to sustain without the assistance of citizen scientists. Today, many organizations work closely with whale-watching companies to gather sightings data (e.g. Pacific Whale Foundation, M.E.E.R. La Gomera, Sea Watch Foundation), and effective interpretation (which citizen science leaders can provide) can increase tourists' knowledge and commitment to protecting both the animals and marine environment (Garcia-Cegarra and Pacheco, 2017).

While marine mammal research can benefit greatly from the use of citizen science, many researchers in the field are reluctant to embrace this approach. Typical concerns relate to the accuracy and validity of the data, but these can be addressed with well-formulated programs and sufficient training (Newman et al., 2003). Because of this reluctance, the contributions by citizen scientists are often hidden in education tracks at scientific meetings, published in outreach sections of journals (Bonney et al., 2014), or not acknowledged in scientific publications. When one searches databases of primary literature using the terms "citizen science" and various synonyms for marine mammals, very few articles are listed. Yet, an informal query of an international marine mammal listserv (MARMAM) about publications "based primarily on data contributed by citizen scientists" resulted in 30 responses and citations for over 30 peer-reviewed articles that included contributions from the public to marine mammal science, and many additional reports, theses, and papers in preparation. Some respondents to this informal query indicated that they used different terms in their work such as "opportunistic" or actively avoid the term "citizen science" – one respondent felt it was an arbitrary distinction since a scientist is "merely another citizen." This issue is not limited to the marine mammal field; as Kullenberg and Kasperowski (2016) had to use a variety of synonyms ("community-based monitoring," "citizen scientist monitoring," and "participatory science"), as well as needing to read the abstracts to identify citizen science publications. In contrast, some researchers include the public contributors as co-authors, such as the Lydersen et al. (2013) publication of an unusual sighting of a white humpback based on tourist photos. While discussion continues on the usefulness of citizen science in marine mammal research, the number of current citizen science projects described in the listserv responses suggest that the field is growing and viewed by researchers and conservationists as an approach with great potential for the study of marine mammals.

## Case study: Whales and Dolphins Under the California Sun

The Southern California Bight is home to a diversity of marine mammal species due to highly productive waters. Large whales such as blues (*Balaenoptera musculus*) and humpbacks (*Megaptera novaeangliae*) visit during the summer months to feed, while grays (*Eschrichtius robustus*) migrate along our coast between their northern feeding grounds and southern breeding lagoons, and minke (*B. acutorostrata*) and fins (*B. physalus*) are year-round residents (Figure 5.1). Dolphin species, including bottlenose (*Tursiops truncatus*), Risso's (*Grampus griseus*), long-beaked (*Delphinus*

FIGURE 5.1   Breaching whales near Dana Point Harbor, CA, USA: (a) humpback whale; (b) minke whale.

*Photos:* Shane Keena Photography.

*capensis*) and short-beaked commons (*D. delphis*) (Figure 5.2), along with pinniped species, primarily harbor seals (*Phoca vitulina*) and California sea lions (*Zalophus californianus*), inhabit the area throughout the year.

This area is also home to some of the largest cities and busiest ports in the world. Thus, these species face a multitude of anthropogenic threats, including vessel traffic, commercial fishing, offshore oil and gas development, and noise and solid-waste pollution. Collisions between whales and vessels have increased as ships get larger

FIGURE 5.2    (a) Bottlenose dolphins in front of harbor entrance; (b) long-beaked common dolphins with calf.

*Photos:* Shane Keena Photography.

and faster and whale populations grow (Laist et al., 2001). Entanglements in fishing gear also can lead to serious injuries or even fatalities; for example, 2016 was a record year for reports of entangled whales off the US West Coast with a concentration off California (NOAA, 2017). There are also less lethal, but still very troubling, threats in terms of the exposure to vessels, as maritime traffic often intersects home ranges or migratory paths. This may cause animals to move their paths further offshore than normal or to alter their surface behavior to avoid large vessels, causing them to expend additional energy (Moore and Clarke, 2002).

While often seen as an environmentally safe activity, whale watching may also be a threat by disturbing the target animals. In a study of gray whales migrating past Ensenada, Mexico, Heckel et al. (2001) found a significant difference in their swimming velocities with and without the presence of whale-watching boats, and observed that the whales displayed avoidance behavior when approached head-on. And orcas in British Columbia spent less time foraging when in the presence of boats than they do otherwise (Lusseau et al., 2009). Such impacts could increase energetic costs while decreasing gains from foraging, and could push an animal past its physiological limits, especially in years of limited prey availability.

Combining the need to investigate anthropogenic impacts on marine mammals off the coast of Southern California with the unique public interest and desire to contribute to conservation of marine mammals, a research project funded by Earthwatch (http://earthwatch.org/) involving the public in collecting data for a long-term monitoring effort of local cetacean species was developed, called Whales and Dolphins under the California Sun. This program serves as a case study through which the field of marine citizen science may draw lessons about involving tourists as citizen scientists in research on charismatic marine species.

## Project goals

The Whales and Dolphins Under the California Sun program was initiated in the winter of 2011 with weekend expeditions timed to coincide with the gray whale migration. It was then expanded to one- to two-week surveys in the summer of 2012 to include the blue and humpback whale season and to provide greater seasonal coverage.

The primary research goal was to establish and maintain a long-term monitoring program to identify influences of human activities on marine mammal populations (Figure 5.3). The project has four general objectives that encompass specific research questions, which range from discrete one- to two-year projects, to ongoing data collection.

*Objective 1: Species Monitoring and Distribution Patterns:* The precise locations of all marine mammal sightings are recorded to determine both daily and seasonal trends in each species' habitat use. Geographic information systems (GIS) maps are then created to show the locations of all marine mammal in relation to a variety of anthropogenic (boat sightings and vessel traffic) and oceanographic factors (sea surface temperature [SST], bathymetry [bottom depth and slope], chlorophyll [measure of primary productivity]) (Figure 5.4). Photographs are used to identify

**FIGURE 5.3**   Recreational boaters surrounding a feeding humpback whale.

*Photo:* Shane Keena Photography.

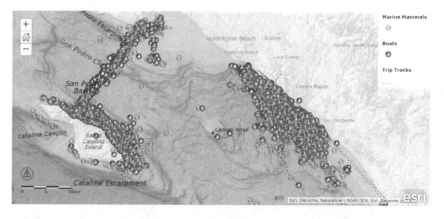

**FIGURE 5.4**   GIS map showing extensive overlap of all sightings of boats ($n = 14,792$) and marine mammals ($n = 5,439$) observed within the Southern California Bight from July 2012 through February 2017. Map created in ArcGIS online (Esri); marine mammal symbols are set at 30% transparent to show the boat symbols underneath.

individual animals to estimate population size, habitat use, site fidelity, and social networks.

*Objective 2: Behavioral Investigations:* To determine habitat use of marine mammals, the activity state of individuals are recorded when sighted. For whales, activity states include Feeding, Traveling, Milling, Socializing, Resting, and Other (or Unknown). Describing dolphin activity is notoriously difficult as there are many individuals in each pod with multiple behaviors occurring at one time, and large groups can make it difficult to record unbiased observations. We have recently developed a detailed ethogram of more than 30 specific behaviors (lateral leap, tail slap, etc.) to allow for more detailed and accurate analyses of discrete behavioral events in relationship to overall pod activity state and habitat use.

*Objective 3: Vessel Disturbance*: The third objective is to map and quantify exposure to vessels, investigate if these vessels comply with existing regulations, and if they act as a disturbance. For the large whales this includes tracking an individual animal's movement patterns, swim speeds, behaviors, and respiration patterns, with simultaneous data collection on boat presence and activity. Specific indicators that vessels are causing a disturbance would include any change in diving and respiratory patterns, a shift in their swim speed or direction of travel, and a change in behavioral state. We are also conducting a study to determine if vessels that observe sea lions resting on a buoy act as a disturbance. Interactions are observed from a jetty with a spotting scope (Figure 5.5); sea lion behavior is recorded with scan-instantaneous sampling while boats are observed continuously. From this work, we hope to contribute evidence-based recommendations for guidelines regarding sustainable whale-watching practices.

*Objective 4: Injury Assessment*: The final objective is focused on describing injury rates to compare species in terms of type of injuries (e.g. natural vs. anthropogenic) and rates within the populations. Photographs collected both for photo-ID efforts and those taken opportunistically are reviewed and scored. These data will provide important information on human impacts and risks faced by the various species.

**FIGURE 5.5**   Observing disturbance of sea lions resting on a buoy near Dana Point Harbor from the jetty using a spotting scope.

*Photo:* Shane Keena Photography.

## Citizen scientist involvement

An important consideration for any citizen science project is recruitment and retention of volunteers. In this case, Earthwatch as an educational environmental tourism organization is responsible for recruiting the volunteers through a variety of media, and facilitate repeated participation by volunteers who got particularly excited about the project. Ranging in age and from all areas of the United States, Earthwatch volunteers pay to participate in trips that involve them in real scientific field research, living with and becoming part of the research crew at the field site.

Training for project volunteers begins with orientation to the research goals, explanation of the field methods, a slide show focused on species identification, and practice with the protocol, technologies, and data sheets on "mock transects" on land. When conducting data collection in the field, the experienced research crew continues to provide close oversight and guidance, especially in the first few days in the field, to verify records are accurate and complete.

Research methodologies involve near-shore transects from charter boats to collect sightings along consistent survey paths for comparison, along with opportunistic recordings from whale-watching boats. Boat-based surveys are done out of Dana Point Harbor and Catalina Island. Observations are also conducted from shore with a theodolite from high elevation vantage points to track animals without our presence acting as a potential disturbance. Dana Wharf Whale Watching has greatly assisted our efforts by providing access to boat charters at a discounted rate and allowing research crew to collect data opportunistically from their regular whale watch trips at no cost when space is available. They also share our research findings via social media and press releases to increase public outreach.

Citizen scientists help in all aspects of data collection, data entry, and preliminary analysis. Data sheets are provided so that participants are clear on what needs to be recorded, and a handheld GPS is used to accurately record the latitude and longitude of all sightings (Figure 5.6). Information that is recorded includes time, location, species, number of animals, activity state, presence of vessels (and their size, type, heading), and notes for additional observations. Sightings data are also recorded on a tablet running Whale mAPP, a mobile app for public contributions of marine mammal sightings (see Box 5.1), so that our data can be freely shared with the public and marine science community. All animals are photographed by multiple people (with DSLR cameras and zoom lenses) to obtain the best images for identification and injury assessment. During focal follows of individual whales, we record respiration patterns and track movements. While observing dolphin pods we use the Collector for ArcGIS (ESRI) app, which we've programmed with a detailed ethogram of dolphin behaviors. When observing a dolphin pod, observers work in pairs and take positions around the boat to conduct two-minute scans and note the frequency of all behaviors from the ethogram; one person acts as the recorder to enter all data on the Collector app. Citizen scientists rotate between the various research activities on 30-minute shifts, for example, starting by recording on the sightings data sheet, then using the GPS, next photographing, then recording boat sightings, and then rotating to a break shift.

**FIGURE 5.6**   Research transects from charter boat. Citizen scientists are involved in all aspects of data collection: observing for animals with binoculars, using a GPS for locations, identifying behaviors with an ethogram, and recording all sightings on data sheets.

---

## BOX 5.1   WHALE MAPP: A MOBILE PLATFORM TO ENCOURAGE BROAD-SCALE PARTICIPATION IN MARINE MAMMAL MONITORING

Whale mAPP was developed to take advantage of the untapped resource of millions of people worldwide who observe marine mammals every year (Hoyt, 2001). This web and mobile application system allows anyone equipped with a GPS-enabled smartphone or tablet to record their sightings and transmit that information to a freely accessible online geodatabase, with an accompanying website that provides instantaneous data in an interactive format (Stelle et al. 2016).

Whale mAPP was designed to contribute to three primary objectives: 1) research, 2) conservation, and 3) education (King 2012). These goals overlap through the creation of datasets on species distributions, abundance, behavior, and habitat use which can be used by researchers, whose findings inform managers developing conservation plans, and users become more educated about the animals and then hopefully invested in supporting conservation efforts. A primary aim was to build a universal platform that could work anywhere in the world, so it is geo-aware and automatically populates region-specific species lists and also can record data without connectivity for use in remote areas. Survey paths are automatically recorded to provide the important effort data for researchers. User engagement was also carefully considered in designing an attractive and easy-to-use application to attract data collectors and keep their attention. Extensive beta testing was conducted to ensure stability and clarity so that anyone could contribute sightings without requiring training. To address concerns about data quality, two accounts are available for users; "experts" provide credentials for approval, while other users are classified as "public"; contributions can then be filtered by user type.

Whale mAPP as of this publication had over 130 registered users from 16 different countries. Most of these users have been recruited via word of mouth or from learning about the program at scientific conferences (e.g. Hann et al. 2015; Stelle and King, 2015), reading journal articles (Stelle, 2015), or via the public media. One concerted effort was led by Courtney Hann, who evaluated the educational and research benefits of the Whale mAPP citizen science project for her M.Sc. thesis work (Marine Resource Management, Oregon State University). In the summer of 2014, Hann recruited 39 volunteers in Southeast Alaska to participate in the study; these volunteers recorded 1,232 marine mammal sightings, composed mostly of humpback whale (~34%), harbor seal (~8%), and sea otter (~8%) sightings. These contributions account for nearly half of the total recordings to date, which suggests that focused recruitment could greatly increase the amount and coverage of sightings.

All of the volunteers in Hann's (2015) study showed a preexisting interest in marine mammals and/or the ocean and most found Whale mAPP engaging. Results from surveys of the volunteer citizen scientists distributed pre- and post-use of Whale mAPP showed improved marine mammal identification skills for less experienced users, and evidence that volunteers sought out more information on the animals through books and the Internet. Further educational development, including expanded content knowledge and changes in attitudes towards the environment, were not seen in this study, and would require additional learning and engagement components to be built into the citizen science project. Results also suggest differences in the experiences with user type. For instance, public users had more technological problems, and would have preferred a simplified app, while expert users' wanted to enter more data on the animal's behavior. To improve the educational components of Whale mAPP, the "learn" component of the website has been expanded to include species facts and video clips, and curriculum is being developed that can be used in the classroom, allowing students to formulate hypotheses that they can immediately "test" with collected data.

Concern regarding the usability of citizen science datasets for research and conservation is often expressed, thus Hann (2015) investigated how accurately home range maps created from the Whale mAPP dataset matched results from previous studies. Species' unique ecological distributions accounted for much of the differences between public and expert datasets, requiring higher sample sizes for highly migratory (humpback whale, killer whale) and discontinuously distributed (Steller sea lion, harbor seal, sea otter) marine mammals, while those with clustered distributions (harbor porpoise and Dall's porpoise) exhibited comparable core- and intermediate-use areas despite their small sample sizes. This limited dataset was useful in describing distribution patterns of higher use, core areas. This short-term study demonstrates the potential benefits that could be obtained with a long-term, large dataset from wide-spread use of Whale mAPP.

Start a trip                Visualize your trip                Record observations

**FIGURE 5.7**   Whale mAPP allows anyone with a mobile device to record and map sightings of marine mammals anywhere in the world.

*Source:* www.Whalemapp.org.

Designated lab time is built into the schedule for data entry and preliminary analyses. Citizen scientists assist by transcribing sightings data into Excel spreadsheets, uploading GPS coordinates, and then creating GIS maps of each days' transect path and sightings of all animals and vessels. They also help to edit and organize the photographs, match individuals (using DARWIN software for dolphin species), and add animals to the photo-ID catalogs. Over the years, we have created, and continually updated, detailed instructions for these protocols to act as a reference for the citizen scientists. All work is double-checked to ensure accuracy, as it is easy to make typos when entering large amounts of coded data. Also, the research crew always trains the citizen scientists on each activity until they feel comfortable doing the work more independently.

The research group is often split into teams with a few citizen scientists per researcher to expand our coverage. For example, one group of three citizen scientists and one to two crew members will go to Catalina for the survey while another group conducts two hours of shore observations followed by data entry and analysis. Other days we may split into three groups and rotate between observations from the whale watch boat, behavioral study of sea lions from the jetty, and data entry. This is one of the major benefits of working with citizen scientists who are able to contribute to the various activities and allow us to greatly increase our productivity.

## Project results

### Species monitoring and distribution

This ongoing project requires long-term data sets to effectively fulfill the conservation goals of the project. We have made progress on each goal and plan continued monitoring. We have created photo-ID catalogs for most of the species we study and collaborate with other research groups to improve our knowledge of individual animals. For example, we have identified over 70 blue whales between 2012 and 2016 but, typically, there are only a few re-sightings between years. Our images and associated details are shared with Cascadia Research Collective, which has a catalog of over 200 blue whales from throughout the North Pacific; some of our sightings are new animals to their database and, for previously known individuals, the re-sightings provide us with important details including locations and dates of other sightings, and in some cases even gender and calving history (Figure 5.8).

### ID0010 "Sleepy"

Zoomed in Right Side Dorsal

Zoomed in Left Side Dorsal

DP20120726_ID0010DR

DP20120726_D0010DL

Left Side Dorsal

DP20120726_ID0010L

Right Side Dorsal

DP20120726_ID0010R

(a)                                                1                          **R**\Redlands

FIGURE 5.8   Blue whale photo-ID catalog example page: (a) images of one animal showing close-up photos or dorsal fins and body from both sides; (b) details on same individual, listing other observation dates and additional details provided by Cascadia Research Collective.

## ID0010 – Additional Information

Sightings:

- 7/26/2012 – Dana Point
- 7/25/2014 – Dana point
  - DP2014IMG_0066 - Copy_ID0010L
  - DP2014IMG_1433_I D0010R

Other Names:

- CRCID: 2056
- Known as "Sleepy"

Gender: Male

(b)      2     

FIGURE 5.8    Continued

Bottlenose dolphins are another commonly observed species in our study area, and most researchers focus on the coastal population that is observed within 2 km of the shore (Defran and Weller, 1999). We have contributed our images to a collaborative catalog, California Dolphin Online Catalog (CDOC), which recently published a catalog of nearly 1,300 individuals to facilitate research (Weller and Defran, 2016). Less is known about the offshore bottlenose dolphins, a distinct ecotype found more than 2 km from shore, but we have developed a catalog of over 315 individual dolphins. The large population size makes it difficult to manually compare images so we use DARWIN, a program to automate the matching process based on traces of dorsal fin images. Plotting the number of identified animals with each survey shows exponential growth; this trend along with low rates of re-sightings suggests that the population is much larger than represented in our catalog and has a large home range (Walters et al., 2016).

We have observed a recent decline in numbers of blue whales with a concurrent increase in sightings of humpback whales in our study area (Figure 5.9). Incorporating oceanographic data with GIS maps of our sighting history, we determined there is a relationship between abundance with sea surface temperature and chlorophyll levels (Laufer and Stelle, 2017). This approach can help us to predict impacts of acute stressors such as El Niño events, and chronic stressors such as climate change, on blue whale abundance.

Common dolphins have a worldwide distribution, yet two species of common dolphins are found in our study area; this sympatric overlap is relatively unusual (Cunha et al., 2015). As part of an undergraduate thesis, Gomez (2017) found significant differences in their habitat use using our citizen science data, with short-beaked common dolphins using deeper habitat further from shore and long-beaked common dolphins being more coastal (Figure 5.10). However, a hot spot analysis of primary feeding areas showed no significant difference. The two species may differ in prey or timing of feeding, which along with reliance on distinct habitats for their other activities might allow for their coexistence.

## Vessel disturbance

Observations of sea lions have established that the animals resting on a buoy near the harbor are exposed to frequent boat traffic from a great variety of vessels. We have observed extreme incidents of harassment, such as jet skis circling the buoy at high speeds, attempting to touch the animals, and shooting them with water guns. Evidence from focal scans shows the sea lions exhibit a significant increase in alert and active behaviors in the presence of boats (Lee et al., 2016; Figure 5.11). With a larger dataset, we hope to determine distances of approach and viewing times to minimize potential disturbance and then share these guidelines with local whale-watching outfits, recreational boat rentals, and yacht clubs.

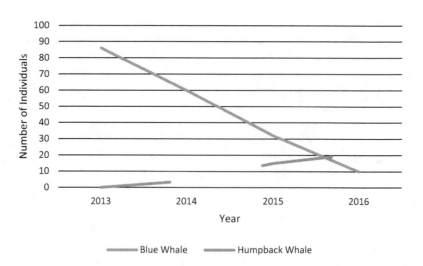

**FIGURE 5.9**  Total number of whales observed each year from 2012–2016; a clear trend is shown with blue whales decreasing and humpback whales increasing since the start of the study.

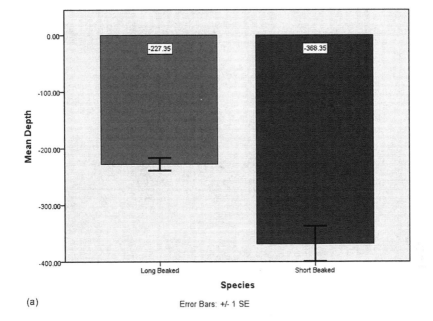

(a)

Error Bars: +/- 1 SE

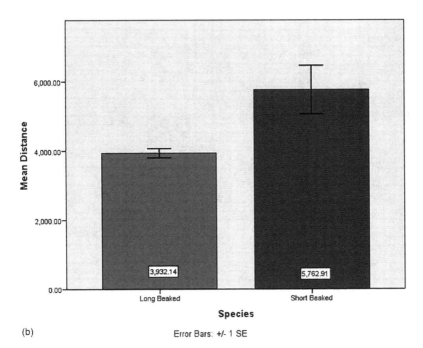

(b)

Error Bars: +/- 1 SE

FIGURE 5.10 Distribution of common dolphin sightings: (a) long-beaked common dolphins were found in significantly shallower waters and (b) significantly closer to shore, compared to short-beaked common dolphins. Average values are shown measured in meters; error bars represent standard error.

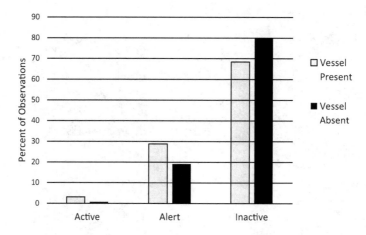

**FIGURE 5.11** Sea lions observed on a buoy outside of Dana Point Harbor. When boats passed by the buoy, the sea lions significantly increased their active and alert behaviors compared to when boats were not in the vicinity.

## Injury assessment

Many animals observed in our study area have evidence of injuries, some clearly caused by human impacts. Weerasinghe (2014) analyzed photos we had collected from 2012 and 2013 and found the highest rate of injuries due to anthropogenic causes in blue whales (17% of the individuals), followed by bottlenose dolphins (9%), and California sea lions (3%). Conner et al. (2011) compared images of gray whales from our study area with photographs collected throughout their migratory path (Baja, Mexico to Canada) and found only 2% of the 1,600 animals showed evidence of anthropogenic injuries (scars from boat propellers and entanglement; Figure 5.12). These values likely underestimate the true incidence of anthropogenic injuries, as both studies relied on photos taken to identify individual animals, which focus on the dorsal fins, flanks, and fluke, and rarely include other body areas more likely to show injuries such as the peduncle or flippers. Thus we have begun taking and storing additional images of the whole body of animals for future analyses.

## Ongoing monitoring

Monitoring studies are difficult to maintain on a long-term basis, but with the support of Earthwatch participants we have developed extensive databases on a variety of marine mammal species, many of which are poorly studied. Our study on common dolphins is the first to examine the habitat segregation of the two sympatric species, which are typically combined in most analyses. Few studies have

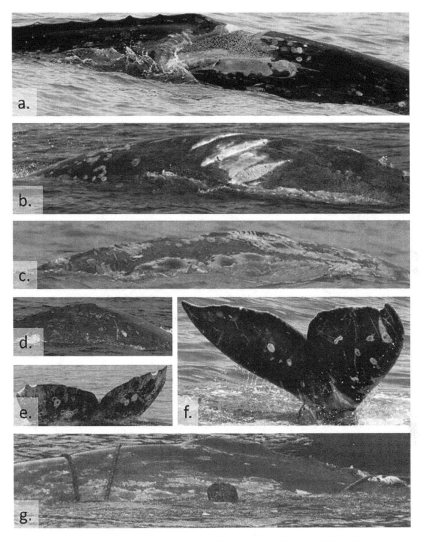

FIGURE 5.12    Examples of injuries seen in photographs of gray whales taken throughout their migratory range: (a) wound; (b) wound (caused by boat propellers); (c) rake marks; (d) scar; (e) fluke missing tips; (f) entanglement
around peduncle; (g) entanglement around body.

*Photos:* Coastal Ecosystem Research Foundation (CERF) and Cascadia Research Collective (CRC;
Brian Gisborne & Jeff Jacobsen) photo-ID catalogs.

examined offshore bottlenose dolphins as they are typically more difficult to access,
so our photo-ID catalog is providing important insight into the population. Collaborations with other researchers is also essential to develop a more thorough

understanding of many of the species as they have very large home ranges or migratory paths. By focusing our efforts in a relatively small study area we can understand marine mammal behaviors and habitat use on a fine scale, and then in conjunction with other projects our findings will contribute to informed management of the local species.

## Benefits to participants

Assessing the educational benefits gained by participants in nature-based tourism is difficult under most circumstances (Ardoin et al., 2015). Because Earthwatch solicits feedback from all their programs' participants with both structured and open-ended survey questions, we can examine their perceptions of how they benefited from this expedition. Over the summer seasons (2013–2015), 35 (37%) of the citizen scientists responded to these evaluation surveys. These respondents described overwhelmingly positive experiences, citing their "sense of involvement in the research" (94%) and "training on field research tasks" (97%). The majority also felt their participation significantly or very significantly increased their understanding of "how the science will be used" (83%), "the importance of the data collected" (87%), and "how the research relates to global environmental issues" (79%). While responses indicated important impacts on participants' self-reported understanding of the science of the project, fewer (but still the majority of respondents) expressed that participation in the project impacted their attitude toward the environment, with fewer citizen scientists stating that their participation had very or significantly "motivated them to include more environmental considerations in daily life" (66%), "increased sense of personal connection to the natural world" (69%), or provided an opportunity to make a meaningful contribution to the planet" (62%). This may reflect that these volunteers are self-selected and already had very pro-environmental attitudes.

Not surprisingly, the citizen scientists reported being excited by their interactions with the study subjects, explaining "it was really valuable to see these animals up close and to be a part of a research team that is working to help protect them" (Figure 5.13), but they also appreciate that they are truly contributing to conservation efforts. We have noticed that citizen scientists also often feel unprepared to collect quality data at the start, but with proper training and supervision they gain confidence: "the data entry was interesting and really helped me feel like I was helping in a significant way." A recurring theme is that citizen scientists want to know they are making real contributions: "I felt like my work was very valued by the team, which I think is an important part of the volunteer experience!"

Many participants have become recurring citizen scientists on Earthwatch projects. One of the citizen scientists who recently participated in this project had completed over 90 expeditions in his 20+ years of retirement; he built photo

**FIGURE 5.13**   Blue whale surprising our citizen scientists when it surfaced near the bow of our boat during a research transect.

*Photo:* Shane Keena Photography.

albums from each project and wrote articles describing his experiences for retirement publications. At the other extreme, another citizen scientist participated in one weekend trip as her first citizen science venture, and she explained that this experience led to a whole new path for her retirement (Box 5.2). According to Earthwatch, 32% of their first-time participants go on to participate in another expedition.

## BOX 5.2 CITIZEN SCIENCE VOLUNTEER: IRENE GILGOFF, MD

When Irene Gilgoff retired after a career as a pediatrician, she was not sure where life would take her. She traveled to the Galapagos Islands and Baja California. While on a whale watching trip, she "*looked into the eye of the gray whale calf that rose in the water beside me, a connection to the natural world became a part of me in a way that it had never been before. That was the beginning of my journey into citizen science.*"

Irene has participated in two Earthwatch expeditions, studying marine mammals in Southern California and leatherback sea turtles in Costa Rica. She describes both as "*wonderful, life changing adventures . . . that introduced (her) to people that I admire and have been able to count as friends and part my new life experiences.*" She currently volunteers twice a week at the Pacific Marine Mammal Center in Laguna Beach, California, to help rescue sea lions and seals, and regularly serves as a whale watch naturalist through the American Cetacean Society (ACS). Irene is enthused that she has the opportunity "*to work with people committed to conservation and maintaining a healthy ocean. This experience has reshaped my life in a personal way. I now practice conservation, recycling, and reusing on a daily basis.*"

She truly embraces all aspects of the work. She was worried about injuries from the physical challenges so hired a personal trainer. She also exemplifies the life-long learner attitude and is taking classes at a local community college in oceanography and marine mammal biology, along with attending scientific conferences. "*Being a citizen scientist has only been a positive experience . . . it has shown me that I can still make a difference.*"

## Challenges and best practices for citizen science on marine mammals

For scientists, there are challenges associated with working with citizen scientists. Many scientists underestimate the additional time commitment required. Training and managing groups of participants requires extensive organization and pre-planning. Field work is inherently unpredictable, so it is essential to have scheduled activities with redundancy plans, and emphasize to the participants the importance of being adaptable. Despite the challenges, Earthwatch scientists have decided the benefits of working with public participants outweigh the challenges (Box 5.3).

Maintaining volunteer engagement is also important but difficult. Earthwatch volunteers are immersed in the project during the expedition, but how can project leaders continue the relationship once volunteers leave the project? Social media

## BOX 5.3 EARTHWATCH PERSPECTIVE ON CITIZEN SCIENCE: INTERVIEW WITH CRISTINA EISENBERG, PH.D., CHIEF SCIENTIST AT EARTHWATCH INSTITUTE

Earthwatch Institute uses a contributory model for citizen science, with the mission to "engage people worldwide in scientific field research and education to promote the understanding and action necessary for sustainable environment" (http://earthwatch.org/about/earthwatch-mission-and-values). Volunteers work directly in the field with scientists and their technicians to collect data. According to Chief Scientist Dr. Cristina Eisenberg, Earthwatch fits into a *"unique niche that tangibly advances citizen science because we require that all the scientists whose projects we support do hypothesis-driven science that leads to peer-reviewed journal article publications."* Citizen scientists keenly interested in science are exposed to and directly participate in cutting-edge, rigorous science that leads to the change. *"Our science matters, because peer-reviewed publications are instrumental in driving policy shifts that can help conserve species at risk of extinction."* For example, contributions by citizen scientists to Earthwatch projects have led to the creation of Marine Protected Areas, and have helped bring back sea turtles from the brink of extinction.

Many prospective citizen scientists express interest in marine-focused projects. The physical requirements of marine work can deter some potential participants, but the opportunity to spend time on boats, snorkel, or even scuba dive attracts many others. Of the 40 projects supported by Earthwatch each year, about one-third are focused on marine conservation, but only three projects study marine mammals.

Earthwatch participants work directly in the field with scientists. This typically leads to rich interactions and mutual learning for volunteers, scientists, and staff, plus it enables the scientists to collect large, high-quality datasets. However, one of the biggest challenges according to Dr. Eisenberg has to do with expectations. Working with citizen scientists requires more labor-intensive management compared to working exclusively with professional technicians to ensure participants' safety, wellbeing, and engagement, and with ensuring the quality of the data. Most PIs find that the benefits of working with citizen scientists greatly outweigh any challenges but scientists new to working with the public typically go through a learning curve. Also, a small proportion of participants join a project expecting their activities to be more recreational or wildlife will be abundant and everywhere. Most participants are passionate about contributing to science directly and so they don't mind these challenges. However, setting expectations well from the outset, before citizen scientists are actually in the field, is critical to ensure project success. PIs working with citizen scientists need to be able to communicate very clearly about the science, framing it in a context accessible and meaningful to everyone.

The premise of Earthwatch is that citizen scientists can help take meaningful action to address the enormous global change problems we face today. Most Earthwatch projects are long-term studies providing necessary data for adaptive management. Participants benefit by learning about and becoming engaged in science and by contributing directly to conservation. It empowers members of the public to be part of that change, using science as a key driver. Many Earthwatch citizen scientists comment afterward that they found their volunteer field research experience "life-changing." One of the biggest benefits is the transformative nature of citizen science on an individual level and for society on a much larger scale. *"This is how we create change for the better and how our society can solve problems. These citizen scientists go home and apply what they learned in the field, share it enthusiastically with others, thereby spreading awareness of science-based conservation."* – Dr. Eisenberg.

can be useful; for example, Facebook can be an effective way to share research updates and news reports, but these tend to be a one-sided communications. A goal is to recruit more past Earthwatch participants as Whale mAPP users so they can continue to contribute to the research. Yet with remote citizen science projects such as mobile apps, it is not uncommon to have the majority of contributions from just a small proportion of users. eBird successfully developed a reward system where users compete with other participants comparing bird counts; this greatly increased the amount of observations (Hochachka et al., 2012). New features are under development in Whale mAPP so users can compare species lists; this approach is based on evidence that gamifying the process can open science to other demographics and engage participants (Newman et al., 2012).

Quality control of data is also a common concern in citizen science projects and can be addressed in a number of ways. For example, Hochachka et al. (2012) suggests using filters such as customized data entry sheets; we utilize that approach with standard data sheets for Earthwatch citizen scientists and dropdown menus on Whale mAPP. These make it clear what information should be recorded, and it's easy to see if there is missing data from blank sections on the forms (or alerts on Whale mAPP). Analytics can be used to identify high quality data retrospectively (Hochachka et al., 2012). Whale mAPP utilizes a script that detects and flags unusual sightings (Guttmacher, 2016). Handling and processing of the data is also challenging. Including the citizen scientists in these steps is useful. For example, for Whales and Dolphins Under the California Sun, the citizen scientists enter their own data and quickly learn the importance of complete and legible entries. This helps them to understand the value of what they are recording when they see the results of their efforts in the form of maps and photo-ID matches.

## Conclusion

Sustaining long-term ecological monitoring is extremely difficult as it requires dedication of a researcher or organization, continued funding, and extensive resources. Citizen science may be one of the few ways to provide these types of data (Dickinson et al., 2010), which are necessary to address many questions related to marine mammal conservation. Since marine mammals are frequently observed from boat and shore by commercial vessels, recreational boaters, and tourists, citizen science can be an effective method for marine mammal research and conservation (Box 5.4).

---

### BOX 5.4  LONG-TERM CITIZEN SCIENCE: AMERICAN CETACEAN SOCIETY/LOS ANGELES GRAY WHALE CENSUS AND BEHAVIOR PROJECT

Alisa Schulman-Janiger has been running the full-season ACS/LA Gray Whale Census and Behavior Project since 1984, taking over from a pilot program started by marine biologist Bill Samaras in 1979. She expanded this shore-based census of gray whales and other species into a full-season census (December to late May), averaging 12 hours of observation every day (Figure 5.14). Many volunteers come from the Cabrillo Whalewatch Program; some have been with the project for over 25 years! The main purpose is to collect baseline data on the gray whales and other marine mammals; the long-term dataset allows for trends and anomalies to be uncovered. Working out of Point Vicente Interpretive Center (Palos Verdes, CA, USA), a publicly accessible location, provides the opportunity to educate the public; sightings are displayed on a whiteboard and volunteers answer questions during breaks between sightings.

Over 30 consecutive seasons of baseline data on migrating gray whales has been used to document changing trends in distribution, abundance, recruitment, and seasonality. For example, they have observed a recent shift to an earlier southbound migration, an extended northbound migration, and dramatic rise in calf counts over the past several years. They have also been able to provide insight into the average migratory speed by tracking unusual sightings with photos from shore. In one case, volunteers sighted a very deformed gray whale with a calf that was re-sighted several days later off Piedras Blancasor, CA, and in another case, a huge group of at least 23 grays were sighted 18 hours later off the coast of San Diego, CA. Data from the census has been used by the International Whaling Commission (IWC) in status reviews of the population and legislative decisions to ban gillnets within 3 miles of shore.

Although the work can be challenging, dedicated volunteers are rewarded with incredible experiences such as breaching whales and sightings of the rare visitors such as killer whales. Gray whale moms and calves frequently use the kelp beds to rest, play, and sometimes nurse; and they just recently observed a mom give birth right in front of the station. Alisa is a proponent of citizen science and emphasizes that *"trained citizen scientists can be crucial tools in collecting data – especially for long-term projects – that would not be possible to do with trained scientists because of budget constraints. Our citizen scientists also have an invaluable opportunity to interact with and educate the public about the habits of our local cetaceans, about safe whale watching practices, and about the scientific process itself."*

**FIGURE 5.14**   Alisa Schulman-Janiger observing gray whales with census volunteers.

*Photo:* Dave Janiger

The Whales and Dolphins Under the California Sun project represents a successful partnership with Earthwatch to reach citizen scientists with an interest in marine mammal research. These citizen scientists can genuinely contribute to the project by increasing the number of eyes on the water, recording a greater variety of data simultaneously, allowing us to split into groups for greater coverage, and assisting with the time-intensive data entry, mapping, and matching images for photo identification. The biggest challenge is the additional time commitment required in planning and organizing before the expeditions, along with the training that must be repeated with each new group of citizen scientists. For some, the interpersonal component could be difficult if you don't enjoy interacting with new people. Fortunately, this can also be one of the greatest benefits as researchers are exposed to fresh perspectives and the citizen scientists gain firsthand experience with the rigors and joys of field research, reinforced by the personal connections.

As a particular kind of vessel traffic, whale-watching vessels can be a double-edged sword for conservation. As whale-watching experiences and other nature-based tourism programs continue to increase, we also must ensure that the practices are sustainable and we aren't "loving them to death." It can be difficult to address the question of whale-watching impacts, especially as the responses can vary with species, behavior, vessel type, vessel approach, and so forth, but increased interest in this topic is leading to new methods and models (New et al., 2015). And citizen science stands to make significant contributions to this area of research. Disturbance from whale watching may be considered minor in comparison to many other anthropogenic harms, but it is one that can be managed, and a small reduction may help species cope with larger-scale impacts (New et al., 2015). By involving the whale watch companies and the tourists in the research, they are more likely to feel invested and likely to exhibit sustainable behaviors. Collaborations between trained scientists, tourism companies, and the public, in addition to providing a way to significantly advance scientific research and conservation, can help break down artificial boundaries between both groups and lead to a shared mission for conservation.

## Literature cited

Ardoin, N.M., Wheaton, M., Bowers, A.W., Hunt, C.A., and Durham, W.H. (2015). Nature-based tourism's impact on environmental knowledge, attitudes, and behavior: A review and analysis of the literature and potential future research. *Journal of Sustainable Tourism*, 23(6), 838–858.

Bonney, R., Shirk, J.L., Phillips, T.B., Wiggins, A., Ballard, H.L., Miller-Rushing, A.J., and Parrish, J.K. (2014). Next steps for citizen science. *Science*, 343(6178), 1436–1437.

Conner, L.M., Stelle, L.L., Najera-Hillman, E., Megill, W.M., and Calambokidis, J. (2011). Using Photo-ID to examine injuries in Eastern Pacific Gray Whales (*Eschrichtius robustus*). *Society for Marine Mammalogy 19th Biennial Conference*, Tampa, Florida, November 27–December 2.

Cunha, H.A., de Castro, R.L., Secchi, E.R., Crespo, E.A., Lailson-Brito, J., Azevedo, A.F., Lazoski, C., and Solé-Cava, A.M. (2015). Molecular and morphological differentiation of common dolphins (*Delphinus* sp.) in the Southwestern Atlantic: Testing the two species hypothesis in sympatry. *PLoS One*, 10(11), e0140251.

Defran, R.H., and Weller, D.W. (1999). Occurrence, distribution, site fidelity, and school size of bottlenose dolphins (*Tursiops truncatus*) off San Diego, California. *Marine Mammal Science*, 15(2), 366–380.

Dickinson, J.L., Zuckerberg, B., and Bonter, D.N. (2010). Citizen science as an ecological research tool: Challenges and benefits. *Annual Review of Ecology, Evolution and Systematics*, 41, 149–172.

Embling, C.B., Walters, A.E.M., and Dolman, S.J. (2015). How much effort is enough? The power of citizen science to monitor trends in coastal cetacean species. *Global Ecology and Conservation*, 3, 867–877.

Gomez, H. (2017). *Common dolphins living in sympatry: Does habitat partitioning explain the coexistence of short-beaked (Delphinus delphis) and long-beaked (Delphinus capensis) common dolphins in Southern California, USA?* B.S. thesis, University of Redlands, CA.

Guttmacher, R.C. (2016). *Automating quality control in a crowd-sourced marine mammal.* Master's thesis, University of Redlands, CA.

Hann, C. (2015). *Citizen science research: A focus on historical whaling data and a current marine mammal citizen science project, Whale mAPP.* Master's thesis, Oregon State University, OR.

Hann, C., Stelle, L.L., Szabo, A., Hanshumaker, B., and Torres, L. (2015). Citizen science: Benefits and limitations for marine mammal research and education. *Society for Marine Mammalogy 21st Biennial Conference*, San Francisco, CA, December 14–18.

Heckel, G., Reilly, S.B., Sumich, J.L., and Espejel, I. (2001). The influence of whalewatching on the behaviour of migrating gray whales (*Eschrichtius robustus*) in Todos Santos Bay and surrounding waters, Baja California, Mexico. *Journal of Cetacean Research and Management*, 3(3), 227–238.

Hochachka, W.M., Fink, D., Hutchinson, R.A., Sheldon, D., Wong, W.K., and Kelling, S. (2012). Data-intensive science applied to broad-scale citizen science. *Trends in Ecology and Evolution*, 27(2), 130–137.

Hoyt, E. (2001). Whale watching 2001: Worldwide tourism numbers, expenditures, and expanding socioeconomic benefits. *International Fund for Animal Welfare*, i–vi; 1–158, Yarmouth Port, MA.

King, M.C. (2012). *Managing marine mammal observations using a volunteered geographic information approach*. Master's thesis, University of Redlands, CA.

Kullenberg, C., and Kasperowski, D. (2016). What is citizen science? – a scientometric meta-analysis. *PLoS One*, 11(1), e0147152.

Laist, D.W., Knowlton, A.R., Mead, J.G., Collet, A.S., and Podesta, M. (2001). Collisions between ships and whales. *Marine Mammal Science*, 17(1), 35–75.

Laufer, A., and Stelle, L.L. (2017). A spatial analysis of marine mammals in the Southern California Bight. *Seventh Los Angeles Geospatial Summit*, Los Angeles, CA, February 24.

Lee, I., Stelle, L.L., and Thiltgen, H. (2016). Human disturbance on California sea lions (*Zalophus californianus*) off Dana Point, California. *Southern California Academy of Sciences Annual Meeting*, Los Angeles, CA, May 6–7.

Lusseau, D., Bain, D.E., Williams, R., and Smith, J.C. (2009). Vessel traffic disrupts the foraging behavior of southern resident killer whales *Orcinus orca*. *Endangered Species Research*, 6(3), 211–221.

Lydersen, C., Øien, N., Mikkelsen, B., Bober, S., Fisher, D., and Kovacs, K.M. (2013). A white humpback whale (*Megaptera novaeangliae*) in the Atlantic Ocean, Svalbard, Norway, August 2012. *Polar Research*, 31(1), 19739. doi:10.3402/polar.v32i0.19739.

Moore, S., and Clarke, J.T. (2002). Potential impact of offshore human activities on gray whales (*Eschrichtius robustus*). *Journal of Cetacean Research and Management*, 4(1), 19–25.

New, L.F., Hall, A.J., Harcourt, R., Kaufman, G., Parsons, E.C.M., Pearson, H.C., Cosentino, A.M., and Schick, R.S. (2015). The modelling and assessment of whale-watching impacts. *Ocean and Coastal Management*, 115, 10–16.

Newman, C., Buesching, C.D., and Macdonald, D.W. (2003). Validating mammal monitoring methods and assessing the performance of citizen scientists in wildlife conservation – "*Sed quis custodiet ipsos custodies?*" *Biological Conservation*, 113(2), 189–197.

Newman, G., Wiggins, A., Crall, A., Graham, E., Newman, S., and Crowston, K. (2012). The future of citizen science: Emerging technologies and shifting paradigms. *Frontiers in Ecology and the Environment*, 10(6), 298–304.

NOAA Fisheries. (2017). *West Coast Entanglement Summary*. [Online] www.westcoast.fisheries.noaa.gov/publications/protected_species/marine_mammals/cetaceans/wcr_2016_whale_entanglements_3-26-17_final.pdf.

O'Connor, S., Campbell, R., Cortez, H., and Knowles, T. (2009). *Whale watching worldwide: Tourism numbers, expenditures and expanding economic benefits*. A special report from the International Fund for Animal Welfare, Yarmouth MA, USA, prepared by Economists at Large, 228.

Parsons, E.C.M. (2012). The negative impacts of whale-watching. *Journal of Marine Biology*, 2012, 1–9.

Reynolds, J.E., III, Marsh, H., and Ragen, T.J. (2009). Marine mammal conservation. *Endangered Species Research*, 7, 23–28.

Roman, J., and Palumbi, S.R. (2003). Whales before whaling in the North Atlantic. *Science*, 301(5632), 508–510.

Schipper, J., Chanson, J.S., Chiozza, F., Cox, N.A., Hoffmann, M., Katariya, V., Lamoreux, J., et al. (2008). The status of the world's land and marine mammals: Diversity, threat, and knowledge. *Science*, 322(5899), 225–230.

Stelle, L.L. (2015). GIS Makes Citizen Science More Accessible: How the General Public Can Regain the Thrill of Scientific Discovery. *ArcNews* (Esri), 27(2), 27.

Stelle, L.L., and King, M. (2015). *Whale mAPP*: Mobile and Web application to encourage citizen science contributions of marine mammal sightings. *Citizen Science 2015*, San Jose, CA, February 11–12.

Stelle, L.L., King, M., and Hann, C. (2016). *Whale mAPP*: Engaging citizen scientists to contribute and map Marine mammal sightings. In *Ocean Solutions, Earth Solutions*, 2nd ed., ed. D.J. Wright, 151–169. Redlands, CA: ESRI Press.

Taylor, B.L., Martinez, M., Gerrodette, T., Barlow, J., and Hrovat, Y.N. (2007). Lessons from monitoring trends in abundance of marine mammals. *Marine Mammal Science*, 23(1), 157–175.

Tonachella, N., Nastasi, A., Kaufman, G., Maldini, D., and Rankin, R.W. (2012). Predicting trends in humpback whale (*Megaptera novaeangliae*) abundance using citizen science. *Pacific Conservation Biology*, 18(4), 297–309.

Walters, E.M., Camper, T., and Stelle, L.L. (2016). Photo-ID of Offshore Bottlenose Dolphins (*Tursiops truncatus*) in Southern California using DARWIN. *Southern California Academy of Sciences Annual Meeting*, Los Angeles, CA, May 6–7.

Weerasinghe, L. (2014). *Using photo-ID to analyze injuries to cetaceans and pinnipeds observed off Dana Point, CA*. B.S. thesis, University of Redlands, CA.

Weller, D.W., and Defran, R.H. (2016). *Coastal bottlenose dolphins off California and Northern Baja California, Mexico: Photo-Identification Catalog 1981–2014*. NOAA Technical Memorandum NMFS. NOAA-TM-NMFS-SWFSC-566. Springfield: National Oceanic and Atmospheric Administration.

# 6

# MARINE LITTER – BRINGING TOGETHER CITIZEN SCIENTISTS FROM AROUND THE WORLD

*Martin Thiel, Sunwook Hong, Jenna R. Jambeck,*
*Magdalena Gatta-Rosemary, Daniela Honorato-Zimmer,*
*Tim Kiessling, Katrin Knickmeier, and Katrin Kruse*

## Introduction

Marine litter is a global problem. Litter (mostly plastics) enters the oceans via multiple sources and in large amounts every day (Lebreton et al., 2012; Maximenko et al., 2012; Lechner et al., 2014; Jambeck et al., 2015). Once reaching the sea, plastics are widely distributed, reaching the deep ocean (Pham et al., 2014), remote seas (Eriksen et al., 2014), polar sea ice (Obbard et al., 2014), and shorelines around the world (Browne et al., 2015). Quantities of litter in the sea appear to have been increasing during the past decades (Thompson et al., 2004; Ryan et al., 2009), and due to the growing impact of plastics on marine life and human health, researchers have requested that harmful plastics be classified as hazardous (Rochman et al., 2013a).

Plastic litter in the oceans impacts marine wildlife in multiple ways (Kühn et al., 2015). Many marine vertebrates (seabirds, mammals, turtles) entangle in large litter items, causing wounds, drowning, and long-term suffocation (Hong et al., 2013; Žydelis et al., 2013; Lawson et al., 2015; Nelms et al., 2015). When breaking down into smaller fragments, many plastic items become accessible to ingestion by fishes, seabirds, and many invertebrates (van Franeker et al., 2011; Goldstein and Goodwin, 2013; Lusher, 2015). Plastic ingestion might cause multiple problems, including transfer of hazardous chemicals from plastics to the organisms (Rochman et al., 2013b, but see also Herzke et al., 2016). In addition, floating plastics may become dispersal vectors for marine organisms, potentially transporting non-indigenous species over long distances and into new, previously uncolonized habitats (Kiessling et al., 2015).

Due to its high visibility, significant impacts on emblematic species, such as seabirds and marine mammals, and the extensive media coverage, there has been an increasing awareness among the general public about the problem of marine litter. This has generated very active participation in cleanup activities (e.g. Kordella et al.,

2013), often including significant commitments by the participating citizens (e.g. Martin, 2013). Working together on marine litter projects also enhances awareness and participation in solutions (Veiga et al., 2016). Even though awareness about the problem of marine litter may be high, only concrete action proposals foster the belief among participants that individual behaviors can contribute to solutions (Jacobs et al., 2015; Gusmerotti et al., 2016).

In addition to coastal cleanups or recycling activities, the participation in scientific research projects on marine litter also contributes to increased environmental awareness among the volunteer participants (Smith et al., 2014; Yeo et al., 2015). Besides enhanced awareness, scientific studies with volunteers also have other important benefits. Volunteer programs can be powerful tools in generating scientific information in regions where no or little information about marine litter abundances, composition, and impacts exists (e.g. Bravo et al., 2009; Hong et al., 2013; Smith et al., 2014). Furthermore, with the participation of many volunteers, these projects can achieve extensive spatial coverage (e.g. Rees and Pond, 1995; Ribic et al., 2010; Ribic et al., 2012a; van der Velde et al., 2017), which is rarely achieved by research projects conducted exclusively by small teams of professional scientists.

During the past decade, the participation of citizen scientists in marine litter research has grown steadily (Hidalgo-Ruz and Thiel, 2015). Thousands of citizen scientists have participated in scientific projects and helped to generate important information about the spatial distribution and temporal trends in marine litter (e.g. Rees and Pond, 1995; Moore et al., 2001; Ribic et al., 2010; Ribic et al., 2012a; Kordella et al., 2013; van der Velde et al., 2017; Zettler et al., 2017). Some of these projects have managed to persist over many years, and have achieved international coverage. The most successful example is the International Coastal Cleanup, which is conducted annually since 1986 and in 2015 gathered data on marine litter from 93 countries with nearly 800,000 volunteers around the world (Ocean Conservancy, 2016). Other citizen science projects are relatively new, but by using simple mobile applications have rapidly achieved extensive international coverage, e.g. the Marine Debris Tracker (Jambeck and Johnson, 2015). By bringing together people from many different backgrounds and nationalities, these programs are raising environmental awareness about marine litter and providing much-needed data. In this chapter, we present some of these projects and we evaluate their role in generating scientific data and contributing to the formation of international ocean citizenship.

## Citizen science projects focused on marine litter

There are many different conservation projects, mostly of local or regional scope, that are focusing on the problem of marine litter. Many of these projects involve the public in taking action and implementing stewardship solutions, but not necessarily with the goal of generating scientific data (e.g. Storrier and McGlashan, 2006). For example, some of the most popular projects are cleanup activities, such as beach sweeps and cleanups (organized by numerous organizations such as

Surfriders, Clean Ocean Action, Ecocolibri, and multiple others). Many dive clubs participate in underwater cleanups (e.g. Al-Najjar and Al-Shiyab, 2011; Smith and Edgar, 2014). There are also many other initiatives that involve citizens as beach users or consumers. For example, recreational fishers are encouraged to recycle used monofilament fishing lines at tackle stores or other locations. Skateboards or sneakers made from old fishing nets get consumers to think about the ocean while buying specific products. Numerous initiatives encourage consumers to avoid disposable one-way products, and instead use reusable items, which is particularly effective for bags and bottles (Newman et al., 2015). The large number of non-governmental organizations (NGOs) and educational projects focusing on marine litter also underlines the strong interest of citizens in helping to keep the oceans clean (Table 6.1).

In many parts of the world, however, many projects have gone beyond the mere collection of litter and cleaning up the shore or seafloor, to involve citizens in actively participating by generating scientific data about marine litter. For example,

**TABLE 6.1** Selected examples of non-governmental organizations focusing on marine litter from all over the world.

| Organization | Main Activities | Geographic Extension | Website |
| --- | --- | --- | --- |
| Algalita | Research, Education | Global (focus US) | algalita.org |
| 5Gyres | Research, Education | Global (focus US) | 5gyres.org |
| OSEAN | Research, Education | East Asia (focus South Korea) | osean.net |
| Plastic Pollution Coalition | Education, Advocacy | Global (focus US) | plasticpollutioncoalition.org |
| JEAN | Education, Advocacy | Japan | jean.jp |
| Surfrider | Campaigns, Advocacy | Global (focus US) | surfrider.org |
| Coastcare | Campaigns, Advocacy | Australia | coastcare.com.au |
| Tangaroa Blue Foundation | Education, Advocacy | Australia | tangaroablue.org |
| NZAEE-Seaweek | Education | New Zealand | seaweek.org.nz |
| Underwater Volunteers NSW | Research, Education | Australia | uvnsw.net.au |
| Ocean Conservancy | Education, Policy | Global | oceanconservancy.org |
| Project Aware | Education, Advocacy | Global | projectaware.org |
| Rozalia Project | Research, Education | US | http://rozaliaproject.org |
| Adventurers and Scientists for Conservation | Research, Education | Global | adventurescience.org |

in the United States, the National Oceanic and Atmospheric Administration (NOAA) has a shoreline monitoring project that trains groups around the country to monitor litter densities through the standardized collection of data in locations chosen by NOAA. A protocol and field guide, as well as training and technical assistance, is provided to these groups. The non-profit Project Aware (Table 6.1) has a global program called Dive Against Debris where SCUBA divers collect submerged litter/debris and report the data to them. The COASST program (Parrish, Chapter 2, this volume) involves hundreds of volunteers in data collection and categorizing marine debris along the coastline from Alaska to California. While these projects may have been born out of the interest to help clean the oceans and data collection became a secondary (add-on) task, for many current citizen science projects the primary goal is sample/data collection, actively involving citizens in scientific studies.

Citizen science projects on marine litter use different approaches, involving volunteer participants in multiple ways (Table 6.2). Consequently, the samples or data gathered by citizen science projects are variable, including (1) observational data of litter impacts, (2) collection of specific litter items, (3) bulk estimates of gross amounts of litter, (4) frequency data on litter types, and (5) quantitative data on litter densities (Figure 6.1).

One program that involves citizen scientists in collecting specific litter items is the International Pellet Watch (Ogata et al., 2009; Yeo et al., 2015; Zettler et al.,

**TABLE 6.2** Objectives of marine-litter citizen science projects.

| Organization | Primary Goal | Secondary Goals | Website |
|---|---|---|---|
| International Pellet Watch | Science | Education | pelletwatch.org/ |
| OSEAN | Advocacy | Science | |
| Ocean Conservancy: International Coastal Cleanup | Campaign | Science, Advocacy | oceanconservancy.org/ our-work/international- coastal-cleanup/ |
| Ocean Conservancy: Clean Swell | App for data collection | Science, Advocacy | oceanconservancy.org/do- your-part/about-clean-swell.html |
| Científicos de la Basura | Education | Science | cientificosdelabasura.cl |
| Following the Pathways of Plastic Litter | Education | Science | save-ocean.org/ |
| Plastikpiraten | Education | Science | wissenschaftsjahr.de/2016-17/ mitmachen/junge-wissenschaft sinteressierte/plastikpiraten.html |
| COASST | Science | Education | http://depts.washington.edu/ coasst/ |
| Marine Debris Tracker | Education | Science | marinedebris.engr.uga.edu/ |

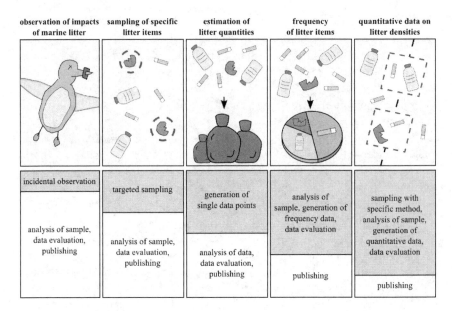

| observation of impacts of marine litter | sampling of specific litter items | estimation of litter quantities | frequency of litter items | quantitative data on litter densities |
|---|---|---|---|---|
| incidental observation | targeted sampling | generation of single data points | analysis of sample, generation of frequency data, data evaluation | sampling with specific method, analysis of sample, generation of quantitative data, data evaluation |
| analysis of sample, data evaluation, publishing | analysis of sample, data evaluation, publishing | analysis of data, data evaluation, publishing | publishing | publishing |

**FIGURE 6.1** Different levels of participation of citizen scientists working on marine litter. The panels above illustrate the employed method of citizen scientists. The panels below describe the involvement of the citizen scientists (gray area) in the scientific process (gray and white areas combined).

2017). Volunteers sample plastic pellets on the beach, bag these in aluminum envelopes, and send them to the central analysis lab in Tokyo, Japan, where they are analyzed by environmental chemists (Heskett et al., 2012). In another project on litter impacts, citizens collected hard plastics on the beach, which they then analyzed for bite marks of fishes (Carson, 2013). Volunteers also participated in projects where they identified plastic items in boluses regurgitated by marine gulls (Lindborg et al., 2012), or helped collect stranded carcasses of northern fulmars for the examination of plastic ingestion (van Franeker et al., 2011).

Most litter projects generate frequency data, which is most common in cleanup activities where volunteers clean all marine litter from the beach and then categorize the different litter items (e.g. Moore et al., 2001; Martin, 2013; Smith et al., 2014). Based on the human activities in which litter items are commonly used (e.g. in households or in fisheries), the different litter types can then be assigned to most probable source sectors, which is fundamental to determine action plans (Ribic et al., 2010; Ribic et al., 2012b; Kordella et al., 2013). Some cleanup projects also produce bulk estimates of litter amounts collected at a site (e.g. Lee and Sanders, 2015). Finally, there are citizen science projects that generate quantitative data on litter, which are reported in the typical scientific units, e.g. total litter items per square meter, or per meter of beach length. Citizen scientists, often guided and accompanied by professional scientists, collect and count all litter items in specific quadrats of standardized surface areas (Bravo et al., 2009; van der Velde et al., 2017) or along transects of standardized length (Hong et al., 2014).

## Case studies

### Impact on wildlife – survey of marine debris impact on wildlife

How widespread are marine debris impacts on wildlife in South Korea? Which species are impacted? Which marine debris items cause serious impacts on wildlife? The Survey of Marine Debris Impact on Wildlife (SMDIW) is a citizen science program designed to answer these questions and to find solutions on how to reduce and mitigate the impacts. Collecting data, fundraising, reporting, and sequential mitigating efforts have been conducted on the basis of volunteer participation.

In general, detection of marine wildlife impacted by marine debris is likely to be opportunistic or anecdotal because entangled animals are widely distributed in the world's oceans, highly migratory, only partially visible at great distance, and quickly disappear (Laist, 1997). Usually, only survivors or stranded, dead individuals are detected (e.g. van Franeker et al., 2011). Consequently, the SMDIW started to work with organizations and individuals who have watched, rescued, or protected wild animals.

The project was initiated in early 2010, and simultaneously a simple website[1] was launched to collect data on the impact of marine debris on wildlife. The website called for participants to report the animal (species or common name), injury types (ingestion or entanglement), marine debris (entanglement material detail, ingestion material detail), together with basic information about the finding (date and place of detection, dead or alive when detected, released alive or disposed of carcass after recording, name and contact of finder, name and contact of reporter if different from finder), and photos including credits (Jang et al., 2012).

Individuals from 10 organizations and their collaborators contributed to the first data collection from February 2010 to March 2012 (Jang et al., 2012). Out of 55 reported cases, 45 cases were examined in detail for ingestion of or entanglement with marine litter. Ten cases were excluded from the analysis because (1) there was no robust evidence that marine debris caused the injury or death of the animal, (2) the organism affected was not a "wild" animal, or (3) the impact was likely due to bycatch of active fishing gear and not due to marine litter. The affected species were identified by veterinarians (Jang et al., 2012). In-depth analysis and documents supplied by experts from various conservation and environmental research fields were essential in enhancing the quality of data and information contributed by non-expert participants (Jang et al., 2012). For example, photographs provided by participants were used to check the accuracy of species identification, allowing validation of the observations by citizen scientists and to avoid errors, which can occur in non-expert surveys (Conrad and Hilchey, 2011).

The confirmed 45 cases of wildlife impacts caused by marine litter were distributed along the coasts of South Korea and consisted of 21 species: mostly birds (18 species, 42 cases), some mammals (2 species, 2 cases), and crustaceans (1 species, 1 case). Internationally endangered species, such as the black-faced spoonbill *Platalea minor*, finless porpoise *Neophocaena phocaenoides*, and water deer *Hydropotes inermis*, were among the affected species (Hong et al., 2013). Ingestion of and entanglement by marine debris were 20 and 25 cases, respectively (Figure 6.2). Fishing lines, hooks, and lead sinkers from recreational fishing activities were the most common cause of damage (73.3%, 33 cases). The result provided a baseline to understand the actual cases of wildlife impacted by marine debris (Hong et al., 2013).

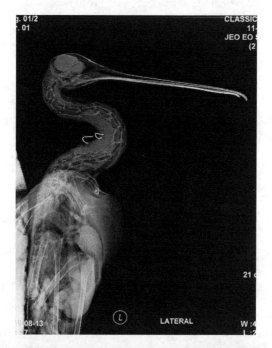

**FIGURE 6.2A** Black-faced spoonbill entangled by recreational fishing hooks.

*Upper, radiography photo:* © Young Jun Kim; *Lower photo:* © Nam Jun Jee.

**FIGURE 6.2B**  Night heron entangled by recreational fishing line.

*Photo:* © Nam Jun Jee.

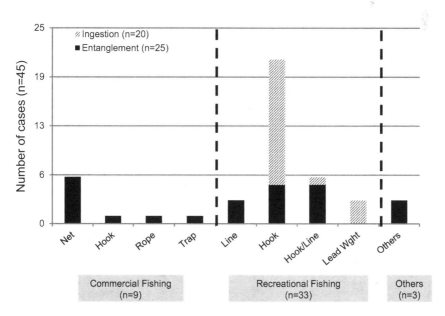

**FIGURE 6.2C**  Survey result showing cases of entanglement and ingestion and recreational fishing gears causing serious threats (Fig. 3 from Hong et al., 2013).

Based on the results, the project produced not only peer-reviewed publications but several education and outreach products. These include a series of booklets for the citizen science contributors, the broader public including children and parents, and government agents and anglers (Jang et al., 2012; Kim et al., 2012; Lee et al., 2014). Findings were also used to create a series of seminars, forums, art exhibitions, and a TV show to educate recreational anglers about the impacts of marine litter running biweekly throughout 2015. This complementary interaction of various audiences via the internet can benefit both non-expert participants and science experts in terms of continuous engagement and contribution to public awareness and solutions.

The SMDIW approach has been sustained and expanded by being adapted to incorporate reports from other countries in Southeast Asia (e.g. Taiwan). Reports on wildlife impacts by marine litter are relatively rare in Southeast Asia (CBD-GEF, 2012) even though this region, which is home to a highly diverse wildlife in marine ecosystems, has been significantly threatened by rapid population growth, destruction of essential habitats, and pollution (Tittensor et al., 2010). With the increasing marine litter impacts on wildlife in the region, the participation of volunteers in documenting these impacts can not only help to determine the species most at risk, but it can also be a powerful tool in raising awareness, as the experience of SMDIW in South Korea has shown.

## Monitoring litter types – marine debris tracker

The Marine Debris Tracker (MDT) is a global mobile app and citizen science program that began in 2011. With multiple goals for data collection, public engagement, and education, MDT was developed for Android and iOS platforms as part of the Southeast Atlantic Marine Debris Initiative (SEA-MDI) citizen science partnership with NOAA. Relatively recent technology has facilitated the global expansion of data collection, aggregation, and analysis (Bonney et al., 2014), and MDT allows crowdsourced citizen scientists to act as human "sensors," reporting litter and marine debris, supplying data to researchers at a scale, speed, and efficiency that was not previously possible before smartphones.

The widespread nature of mobile apps today makes them an innovative yet simple tool for development and use. In particular, the MDT app lets individuals record the location and description of marine debris items on their smartphones instead of on a paper data card. Unless noted that an item is not collected or it is observed in the open ocean, the users of MDT are encouraged to clean up the items as they log (using NOAA protocols while on the coastline, if possible; Opfer et al., 2012), so the data collected by this app are documenting a global-wide effort to remove litter and debris from our environment, keeping it out of the oceans and protecting ecosystems, wildlife, and human health.

The app's flexibility works across many missions, from beachgoers, to people participating in organized cleanups, and even scientists studying the issue. Data are posted on a publicly available web portal,[2] with the five most recent data reports appearing in a dynamic feed that updates every time a debris item is recorded. Data are also viewable and filterable (by user, time, and category, such as plastic, metal, etc.) on an interactive map. An individual user may download their data with their username and password; the entire data set (minus usernames, to protect privacy) is available for download from the website. The app has had over 15,000 downloads and over 1,300 registered users logging debris. The map of debris on the website has had more than 260,149 views from 200 countries, with an average of 135 visits per day in 2016–2017.

Behind the app is a MySQL database housed at the University of Georgia (UGA) that provides data security, storage, access, and backup. A PHP-based web service allows for any programmable, internet-capable device to securely log marine debris items by accepting the debris data collected, user identification data (if not anonymous), and metadata about the upload itself. The principal investigators (PIs) of MDT, in Computer Systems and Environmental Engineering at UGA, oversee the database comprising eight categories of various items commonly found, plus an "Other" category for write-in values (Table 6.3). Users may also add written descriptions, add a quantity for each item, and take a photo. The metadata collected by the app, which include GPS, time, date, altitude, and radius, allow for quality control (e.g. data are not aggregated spatially into a smaller granularity than the error radius). The PIs examine the data periodically, and also before compiling any reports, for any non-typical entries. For example, data entries that are over 10,000 items are investigated to determine accuracy. Users can be contacted by email to verify the accuracy of the entries. For some of the most frequent users of MDT,

**TABLE 6.3**  The Marine Debris Tracker (MDT) database (24 March 2017). The data reported here illustrates the frequency, quantity, and characteristics of what people are collecting, with plastic items being by far the most frequently logged item.

| Category | Number of Entries | Number of Items |
|---|---|---|
| Plastic (straws; cigarettes) | 98,944 | 784,273[1] |
| Lumber (wood or paper; food wrappers) | 10,572 | 47,319 |
| Metal (aluminum cans) | 8,443 | 36,353 |
| General (test item; items not on the list) | 2,194[2] | 10,994[2] |
| Fishing gear (monofilament line) | 6,200 | 53,635 |
| Cloth (clothing) | 3,629 | 9,067 |
| Glass (beverage bottle) | 3,925 | 31,893 |
| Rubber (tires; flip-flops) | 965 | 2,781 |
| **Total** | **134,872** | **976,315** |

1  Contains items of 38,875, 15,496, and 12,594 cigarette butts. Microplastic estimates of 80,000, 13,500, and 13,500 were removed for this table.

2  10,454 test entries and 24,143 test items removed for this table.

Note: The data in this table include all the items that have been logged to date. In each list, an entry called "test item" is available so that users can test the app before logging real data; this was added in the second version of the app.

and especially group users, there has been direct communication and dialogue with the PIs as they have developed their program to utilize the app using NOAA protocols (Opfer et al., 2012). The MDT community is very active and supportive of each other, and is facilitated by social media: users share photos and stories of their cleanup activities on Facebook and tagging @DebrisTracker on Twitter, which can be done directly from the mobile app. MDT and its associated Web platform also engage citizen scientists by creating social incentives to contribute. The "Top Trackers" are showcased on the website, with users who move up in the rankings receiving marine animal icons at various stages. The statistics of the most active contributors to MDT are also visualized on the website (Table 6.4).

**TABLE 6.4** MDT top tracker data (24 March 2017).

| User Name | User Type | Description | Items | Entries |
|---|---|---|---|---|
| GSTC Citizen Science | Group | The Georgia Sea Turtle Center is a marine turtle rehabilitation, research, and education facility on Jekyll Island. The Center's Marine Debris Citizen Science participants keep Jekyll Island's beaches free of marine debris. | 228,256 | 35,508 |
| OldMarketPhoto | Individual | Old Market Photo has a passion for photographic light and to take 10,000 steps a day. The path behind him is cleaner than what faces him because he picks up litter and documents it all with MDT! Find him on Twitter @oldmarketphoto. | 84,705 | 10,567 |
| muvemiami | Group | Museum Volunteers for the Environment (MUVE) is Patricia and Phillip Frost Museum of Science volunteer based restoration project. Conserving coastal habitats in South Florida. #citizenscience | 44,397 | 7,490 |
| FOHI Turtles | Group | In cooperation with South Carolina Department of Natural Resources and the US Fish and Wildlife Service, the volunteers of the Sea Turtle Conservation Project commit their early mornings from May through mid-October to walk the beaches of Hunting Island State Park, locating and protecting nests, relocating nests when necessary, and conducting nest inventories after the hatchlings emerge. | 11,038 | 5,480 |

| User Name | User Type | Description | Items | Entries |
|---|---|---|---|---|
| treehuggerlisa | Individual | Lisa is an avid sailor, surfer, paddleboard yogi, beach sweeper, and SCUBA diver certified as a PADI divemaster. She works as a Solid Waste Assistant Director for local government with a focus on resource management at the coast including proper disposal, marine debris prevention and removal, environmental education, waste reduction, and recycling. | 36,103 | 4,228 |
| Mote HAP Interns | Group | Dedicated Tracker | 7,835 | 4,070 |
| saunieindiego | Individual | We will lie down for such a long time after death that it is worthwhile to keep standing while we are alive. Let us work now; one day we will rest. Follow Saunie on Twitter @ saunieindiego. | 12,454 | 2,576 |
| IslandLife | Individual | Dedicated Tracker | 11,415 | 1,795 |
| ParleyxRozalia | Group | Rozalia Project for a Clean Ocean teamed up with Parley for the Oceans for ParleyxRozalia: An Expedition for the Oceans to clean remote islands and hard to reach shorelines in the Gulf of Maine. Our volunteers sailed over 800 miles on *American Promise* to not just collect marine debris, but make sure that none of it ended up in landfills. Instead, the trash was upcycled, recycled, and sent to waste to energy. | 64,253 | 1,622 |

MDT can provide motivation for anyone to help with a global conservation effort to remove litter and debris from the environment to protect ecosystems, wildlife, and human health, and the PIs and other partners have used the app and subsequent data for classroom teaching, engagement of volunteers in a specific program, and policy efforts. MDT is a powerful tool to provide data directly to a user who can communicate relevant information through data compilation, charts, graphs, and maps to a decision-maker. The PIs are examining regional characteristics of debris identified in the United States. Funded by NOAA, this work will be completed in summer 2017 and published thereafter.

MDT has been used in the curriculum at UGA for a First-Year Odyssey course and a second-year design project-based course in environmental engineering in cooperation with the campus Watershed UGA program. MDT has also been used in UGA Public Service and Outreach (PSO) projects, along with the PIs. Seventh grade students along the coast of Georgia in Glynn County are introduced to marine debris and MDT in their curriculum, and then students can further participate as a Salt Marsh Soldier, cleaning up and collecting data on debris found near their school, keeping it out of the ocean. Also in Glynn County, the Georgia Sea Turtle Center (GSTC), the largest user of MDT, has been successful in analyzing and publishing data from its citizen science initiative, using the MDT app to discuss the interaction of debris that volunteers find with the turtles rescued and rehabilitated, as well as the success of its volunteer campaign (Martin, 2013; Martin et al., 2015).

For conservation policy, MDT data has been compiled and used by the authors of the plastics Better Alternatives Now (BAN) list, which is "an analysis and call-to-action to phase out the most harmful plastic products used in California" (Eriksen et al., 2016). The list ranks the most detrimental litter items by frequency found, polymer type, hazard in manufacturing, environmental persistence, potential to accumulate toxic chemicals in the environment, and recovery for reuse, recycling, or composting (Eriksen et al., 2016). With a report showing that if the debris in Orange County, CA, was reduced by just 25%, it would save residents roughly $32 million in reduced travel to other beaches (Leggett et al., 2014). Eriksen et al. (2016) used MDT and other data to prioritize items for source reduction to reduce leakage into the environment. MDT use is not limited to the continental United States, and the app has expanded to global use, with data collected in 37 countries worldwide, including small island states. The largest datasets are in Puerto Rico, Canada, the Galapagos Islands, Norway, and Vietnam (Figure 6.3).

## Litter abundances – following the pathways of plastic litter

Which are the most contaminated beaches along the German and Chilean coasts? What are the most common litter items? And where does this litter come from? These and other questions are answered in the citizen science project, Following

**FIGURE 6.3**    Litter and debris items picked up and logged with Marine Debris Tracker (MDT) globally.

the Pathways of Plastic Litter, an international network between K-12 students, K-12 teachers, and professional scientists. The project is a collaboration between two outreach programs, the Kieler Forschungswerkstatt (Kiel Science Factory) of the University of Kiel (Germany), and the Científicos de la Basura (Litter Scientists) of the Universidad Católica del Norte (Chile).

The project has three main goals: (1) teach students the scientific method, (2) generate useful environmental data (quantitative estimates of litter densities), and (3) foster environmental awareness among the participating K-12 students. Particular emphasis is placed on students exchanging experiences and comparing findings, first within each country, but then also between the two participating countries. To compare their data, students quantify litter densities following standardized protocols (see below; for general synthesis see also Eastman et al., 2014). By investigating litter on beaches and within their domestic environment, students learn that their own actions are part of the problem and thereby also part of the solution. Sharing their newly acquired knowledge with their partners from the other country enhances the learning experience (Box 6.1).

---

## BOX 6.1   TESTIMONY FROM SUSANA RUIZ, K-12 TEACHER FROM ARICA, CHILE

The participation of our school group in this project was very important for the generation of scientific data about the problem of litter on Chilean beaches. The students understood that with our work we could do our bit to contribute to the project.

The most important learning experience for the students was the application of the scientific method within the framework of a real investigation that also put emphasis on teamwork, working together with students from Chile and Germany, taking field samples, and classifying/analyzing data for an international study about the huge problem that is marine litter.

My students took great pride and dedication while working on this project. They did serious, systematic work, trying to follow and responsibly fulfill every single step of the scientific method. They were enthusiastic and committed, enjoying their activities, which became a very beneficial pedagogical experience for them, promoting their educational training. It was evident that they felt happy for being part of a national and international scientific investigation.

Given that the marine litter problem is still little known and poorly addressed by society, it would be very positive to deliver these research results to our governmental authorities, in order to demand a more effective commitment for possible solutions to the problem. It is important that we all become aware of the present and future damage, all of which could be prevented. At the same time, I hope that this project's learning experience will be made accessible to everyone, making the study of the marine litter problem a cross-curricular topic in the Teaching Programs of the Education Ministry of Chile.

The investigation of litter on the beaches from the Chilean and German coasts follows a standardized methodology (Eastman et al., 2014). A beach is divided into several transects, each with several (two to six) stations where litter is sampled in a 3 × 3 m quadrat (Figure 6.4). At each station students collect all litter, sort it into basic categories, and count it to obtain quantitative estimates of litter densities (Figure 6.5). Data are entered into simple worksheets on computers, which automatically calculate the percentages of litter items and density of total litter items per square meter (i.e. items m$^{-2}$, a commonly used unit for litter densities).

During sampling activities, teachers and students are typically accompanied by project coordinators and/or scientific advisors. These advisors, many of whom voluntarily share their time with the teachers and schools, are typically biologists or other professionals with scientific backgrounds; they participate in the field samplings, instruct teachers and student participants, and supervise the sampling activities (Eastman et al., 2014). Occasionally, these scientific advisors have expressed concerns about the data gathered by individual schools, which could result in the elimination of their data from the dataset. In the case of more complicated analyses,

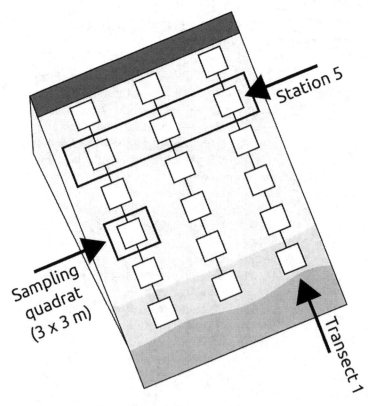

**FIGURE 6.4** Litter sampling scheme for sandy beaches. Sampling stations of 9 m$^2$ (3 × 3 m) area established on transects, ranging from the waterline to the upper shore. Modified after Bravo et al., 2009.

and whenever feasible, samples have also been sent to our central laboratory, where they have been evaluated by trained experts (Hidalgo-Ruz and Thiel, 2013).

This bilateral approach partnering students from Germany and Chile is adding an important new aspect to this citizen science project, which has already completed several investigations in Chile (Bravo et al., 2009; Eastman et al., 2013; Hidalgo-Ruz and Thiel, 2013; Rech et al., 2015): by being able to share and compare their experiences with students from the respective other country, the participating students have additional motivation to report their own findings. This offers the opportunity to actively involve students in the evaluation and interpretation of their data (Nicosia et al., 2014; Ballard et al., 2017; see Chapter 11). The scientific information gathered by the participating schools has been published by the Chilean forerunner project (for synthesis see Thiel et al., 2011; Eastman et al., 2014), and some of the data collected by the binational pathway project have recently been utilized to highlight differences in beach litter abundances between several locations along the Chilean coast (Kiessling et al., 2017).

The project includes five main aspects that ensured the success of the scientific investigation and successful learning among the participating students in this case: (1) accompanying course materials, (2) project website serving as communication platform, (3) reliable and comparable scientific method, (4) presentation of the results, and (5) evaluation of the project, as recommended for citizen science projects (Bonney et al., 2009).

> *Course Material*: A workbook designed to prepare students to conduct investigations of marine litter on the beach introduces the students to the "ocean ecosystem." Students engage with the complex and interdisciplinary problem of marine litter through informational texts and activities that focus on the properties of plastic litter and the impacts they cause to marine wildlife. The workbook contains the standardized sampling method and simple worksheet tables for the evaluation of the collected data. After having synthesized their own results and compared them with those from other localities, students are encouraged to deduce the causes of the problem and, based on this, propose solutions.
>
> *Project Website*: The website[3] enables communication between schools in Germany and Chile that are matched and paired by grade level. The interactive sections on the website allow for direct exchange between the participating schools. Each student creates a personal profile where they can share information, experiences, and images or videos, which are uploaded to the built-in website blog. The project website also serves for mapping of data (Figure 6.5). The cultural exchange allows students to learn about different perspectives of the problem and different approaches to solve the problem, facilitated by project coordinators and teachers (Box 6.1).
>
> *Students Collaborate on Findings and Conservation Strategies*: Following the sampling and analysis of the data, students interpret their results, search for solutions, and disseminate their findings. Students are encouraged to discuss possible

FIGURE 6.5    Chilean and German K-12 students sampling litter during the Following the Pathways of Plastic Litter project. (a) Students from Escuela Humberto Valenzuela García in Arica, Chile, © Susana Ruiz. (b) Students from Alexander-von-Humboldt Schule in Neumünster, Germany, © Anna Thielisch. (c) Using the save-ocean.org website, children and teachers could visualize their results. (d) Regional newspapers also showed an interest in the project (*Lübecker Nachrichten*, 22 June 2016).

solutions with their partner schools from the other country. They are also encouraged to agree on one specific solution that they will put into action in their respective community, such as using reusable products and other ways to reduce waste in their homes. By evaluating the feasibility of alternative courses of action, and their involvement in a scientific study, students experience a positive impact on their understanding of the scientific method and environmental awareness and commitment to take actions.

*Presentation of Results:* The data gathered by the participating schools are used to inform the public and national administrators. Within the framework of this project, the participating schools from Chile, which come from coastal communities across the entire country (spanning a coastline of >4000 km), have been participating in the 3rd National Sampling of Litter on the Beaches (2008, 2012, and 2016). The data of previous samplings have been published in the primary scientific literature (Bravo et al., 2009; Thiel et al., 2011; Eastman et al., 2014) and other media (Figure 6.5). These communications have helped to raise public awareness, and together with innovative initiatives from other groups contributed to increasing concerns about littering. As a result of growing public awareness, currently important modifications to existing laws about litter management and a new law about extended producer responsibility have been implemented by the Chilean parliament (Ministerio del Medio Ambiente de Chile, 2016).

The litter pathway project is supported by public and private institutions in both participating countries. This broad multi-institutional support across countries enhances not only the visibility but also emphasizes the relevance of the marine litter topic (1) within these different funding institutions, (2) to visitors of the website, and (3) to the audience of media communications.

## Lessons learned

### Goals of litter citizen science projects

Projects in which citizens collect scientific samples or scientific data on marine litter can serve several goals, ranging from science to education and concrete actions (Table 6.2). Many citizen science projects pursue multiple goals including conservation and education (Bonney et al., 2009; see also Chapters 8 and 11), which does not necessarily compromise the quality of the scientific data collected, as long as the type and quality of the data by citizen volunteers is clearly identified. For example, some of the earliest citizen science projects simply organized observations by hobby naturalists in standardized databases (Miller-Rushing et al., 2012). In the context of marine litter projects with volunteer participants, the initial emphasis has been on cleanup activities (e.g. Sheavly and Register, 2007), but in recent years the emphasis has shifted to an increasing number of projects that focus on generating relevant scientific data (e.g. Eastman et al., 2014; van der Velde et al., 2017). Citizen science projects about marine litter are currently conducted in many countries around the world (for a recent review, see Hidalgo-Ruz and Thiel, 2015).

Working with untrained volunteers may require adjustments of the data collection methods, because some complex tasks can only be completed by trained research participants. Some projects with relatively simple tasks provide written instructions (usually downloadable from websites) that contain the basic information for the collection of samples/data. For example, the instructions for the International Pellet Watch[4] can be downloaded from the project website, and with this information volunteers can go to the beach and collect pellets that are sent to the central analysis lab in Japan (Yeo et al., 2015). Many programs also have a section of frequently asked questions (FAQ) on their websites, where people can ask questions about sampling, which are then answered by the program coordinators and displayed in the FAQ sections for future volunteers to read.

The preceding cases demonstrate that like most citizen science programs, marine litter citizen science projects require very active coordinators. While technological advances can facilitate communication with interested citizens and also data administration, it is fundamental to maintain fluent communication with citizens. These tasks are time-consuming, and they also require good communication skills (Eastman et al., 2014). For example, about 40 school classes from across Chile are participating in the Litter Pathways project, and during the activities one person is working full time in coordinating the different project activities, including the scientific sampling of litter on the beach. Generating the materials and websites for citizen science programs, and regularly updating them requires specific skills and effort. All these aspects need to be accounted for when planning and conducting a citizen science project.

## Data quality control

One lesson learned across these projects is that citizen science projects should include data quality control procedures that do not overburden the volunteers. While citizens want to participate in science, and engagement in the science directly is important to them, getting bogged down in the data analysis can limit the number of people that want to participate. Using technology to your advantage (like with MDT) means that data collection is simple from the perspective of a citizen scientist, yet the data are robust for the investigators.

In citizen science, the data quality is fundamental (Crall et al., 2010; Hunter et al., 2013; Forrester et al., 2015; Zettler et al., 2017), and quality control can be a critical part to determine the accuracy and precision (Peckenham et al., 2012; Worthington et al., 2012). Some studies have shown that marine debris data collected by citizen science are of similar quality as those collected by experts (e.g. Hidalgo-Ruz and Thiel, 2013; van der Velde et al., 2017). Nevertheless, there are also tradeoffs between data quantity and quality, and this should be considered by the project designer. In the case of the MDT, the data are opportunistic, working towards large quantities to be able to make conclusions about the data. In the case of the Litter Pathways, during the field sampling of litter on the beaches, trained scientists (mostly marine biologists) are recruited as volunteers to accompany the teachers and their students: they provide practical advice in the field, supervise the sampling, and identify potential problems with the collected data.

## Limitations and challenges

There are, however, also limitations to marine litter citizen science for coastal conservation that are hard to overcome. The coastline is not a homogenous environment, and some locations and terrains are challenging to access. In general, and especially for opportunistic data, citizens will only go to easily accessible areas such as sandy beaches. This means that some treacherous or less-desirable terrain will not have data collected from it. This is a gap and limitation with the collection of any coastal data, and in this case, especially marine debris, since some of the non-sandy beaches tend to act as catchments for debris and litter (Aguilera et al., 2016).

## Publication and communication

Citizen science projects focused on marine litter have resulted in several scientific publications. Projects with specific, well-defined research questions have been most successful in using the samples or data collected by citizen scientists to respond to these questions and publish the results in a timely fashion. The time from collection of samples/data to publication has been relatively brief (e.g. Bravo et al., 2009; Hong et al., 2013; Hong et al., 2014; Rech et al., 2015) to moderately long (e.g. Ogata et al., 2009; Heskett et al., 2012; Ribic et al., 2012a; Yeo et al., 2015; van der Velde et al., 2017), allowing the findings and scientific publications to be shared with the participating citizens shortly after sampling. Many programs are also efficient in communicating their findings with the local, national, and international media, as in the cases discussed in this chapter, suggesting that citizen science projects have contributed importantly to the growing awareness about marine litter.

## Impact of citizen science projects on marine litter awareness and policies

Data collected through citizen science can be used to help with policy and decision-making (McKinley et al., 2016), and this is also true for marine litter citizen science projects. For example, with the Marine Debris Tracker program, the data have been used in a compilation of litter clean-up data in California to inform and prioritize specific litter items for upstream solutions (Eriksen et al., 2016). In addition, research is underway at UGA to compare and contrast the NOAA Marine Debris Program's five different regions in the United States for marine debris and litter characterization. With those data, policy makers and decision-makers can target outreach, education, and policy initiatives to each region's specific issues. Several citizen science programs also identify litter and debris items by location, and integrating these spatial data sets can help researchers to identify ecological debris hotspots around the world (Zettler et al., 2017). The data results from South Korea have provided baseline data over nine years to date with the objectives to quantitatively assess the level of beach debris pollution; to identify geographic hotspots, major types, composition, and sources of litter; and to determine management priorities nationwide (Hong et al., 2014). Urgent issues, such as increased expanded polystyrene (Styrofoam) buoy debris from aquaculture, have been incorporated in the national marine debris management policy (Hong et al., 2014; Lee et al., 2015; KMOF, MOE, and KCG, 2013). The SMDIW aims to uncover the impacts of marine litter on wildlife, a topic that had not been well-known. The information was used to raise awareness about the main sources of litter that is impacting wildlife and to design efficient management policies (Hong, 2015).

The Litter Pathways project has made an important contribution to awareness of marine litter in Chile and Germany. The scientific information generated in Chile has been fundamental in informing the general public and lawmakers about the extent of the problem (Thiel et al., 2011; Kiessling et al., 2017). Furthermore, the initiatives proposed and implemented by the participating K-12 students have contributed to an increase in environmental awareness, similar to that reported for comparable initiatives (Hartley et al., 2015; Wyles et al., 2016). In Chile, recently the law about Extended Producer Responsibility has been passed by the national congress (Ministerio del Medio Ambiente de Chile, 2016); it is likely that the continuing information generated by the Litter Pathways program has helped to sensitize lawmakers. In Germany, the student-focused Pathways of Plastic Litter program has enhanced the visibility of the citizen science approach, and another project from the Federal Ministry of Education and Research has followed: "Plastikpiraten – das Meer beginnt hier!" ("Plastic pirates – the ocean starts here!"). This Germany-wide marine litter project asks schools to collect data about litter in freshwater ecosystems like rivers. These and many other citizen science programs on marine litter have potentially affected public awareness of environmental problems, science, education, outreach, and science communication, generating new scientists and skilled specialists, extending up to decision-makers (Figure 6.6).

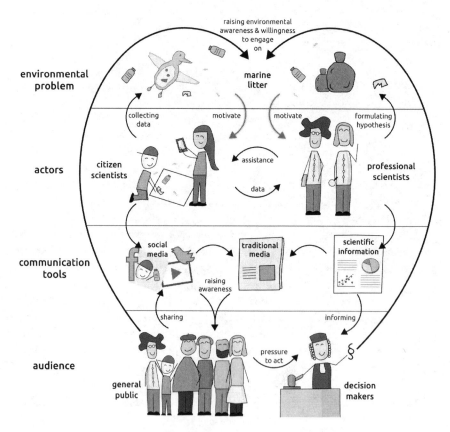

**FIGURE 6.6**  The important role of citizen scientists in raising awareness and advancing active engagement on the marine litter problem: Citizen scientists contribute valuable scientific data to professional scientists and may influence the general public by reporting about their experience, for example in the form of social media. This, in turn, encourages the general public and eventually decision-makers to act on the environmental problem in question.

*Figure authors:* Tim Kiessling and Martin Thiel (Creative Commons BY-NC 4.0 license).

Many citizen science programs on marine litter have been maintained over many years, and there is an increasing tendency for successful programs to become more international. Social media, websites, and smartphone applications facilitate this internationalization process through virtual and online communities. These communities support each other's efforts through common social media sites like Facebook, Twitter, Instagram, and Pinterest. Participants in campaigns will post photos illustrating the problem (e.g. litter in our environment or highlighting their accomplishments, total litter items collected during a cleanup), sharing these events with their local and international community. While social media have allowed for many groups to communicate internationally, they also provide an excellent platform for reaching local participants for cleanups and data collection events.

## Conclusions

A diverse range of citizen science programs have contributed to advance knowledge and awareness about marine litter. These programs involve various degrees of participation by the public, ranging from collection of samples to recording of opportunistic observations and to rigorous sampling of quantitative data. Some of these programs have made important contributions to the advancement of scientific knowledge. However, individual programs investigate mostly macro-litter or meso-litter, with a focus on the description of patterns (e.g. distribution and composition of marine litter). Processes such as transport, degradation, or ingestion of litter by marine organisms are rarely investigated by citizen scientists, which is an important consideration in designing citizen science projects.

Most litter survey programs are based on reciprocal interactions between citizens, scientists, stakeholders, and decision-makers (Figure 6.6). Citizen scientists can also educate the general public about the coastal litter (or any other environmental) problem. This is done by sharing their personal experience, for example via social media. This, in turn, may influence the public (bottom-up) and decision-makers (top-down) to act on the initial environmental problem (Figure 6.6). For the issue of marine litter and its impacts on oceans and coastlines, citizen science can effectively impact both the science and public environmental awareness that contribute to conservation solutions.

## Acknowledgements

Foremost, we would like to thank all the volunteers who have contributed to the projects presented in this contribution – their participation is fundamental to improve the conservation of the oceans. We are grateful to Susana Ruiz for sharing her experiences. Funding has been received from the Science Outreach Program EXPLORA of the Chilean Science Foundation CONICYT, the US Embassy in Santiago, Chile, Millennium Nucleus ESMOI (ICM 120030), National Oceanic and Atmospheric Administration, 11th Hour Racing, and the Lighthouse Foundation.

## Web resources

1 www.osean.net.
2 http://marinedebris.engr.uga.edu/.
3 www.save-ocean.org.
4 www.pelletwatch.org.

## Literature cited

Aguilera, M., Broitman, B., and Thiel, M. (2016). Artificial breakwaters as garbage bins: Structural complexity enhances anthropogenic litter accumulation in marine intertidal habitats. *Environmental Pollution*, 214, 737–747.

Al-Najjar, T., and Al-Shiyab, A. (2011). Marine litter at (Al-Ghandoor area) the most northern part of the Jordanian coast of the Gulf of Aqaba, Red Sea. *Natural Science*, 3(11), 921–926.

Ballard, H., Dixon, C., and Harris, E. (2017). Youth-focused citizen science: Examining the role of environmental science learning and agency for conservation. *Biological Conservation*, 208, 65–75.

Bonney, R., Cooper, C., Dickinson, J., Kelling, S., Phillips, T., Rosenberg, K., and Shirk, J. (2009). Citizen science: A developing tool for expanding science knowledge and scientific literacy. *BioScience*, 59(11), 977–984.

Bonney, R., Shirk, J., Phillips, T., Wiggins, A., Ballard, H., Miller-Rushing, A., and Parrish, J. (2014). Next steps for citizen science. *Science*, 343(6178), 1436–1437.

Bravo, M., de los Ángeles Gallardo, M., Luna-Jorquera, G., Núñez, P., Vásquez, N., and Thiel, M. (2009). Anthropogenic debris on beaches in the SE Pacific (Chile): Results from a national survey supported by volunteers. *Marine Pollution Bulletin*, 58(11), 1718–1726.

Browne, M., Chapman, M., Thompson, R., Amaral Zettler, L., Jambeck, J., and Mallos, N. (2015). Spatial and temporal patterns of stranded intertidal marine debris: Is there a picture of global change? *Environmental Science & Technology*, 49(12), 7082–7094.

Carson, H. (2013). The incidence of plastic ingestion by fishes: From the prey's perspective. *Marine Pollution Bulletin*, 74(1), 170–174.

Conrad, C., and Hilchey, K. (2011). A review of citizen science and community-based environmental monitoring: Issues and opportunities. *Environmental Monitoring and Assessment*, 176(1–4), 273–291.

CBD – GEF. (2012). *Impacts of marine debris on biodiversity: Current status and potential solutions*. Montreal, Canada. Technical Series No. 67, 61 pp.

Crall, A., Newman, G., Jarnevich, C., Stohlgren, T., Waller, D., and Graham, J. (2010). Improving and integrating data on invasive species collected by citizen scientists. *Biological Invasions*, 12(10), 3419–3428.

Eastman, L., Hidalgo-Ruz, V., Macaya, V., Nuñez, P., and Thiel, M. (2014). The potential for young citizen scientist projects: A case study of Chilean schoolchildren collecting data on marine litter. *Revista de Gestão Costeira Integrada*, 14(4), 569–579.

Eastman, L., Núñez, P., Crettier, B., and Thiel, M. (2013). Identification of self-reported user behavior, education level, and preferences to reduce littering on beaches – a survey from the SE Pacific. *Ocean & Coastal Management*, 78, 18–24.

Eriksen, M., Lebreton, L., Carson, H., Thiel, M., Moore, C., Borerro, J., Galgani, F., Ryan, P., and Reisser, J. (2014). Plastic pollution in the world's oceans: More than 5 trillion plastic pieces weighing over 250,000 tons afloat at sea. *PLoS One*, 9(12), e111913.

Eriksen, M., Prindiville, M., and Thorpe, B. (2016). *The plastics better alternative now list*. [Online] http://upstreampolicy.org/wp-content/uploads/2016/11/5Gyres_BANList2016_REV110416.pdf. [Accessed March 24, 2017].

Forrester, G., Baily, P., Conetta, D., Forrester, L., Kintzing, E., and Jarecki, L. (2015). Comparing monitoring data collected by volunteers and professionals shows that citizen scientists can detect long-term change on coral reefs. *Journal for Nature Conservation*, 24, 1–9.

García-Cegarra, A., and Pacheco, A. (2017). Whale-watching trips in Peru lead to increases in tourist knowledge, pro-conservation intentions and tourist concern for the impacts of whale-watching on humpback whales. *Aquatic Conservation: Marine and Freshwater Ecosystems*, doi:10.1002/aqc.2754.

Goldstein, M., and Goodwin, D. (2013). Gooseneck barnacles (*Lepas* spp.) ingest microplastic debris in the North Pacific Subtropical Gyre. *PeerJ*, 1, e184.

Gusmerotti, N., Corsini, F., Testa, F., Borghini, A., and Iraldo, F. (2016). Predicting behaviours related to marine litter prevention: an empirical case based on junior high school students in Italy. *International Journal of Sustainable Society*, 8(1), 1.

Hartley, B., Thompson, R., and Pahl, S. (2015). Marine litter education boosts children's understanding and self-reported actions. *Marine Pollution Bulletin*, 90(1–2), 209–217.

Herzke, D., Anker-Nilssen, T., Nøst, T., Götsch, A., Christensen-Dalsgaard, S., Langset, M., Fangel, K., and Koelmans, A. (2016). Negligible impact of ingested microplastics on tissue concentrations of persistent organic pollutants in Northern Fulmars off Coastal Norway. *Environmental Science & Technology*, 50(4), 1924–1933.

Heskett, M., Takada, H., Yamashita, R., Yuyama, M., Ito, M., Geok, Y., Ogata, Y., Kwan, C., Heckhausen, A., Taylor, H., Powell, T., Morishige, C., Young, D., Patterson, H., Robertson, B., Bailey, E., and Mermoz, J. (2012). Measurement of persistent organic pollutants (POPs) in plastic resin pellets from remote islands: Toward establishment of background concentrations for International Pellet Watch. *Marine Pollution Bulletin*, 64(2), 445–448.

Hidalgo-Ruz, V., and Thiel, M. (2013). Distribution and abundance of small plastic debris on beaches in the SE Pacific (Chile): A study supported by a citizen science project. *Marine Environmental Research*, 87–88, 12–18.

Hidalgo-Ruz, V., and Thiel, M. (2015). The contribution of citizen scientists to the monitoring of marine litter. In *Marine Anthropogenic Litter*, ed. M. Bergmann, L. Gutow, and M. Klages, 429–447. Berlin: Springer.

Hong, S. (2015). TV show launched, targeting anglers' littering in Korea. *Marine Litter News*, 6(2), 7–9. ISSN: 2287–8971. [Online] http://cafe.naver.com/osean/1834 [Accessed March 1, 2016].

Hong, S., Lee, J., Jang, Y., Kim, Y., Kim, H., Han, D., Hong, S., Kang, D., and Shim, W. (2013). Impacts of marine debris on wild animals in the coastal area of Korea. *Marine Pollution Bulletin*, 66(1–2), 117–124.

Hong, S., Lee, J., Kang, D., Choi, H.W., and Ko, S.H. (2014). Quantities, composition, and sources of beach debris in Korea from the results of nationwide monitoring. *Marine Pollution Bulletin*, 84, 27–34.

Hunter, J., Alabri, A., and van Ingen, C. (2013). Assessing the quality and trustworthiness of citizen science data. *Concurrency and Computation: Practice and Experience*, 25, 454–466.

Jacobs, S., Sioen, I., De Henauw, S., Rosseel, Y., Calis, T., Tediosi, A., Nadal, M., Marques, A., and Verbeke, W. (2015). Marine environmental contamination: Public awareness, concern and perceived effectiveness in five European countries. *Environmental Research*, 143, 4–10.

Jambeck, J.R., Geyer, R., Wilcox, C., Siegler, T.R., Perryman, M., Andrady, A., Narayan, R., and Law, K.L. (2015). Plastic waste inputs from land into the ocean. *Science*, 347, 768–771.

Jambeck, J.R., and Johnsen, K. (2015). Citizen-based litter and marine debris data collection and mapping. *Computing in Science & Engineering*, 17, 20–26.

Jang, Y.C., Hong, S., Lee, J., and Lee, M. (2012). The impact of marine debris on wildlife in South Korea: Cases and photographs. Our Sea of East Asia Network, Design Jiho, 101 pp. ISBN: 978-89-969258-0-4. [Online] http://cafe.naver.com/osean/1846 [Accessed March 21, 2017].

Kiessling, T., Gutow, L., and Thiel, M. (2015). Marine litter as habitat and dispersal vector. In *Marine Anthropogenic Litter*, ed. M. Bergmann, L. Gutow, and M. Klages, 141–181. Berlin: Springer.

Kiessling, T., Salas, S., Mutafoglu, K., and Thiel, M. (2017). Who cares about dirty beaches? Evaluating environmental awareness and action on coastal litter in Chile. *Ocean & Coastal Management*, 137, 82–95.

Kim, J.A., Hong, S., Lee, J., and Jang, Y.C. (2012). Marine Litter Activity Book: Listen to the Voice of the Ocean, Our Sea of East Asia Network, 20 pp. ISBN: 978-89-969258-2-8 73370. [Online] http://cafe.naver.com/osean/1503 [Accessed March 21, 2017].

KMOF (Ministry of Ocean and Fisheries), MOE (Ministry of Environment), KCG (Korea Coast Guard). (2013). The 2nd National Plan for Marine Litter Management (2014–2019).

Kordella, S., Geraga, M., Papatheodorou, G., Fakiris, E., and Mitropoulou, I.M. (2013). Litter composition and source contribution for 80 beaches in Greece, Eastern Mediterranean: A nationwide voluntary clean-up campaign. *Aquatic Ecosystem Health & Management*, 16, 111–118.

Kühn, S., Rebolledo, E.L.B., and van Franeker, J.A. (2015). Deleterious effects of litter on marine life. In *Marine Anthropogenic Litter*, ed. M. Bergmann, L. Gutow, and M. Klages, 75–116. Berlin: Springer.

Laist, D.W. (1997). Impacts of marine debris: Entanglement of marine life in marine debris including a comprehensive list of species with entanglement and ingestion records. In *Marine Debris – Sources, Impacts and Solutions*, ed. J.M. Coe and D.B. Rogers, 99–139. New York: Springer Verlag.

Lawson, T.J., Wilcox, C., Johns, K., Dann, P., and Hardesty, B.D. (2015). Characteristics of marine debris that entangle Australian fur seals (*Arctocephalus pusillus doriferus*) in southern Australia. *Marine Pollution Bulletin*, 98, 354–357.

Lebreton, L.M., Greer, S.D., and Borrero, J.C. (2012). Numerical modelling of floating debris in the world's oceans. *Marine Pollution Bulletin*, 64, 653–661.

Lechner, A., Keckeis, H., Lumesberger-Loisl, F., Zens, B., Krusch, R., Tritthart, M., Glas, M., and Schludermann, E. (2014). The Danube so colourful: A potpourri of plastic litter outnumbers fish larvae in Europe's second largest river. *Environmental Pollution*, 188, 177–181.

Lee, J., Hong, S., Jang, Y.C., Lee, M.J., Kang, D., and Shim, W.J. (2015). Finding solutions for the styrofoam buoy debris problem through participatory workshops. *Marine Policy*, 51, 182–189.

Lee, K., Hong, S., Si, J., Jang, Y.C., and Lee, J. (2014). *Please save the black-faced spoonbills from recreational fishing debris*. Waterbird Network Korea, Our Sea of East Asia Network, Si Design, 12 pp. ISBN: 978-89-956179-7-7. [Online] http://cafe.naver.com/osean/ 1847 [Accessed 1 March 2016].

Lee, R.F., and Sanders, D.P. (2015). The amount and accumulation rate of plastic debris on marshes and beaches on the Georgia coast. *Marine Pollution Bulletin*, 91, 113–119.

Leggett, C., Scherer, N., Curry, M., and Bailey, R. (2014). Assessing the economic benefits of reductions in marine debris: A pilot study of beach recreation in Orange County, California. *NOAA Marine Debris Program Industrial Economics, Inc.*

Lindborg, V.A., Ledbetter, J.F., Walat, J.M., and Moffett, C. (2012). Plastic consumption and diet of glaucous-winged gulls (*Larus glaucescens*). *Marine Pollution Bulletin*, 64, 2351–2356.

Lusher, A. (2015). Microplastics in the marine environment: Distribution, interactions and effects. In *Marine Anthropogenic Litter*, ed. M. Bergmann, L. Gutow, and M. Klages, 245–307. Berlin: Springer.

Martin, J.M. (2013). Marine debris removal: One year of effort by the Georgia Sea turtle-center-marine debris initiative. *Marine Pollution Bulletin*, 74, 165–169.

Martin, J.M., Higgins, K., Lee, K., Stearns, K., and Hunt, L. (2015). Integrating science education and marine conservation through collaborative partnerships. *Marine Pollution Bulletin*, 95, 520–522.

Maximenko, N., Hafner, J., and Niiler, P. (2012). Pathways of marine debris derived from trajectories of Lagrangian drifters. *Marine Pollution Bulletin*, 65, 51–62.

McKinley, D., Miller-Rushing, A.J., Ballard, H., Bonney, R., Brown, H., Cook-Pattone, S.C., Evans, D.M., French, R.A., Parrish, J.K., Phillips, T.B., Ryan, S.F., Shanley, L.A., Shirk, J.L., Stepenuck, K.F., Weltzink, J.F., Wiggins, A., Boyle, O.D., Briggs, R.D., Chapin, S.F., III, Hewitt, D.A., Preuss, P.A., and Soukup, M.A. (2017). Citizen science can improve conservation science, natural resource management, and environmental protection. *Biological Conservation*, 208, 15–28. http://dx.doi.org/10.1016/j.biocon.2016.05.015.

Miller-Rushing, A., Primack, R., and Bonney, R. (2012). The history of public participation in ecological research. *Frontiers in Ecology and the Environment*, 10, 286–290.

Ministerio del Medio Ambiente de Chile. (2016). *Ley Marco para la Gestión de Residuos, la Responsabilidad Extendida del Productor y Fomento al Reciclaje; Ley 20920*. [Online] http://portal.mma.gob.cl/wp-content/uploads/2015/06/Ley-REP-Ley-No20920.pdf [Accessed March 20, 2017].

Moore, S.L., Gregorio, D., Carreon, M., Weisberg, S.B., and Leecaster, M.K. (2001). Composition and distribution of beach debris in Orange County, California. *Marine Pollution Bulletin*, 42, 241–245.

Nelms, S., Duncan, E., Broderick, A., Galloway, T., Godfrey, M., Hamann, M., Lindeque, P., and Godley, B. (2015). Plastic and marine turtles: A review and call for research. *ICES Journal of Marine Science: Journal du Conseil*, 73(2), 165–181.

Newman, S., Watkins, E., Farmer, A., ten Brink, P., and Schweitzer, J.P. (2015). The economics of marine litter. In *Marine Anthropogenic Litter*, ed. M. Bergmann, L. Gutow, and M. Klages, 367–394. Berlin: Springer.

Nicosia, K., Daaram, S., Edelman, B., Gedrich, L., He, E., McNeilly, S., Shenoy, V., Velagapudi, A., Wu, W., Zhang, L., Barvalia, A., Bokka, V., Chan, B., Chiu, J., Dhulipalla, S., Hernandez, V., Jeon, J., Kanukollu, P., Kravets, P., Mantha, A., Miranda, C., Nigam, V., Patel, M., Praveen, S., Sang, T., Upadhyay, S., Varma, T., Xu, C., Yalamanchi, B., Zharova, M., Zheng, A., Verma, R., Vasslides, J., Manderson, J., Jordan, R., and Gray, S. (2014). Determining the willingness to pay for ecosystem service restoration in a degraded coastal watershed: A ninth grade investigation. *Ecological Economics*, 104, 145–151.

Obbard, R.W., Sadri, S., Wong, Y.Q., Khitun, A.A., Baker, I., and Thompson, R.C. (2014). Global warming releases microplastic legacy frozen in Arctic Sea ice. *Earth's Future*, 2, 315–320.

Ocean Conservancy. (2016). *International coastal cleanup 2015 – data report*. [Online] www.oceanconservancy.org [Accessed August 24, 2016].

Ogata, Y., Takada, H., Mizukawa, K., Hirai, H., Iwasa, S., Endo, S., Mato, Y., Saha, M., Okuda, K., Nakashima, A., Murakami, M., Zurcher, N., Booyatumanondo, R., Zakaria, M., Dung, L., Gordon, M., Miguez, C., Suzuki, S., Moore, C., Karapanagioti, H., Weerts, S., McClurg, T., Burres, E., Smith, W., Velkenburg, M., Lang, J., Lang, R., Laursen, D., Danner, B., Stewardson, N., and Thompson, R. (2009). International Pellet Watch: Global monitoring of persistent organic pollutants (POPs) in coastal waters. 1. Initial phase data on PCBs, DDTs, and HCHs. *Marine Pollution Bulletin*, 58(10), 1437–1446.

Opfer, S., Arthur, C., and Lippiatt, S. (2012). *NOAA marine debris shoreline survey field guide*. [Online] https://marinedebris.noaa.gov/sites/default/files/ShorelineFieldGuide2012.pdf [Accessed April 6, 2017].

Peckenham, J.M., Thornton, T., and Peckenham, P. (2012). Validation of student generated data for assessment of groundwater quality. *Journal of Science Education and Technology*, 21, 287–294.

Pham, C.K., Ramirez-Llodra, E., Alt, C.H., Amaro, T., Bergmann, M., Canals, M., Company, J.B., Davies, J., Duineveld, G., Galgani, F., Howell, K.L., Huvenne, V.A.I., Isidro, E., Jones, D.O.B., Lastras, G., Morato, T., Gomes-Pereira, J.N., Purser, A., Stewart, H., Tojeira, I., Tubau, X., van Rooji, D., and Tyler, P.A. (2014). Marine litter distribution and density in European seas, from the shelves to deep basins. *PLoS One*, 9(4), e95839.

Rech, S., Macaya-Caquilpán, V., Pantoja, J., Rivadeneira, M., Kroeger Campodónico, C., and Thiel, M. (2015). Sampling of riverine litter with citizen scientists – findings and recommendations. *Environmental Monitoring & Assessment*, 187, 335.

Rees, G., and Pond, K. (1995). Marine litter monitoring programmes – a review of methods with special reference to national surveys. *Marine Pollution Bulletin*, 30, 103–108.

Ribic, C.A., Sheavly, S.B., Rugg, D.J., and Erdmann, E.S. (2012a). Trends in marine debris along the US Pacific Coast and Hawai'i 1998–2007. *Marine Pollution Bulletin*, 64, 994–1004.

Ribic, C.A., Sheavly, S.B., and Klavitter, J. (2012b). Baseline for beached marine debris on Sand Island, Midway Atoll. *Marine Pollution Bulletin*, 64, 1726–1729.

Ribic, C.A., Sheavly, S.B., Rugg, D.J., and Erdmann, E.S. (2010). Trends and drivers of marine debris on the Atlantic coast of the United States 1997–2007. *Marine Pollution Bulletin*, 60, 1231–1242.

Rochman, C.M., Browne, M.A., Halpern, B.S., Hentschel, B.T., Hoh, E., Karapanagioti, H.K., Rios-Mendoza, L.M., Takada, H., Teh, S., and Thompson, R.C. (2013a). Policy: Classify plastic waste as hazardous. *Nature*, 494, 169–171.

Rochman, C.M., Hoh, E., Kurobe, T., and Teh, S.J. (2013b). Ingested plastic transfers hazardous chemicals to fish and induces hepatic stress. *Scientific Reports*, 3, 3263.

Ryan, P.G., Moore, C.J., van Franeker, J.A., and Moloney, C.L. (2009). Monitoring the abundance of plastic debris in the marine environment. *Philosophical Transactions of the Royal Society of London B: Biological Sciences*, 364, 1999–2012.

Sheavly, S.B., and Register, K.M. (2007). Marine debris & plastics: environmental concerns, sources, impacts and solutions. *Journal of Polymers and the Environment*, 15, 301–305.

Smith, S.D., and Edgar, R.J. (2014). Documenting the density of subtidal marine debris across multiple marine and coastal habitats. *PLoS One*, 9(4), e94593.

Smith, S.D., Gillies, C.L., and Shortland-Jones, H. (2014). Patterns of marine debris distribution on the beaches of Rottnest Island, Western Australia. *Marine Pollution Bulletin*, 88, 188–193.

Storrier, K.L., and McGlashan, D.J. (2006). Development and management of a coastal litter campaign: The voluntary coastal partnership approach. *Marine Policy*, 30, 189–196.

Thiel, M., Bravo, M., Hinojosa, I.A., Luna, G., Miranda, L., Núñez, P., Pacheco, A.S., and Vásquez, N. (2011). Anthropogenic litter in the SE Pacific: An overview of the problem and possible solutions. *Journal of Integrated Coastal Zone Management*, 11, 115–134.

Thompson, R.C., Olsen, Y., Mitchell, R.P., Davis, A., Rowland, S.J., John, A.W., McGonigle, D., and Russell, A.E. (2004). Lost at sea: Where is all the plastic? *Science*, 304, 838.

Tittensor, D.P., Mora, C., Jetz, W., Lotze, H.K., Ricard, D., Vanden Berghe, E., and Worm, B. (2010). Global patterns and predictors of marine biodiversity across taxa. *Nature*, 466, 1098–1101.

van der Velde, T., Milton, D.A., Lawson, T.J., Wilcox, C., Lansdell, M., Davis, G., Perkins, G., and Hardesty, B.D. (2017). Comparison of marine debris data collected by researchers and citizen scientist: Is citizen science data worth the effort? *Biological Conservation*, 208, 127–138. http://dx.doi.org/10.1016/j.biocon.2016.05.025

van Franeker, J.A., Blaize, C., Danielsen, J., Fairclough, K., Gollan, J., Guse, Hansen, P., Heubeck, M., Jensen, J., Guillou, G.L., Olsen, B., Olsen, K., Pedersen, J., Stienen, E.W.M., and Turner, D.M. (2011). Monitoring plastic ingestion by the northern fulmar *Fulmarus glacialis* in the North Sea. *Environmental Pollution*, 159, 2609–2615.

Veiga, J.M., Vlachogianni, T., Pahl, S., Thompson, R.C., Kopke, K., Doyle, T.K., Hartley, B.L., Maes, T., Orthodoxou, D.L., Loizidou, X.I., and Alampei, I. (2016). Enhancing public awareness and promoting co-responsibility for marine litter in Europe: The challenge of MARLISCO. *Marine Pollution Bulletin*, 102, 309–315.

Worthington, T., Kemp, P.S., Osborne, P.E., Dillen, A., Coeck, J., Bunzel-Drüke, M., Naura, M., Gregory, J., and Easton, K. (2012). A spatial analytical approach for selecting reintroduction sites for burbot in English rivers. *Freshwater Biology*, 57, 602–611.

Wyles, K.J., Pahl, S., Holland, M., and Thompson, R.C. (2016). Can beach cleans do more than clean-up litter? Comparing beach cleans to other coastal activities. *Environment and Behavior*, 49(5) 509–553. doi:10.1177/0013916516649412.

Yeo, B.G., Takada, H., Taylor, H., Ito, M., Hosoda, J., Allinson, M., Connell, S., Greaves, L., and McGrath, J. (2015). POPs monitoring in Australia and New Zealand using plastic resin pellets, and International Pellet Watch as a tool for education and raising public awareness on plastic debris and POPs. *Marine Pollution Bulletin*, 101, 137–145.

Zettler, E.R., Takada, H., Monteleone, B., Mallos, N., Eriksen, M., and Amaral-Zettler, L.A. (2017). Incorporating citizen science to study plastics in the environment. *Analytical Methods*, 9, 1392–1403.

Žydelis, R., Small, C., and French, G. (2013). The incidental catch of seabirds in gillnet fisheries: A global review. *Biological Conservation*, 162, 76–88.

# 7

# USING CITIZEN SCIENCE TO INFORM OCEAN AND COASTAL RESOURCE MANAGEMENT

*Ryan Meyer, Erin Meyer, Leila Sievanen, and Amy Freitag*

## Introduction

Citizen science projects in coastal and marine systems may have different goals, such as science education, environmental stewardship, academic or applied research, and social justice (Bonney et al., 2014). One goal that is often invoked but which has received little focused attention is that of informing natural resource management in these systems (Cigliano et al., 2015). The recent shift in management to an emphasis on ecosystem-level protections and adaptive management schemes has increased the reliance of management on scientific data to inform decisions and evaluate the effects of policy implementation (Biber, 2011). Managers charged with environmental monitoring face a wide array of science and data needs, some of which may be well-suited to citizen science approaches. How should managers and citizen science groups negotiate the challenges of including non-conventional forms of participation and knowledge? How can they capitalize on partnership opportunities?

In this chapter, we explore these questions at three different levels. We begin with an overview of potential opportunities and challenges associated with linking citizen science with natural resource management. We then present the case study of California's Statewide Marine Protected Area (MPA) Monitoring Program. Along with the general description of the Monitoring Program we present mini-cases to illustrate how citizen science can contribute to MPA monitoring.

### Background

In our discussion, we focus primarily on the use of citizen science-generated data to support natural resource management. While the primary aim of this activity is not to formulate new policies, it can lead to adjustments in policy through an adaptive management process. Policy, or "the ongoing interaction of people in their efforts to achieve what they value" (Clark, 2002, 6), is often used in tandem or interchangeably with "management." For simplicity, we use "management" to refer to the professionals and institutions that govern natural resources.

Many of the challenges of linking new knowledge to natural resource management are not unique to citizen science. Even when relevant to a given problem, new knowledge is rarely used in the absence of institutions that mediate and encourage communication between knowledge producers and users (for useful reviews of this general problem see Cash et al., 2003; Lemos, Kirchhoff, and Ramprasad, 2012; McNie, 2007). Knowledge considered to be salient, credible, and legitimate is more likely to be used (Cash et al., 2003). Designing processes for knowledge "co-production" (Cash et al., 2003) and enhancing trust and institutional capacity between knowledge producers and users (Guston, 2001; Lemos et al., 2012; Parker and Crona, 2012; see also Chapter 13) is also important. These themes are applicable in various ways in our discussion of the links between citizen science and management. It is important to keep potential overlaps between the broader science/policy boundary and the citizen science discussion in mind.

Nevertheless, a specific focus on linking *citizen* science with management is timely given the rapid increase in attention that governments are paying to this newly prominent and rapidly growing field (Bonney, Cooper, and Ballard, 2016). Informing management is just a subset of the many ways that marine citizen science might have an impact on coastal and marine conservation (Cigliano et al., 2015), but some surveys suggest that this is a common goal of citizen science projects and an area of great potential (Aceves-Bueno et al., 2015; Freitag and Pfeffer, 2013; Roy et al., 2012).

It is also important to keep in mind the overlaps and distinctions between citizen science in the coastal and marine context and other contexts (see Cigliano et al., 2015; Hyder et al., 2015; Thiel et al., 2014). A survey by Roy et al. (2012) found relatively fewer marine-based citizen science programs than terrestrial or freshwater-based programs. However, there are strong parallels between marine and terrestrial citizen science in terms of the diversity of programs and the rapid expansion of activity that has been underway in recent years (Thiel et al., 2014). Our overview of benefits and challenges of informing management considers a wide variety of cases as there are important lessons that translate across these arenas.

## Potential benefits of partnering citizen science and management

In this section, we explore why citizen scientists and managers might choose to form a relationship and examine how such efforts might contribute to or conflict with other goals of citizen science programs. The potential benefits of citizen science for natural resource management and policy have been explored in general by McKinley et al. (2015) and McKinley et al. (2017) and also by Hyder et al. (2015) with a specific focus on marine policy which in their formulation encompasses marine resource management. Our discussion draws on these and other studies to set the stage for our discussion of MPA monitoring in California. By first under-standing the range of potential benefits of citizen science, we can then explore how different models for engaging with management relate to those benefits. These benefits can transfer into incentives when clearly understood and documented.

## Benefits for managers

There are many potential motivations for managers to engage citizens in research and monitoring. To begin with, the large number of volunteers of some citizen sci-ence programs can improve and broaden environmental knowledge through more comprehensive monitoring across time and space. When data on a large scale are needed, citizen science may be the only viable approach (McKinley et al., 2015; McKinley et al., 2017). Large datasets from citizen science can also fill informa-tion gaps left by de-funded baseline surveys, ensuring monitoring data at the scale needed for management (Carr, 2004). Citizen science projects may be more sus-tainable than projects conducted by an outside (often distant) agency or university scientist conducting monitoring across many different regions (Danielsen et al., 2009; Cigliano et al., 2015).

Monitoring activities needed to inform management are notoriously difficult to fund sustainably, and they are often chronically under-resourced. They typically rely on the sacrifice of time and money from a small group of government or industry actors, making monitoring costs hard to justify by these actors in the short-term given that the benefits may not be realized for many years (Biber, 2011). Citizen science has the potential to address perennial funding issues by lowering operating costs, diversifying funding sources, and broadening both the benefits and constitu-encies of monitoring (see also Chapter 3 for a discussion of a project that also pro-vides research funding). However, the challenges of managing diverse partnerships to achieve cost-effective monitoring would not necessarily be reduced through citizen science approaches (OST, 2014b).

The use of citizen science can potentially provide benefits to managers beyond data collection. Citizen science may bring more (and more diverse) people into scientific processes related to management (Aceves-Bueno et al., 2015; Hyder et al., 2015; McKinley et al., 2015; McKinley et al., 2017; Thiel et al., 2014). Citizen science may increase perceived legitimacy of management decisions and public awareness of management issues (Wiederhold, 2011), which may also benefit man-agers seeking public engagement. Public participation in the knowledge-gathering process that leads to management decisions may result in greater stakeholder buy-in (Burgman et al., 2011). Involvement of citizens in priority research areas may also increase public awareness of management challenges and needs. This awareness and engagement may translate to support for funding by government foundations and others in support of those challenges and needs (Gouveia et al., 2004). One study found that, possibly because of this kind of leverage, European monitoring schemes involving stakeholders result in management action at the local scale in less than a year as opposed to three to nine years for academic scientist–executed schemes (Danielsen et al., 2010). Thus, involving citizens in gathering knowledge and applying that science to meet agency science needs could lead to more timely or immediate management actions.

Scholarship on citizen science and management discussed earlier suggests that citizen science, while certainly not free, may in some cases be a more resilient, cost-effective approach to monitoring required by natural resource managers, and may confer multiple benefits beyond the provision of data. We caution, however, that these additional benefits are not guaranteed outcomes. Collecting data is not necessarily the same as participating in management processes, and volunteers may not always experience the kinds of learning empowerment and engagement that are described in the reviews and cases cited earlier. It is incumbent upon managers and citizen science practitioners to as appropriate or as needed build programs and collaborations in ways that enable and promote these benefits.

## Benefits for citizen science programs

There are many potential motivations for people to sign up for and participate in citizen science programs. In fact, clear evidence that data inform management decisions may help to attract retain and motivate volunteers. One survey of volunteer motivations (Rotman et al., 2012) found two management-related factors that were critical for volunteers to continue participating: positive community impacts and advocacy for related environmental policies. Volunteer satisfaction was shown to be enhanced by a well-established, clear connection between a citizen science program and effective management.

Citizen science programs with demonstrated success in informing natural resource management processes may see improved outcomes in stewardship and civic engagement. When citizen scientists witness connections between the data they collect and subsequent management decisions they may gain personal insight into science-based decision-making and identify additional ways of becoming involved in the process (Carr, 2004; Haywood et al., 2016). Gaining insight into the process may encourage citizens to bring results directly to their local officials who have jurisdiction to act on local issues (Carr, 2004; Haywood et al., 2016). Thus, citizen science can be a pathway to participation in stakeholder-driven management and policy.

Taking this a step further, Bonney et al. (2009) found that when citizen scientists learn more about decision-making processes they gain confidence in asking for a place at the table in community planning and local politics. On a personal level, volunteers also gain a better understanding of related individual decisions such as who to vote for, what to donate money to, and what to spend time on (Brossard et al., 2005). Through these avenues citizen science can increase individual agency and foster higher levels of engagement in participatory processes both scientific and political. Moving up to the regional state and national level, volunteers can invoke their right to participate in agenda-setting for which science gets publicly funded (Carr, 2004), and leverage their collective participation in science to gain better access to, and influence on, policy makers (Conrad and Hilchey, 2011). Citizen science groups with a goal of producing action on a given subject could benefit by engaging with management directly as part of their program.

### Reasons citizen science programs may choose not to engage with managers

Despite the potential benefits outlined earlier, citizen science participants and leaders sometimes choose not to engage with managers. For example, credibility is the main priority of the Global Community Monitor's air monitoring program. In an effort to distance itself from activism or lobbying, this group only provides scientific information to other groups that engage with managers (Conrad and Hilchey, 2011). This example shows that occasionally program priorities may be perceived to be in conflict. Another reason citizen science programs may distance themselves from managers is the feeling also held by some professional scientists that data should speak for themselves, or that applied science is less credible than basic science.

If informing management is not the primary goal of a citizen science program, citizen science program coordinators may not allocate the extra time or resources this kind of link requires. Program coordinators and volunteers may not know how best to connect to management or have the personal relationships established to easily do so, and thus choose not to devote time to overcoming these obstacles (Lawrence and Turnhout, 2010). Activities required for connecting with management, such as organizing or attending meetings with managers or producing analyses and other materials that address manager needs, require extra resources that a group may not have at its disposal. Sometimes volunteer participants desire limited participation in data collection only and do not want to donate time to such activities (Dietz and Stern, 2008). This puts the pressure on citizen science program coordinators to take on the additional responsibilities associated with connecting with management, including any related data management, communications, and methods/training evaluation activities. Project staff may find themselves torn between activities that directly support and retain volunteers and activities that promote the relevance and utility of the data collected by those volunteers.

### Case study: California's statewide MPA monitoring program

To illustrate the benefits and challenges described earlier, we discuss MPA monitoring in California (Figure 7.1). This case affords multiple examples of citizen science projects working to inform adaptive management of MPAs under a common framework. Each project is unique due to factors such as the structure and complexity of data collection, programmatic structure of the citizen science activity, institutional arrangements, and data needs of the overarching program. We begin with an overview of the MPA monitoring program and its orientation toward

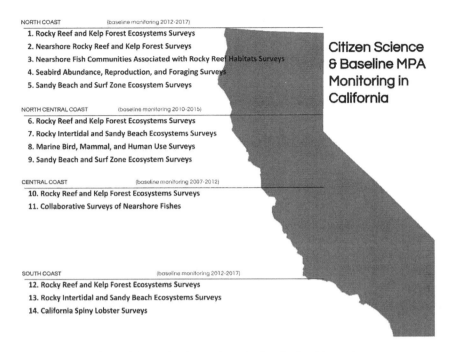

NORTH COAST          (baseline monitoring 2012-2017)

1. Rocky Reef and Kelp Forest Ecosystems Surveys
2. Nearshore Rocky Reef and Kelp Forest Surveys
3. Nearshore Fish Communities Associated with Rocky Reef Habitats Surveys
4. Seabird Abundance, Reproduction, and Foraging Surveys
5. Sandy Beach and Surf Zone Ecosystem Surveys

NORTH CENTRAL COAST          (baseline monitoring 2010-2015)

6. Rocky Reef and Kelp Forest Ecosystems Surveys
7. Rocky Intertidal and Sandy Beach Ecosystems Surveys
8. Marine Bird, Mammal, and Human Use Surveys
9. Sandy Beach and Surf Zone Ecosystem Surveys

CENTRAL COAST          (baseline monitoring 2007-2012)

10. Rocky Reef and Kelp Forest Ecosystems Surveys
11. Collaborative Surveys of Nearshore Fishes

SOUTH COAST          (baseline monitoring 2012-2017)

12. Rocky Reef and Kelp Forest Ecosystems Surveys
13. Rocky Intertidal and Sandy Beach Ecosystems Surveys
14. California Spiny Lobster Surveys

**Citizen Science & Baseline MPA Monitoring in California**

**FIGURE 7.1**    Baseline MPA monitoring projects that involved a citizen science component.

citizen science and then describe three different examples of citizen science playing a role in recent years.

In presenting these case studies, all four authors are writing from a perspective gained while working at the California Ocean Science Trust (OST), a 501(c)(3) non-profit "boundary organization" (Guston, 2001) established pursuant to state legislation (CORSA, 2000). OST uses science to bring together government scientists and communities (e.g. Meyer et al., 2015; Pietri et al., 2011), and since 2007 has been collaborating closely with state agencies (particularly the California Ocean Protection Council and California Department of Fish and Wildlife) and many other partners to design and implement California's Statewide MPA Monitoring Program (more information in OPC, 2014).

California's statewide MPA network consists of 124 MPAs and 15 special closures that span the entire coast from mean high tide to three nautical miles offshore (state waters), including state waters around offshore islands such as the Farallon Islands and Channel Islands. This network encompasses 852 square miles of marine habitat covering 16% of state waters, 9% of which is within no-take State Marine Reserves. The network was finalized in 2012 following the passage of the Marine Life Protection Act (MLPA) of 1999, which required California to re-design its MPAs to meet six high-level goals including protecting ecosystem structure function and integrity; providing recreational educational and study opportunities; and protecting marine national heritage (MLPA, 1999). Beyond requiring the state to establish a network of MPAs, the MLPA established a governance structure requiring comprehensive management of the MPA network across four focal areas: outreach and education; enforcement and compliance; research and monitoring; and policy and permitting.

California adopted a two-phased approach to monitoring the health of ecosystems and socioeconomic conditions in and around the MPAs: regional *baseline* monitoring and statewide *long-term* monitoring.[1] Baseline monitoring occurs during the first five years following MPA implementation in each region to establish a baseline or "benchmark" of ecological and socioeconomic conditions and assess any initial changes. Each regional program is composed of a set of state-funded projects with the goal of building a comprehensive baseline across as many ecosystems and human uses as feasible within the temporal financial and methodological constraints. There are currently no specific benchmarks for the performance of individual MPAs or the MPA network at the regional or statewide scales. However, in 2017 the state will start developing a document to guide long-term monitoring that will include management effectiveness questions which will necessitate metrics of performance. Phase two of the MPA monitoring program – long-term monitoring – began in 2016, including data collection in three ecosystems across three regions, maintaining state capacity to collect data with equipment upgrades, and expanding state science capacity to fund three post-doctoral positions. In the future, after the guidance document is completed, long-term monitoring will continue to reflect and be responsive to state priorities and management needs.

The monitoring framework and monitoring plans focus on condition (the state of the system) and trends (how it is changing), and on management effectiveness (or the role that management actions are playing in the changes that are occurring in the ocean). This structure is designed to be adaptable to these and other priorities that emerge.

### A role for citizen science

A science-based monitoring framework guides monitoring activities across 10 "Ecosystem Features" (Table 7.1). This framework explicitly acknowledges the strengths of developing sets of multi-tiered metrics, some of which are less technically or methodologically demanding. Data collected on a set of metrics reveal the condition or status of ecosystems, and when collected over multiple years these data provide an understanding of how conditions are changing (i.e. trends over time). The approach to condition and trends monitoring as laid out by the framework includes two implementation options – "check-ups" and "assessments" – each with a separate set of metrics that when monitored together provide insight into both the condition and trends of an ecosystem. *Check-ups* provide a coarse evaluation of conditions and trends in ecosystems and human uses contributing to our understanding of ecosystem health and MPA performance. They are designed to take advantage of existing capacity presented by citizen science and community groups, and the role these can play in MPA monitoring. By comparison, *assessments* demand

**TABLE 7.1** Ecosystem features in California's science-based statewide MPA monitoring framework. More information at http://oceanspaces.org/monitoring.

Rocky Intertidal Ecosystems
Kelp and Shallow Rock Ecosystems (0–30 m)
Mid-depth Rock Ecosystems (30–100 m)
Estuarine and Wetland Ecosystems
Soft-bottom Intertidal and Beach Ecosystems
Soft-bottom Subtidal Ecosystems (0–100 m)
Deep Ecosystems and Canyons (>100 m)
Nearshore Pelagic Ecosystems (i.e. the water column habitat within state waters in depths > 30 m)
Consumptive Uses
Non-consumptive Uses

a higher level of detail and often require more complex or time-consuming monitoring methods.

That said, the monitoring framework does not assume that citizen science can only contribute simpler "check-ups," and indeed some programs are able to provide data with the breadth, quality, and sophistication expected in "assessments" (e.g. Reef Check California).[2] Regional monitoring plans (e.g. OST, 2014a),[3] which are guided by the framework and designed to be adaptable and responsive to changing state priorities and scientific advancements, call for well-developed training programs and formalized data quality assurance and quality control (QA/QC). The monitoring framework and monitoring plans guide the implementation of California's MPA monitoring program in both the baseline and long-term phases.

Of the 38 state-funded projects, 14 had one or more citizen science components. The citizen science activities that occurred as part of baseline monitoring vary greatly in their structure, the nature and scale of the activity, the makeup of their participants, and other facets (Table 7.2). With long-term monitoring in the beginning stages, it is unclear exactly what role citizen science will play going forward. However, the state agencies recognize not only the valuable data that can be produced by citizen science programs but also the political capital and buy-in that results from engaging citizens in data-collection efforts.

## Why use citizen science for MPA monitoring?

The decision to design California's Statewide MPA Monitoring Program with an explicit openness to citizen science reflects a variety of considerations. From the beginning of the MLPA implementation process, there has been a strong emphasis on public participation (Fox et al., 2013; Kirlin et al., 2013; Sayce et al., 2013). Incorporating a role for citizen science is a natural extension of this value.

From the beginning, the monitoring program was also based on a partnerships approach (OPC, 2014), recognizing that no single agency or entity could fully realize a comprehensive monitoring program on its own. To succeed, the program would need to take advantage of the considerable capacity for research and monitoring of coastal ecosystems already in place throughout California. In other words, the program is aimed at finding the most cost-effective approaches, which may include citizen science. This approach also requires innovation and adaptability. To succeed, the implementing agencies must be attuned to partnership opportunities that arise, and they must be willing to try out collaborative approaches and to adapt based on what is learned from their experiences. Additionally, some citizen science partnerships were funded with an explicit goal of exploring future collaboration rather than obtaining needed data in the near-term (e.g. LiMPETS, Chapter 11). In this way, the principles of adaptive management that by law govern the MPA network (MLPA, 1999) are also at the core of the monitoring program (OST, 2014a).

Another element to the evolving role of citizen science in MPA monitoring is how a monitoring program can maintain relevance, utility, and support over the long term. One way is by expanding the constituency for monitoring – the group of people who participate and see the value in data collection. Another way is the apparent establishment of feedback loops between participation of citizen scientists in data collection and participation of those same citizens in public meetings related to planning and priority setting for MPA monitoring. There may be similar feedback loops between citizen science involvement and other MPA implementation goals related to education and outreach and enforcement and compliance.

## Case studies of citizen science involvement in MPA monitoring

Here we provide a brief overview of citizen science involvement in baseline monitoring. These cases span all four regions, and some of them occurred across multiple regions (Table 7.2). We describe two of those cases in further detail to illustrate the diversity of experiences accrued during the baseline phase of MPA monitoring across the state.

### California spiny lobster project

The California spiny lobster (*Panulirus interruptus*) fishery is one of the most economically important in California, supporting both a commercial and recreational fishery (Miller, 2014). There have been cases in other parts of the world in which spiny lobster populations have rapidly risen within MPAs after establishment and have even spilled over to enhance adjacent fisheries (e.g. Goñi et al., 2006; Kelly and MacDiarmid, 2003). Thus, there is a great deal of interest by fishermen[4] scientists and managers in how MPAs affect these organisms in California. The Southern California Lobster Research Group was formed in 2011 and received state funds to conduct baseline monitoring on the abundance, size, distribution, and behavior of California spiny lobsters in South Coast MPAs (Hovel et al., 2014). Five sites inside and outside of newly established MPAs in the South Coast were chosen for monitoring. This part of the South Coast region was chosen because it generates a substantial portion of statewide annual landings and because historical baselines of fishing effort exist for the most productive spiny lobster fishing groups in the area (Hovel et al., 2014).

**TABLE 7.2** Description of projects involving citizen science as part of baseline MPA monitoring in California.

| Baseline Project(s)* | Organization** | Pre-existing? | Organization Type(s) | Activity Description | Participant Description |
|---|---|---|---|---|---|
| 1, 6, 10, 12 | RCCA | yes | NGO | Scientists and volunteer divers with Reef Check California surveyed fish, invertebrates, and habitats of rocky reefs and kelp forests. | volunteer divers |
| 7 | LiMPETS (CAS, FMSA, PGMNH, UCSC) | yes | NGO/ government | LiMPETS program coordinators analyzed existing, long-term data collected by middle and high school students on invertebrates and algae in sandy beach and rocky intertidal ecosystems. | grade school students |
| 9, 13 | LiMPETS, SSU, UCSB | no | NGO/ government, academic | Scientists compared their data with LiMPETS data, collected by middle and high school students, and tested LiMPETS beach monitoring protocols. | grade school students |
| 11 | CCFRP (CalPoly, MLML) | yes | Academic | Volunteer anglers collected data on rocky reef fish populations. | volunteer anglers |
| 8 | Beach Watch (FMSA, GFNMS) | yes | NGO/ government | Beach Watch program coordinators analyzed existing, long-term data collected by volunteers who surveyed marine birds and mammals (alive and dead), and human uses on beaches within the Gulf of the Farallones and Monterey Bay National Marine Sanctuaries. | volunteers (general) |
| 14 | CDFW, Scripps, SDSU | no | Academic/ government | Scientists from CDFW, Scripps, and SDSU partnered with the California Lobster Trap Fishermen's Association, and volunteers from the San Diego Oceans Foundation participated in a tag-recapture program to estimate lobster abundance and distribution across MPA boundaries. | lobster fishermen; volunteers (general) |
| 2 | HSU | no | Academic | Commercial urchin fishermen partnering with academic scientists to collect data on rocky reef and kelp forest invertebrates (mainly urchins), which will be compared to data collected by academic researchers. | commercial urchin fishermen |

*(Continued)*

**TABLE 7.2** (Continued)

| Baseline Project(s)* | Organization** | Pre-existing? | Organization Type(s) | Activity Description | Participant Description |
|---|---|---|---|---|---|
| 3 | HSU | no | Academic | Academic scientists, recreational anglers, and sport fishing boat captains collaborate to survey rocky reef fish communities. | volunteer anglers; boat captains |
| 4 | HSU, PBCS | no | Academic/ NGO | Scientists and volunteers conduct shore-based surveys of seabird populations, focused on common murre, Brandt's cormorant, double-crested cormorant, pelagic cormorant, and Western gull. | volunteers (general) |
| 4 | HSU | no | Academic | Crowd-sourced and other volunteers code video footage of seabird breeding and foraging behavior on Castle Rock. | volunteers (general) |
| 5, 9 | BML/UCD, SFSU, SSU, HSU | no | Academic | Scientists partner with recreational anglers to survey surf zone fishes (e.g. surfperch) | volunteer anglers |

* See Figure 7.1 for representation of the four regions, and a key to project numbers.
** Organization acronyms are as follows: Bodega Marine Laboratories (BML), California Academy of Sciences (CAS), California Collaborative Fisheries Research Program (CCFRP), California Department of Fish and Wildlife (CDFW), California Polytechnic State University San Luis Obispo (CalPoly), Farallones Marine Sanctuary Association (FMSA), Gulf of the Farallones National Marine Sanctuary (GFNMS), Humboldt State University (HSU), Long-term Monitoring Program and Experiential Training for Students (LiMPETS), Moss Landing Marine Laboratories (MLML), Pacific Grove Museum of Natural History (PGMNH), Reef Check California (RCCA), San Francisco State University (SFSU), San Diego State University (SDSU), Scripps Institute of Oceanography (Scripps), Sonoma State University (SSU), University of California Davis (UCD), University of California Santa Barbara (UCSB), University of California Santa Cruz (UCSC).

In this three-year tag-recapture study, scientists from San Diego State University Scripps Institute of Oceanography and the California Department of Fish and Wildlife partnered with lobster fishermen from San Diego, Laguna Beach, and Palos Verdes. The program relied on commercial fishermen's boats as well as their knowledge of the sites. The fishermen donated their time but were compensated for the cost of fuel, insurance, and wear-and-tear on their vessels. Project leaders also partnered with the San Diego Oceans Foundation, a non-profit organization focusing on educating the public about ocean stewardship and implementing projects to improve ocean health. The project took advantage of San Diego Oceans Foundation's large membership database for recruiting, which resulted in hundreds of Southern California residents applying to help the lobster fishermen and scientists collect and record data (Freiwald et al., submitted). Applicants were interviewed, and those who went to sea read and were tested on a volunteer manual. Their training covered their responsibilities, what to expect at sea, basic safety protocols aboard a vessel, and how to accurately collect data (Freiwald et al., submitted). The only requirements were the ability to record data availability one day per month, and comfort on small boats. Most volunteers recorded data on spiny lobster abundance, size, distribution, sex, reproductive status, and movement; some more experienced volunteers occasionally assisted with lobster tagging (Freiwald et al., submitted).

This research collaboration among fishermen scientists and the public is a valuable model for promoting education legitimacy and scientific understanding of MPAs. Fishermen who participate in monitoring (and others in their community) may be more likely to find the results legitimate and credible (Kay et al., 2012; McCay and Jentoft, 1996). It was also a cost-effective means of generating high quality data, as time and equipment were donated by volunteers. To ensure data quality, data sheets were checked daily or weekly by trained project staff for inconsistencies, and any inconsistencies were resolved with the data recorder or scientists. Any unclear data were discarded (Hovel et al., 2014). In partnering with a non-profit organization (San Diego Oceans Foundation) with a mission of education and stewardship, the project could draw in many volunteers who were educated about California MPAs and monitoring. San Diego Oceans Foundation staff (many of whom were volunteers themselves) devoted hundreds of hours of time to vet potential volunteers and train them. The large number of people meant that project leaders could carry out several monitoring components that contributed complementary information (e.g. boat-based tagging, SCUBA-based surveys, data entry, data analysis). While most of the volunteers were accurate in data recording, some were not. Those volunteers were not invited back (Freiwald et al., submitted).

This project was designed by academic scientists specifically to provide baseline information on spiny lobster abundance size distribution growth and behavior as part of South Coast MPA baseline monitoring. This sets it apart from the other two examples discussed here which existed prior to their involvement in MPA monitoring. Through the capture and tagging of over 19,000 spiny lobsters in and around the MPAs, the project established baseline conditions of spiny lobster populations and behavioral information that provides a benchmark against which future changes can be measured. These data may also be useful for current efforts to assess and model spiny lobster populations in support of fisheries management.

## Long-term Monitoring Program and Experiential Training for Students (LiMPETS)[5]

In two of the regional baseline programs – North Central Coast and South Coast – researchers studying sandy beach and rocky intertidal ecosystems collaborated with the LiMPETS program, which involves students in data collection on sandy beach and rocky intertidal ecosystems (see detailed account in Chapter 11). LiMPETS was created in 2002 and is run through a partnership of California's National Marine Sanctuaries Farallones Marine Sanctuary Association Marine Science Institute, at the University of California at Santa Barbara and the Pacific Grove Museum of Natural History.[6] Through its work with educators, students, and local communities, LiMPETS has involved a very large number of citizen scientists in MPA monitoring. For example, in the North Central Coast, LiMPETS engaged 3,300 students from across 60 schools over just three years (Dean et al., 2013). By reaching many students, the benefits of LiMPETS' work go well beyond the science including MPA education, raising awareness, and inspiring lasting ocean stewardship.

Across the state, teachers and students are trained to use standardized protocols to collect and analyze data on marine populations, providing an invaluable hands-on experiential learning opportunity. Prior to going into the field, teachers attend a mandatory eight-hour workshop introducing them to the LiMPETS program and data collection protocols. This is followed by one- to three-hour student trainings that occur in the classroom covering field methods and protocols and species identifications.[7] After the trainings are complete, all students must pass a "readiness quiz" before participating in data collection. In 2016, LiMPETS finalized a quality assurance project plan (QAPP) that provides specific guidelines to standardize quality assurance/quality control (QA/QC) protocols across the program. All field surveys are supervised by experienced LiMPETS personnel who oversee in-field QA/QC; they ensure methods and protocols are followed and that datasheets are completed accurately and thoroughly.

Youth-focused citizen science programs come with challenges like any citizen science program. There are many teachers who have been with the program for several years, but there is no actual "volunteer" retention from survey to survey: by default, teachers are taking new sets of students out each year. Also, protocols are restricted to include only areas above the surf zone due to safety concerns, which, as is the case with sand crabs, can result in missing an entire size class (Meyer et al., 2014). While working with youth citizen scientists presents its challenges, the broad reach of this program – 27 sites statewide, some of which were surveyed 20 times per year – presents the motivation to explore how best to take advantage of this capacity.

LiMPETS involvement in baseline MPA monitoring was in many ways exploratory, with the main goal of understanding complementarity and inconsistencies between their results and those produced by academic researchers. LiMPETS, together with academic researchers, generated recommendations for aligning targeted metrics with those identified in the monitoring plans and how to fine-tune protocols to ensure more precise and accurate results. For example, beach monitoring recommendations included using a dynamic sampling grid to be more adaptive to how targeted species (e.g. sand crabs) move in response to changing beach conditions, and to decrease the amount of time participants spend in the swash zone to reduce disturbance of highly mobile species (Dugan et al., 2015). Long-standing citizen science programs like LiMPETS can also offer historical datasets that can be an invaluable resource for interpreting current and future population trends.

## Reef Check California

The only citizen science program that has participated in baseline monitoring across all four regions is Reef Check California (RCCA), a non-profit organization established in 2005 with the dual goals of collecting rigorous useful data and promoting environmental stewardship through education. Volunteer SCUBA divers with RCCA are trained to conduct surveys of fish and invertebrates in kelp forest (Figure 7.2) and shallow rock habitats. They do this work in groups overseen by program staff and experienced volunteers. Volunteers must meet strict requirements before they can begin the required training, and the program engages in a wide range of activities and follows rigid guidelines designed to ensure data quality and enhance the usability and credibility of its results (Freitag et al., 2016). Such activities and guidelines include volunteer training and retraining requirements; field surveys led by RCCA staff or experienced volunteers; and quality control measures (Figure 7.3). As of 2014 RCCA had trained over 1,000 volunteer divers with an

**FIGURE 7.2** A volunteer Reef Check diver surveys algae at Anacapa Island.

*Photo credit:* Michelle Hoalton.

**FIGURE 7.3** Volunteers review datasheets after a Reef Check dive in Palos Verdes, Los Angeles County.

*Photo credit:* Colleen Wisniewski.

active team of roughly 250 new and returning citizen scientists participating each year (Freiwald and Wisniewski, 2014).

Although an independent organization, RCCA has worked closely with academic scientists, state agencies, and other partners involved in MPA implementation in California since its inception. Of note is the program's close relationship with the Partnership for Interdisciplinary Studies of Coastal Oceans (PISCO), a network of researchers that has been monitoring ecosystems along the US West Coast since 1999.[8] Through both formal data comparison (e.g. Gillett et al., 2012) and regular interaction over that last decade, RCCA has partnered with and learned from PISCO researchers. Both programs have learned from each other about the potential for coordination and collaboration in their monitoring activities (based on personal communications with staff from each program; see also Pondella et al., 2014).

The RCCA model is in many ways ideal for California's Statewide MPA Monitoring Program. It has proven an ability to provide high quality data and an ability to work closely with high-performing academic programs focused on the same ecosystems along the California coast. As such, RCCA has the potential for cost-effectiveness (e.g. time and equipment donated by volunteers). The program also presents a leveraging opportunity with its track record of attracting philanthropic funds. Finally, the mission of education and stewardship combined with the goal of producing high quality useful data is yet another opportunity for the broader monitoring program. On the other hand, RCCA's volunteer base may not be particularly scalable within California – or beyond for Reef Check programs and projects in other regions and parts of the world – given the high bar for entry and the heavy training requirements. Compared with LiMPETS, for example, which engages middle school students and teachers, there is less potential for engaging and impacting large numbers of participants outside the academic science community.

## Lessons learned

The cases described earlier and those outlined in Table 7.2 illustrate the diversity of projects that have productively contributed to MPA monitoring in California, as well as the range of models that natural resource managers might consider as they explore the opportunity of citizen science.

A major factor in the various examples is whether they were pre-existing programs that became part of state-funded baseline monitoring, or were new projects created specifically for MPA baseline monitoring. Each has advantages and disadvantages for informing natural resource management. Newly created efforts, such as the spiny lobster surf zone fish and kelp forest invertebrate projects (Table 7.2), allow for tailoring data collection to meet specific needs identified at the time of project inception. In some cases, this work was nested within a larger project run by academic scientists. This closer relationship created opportunities for scientists to interact with new communities, build new partnerships, and generally expand the reach of MPA monitoring. Such activities require significant investment of time and resources on the part of organizers. But broadening the collaborator base and bringing outside perspectives to the fore is beneficial for all parties involved from the citizen science groups and academics to the funders and users of the results.

On the other hand, sustainability can be a challenge for newly created projects if funding is not available on a yearly basis.[9] For example, the surf zone fish project

(Table 7.2), though seen as a success by many (based on personal communications), has not continued in the North Central Coast region now that the baseline monitoring is completed. While it might be possible to spin up the effort once again, this would involve significant investments in time and energy.

Pre-existing projects and programs often have multiple sources of support and thus may be able to keep up activities relationships and overall capacity in off-years to maintain a long-term monitoring program. For example, the California Collaborative Fisheries Research Program (Table 7.2) has continued collecting data in the Central Coast using grants from a variety of sources, though they have not received state funds for MPA monitoring in recent years. The state has provided funding to this group once again (for 2016–2017) as part of long-term MPA monitoring, leveraging investments from other sources both in the interim years and these years. Through this new investment, the state can take advantage of data generated in the "gap" years – a significant advantage from a leveraging standpoint.

But pre-existing programs have many different partnerships and priorities which must be balanced with those of California's Statewide MPA Monitoring Program (OST, 2014b). The LiMPETS (Chapter 11) program has a strong focus on education in addition to informing management and promoting stewardship. It may not always be the case that the data collection best suited to youth learning in the field will also match with the state's needs. Similarly, other pre-existing programs may find themselves torn between manager needs from different agencies as there are multiple relevant mandates across the state and federal governments.

An important factor across these cases is the MPA monitoring framework and partnerships approach, which enabled these collaborations and laid the groundwork for continually building and improving the role for citizen science and other forms of knowledge in the management of MPAs.

## Next steps

As the final baseline period (in the North Coast) ends in 2018 and California looks toward long-term monitoring of MPAs, there is a renewed commitment to the partnerships-based approach to monitoring and MPA implementation more broadly. California has put forward a "Partnerships Plan" for MPAs formally adopted by the California Ocean Protection Council (OPC, 2014) and assembled a MPA Statewide Leadership Team consisting of agencies and other partners who have significant statewide authority affecting MPAs (OPC, 2015). This team is charged with working together on implementation issues relevant beyond research and monitoring to include the broad governance spectrum from regulation compliance to outreach needs.

As citizen scientists and related programs continue to be an integral part of California's Statewide MPA Monitoring Program, there are important questions to ask about the broader long-term outcomes. How might long-term citizen science involvement contribute to stewardship activities and education outcomes related to MPAs? How might it change the work of collaborating academic scientists? Can the monitoring program help to link these citizen science efforts to one another and create a network? The high-level framework that guides our work in this area has created fertile ground for both investigating and improving upon the relationships between citizen science and ocean and coastal resource management. And the broad suite of partnerships established through baseline monitoring is poised to face this challenge.

## Notes

1  To learn more about this two-phased approach to monitoring visit http://oceanspaces. org/monitoring.
2  www.reefcheck.org/california/ca-overview/rcca_home.php.
3  Other regional MPA monitoring plans can be found at http://oceanspaces.org/ monitoring.
4  We use the term "fishermen" in this chapter because it is how men and women catching or harvesting fish in California describe themselves.
5  LiMPETS is the subject of Chapter 11.
6  More information at: http://limpets.org/.
7  Methods and protocols vary by habitat – rocky intertidal vs. beaches – and can also vary by site. More detailed information about survey methods can be found online: http://limpets. org/rocky-intertidal-monitoring/ and http://limpets.org/sandy-beach-monitoring/.
8  More information at www.piscoweb.org/what.
9  This is likely for many of the ecosystem features in the MPA monitoring framework (Table 7.1) due to the geographic and ecological scale of the program.

## Literature cited

Aceves-Bueno, E., Adeleye, A., Bradley, D., Tyler Brandt, W., Callery, P., Feraud, M., Garner, K., Gentry, R., Huang, Y., McCullough, I., Pearlman, I., Sutherland, S., Wilkinson, W., Yang, Y., Zink, T., Anderson, S., and Tague, C. (2015). Citizen science as an approach for overcoming insufficient monitoring and inadequate stakeholder buy-in in adaptive management: Criteria and evidence. *Ecosystems*, 18(3), 493–506.

Biber, E. (2011). The problem of environmental monitoring. *University of Colorado Law Review*, 83(1), 1–82.

Bonney, R., Cooper, C.B., Dickinson, J., Kelling, S., Phillips, T., Rosenberg, K.V., and Shirk, J. (2009). Citizen science: A developing tool for expanding science knowledge and scientific literacy. *BioScience*, 59(11), 977–984.

Bonney, R., Cooper, C., and Ballard, H. (2016). The theory and practice of citizen science: Launching a new journal. *Citizen Science: Theory and Practice*, 1(1), 1, http://doi. org/10.5334/cstp.65.

Bonney, R., Shirk, J.L., Phillips, T.B., Wiggins, A., Ballard, H.L., Miller-Rushing, A.J., and Parrish, J.K. (2014). Next steps for citizen science. *Science*, 343(6178), 1436–1437.

Brossard, D., Lewenstein, B., and Bonney, R. (2005). Scientific knowledge and attitude change: The impact of a citizen science project. *International Journal of Science Education*, 27(9), 1099–1121.

Burgman, M., Carr, A., Godden, L., Gregory, R., McBride, M., Flander, L., and Maguire, L. (2011). Redefining expertise and improving ecological judgment. *Conservation Letters* 4(2), 81–87. http://doi.org/10.1111/j.1755-263X.2011.00165.x.

Carr, A.J.L. (2004). Policy reviews and essays: Why do we all need community science? *Society & Natural Resources*, 17(9), 841–849.

Cash, D.W., Clark, W., Alcock, F., Dickson, N.M., Eckley, N., Guston, D.H., . . . Mitchell, R.B. (2003). Knowledge systems for sustainable development. *Proceedings of the National Academy of Sciences of the United States of America*, 100, 8086–8091.

Cigliano, J.A., Meyer, R., Ballard, H.L., Freitag, A., Phillips, T.B., and Wasser, A. (2015). Making marine and coastal citizen science matter. *Ocean & Coastal Management*, 115, 77–87.

Clark, T.W. (2002). *The Policy Process: A Practical Guide for Natural Resources Professionals*. New Haven, CT: Yale University Press.

Conrad, C., and Hilchey, K. (2011). A review of citizen science and community-based environmental monitoring: Issues and opportunities. *Environmental Monitoring and Assessment*, 176(1–4), 273–291.

CORSA. California Ocean Resources Stewardship Act (2000).

Danielsen, F., Burgess, N.D., Balmford, A., Donald, P.F., Funder, M., Jones, J.P.G., . . . Yonten, D. (2009). Local participation in natural resource monitoring: A characterization of approaches. *Conservation Biology: The Journal of the Society for Conservation Biology*, 23(1), 31–42.

Danielsen, F., Burgess, N.D., Jensen, P.M., and Pirhofer-Walzl, K. (2010). Environmental monitoring: The scale and speed of implementation varies according to the degree of peoples involvement. *Journal of Applied Ecology*, 47(6), 1166–1168.

Dean, A., Young, A.N., Nickels, A., Pearse, J., & Wasser, A. (2013). An analysis of citizen science data from LiMPETS: In support of the North Central Coast Baseline Characterization Project. San Francisco. Retrieved from https://caseagrant.ucsd.edu/sites/default/files/RMPA-7_LiMPETS_FinalReport.pdf

Dietz, T., and Stern, P. (2008). *Public Participation in Environmental Assessment and Decision Making*. Washington: National Academies Press.

Dugan, J.E., Hubbard, D.M., Nielsen, K.J., Altstatt, J., and Bursek, J. (2015). *Baseline characterization of Sandy Beach ecosystems along the South Coast of California: Final report*. https://caseagrant.ucsd.edu/sites/default/files/SCMPA-24-Final-Report-Appendices.pdf.

Fox, E., Hastings, S., Miller-Henson, M., Monie, D., Ugoretz, J., Frimodig, A., Shuman, C., Owens, B., Garwood, R., Connor, D., Serpa, P., and Gleason, M. (2013). Addressing policy issues in a stakeholder-based and science-driven marine protected area network planning process. *Ocean & Coastal Management*, 74, 34–44.

Freitag, A., Meyer, R., and Whiteman, L. (2016). Strategies employed by citizen science programs to increase the credibility of their data. *Citizen Science: Theory and Practice*, 1(1), 2.

Freitag, A., and Pfeffer, M. (2013). Process, not product: Investigating recommendations for improving citizen science "success". *PLoS One*, 8(5), e64079.

Freiwald, J., Caselle, J., Meyer, E., Blanchette, R.M., Hovel, C., Neilson, K.A., . . . Burse. (n.d.). Citizen science monitoring of marine protected areas: Case studies and recommendations for integration among monitoring programs. *Marine Ecology*.

Freiwald, J., and Wisniewski, C. (2014). *Reef check California: Citizen scientist monitoring of rocky reefs and kelp forests: Creating a baseline for California's South Coast*. [Online] https://caseagrant.ucsd.edu/sites/default/files/SCMPA-21-Final-Report_0.pdf.

Gillett, D., Pondella, D., Freiwald, J., Schiff, K., Caselle, J., Shuman, C., and Weisberg, S. (2012). Comparing volunteer and professionally collected monitoring data from the rocky subtidal reefs of Southern California, USA. *Environmental Monitoring and Assessment*, 184(5), 3239–3257.

Goñi, R., Quetglas, A., and Reñones, O. (2006). Spillover of spiny lobsters *Palinurus elephas* from a marine reserve to an adjoining fishery. *Marine Ecology Progress Series*, 308, 207–219.

Gouveia, C., Fonseca, A., Câmara, A., and Ferreira, F. (2004). Promoting the use of environmental data collected by concerned citizens through information and communication technologies. *Journal of Environmental Management*, 71(2), 135–154.

Guston, D. (2001). Boundary organizations in environmental policy and science: An introduction. *Science, Technology & Human Values*, 26(4), 399–408.

Haywood, B., Parrish, J., and Dolliver, J. (2016). Place-based and data-rich citizen science as a precursor for conservation action. *Conservation Biology*, 30(3), 476–486.

Hovel, K.A., Neilson, D.J., and Parnell, E. (2014). *Baseline characterization of California spiny lobster (Panulirus interruptus) in South Coast marine protected areas.* https://caseagrant.ucsd.edu/sites/default/files/SCMPA-25-Final-Report.pdf.

Hyder, K., Townhill, B., Anderson, L., Delany, J., and Pinnegar, J. (2015). Can citizen science contribute to the evidence-base that underpins marine policy? *Marine Policy*, 59, 112–120.

Kay, M., Lenihan, H., Guenther, C., Wilson, J., Miller, C., and Shrout, S. (2012). Collaborative assessment of California spiny lobster population and fishery responses to a marine reserve network. *Ecological Applications*, 22(1), 322–335.

Kelly, S., and MacDiarmid, A. (2003). Movement patterns of mature spiny lobsters, *Jasus edwardsii*, from a marine reserve. *New Zealand Journal of Marine and Freshwater Research*, 37(1), 149–158.

Kirlin, J., Caldwell, M., Gleason, M., Weber, M., Ugoretz, J., Fox, E., and Miller-Henson, M. (2013). California's Marine Life Protection Act initiative: Supporting implementation of legislation establishing a statewide network of marine protected areas. *Ocean & Coastal Management*, 74, 3–13.

Lawrence, A., and Turnhout, E. (2010). Personal meaning in the public sphere: The standardisation and rationalisation of biodiversity data in the UK and the Netherlands. *Journal of Rural Studies*, 26(4), 353–360.

Lemos, M., Kirchhoff, C., and Ramprasad, V. (2012). Narrowing the climate information usability gap. *Nature Climate Change*, 2(11), 789–794.

McCay, B., and Jentoft, S. (1996). From the bottom up: Participatory issues in fisheries management. *Society & Natural Resources*, 9(3), 237–250.

McKinley, D.C., Miller-Rushing, A.J., Ballard, H.L., Bonney, R., Brown, H., Cook-Patton, S.C., Evans, D.M., French, R.A., Parrish, J.K., Phillips, T.B., and Ryan, S.F. (2017). Citizen science can improve conservation science, natural resource management, and environmental protection. *Biological Conservation*, 208, 15–28. http://doi.org/10.1016/j.biocon.2016.05.015.

McKinley, D.C., Miller-Rushing, A.J., Ballard, H.L., Bonney, R., Brown, H., Evans, D.M., . . . Soukup, M.A. (2015). Investing in citizen science can improve natural resource management and environmental protection. *Issues in Ecology*, 19. http://pubs.er.usgs.gov/publication/70159470.

McNie, E. (2007). Reconciling the supply of scientific information with user demands: An analysis of the problem and review of the literature. *Environmental Science & Policy*, 10(1), 17–38.

Meyer, E.M., Rindge, H., and Whiteman, E. (2014). *California North Central Coast: Marine Protected Area Baseline Monitoring Summary Report 2010–2013.* California Ocean Science Trust, Oakland, CA.

Meyer, R., McAfee, S., and Whiteman, E. (2015). How California is mobilizing boundary chains to integrate science, policy and management for changing ocean chemistry. *Climate Risk Management*, 9, 50–61.

Miller, E.F. (2014). Status and trends in the southern California spiny lobster fishery and population: 1980–2011. *Bulletin Southern California Academy of Sciences*, 113(1), 14–33.

Miller-Rushing, A., Primack, R., and Bonney, R. (2012). The history of public participation in ecological research. *Frontiers in Ecology and the Environment*, 10(6), 285–290.

MLPA. California Marine Life Protection Act (1999).

OPC. (2014). *The California Collaborative Approach: Marine Protected Areas Partnership Plan*. Sacramento, CA. www.opc.ca.gov/webmaster/ftp/pdf/docs/mpa/APPROVED_FINAL_MPA_Partnership_Plan_12022014.pdf.

OPC. (2015). *Marine Protected Area (MPA) Statewide Leadership Team Work Plan FY 15/16–17/18*. California Ocean Protection Council, Sacramento, CA.

OST. (2014a). *Central Coast MPA Monitoring Plan*. Oakland, CA. http://oceanspaces.org/sites/default/files/regions/files/central_coast_monitoring_plan_final_october2014.pdf.

OST. (2014b). *Citizen Science & Ocean Resource Management in California: Guidance for Forming Productive Partnerships*. California Ocean Science Trust, Oakland, CA.

Parker, J., and Crona, B. (2012). On being all things to all people: Boundary organizations and the contemporary research university. *Social Studies of Science*, 42(2), 262–289.

Pietri, D., McAfee, S., Mace, A., Knight, E., Rogers, L., and Chornesky, E. (2011). Using science to inform controversial issues: A case study from the California ocean science trust. *Coastal Management*, 39(3), 296–316.

Pondella, D.J., Caselle, J.E., Claisse, J.T., Williams, J.P., Davis, K., Williams, C.M., and Zahn, L.A. (2014). *South Coast baseline program final report: Kelp and Shallow rock ecosystems shallow rock ecosystems*. http://oceanspaces.org/projects/south-coast-baseline-characterization-kelp-shallow-rock-ecosystems.

Rotman, D., Preece, J., Hammock, J., Procita, K., Hansen, D., Parr, C., Lewis, D., and Jacobs, D. (2012). Dynamic changes in motivation in collaborative citizen-science projects. In *Proceedings of the ACM 2012 Conference on Computer Supported Cooperative Work*, 217–226. New York: ACM Press.

Roy, H.E., Pocock, M.J.O., Preston, C.D., Roy, D.B., Savage, J., Tweddle, J.C., and Robinson, L.D. (2012). *Understanding citizen science and environmental monitoring*. Final report on behalf of UK Environmental Observation Framework.

Sarewitz, D., and Pielke, R. (2007). The neglected heart of science policy: Reconciling supply of and demand for science. *Environmental Science & Policy*, 10(1), 5–16.

Sayce, K., Shuman, C., Connor, D., Reisewitz, A., Pope, E., Miller-Henson, M., Poncelet, E., Monié, D., and Owens, B. (2013). Beyond traditional stakeholder engagement: Public participation roles in California's statewide marine protected area planning process. *Ocean & Coastal Management*, 74, 57–66.

Thiel, M., Penna-Díaz, M.A., Luna-Jorquera, G., Salas, S., Sellanes, J., and Stotz, W. (2014). Citizen scientists and marine research: Volunteer participants, their contributions, and projection for the future. *Oceanography and Marine Biology: An Annual Review*, 52, 257–314.

Wiederhold, B. (2011). Citizen scientists generate benefits for researchers, educators, society, and themselves. *Cyberpsychology, Behavior, and Social Networking*, 14(12), 70.

# 8

# ENGAGEMENT IN MARINE CONSERVATION THROUGH CITIZEN SCIENCE

## A community-based approach to eelgrass restoration in Frenchman Bay, Maine, USA

*Jane E. Disney, Emma L. Fox, Anna Farrell, Carrie LeDuc, and Duncan Bailey*

## Introduction

Citizen science has historically involved the collection of natural resource data by citizens (Wiggins and Crowston, 2011); the citizen scientist typically participates in a "contributory" capacity by recording the status of key measurable indicators for research (Bonney et al., 2009). Shirk et al. (2012) describe five models of citizen contribution to research science, which are based on the degree of public participation in scientific research (PPSR). These models range from *contractual projects* on one end of the spectrum to *collegial contributions* on the other. In contractual projects, communities ask professional scientists to engage in a specific research project and provide feedback, while in collegial contributions, citizen scientists conduct research independent of professional scientists.

The roles that citizen scientists have had in research and habitat restoration have been diverse, from monitoring and assessment (Huddart et al., 2016) to project design/development (Shirk et al., 2012), and even collaboration of the public in the scientific process, from hypothesis formation to evaluation (Haklay, 2013).

Coastal and marine restorations are multifaceted endeavors that require sustained efforts across multiple fronts over many years. Community engagement can be the key to project success. Early stage engagement for any restoration project includes baseline monitoring and mapping of existing habitat and associated resources. Roelfsema et al. (2016) demonstrate the extensive role that citizens have played in monitoring and mapping coral reef communities in Australia. Frey and Berkes (2014) provide a case study of how engagement of a fishing community paved the way for coral reef restoration in Bali.

From our work in marine conservation in Frenchman Bay, Maine, USA, over the last decade, we recognize the importance of including community members in early-stage monitoring and planning as well as examining impacts of unsustainable fishing practices on marine habitats. In our case, the focus was on eelgrass restoration; citizen engagement continued through restoration project implementation and evaluation.

Our conservation goals include restoring historic eelgrass areas (important habitat for juvenile fishes and invertebrates of all life stages) and maintaining good water quality in upper Frenchman Bay. Specifically, we hope to return to 1996 eelgrass levels where possible. Over the last decade, we have successfully engaged citizen scientists in all aspects of eelgrass habitat restoration and evaluation all along the contractual-collegial participation spectrum.

In this chapter, we identify citizen science engagement patterns in our eelgrass restoration work, for example, scenarios of citizen participation in restoration that include initiation, orientation, implementation, and opportunity for re-engagement and/or application of knowledge through future project planning and development. We extend existing models of public participation in scientific research (Shirk et al., 2012) to describe a continuum of engagement and autonomy in goal setting for citizen scientists that will help inform intentional frameworks for marine restoration project development in the future.

In parallel with the citizen science work, we describe a restoration project cycle (providing multiple entry points for citizen participation) and identify an additional level of engagement, which we call *citizen-created contextual projects*, as some individual citizen scientists have envisioned and initiated their own projects within the context of our eelgrass restoration work. Finally, we build on the discussion of citizen scientist participation in habitat restoration by reflecting on the evolving role of citizen scientists in our own restoration initiatives. In doing so, we provide a model for developing and managing successful and sustainable engagement of citizen scientists within the life cycle of marine habitat restoration projects.

## Restoration ecology and citizen science

Citizen science can be an effective tool to accomplish conservation goals because it has the potential to integrate public outreach and research at local, regional, and geographic scales (Cooper et al., 2007). The engagement of citizens increases the probability of sustaining projects over the long term, in part because their in-kind contributions lower the costs of restoration (Bayraktarov et al., 2015; Huddart et al., 2016), and because they can fill gaps in data collection such as evaluation of restoration outcomes (Huddart et al., 2016). Coastal and marine citizen science projects based in habitat restoration range from assisting in *passive restoration* (removing the environmental stressor that prevents the natural recovery of an ecosystem) to assisting in *active restoration* (habitat is restored using techniques such as transplanting or planting of seedlings; Davis et al., 2009; Perrow and Davy, 2002; Short et al., 2002). Within the context of either of these kinds of restoration, citizen science can provide important pre-project baseline and post-project evaluation data to track the recovery of the habitat and any target species of concern. For example, citizen scientists assessed molluscan community recovery after the partial tidal restoration of an estuary (Thelen and Thiet, 2009) and aided mangrove restoration work in Kenya by planting seedlings and assisting in long-term monitoring of the recovery (Chapter 3).

## Eelgrass restoration and citizen science

Since 2007, we have worked with diverse groups of community partners and stake-holders, engaging them in a variety of ways, including citizen science projects, in order to restore eelgrass to its former coverage, as part of the Community Environmental Health Laboratory at MDI Biological Laboratory in Bar Harbor, Maine. Our leadership team includes staff scientists, AmeriCorps members, project partners from other non-profit institutions, and undergraduate and high school research fellows affiliated with the projects and programs of the Community Environmental Health Laboratory. Together we engage community members, including teachers and students, participants in summer camps and related programs, and individual community members of many ages in restoration and pre- and post-restoration monitoring and evaluation efforts.

One of our primary research and restoration areas is at Hadley Point in upper Frenchman Bay (Figure 8.1). We based our site selection decision on conservation

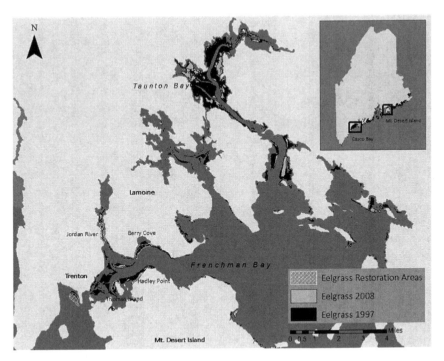

**FIGURE 8.1** Eelgrass in Frenchman Bay and along the coast of Maine 1996–2008. Restoration sites in upper Frenchman Bay are outlined.

*Source:* Jane E. Disney.

goals as well as on practical concerns: this site, like other places in the bay, has experienced a significant decline in eelgrass coverage since 1996. Unlike other sites, however, Hadley Point is accessible by foot at low tide, making it ideal for involving citizen scientists of all ages and abilities in all aspects of eelgrass restoration.

As with any habitat restoration project, eelgrass restoration involves much pre-planning and community engagement. Before initiating eelgrass restoration, we conduct a thorough suitability assessment of potential restoration sites. This typically involves mapping existing eelgrass, assessing water quality, and in some cases analyzing sediment composition. Equally important is the process of engaging local stakeholders and developing formal or informal conservation agreements (for example, we have an agreement with local mussel harvesters who voluntarily relinquish their right to drag in eelgrass restoration areas). In Maine, coastal restoration projects require permitting from both the Army Corps of Engineers and the Department of Environmental Protection, as well as official "Timing of Restoration" approval from the Department of Marine Resources. Finally, there is the actual work of restoration: designing methods, harvesting plants or collecting seeds, transferring plants or seeds to restoration sites, and monitoring restoration success over time.

Ecological restoration is a process, not an event. It may take many years to accomplish restoration goals, and work plans may undergo changes within that time frame. We find that often, projects form within projects over the lifetime of a coastal restoration endeavor. This creates numerous points of entry and opportunities for citizen engagement. Citizen science within the context of a restoration project does not have to be restricted to data collection; we find that the line is blurred between those who might be considered volunteers or environmental stewards in other project contexts and those who we consider to be citizen scientists. Often, the process of restoration draws project volunteers deep into the methodology and the scientific process as a whole, whether they are involved in early stages or later stages of what we are calling the Citizen Science Restoration Project Cycle (Figure 8.2), and across the range of "contributory, collaborative, and co-created" projects as defined by Shirk et al. (2012). There are many entry points into this cycle; the point of entry may define a citizen's participation as "contributory," "collaborative," or "co-created" (see discussion in Chapter 1).

Through the questions that project participants ask or suggestions that they make, they have the potential to actively shape conservation-based research. Thus, we generally consider everyone involved in our restoration projects to be citizen scientists. In the case of eelgrass restoration in Maine, those points of engagement have evolved over time and crystallized into what we define as the Citizen Science Eelgrass Restoration Project Cycle (Figure 8.3). This model has applications to other coastal and marine restoration projects around the world by expanding the role of citizen scientists and providing multiple and repeated entry points for public engagement in the restoration process.

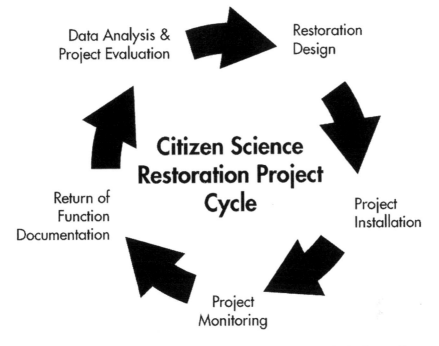

**FIGURE 8.2** A generalized Citizen Science Restoration Project Cycle that applies to any restoration project on land or in aquatic (estuarine or marine) contexts.

**FIGURE 8.3** Eelgrass Restoration-Specific Citizen Science Project Cycle. All of the listed activities can by conducted by citizens, in contributory, collaborative, co-created, or citizen-created contexts.

Our goals in engaging citizen scientists in eelgrass restoration efforts in upper Frenchman Bay are threefold:

**Goal 1:** *Restore a sufficient area of eelgrass to function as nursery and habitat for species that historically thrived in Frenchman Bay.* With the help of citizen scientists, develop and test new methodologies for restoration work, collect data on new and existing restoration sites, and compare data across time and distance to look for indications of success.

**Goal 2:** *Sustain or improve water quality in upper Frenchman Bay to the benefit of all estuarine and marine species.* Involve citizen scientists in gathering baseline data on water quality in proposed restoration sites, as well as in ongoing water quality monitoring in restored areas.

**Goal 3:** *Raise awareness about the importance of eelgrass habitat in order to help conserve it for the future health of Frenchman Bay.* Use eelgrass restoration as a meaningful way to connect environmental education and citizen science with conservation. This eelgrass conservation narrative can provide context for science and environmental curricula, bay management initiatives, and other coastal and marine restoration endeavors.

## The importance of eelgrass

Eelgrass (*Zostera marina*) is a unique flowering plant, occurring in widespread meadows in subtidal zones along the coast of Maine. Eelgrass oxygenates both the water surrounding it and the mud in which it is rooted, and draws nutrients from the water column, thus improving water quality. Its roots stabilize bottom sediments, preventing erosion and contributing to water clarity. Eelgrass serves as a substrate for the growth of organisms, such as epiphytic algae and epizootics (anemones, sponges, and bryozoans), which are themselves consumed by larger organisms (Hemminga and Duarte, 2000). Eelgrass is an effective carbon sink, helping to offset climate change impacts (Nellemann et al., 2009). In addition, eelgrass beds function as nursery habitat for many larger fishes such as winter flounder, striped bass, and Atlantic cod (Gotceitas et al., 1997), and serve as a settling site for invertebrates, including juvenile blue mussels (Newell et al., 2010; Disney et al., 2011). Eelgrass beds may be the single most important key to the sustainability of fisheries in Maine; they enhance local populations of mussel, lobster (Short et al., 2001), and forage fish, such as herring, eels, and alewives, that serve as prey for larger fishes (Hughes et al., 2002).

## Threats to eelgrass

Although eelgrass plays a crucial role in the ecology of coastal areas throughout temperate regions of the world, it has experienced recent declines. Our Frenchman Bay study areas are no exception (Figure 8.1). Frenchman Bay had 3,174 acres of eelgrass in 1996. By 2008, there were 1,076 acres left, a net loss of 66% (determined using geographic information systems [GIS] maps prepared by Seth Barker, Maine

Department of Marine Resources). In other areas of the world, eutrophication has played a major role in eelgrass decline (Ralph et al., 2006). However, Frenchman Bay has excellent water quality; eutrophication does not explain the loss of eelgrass habitat over the last two decades.

One contributor to eelgrass loss in Frenchman Bay has been the destruction caused by commercial mussel dragging. Mussels often inhabit the same low inter-tidal and subtidal areas as eelgrass. In the summer of 2005, there was an unusually prolonged and widespread occurrence of the *Alexandrium* algae responsible for "red tide" throughout Maine coastal waters, except for Frenchman Bay. As a result, the Maine Department of Marine Resources closed most of the Maine coastline to the harvesting of shellfish, leaving Frenchman Bay open and vulnerable to overharvesting of shellfish. For many weeks, numerous mussel-dragging boats from areas around the state came to Frenchman Bay and extensively dragged for mussels. Based on stud-ies of the impact of mussel dragging on eelgrass beds (Neckles et al., 2005) and our knowledge of the intense harvest of mussels within Frenchman Bay during the 2005 red tide event, we infer that legal but unsustainable harvesting practices may have contributed to initial eelgrass disruption in Frenchman Bay. In recent years, mussel harvesters have refrained from dragging in eelgrass beds, but eelgrass has continued to decline in some areas. This may be attributable to increases in invasive European green crab populations (Neckles, 2015). Green crab census work by citizen scientists in the Frenchman Bay area has shown an increase in crab populations in recent years.

## Contexts and opportunities for citizen participation in eelgrass restoration

Our understanding of the Citizen Science Eelgrass Restoration Project Cycle (Fig-ure 8.3) has changed as we have repeatedly engaged with citizen scientists in the context of local projects. Over the last decade, citizen scientists from middle school children through adults have contributed to eelgrass restoration efforts in different and meaningful ways. These include:

- Assessing sediment characteristics to make predictions about best sites for restoration
- Designing and testing restoration project methods
- Documenting project success by assessing the habitat function in restored areas
- Mapping eelgrass spread from restored patches
- Contributing to an online project at Anecdata.org called "Eelgrass in Maine"[1] to document the extent of the loss in Frenchman Bay and along the coast of Maine.

Some of these endeavors were initiated by citizen scientists and were not originally envisioned as part of the research projects designed by members of our scientific leadership team. For example, an earth science teacher who had formerly worked as a geologist for an environmental consulting firm was curious about sediment com-position in eelgrass restoration areas and engaged students in performing sediment analyses over two summers. They found natural sediment composition differences between sites that may have influenced eelgrass restoration success at those sites. However, transplantation methods also make a difference in project success; some methods are more successful and scalable in some areas than others (often due to current strength, wind direction, or water depth). As another example, the parent of a student volunteer recognized the challenges in scalability of restoration efforts using wooden biodegradable grids and suggested that ceramic engineering students at her university might be able to design a way to weight plants without frames. Alfred University students invented a small ceramic disk, which has turned out to be superior to grids in multiple ways, turning deployment into an easily scalable and more mobile process. These two examples, discussed in detail below, serve as documentation of an additional category of PPSR projects, which we call citizen-created contextual projects.

## Citizen-created contextual projects

Citizen-created contextual projects *achieve an independent goal, set by citizen scientists themselves, to help achieve the larger goal established by scientists, or in our case, our project leadership team.* While similar to co-created citizen science projects (Bonney et al., 2009), and extreme citizen science (Haklay, 2013), *contextual projects* are projects within projects, created by citizen scientists, and related to, embedded within, or expanding from a larger scientist-driven project. They may not be wholly independent, but use the resources and expertise of the original scientist-driven project as a foundation to create a new citizen-driven research project. This was an unanticipated result of engaging citizen scientists in restoration projects; however, these contextual projects have become instrumental in moving the entire eelgrass restoration initiative forward in Maine. Unlike the various citizen science typologies described by Wiggins and Crowston (2011), but similar to Haklay (2013) and Shirk et al. (2012), citizen-created contextual projects embrace more fully the entire scientific process, rather than a piece of it (such as observation, monitoring, or data recording). In a true contextual project, citizen scientists *ask the research questions* and *develop the experimental design* within existing restoration work. In our experience, citizen scientists creating projects in this capacity have some level of expertise, often in a different discipline (geology, in the case of the teacher who spearheaded analyses of sediments; ceramic engineering, in the case of undergraduates who designed a new method of eelgrass restoration using ceramic disks). Interdisciplinary approaches to problem solving can arise when broad participation in citizen science endeavors is encouraged and citizen input is invited.

Dillon et al. (2016) adapted previously published models to provide an overview of different possible configurations of citizen science. Their heuristic model has two axes: a horizontal (participation) axis, representative of the continuum of citizen participation in science initiatives; and a vertical (goal) axis, representative of the range of possibilities for citizen involvement in setting goals and objectives in science initiatives. In their model, the resulting quadrants correspond to a particular category or type of citizen science. To illustrate the range of citizen participation in

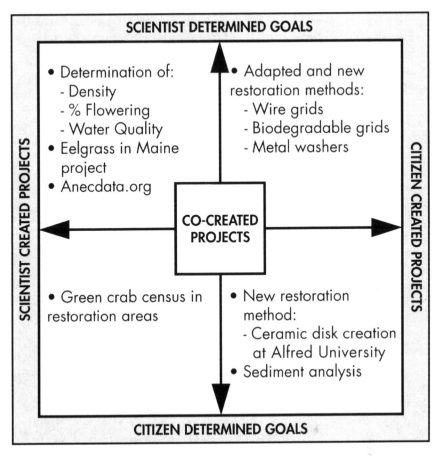

**SCIENTIST DETERMINED GOALS**

**SCIENTIST CREATED PROJECTS**

**CITIZEN CREATED PROJECTS**

- Determination of:
  - Density
  - % Flowering
  - Water Quality
- Eelgrass in Maine project
- Anecdata.org

- Adapted and new restoration methods:
  - Wire grids
  - Biodegradable grids
  - Metal washers

**CO-CREATED PROJECTS**

- Green crab census in restoration areas

- New restoration method:
  - Ceramic disk creation at Alfred University
- Sediment analysis

**CITIZEN DETERMINED GOALS**

**FIGURE 8.4** Citizen science engagement model for eelgrass. This model depicts a continuum of participation on the horizontal access and a continuum of engagement in goal setting on the vertical axis. Projects within the over-arching eelgrass restoration project are listed in the four quadrants. (Adapted from Dillon et al., 2016.)

eelgrass restoration-related activities and the depth of citizen engagement in setting goals within those activities, we extend the model of Dillon et al. (2016) to capture our own experience with citizen participation in restoration. In our model, we represent with the horizontal axis the range from scientist-created projects to citizen-created contextual projects. We provide examples within the resulting quadrants of our extended model (Figure 8.4).

## Methods of eelgrass restoration invite different levels of citizen participation

In the early years of eelgrass restoration in Frenchman Bay, we adapted a method developed by Fred Short at the University of New Hampshire called TERFS

(Transplanting Eelgrass using Remote Frame Systems) (Short et al., 2002). Our method involved using 0.186 m² wire grids made of heavy gauge lobster-trap material, with two bricks wired to each side for weight as a means for transplanting eelgrass shoots. Individual plants were tied to these weighted grids with biodegradable twist ties made of floral tape; then grids loaded with plants were deployed in our study site off of Hadley Point in Frenchman Bay (Figure 8.1). We transplanted 36.4 m² of eelgrass over 14 acres in 2007 and 2008; by 2009, this had expanded to 537.5 m², a nearly 15-fold increase (Disney and Kidder, 2010).

Citizen scientists in our projects (students, parents, teachers, and citizens of all ages from the local community), were involved in every stage of the process: harvesting (Figure 8.5a) and tying eelgrass to grids (Figure 8.5b), conducting underwater videography, and assessing percent coverage by calculating the percentage of time that eelgrass appeared in the recording. To evaluate restoration success, citizen scientists donned wetsuits and traversed the eelgrass area at low tide, measuring the perimeter of each eelgrass patch with meter sticks and recording patch location using handheld GPS units. Despite the intense nature of the work, the role of citizen scientists in these early years of restoration was mostly "contributory."

During the summer of 2009, after a few field seasons to familiarize ourselves with transplantation work, we continued to involve citizen scientists in restoration

FIGURE 8.5A   Harvesting eelgrass.

*Source:* Jane E. Disney.

**FIGURE 8.5B**   Tying eelgrass to biodegradable grids.

*Source:* Jane E. Disney.

assessment and monitoring at Hadley Point. While still using our modified TERFS method, we began experimenting with the efficacy of other methods (Kidder et al., 2015). This experimentation became more formalized with the help of citizen scientists, who took on a direct role in assisting with assessment of the relative success of these methodological experiments and helped us determine best restoration methods for use in Maine.

By 2011, we had transplanted 73.6 m² of eelgrass at Hadley Point using a variety of methods, including the substitution of biodegradable grids for the wire frames. Our uniquely designed biodegradable grids were composed of a wooden frame with loose sisal twine or burlap mesh, weighted with sandbags at each corner (Figure 8.5b). Community volunteers and students worked with us at the shoreline to tie plants to the sisal twine or weave plants into the burlap mesh. The only real drawback we experienced with biodegradable grids was the amount of time and labor required for fabrication. These grids were a great solution for small-scale projects, but we needed a solution for larger-scale restoration efforts.

Because it was so labor-intensive to construct the biodegradable grids, we invited our cadre of citizen scientists to think of other methods. Students in one of our "Young Environmental Leaders" programs focused on engaging youth in and out of schools in eelgrass restoration science, suggested that we forgo the frames and just tie sandbag weights to long burlap strips. Students tried this novel method, harvesting eelgrass and weaving it in and out of the burlap strips as they had with burlap on frames. They tested their "restoration runners" by rolling them out in the subtidal area alongside biodegradable grids. Some of the students returned to the study site at a later date to document which method fared better. The students discovered that the restoration runners worked well in areas protected from strong currents, but the weighted grids worked better in areas with strong currents, onshore winds, and potential disruption by other bay activities.

Hearing about the use of metal washers to weight plants in Canada, some students suggested we try washers as a way to accomplish restoration goals. Reluctant to deposit thousands of metal washers in the ocean, other students suggested tying eelgrass to stones as weights. We challenged students to find irregularly shaped rocks to which eelgrass could be tied without the ties slipping off the rocks. The students helped to harvest eelgrass, tie it on rocks with floral tape, and toss from a boat to the ocean bottom. In testing their delivery method, students found that most plants slipped out from under the floral tape as the rocks hit the water.

These students were all involved in co-creating new methods with us and then testing their hypotheses by assessing and revising these methods. By providing opportunity for input from students, our Frenchman Bay eelgrass restoration swiftly evolved from a strictly contributory model of citizen engagement to a fully collaborative one with citizen input and evaluation.

It was difficult to find enough well-shaped rocks to accomplish large-scale restoration, so we discussed getting high school or adult education students enrolled in pottery classes to create ceramic washers for eelgrass restoration. A parent of one of our Young Environmental Leaders suggested that ceramic engineering students at Alfred University, where she worked, might be able to design an effective ceramic washer. When presented with this challenge, ceramic engineering students designed a 7-inch ceramic disk perforated with five to seven holes. The intent was to have citizens tie eelgrass to the holes; however, we later discovered that we could weave the plants through the holes as we had with burlap (Figure 8.6a, 8.6b). The students tested various prototypes before deciding on a model to manufacture for our use. Representatives from the ceramic engineering department traveled to Maine to participate in implementation and assessment of this new method of eelgrass restoration. At this point, we saw our eelgrass restoration project evolve into a truly citizen-created model, as others were envisioning new methods of restoration, and creating and testing them.

We worked with citizen scientists over two summers to test the ceramic disks under varying conditions, and discovered that disks are superior to biodegradable grids for restoring eelgrass. In a comparison study, we documented a 2.5-fold increase in the number of plants on and around biodegradable grids, but a 4.8-fold increase in the number of plants on and around ceramic restoration disks.

**FIGURE 8.6A** Weaving eelgrass into ceramic disks.

*Source:* Jane E. Disney.

Ceramic Disk

**FIGURE 8.6B** Disks with eelgrass ready for transplanting.

*Source:* Jane E. Disney.

## Citizen engagement scenarios

The eelgrass restoration projects described earlier unfolded under a variety of volunteer engagement scenarios (Table 8.1). There are four phases that all of our citizen engagement scenarios have in common regardless of the entry point of citizen scientists into the project cycle (Figure 8.3):

*Initiation*: Recruitment "kick-starts" engagement. This recruitment can be scientist-driven or more organic, inspired by community members or citizen scientists already engaged in the work of restoration. Recruitment often takes the form of outreach from our laboratory to local schools or community groups, citizen inquiries about the project from within or outside of the community, or a grant opportunity that allows expansion of restoration and testing of new methods.

*Orientation*: Citizen scientists learn the details of our local conservation backstory: why eelgrass is important in Frenchman Bay, how this valuable resource was lost, how they can be involved in restoration, and what difference it will make.

*Implementation*: Citizen scientists enter the eelgrass restoration project cycle, which involves restoration activities, monitoring or research activities. They help with designing and/or constructing grids, harvesting eelgrass, tying eelgrass to grids or weaving into disks in preparation for deployment, helping to deploy the grids/disks, following up on transplantation success by measuring eelgrass density, documenting return of habitat function, and/or mapping restored eelgrass.

*Re-engagement and/or Application of Knowledge*: Depending on where volunteers entered the project cycle, they may re-engage with the project at a later stage. This is encouraged for various reasons. For example, those who constructed the grids know the rationale behind the design of the grids. It is more intuitive for these volunteers to tie eelgrass to the grids than those who have no familiarity with the grids. These citizen scientists become educators and mentors, helping new project participants understand the rationale for handling the plants and grids in particular ways. Those who re-engage or enter the project cycle "late in the game," for example documenting plant density or mapping eelgrass in restoration areas, may be ready to apply knowledge about restoration success to advocacy for eelgrass protection, or participate in data sharing to monitor eelgrass in Maine.

*Scenario 1. School-Based Citizen Science*: We reached out to local high school teachers to seek help in construction of wooden biodegradable grids. An AP science teacher decided to undertake construction of the wooden frames as a final project for the school year. The students participated in a restoration project at the end of the school year, re-engaging at the next phase of restoration by tying eelgrass to grids. Some of these students returned in a subsequent year to help measure eelgrass spread and map restoration areas.

**TABLE 8.1** Scenarios for eelgrass restoration. These represent the types of scenarios in which eelgrass restoration projects were implemented. All scenarios have the stages of initiation, orientation, implementation, and potential for re-engagement or application in common.

| Project Stage | Scenario 1 | Scenario 2 | Scenario 3 | Scenario 4 | Scenario 5 |
|---|---|---|---|---|---|
| Initiation | High School AP science teachers were asked if their students could participate in construction of wooden biodegradable grids. | EPA Environmental Education grant-funded middle school project "Seagrasses in Classes" was launched in four schools. | Camp directors sought opportunities for campers to contribute to environmental efforts in local communities. | EPA Environmental Education grant-funded high school teacher–student research teams adopted restoration sites in Frenchman Bay. | Established "Eelgrass in Maine" as a project on Anecdata.org to collect observations of eelgrass presence and absence. |
| Orientation | Students received an introduction to eelgrass basics and issues surrounding eelgrass loss as an in-class presentation. | Middle school students learned how to care for eelgrass tanks. Their teachers nominated some of them for our "Young Environmental Leaders" program. | Campers received an orientation to eelgrass issues and presentation on basics of eelgrass. | Teacher–student research teams returned over multiple summers; documenting eelgrass density, mapping eelgrass, characterizing sediments, monitoring water quality. | Put out press releases to inform the public about the project and solicit input. |

(*Continued*)

**TABLE 8.1** (Continued)

| Project Stage | Scenario 1 | Scenario 2 | Scenario 3 | Scenario 4 | Scenario 5 |
|---|---|---|---|---|---|
| Implementation | Students devoted weeks after the completion of their AP exams to grid construction. They worked with students from a woodworking class who had suggestions for easier construction of the grids. | Young Environmental Leaders participated in grid construction, re-design, eelgrass harvest, restoration, post-restoration eelgrass and water quality monitoring. | Campers arrived on the beach on the day of restoration and helped to tie plants to grids. Some campers had wetsuits and helped to deploy grids in the ocean as well. | Teacher-student research teams honed field research, data analysis, GIS mapping, and laboratory research skills. | Collected input from citizens around Maine to help understand where and why eelgrass is disappearing. |
| Re-engagement and/or Application | Students participated in a restoration event, tying eelgrass to grids on the shore. | Students asked if they could return in year 2 and beyond. "Advanced Young Environmental Leaders" visited eelgrass restoration sites to document plant density and spread over many years. | Some camps returned the following day to document restoration project status. Some returned in subsequent years to document project success in terms of plant density and spread. | Teacher-student research teams brought expertise back to high schools; inspired new teachers and students to participate in subsequent years; translated skills to classrooms. | Hosted a biennial meeting of eelgrass researchers and stakeholders to share data and identify next steps for addressing eelgrass loss. |

*Scenario 2. Out of School–Based Citizen Science:* We were awarded an EPA Environmental Education Grant to develop an outreach program for middle schools called "Seagrasses in Classes" (NE-961063-961001). The program involved visiting classrooms and discussing the importance of eelgrass habitat; helping students set up eelgrass aquaria in classrooms or school yards; and teaching students how to monitor water quality, measure eelgrass growth, and document food webs in eelgrass habitat. Teachers nominated interested students to participate in our weeklong summer Young Environmental Leaders (YELP) program. These students entered the "Citizen Science Project Cycle" at this point. During the program week, students participated in a restoration project from beginning to end. The YELP program inspired an Advanced Young Environmental Leaders program to accommodate students' persistent interest in eelgrass restoration (Disney and Crossman-Turner, 2014). Some of these students returned in subsequent years and volunteered in various aspects of the program, including harvesting plants, restoring plants, re-designing restoration methods, and monitoring restoration sites.

*Scenario 3: Summer Camp–Based Citizen Science:* Various summer camp groups have participated in eelgrass restoration over the past decade. Most have been involved in tying eelgrass to grids on the shore. Some have joined us for eelgrass harvesting. Some have stayed after the restoration project was over, taking advantage of the next day low tide, to collect critical baseline data on the newly deployed grids, or to determine plant density in former eelgrass restoration sites, thus furthering long-term restoration monitoring work. One group, Sustainable Ocean Studies, a joint program of Chewonki Foundation and Waynflete School for 10th, 11th, and 12th graders, has returned over multiple years and has participated at every stage of the Eelgrass Restoration Project Cycle.

*Scenario 4: Summer Teacher-Student Research Teams as Citizen Scientists:* We were awarded an Environmental Education Grant (NE-961528-961501) to follow up on Seagrasses in Classes and bring inland teachers to the coast. These teachers, from six different schools in Maine, spent a week in our lab as interns, learning firsthand how to plan and implement environmental stewardship projects. Some of them wanted to return with students. In subsequent years, teachers and students from Waterville High School returned and participated in restoration, follow-up monitoring of plant density and mapping in restoration areas, water quality monitoring, and invasive green crab surveys. Teachers and students from Bangor High School did the same, and added their own sediment composition project to the suite of restoration-related activities. The teacher-student teams were able to engage in all aspects of the Citizen Science Project Cycle in their week at the laboratory, and spanned the continuum of contributory, collaborative, co-created, and citizen-created contextual engagement.

*Scenario 5: Crowdsourcing Information on Eelgrass in Maine:* In spring 2013, we noticed that eelgrass was completely missing from upper Frenchman Bay. We created a web portal called "Eelgrass in Maine" that, unlike other citizen science websites available at the time, allowed users to note where eelgrass was absent, as well as present. We sent the link to the "Eelgrass in Maine" website to everyone we knew who was studying eelgrass along Maine's coast. We put out press releases in local papers and contacted summer camps and environmental programs. The presence of eelgrass was reported for 46 locations; eelgrass loss was reported for 13 locations, most of them in Frenchman Bay. With input from all of these sources, 59 reports in all, we were able to determine that there was extensive eelgrass loss in some areas of Casco Bay and throughout upper Frenchman Bay and Taunton Bay (Figure 8.1), but that eelgrass was not lost everywhere. Eelgrass loss seemed to be restricted to upper bay areas. More exposed areas of the outer coast and coastal islands appeared to be largely unaffected (Bailey et al., 2014). We later transformed "Eelgrass in Maine" into Anecdata.org, a free, full-fledged citizen science platform supporting a wide range of data for similar environmental crowd-sourcing efforts, including numerous coastal and marine projects.

These five scenarios (Table 8.1) show that participant groups are diverse and varied and there are multiple ways for citizen scientists to engage with coastal restoration projects. Coastal restoration requires a long-term commitment by scientists and citizen scientists alike. By engaging diverse groups, being open about the point of entry for project participants, and recognizing that people have different capacities at different times to fully engage in a project, we ensure that projects can be sustained until restoration goals have been achieved.

## Models of training and data quality assurance

*Training*: Citizen scientists are trained in various ways, depending on the participant group and the length of time for engagement in restoration work. Training is often task-specific, but no matter where citizen scientists enter the Eelgrass Restoration Project Cycle (Figure 8.3), they all receive an introduction to eelgrass, its role as habitat, and our local conservation history. We give a mini-lecture, providing them with a quick overview of the anatomy of eelgrass, potential threats, possible reasons for loss, history of our restoration efforts, and examples of local restoration success.

School groups often receive a more involved presentation in class. When possible, eelgrass plants are brought into the classroom for exploration by students. Students identify the plant parts (root, shoot, rhizome, meristem, spathe) and use microscopes to look for small marine invertebrates. For summer camps or visiting groups, our Web pages have information and links to reports that groups can use to orient themselves before arriving. When possible, we make a presentation to these groups when they arrive, before making grids or embarking on a field trip to, for example, restore eelgrass or measure plant density in restored or comparison eelgrass areas.

*Data Quality Assurance/Quality Control Procedures*: Unlike some citizen science programs, individuals and groups engaged in eelgrass restoration do not work independently; someone from our laboratory group always accompanies them. The oversight of an experienced eelgrass researcher ensures that citizens collect quality data. We have created explicit field sheets for plant density and water quality studies that ensure that citizens collect consistent data. Additionally, citizen scientists who participate in data entry or data analysis have their work checked by another volunteer or staff member from our laboratory.

## Achieving conservation, education, and community engagement goals

*Achieving Conservation Goals:* By working with citizen scientists, we are making progress in restoring historic eelgrass beds. We have documented that plants in restored areas produce flowers and distribute seeds beyond our restoration sites. Our most recent mapping studies reveal that eelgrass is returning to historic levels in two of the four sites we monitor in upper Frenchman Bay. At Hadley Point, where there are 12 acres along a 1.6 km stretch of shoreline inside of a bottom mussel aquaculture site, eelgrass is fully restored (Figure 8.7). Other sites, for example, at Thomas Island (Figure 8.1), present challenges due to sediment changes and human activities on the bay.

The area around Thomas Island previously had extensive eelgrass beds along the shoreline. In all of our attempts to restore eelgrass, the grids sank into the substrate

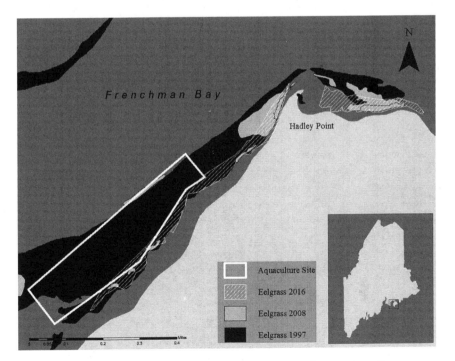

**FIGURE 8.7**    Eelgrass return to Hadley Point after 10 years of restoration efforts.

and plants became buried in sediment over time. As mentioned earlier, a teacher-student citizen science team from Bangor High School spent two summers doing sieve analyses of sediments in historic eelgrass areas in order to develop a predictive model for eelgrass restoration success. They found that areas where eelgrass restoration was least successful had the highest percentage of silt/clay in sediments. For example, Hadley Point, where eelgrass restoration has been successful, has an average of 45% silt/clay, whereas Thomas Island, where eelgrass restoration was not successful, has an average of 77% silt/clay. The high school team repeated this comparison study in a second year at the same sites, which confirmed the earlier result. Sediments have probably changed since the time when eelgrass last grew around Thomas Island, making achieving conservation goals in this area impossible.

We have chosen transparency as a metric for water quality, as good water clarity is characteristic of clean water and transparency is a metric easily measured by citizen scientists. Eelgrass can help to maintain good water quality by absorbing nutrients that might otherwise lead to algal blooms and stabilizing bottom sediments in near-shore areas. Based on historic water quality data, we have set a goal of maintaining a transparency of 3–4 m throughout the upper bay. The most recent upper bay transparency average, based on four monthly measurements at eight different sites using a Secchi disk methodology, is 3.32 m, hence our efforts at maintaining water quality through eelgrass restoration appear to be successful thus far.

*Achieving Education Goals:* We have educated a cohort of students from local middle schools and high schools. Eleven schools and 605 students have been involved over the last decade. As we discovered with our Young Environmental Leaders program, students who learn about the importance of seagrasses in school are likely to volunteer outside of school for restoration projects. We know that some of these students have gone on to college to major in marine biology, engineering, and other STEM majors. We engaged many undergraduate interns and AmeriCorps Environmental Stewards in both eelgrass restoration projects and in working with the Seagrasses in Classes and/or the Young Environmental Leaders program. Some undergraduates and AmeriCorps Stewards have gone on to graduate studies in coastal restoration, marine microbiology, environmental economics, sustainable aquaculture, and science education.

*Achieving Community Development Goals:* Our eelgrass restoration project has been the impetus for stakeholder engagement around additional conservation goals. In 2011, we engaged multiple community partners in a discussion of priority areas for eelgrass restoration. In doing so, we heard about other priorities around French-man Bay. After follow-up stakeholder meetings, we decided to create a formal coalition called Frenchman Bay Partners (hereinafter the Partners). The Partners used a Conservation Action Planning process to create a bay plan where we clarified our goals for eelgrass restoration and set goals for other conservation targets: mudflats, benthic habitats, diadromous fishes, and rockweed. The Partners have been actively involved in facilitating communication and participation among bay users over the last six years and launching projects to achieve goals laid out in the bay plan.

One of the pivotal discussions facilitated by the Partners was between mussel harvesters, bottom mussel aquaculture lease holders, and eelgrass researchers, all user groups with conflicting interests in the subtidal zone of the bay. During our discussion, we projected an ArcGIS map of Frenchman Bay on a screen and used a consensus process to identify eelgrass conservation areas. In all, 228 acres were designated as restoration areas or refugia. The map was printed, and signed by all. The resulting map is a Voluntary Conservation Agreement and has been instrumental in obtaining funding for community-based eelgrass restoration and education.

*Funding*: Funding has been key in achieving our conservation goals. Over a decade, our eelgrass restoration work has been funded from diverse sources including federal and private foundation science and education grants. Each grant project had specific restoration, education, and community engagement goals, but all served the ultimate goal of a healthy future for Frenchman Bay. Funding restoration, monitoring, and research has been challenging, but the partnerships that have grown out of the work have simultaneously helped push the work forward. These grant-funded projects included teachers, students, individual community members, shorefront property owners, non-profit partners, land trusts, local mussel harvesters, water dependent businesses, aquaculture leaseholders, municipal officials and committee members, representatives of government agencies, summer camps, school groups, and others.

*Final Analysis*: In Table 8.2, we present an overall picture of how many people of all kinds were engaged, what we accomplished, and total costs over a decade of

**TABLE 8.2** Eelgrass restoration by the numbers (2007–2016).

| Category | Restoration Facts | Numbers |
|---|---|---|
| Eelgrass | # of summers of restoration | 10 |
| | # of acres restored | 12.8 |
| | # of acres set aside as restoration areas | 228 |
| | # of acres set aside as "donor sites" | 39 |
| | # of tried methods | 9 |
| Funding | Funding for eelgrass-related work | $1,023,694 |
| | # of different funding sources | 22 |
| | % for eelgrass research and restoration | 44% |
| | % for eelgrass outreach and education | 40% |
| | % for building partnerships | 16% |
| People | # of full and part-time staff | 6 |
| | # of AmeriCorps terms of service (8 members) | 11 |
| | # of volunteers | 584 |
| | # of volunteer hours | 3,617 |
| | # of student interns | 30 |
| | # of teacher interns | 17 |
| | # of organizational partners | 48 |
| Education | # of schools involved | 11 |
| | # of students involved | 605 |

effort. It is clear that marine restoration requires a sustained effort by a large number of people and considerable financial resources.

## Conclusion

Given the nature of eelgrass restoration and the multiple points of entry for citizen scientists into related projects, there are ways for people of most ages, skill levels, and types of interest to become involved in the work of restoration and shape future projects and research methods. We offer here some parameters in planning ecological restoration projects with citizen scientists. In our experience, it is easiest to engage large numbers of people in constructing grids, harvesting plants, tying or weaving plants on grids with twine or burlap, or weaving plants into ceramic restoration disks. It is more difficult to engage a broad cross-section of people in deploying grids and disks in the water or collecting water quality data at the time of deployment, given the constraints of working in and on the water. The number of wet suits available or the number of people we can fit on the boat at one time limits participation. Likewise, when assessing restoration success, the participation of citizen scientists is constrained by wet suit and boat availability. To the extent possible, we rotate groups of citizen scientists out to restoration sites at low tide. There, they can participate in assessing plant density by tossing quadrats and counting shoots, or assessing water quality. As compared to some citizen projects in which individuals can participate at will, community-based eelgrass restoration works best with groups of people who can be oriented in the field and participate together with scientists, such as those described in the various scenarios. Despite these constraints, project participants as young as middle school age have the capacity to engage in more advanced collaborative and co-constructed levels, if given the opportunity. In our experience, students as young as high school age have the capacity to create novel projects within the larger context of eelgrass restoration.

We believe we have created a model of citizen engagement and methods of marine restoration for our region that can be transferrable to other places. To that end, we continue to share our methods with neighboring communities in a continued effort to restore eelgrass habitat and bring awareness to the community about the valuable resource just offshore, just out of sight, but providing critical marine ecosystem services such as clarifying the water, sequestering carbon, mitigating wave energy, preventing erosion, and providing habitat for diverse marine species.

## Acknowledgements

We acknowledge the collaborative efforts of a variety of organizations and individuals, including the Maine Coast Heritage Trust, College of the Atlantic, Lamoine Conservation Commission, Maine Coast Heritage Trust, and the Maine Mussel Harvesters Association. Funding came from National Fish and Wildlife Foundation, Maine Sea Grant, Alex C. Walker Foundation, The Long Cove Foundation, The Davis Conservation Fund, The Nature Conservancy, EPA Environmental

Education grants NE-961528–961501 and NE 961063–961001, the Manzanar Project, and private sources. We appreciate the leadership of undergraduate interns Casie Reed, Kavita Balkaran, Annie Evankow, Shira Bleicher, Megan May, Alden Dirks, Mary Badger, Hannah Mogensen, Lukas Thorburn, Kat Gillies-Rector, and Bernice O'Brien (supported by NSF REU DBI-1005003); high school interns Ellen Daily and Eli Peirce (supported by NIEHS STEER R25-ES5016254), Megan Hooper, Ming Feng Schnorr, and Leah Berry-Sandelin; undergraduate Dakota Holmes (supported by the James Slater Murphy, MD Fund); and teachers and students from Waterville High School, James F. Doughty School in Bangor, and Bangor High School (supported in part by COSEE-OS NSF OCE-1038786 and Maine Community Foundation), Ariel Durrant, Molly Miller, Shannon White, and Jirias Charabati (AmeriCorps environmental stewards), and Dr. George Kidder III.

## Note

1 Find and contribute citizen science data to the "Eelgrass in Maine" project at www.anecdata.org/projects/view/eelgrass-in-maine.

## Literature cited

Bailey, D., Bailey, J., Kidder, G.W., and Disney, J.E. (2014). A citizen science approach to mapping eelgrass (*Zostera marina* L.) loss in Maine. *Bulletin Mt. Desert Island Biological Laboratory*, 53, 25.

Bayraktarov, E., Saunders, M., Abdullah, S., Mills, M., Beher, J., Possingham, H., Mumby, P., and Lovelock, C. (2015). The cost and feasibility of marine coastal restoration. *Ecological Applications*, 26(4), 1055–1074.

Bonney, R., Ballard, H., Jordan, R., McCallie, E., Phillips, T., Shirk, J., and Wilderman, C.C. (2009). *Public participation in scientific research: Defining the field and assessing its potential for informal science education*. A CAISE Inquiry Group Report. Washington, DC: Center for Advancement of Informal Science Education (CAISE).

Cooper, C., Dickinson, J., Phillips, T., and Bonney, R. (2007). Citizen science as a tool for conservation in residential ecosystems. *Ecology and Society*, 12(2), 11. [Online] www.ecologyandsociety.org/vol12/iss2/art11/.

Davis, R.C., and Short, F.T. (1997). Restoring eelgrass, *Zostera marina*, habitat using a new transplanting technique: The horizontal rhizome method. *Aquatic Botany*, 59(1), 1–15.

Dillon, J., Stevenson, R.B., and Wals, A.E.J. (2016). Introduction to the special section: Moving from citizen to civic science to address wicked conservation problems. Corrected by erratum 12844. *Conservation Biology*, 30, 450–455. doi:10.1111/cobi.12689.

Disney, J.E., and Crossman-Turner, T. (2014). Young environmental leaders: Building environmental stewardship skills and self-confidence in students through eelgrass research and restoration. *Current: Journal of Marine Education*, 29(1), 22–30.

Disney, J.E., and Kidder, G.W. (2010). Community-based eelgrass (*Zostera marina*) restoration in Frenchman Bay. *Bulletin Mt. Desert Island Biological Laboratory*, 49, 108–109.

Disney, J.E., Kidder, G.W., Balkaran, K., Brestel, C., and Brestel, G. (2011). Blue mussel (*Mytilus edulis*) settlement on restored eelgrass (*Zostera marina*) is not related to proximity of eelgrass beds to a bottom mussel aquaculture lease site in Frenchman Bay. *Bulletin Mt. Desert Island Biological Laboratory*, 50, 80–82.

Frey, J.B., and Berkes, F. (2014). Can partnerships and community-based conservation reverse the decline of coral reef social-ecological systems? *International Journal of the Commons*, 8(1), 26–46. http://doi.org/10.18352/ijc.408.

Gotceitas, V., Fraser, S., and. Brown, J.A. (1997). Use of eelgrass beds (*Zostera marina*) by juvenile Atlantic cod (*Gadus morhua*). *Canadian Journal of Fisheries and Aquatic Sci*ences, 54, 1306–1319.

Haklay, M. (2013). Citizen science and volunteered geographic information – overview and typology of participation. In *Crowdsourcing Geographic Knowledge: Volunteered Geographic Information (VGI) in Theory and Practice*, ed. D.Z. Sui, S. Elwood, and M.F. Goodchild, 105–122. Berlin: Springer.

Hemminga, M.A., and Duarte, C.M. (2000). *Seagrass Ecology*. Cambridge: Cambridge University Press.

Huddart, J.E.A., Thompson, M.S.A., Woodward, G., and Brooks, S.J. (2016). Citizen science: From detecting pollution to evaluating ecological restoration. *WIREs Water*, 3, 287–300.

Hughes, J.E., Deegan, L.A., Wyda, J.C., Weaver, M.J., and Wright, A. (2002). Effects of eelgrass habitat loss on estuarine fish communities in Southern New England. *Estuaries*, 25, 235–249.

Kidder, G.W., Whit, S., Miller, M.F., Norden, W.S., Taylor, T., and Disney, J.E. (2015). Biodegradable grids: An effective method for community-based *Zostera marina* (Eelgrass) restoration in Maine. *Journal of Coastal Research*, 31(4), 900–906.

Neckles, H.A. (2015). Loss of eelgrass in Casco Bay, Maine, linked to Green Crab disturbance. *Northeastern Naturalist*, 22(3), 478–500.

Neckles, H.A., Short, F.T., Barker, S., and Kopp, S.B. (2005). Disturbance of eelgrass *Zostera marina* by commercial mussel *Mytilus edulis* harvesting in Maine: Dragging impacts and habitat recovery. *Marine Ecology Progress Series*, 285, 57–73.

Nellemann, C., Corcoran, E., Duarte, C.M.,Valdés, L., DeYoung, C., Fonseca, L., and Grimsditch, G. (Eds.). (2009). *Blue carbon: A rapid response assessment*. United Nations Environment Programme, GRID-Arendal. www.grida.no.

Newell, C.R., Short, F.T., Hoven, H., Healey, L., Panchang, V., and Cheng, G. (2010). The dispersal dynamics of juvenile plantigrade mussels (*Mytilus edulis*) from eelgrass (*Zostera marina*) meadows in Maine, USA. *Journal of. Experimental Marine Biology and Ecology*, 394, 45–52.

Perrow, M., and Davy, A. (Eds.). (2002). *Handbook of Ecological Restoration*. Cambridge: Cambridge University Press.

Ralph, P.J., Tomasko, D., Moore, K., Seddon, S., and Macinnis-Ng, C.M.O. (2006). Human impacts on seagrasses: Eutrophication, sedimentation, and contamination in seagrasses. In *Biology, Ecology and Conservation*, ed. A.W.D. Larkum et al., 567–593. Dordrecht, the Netherlands: Springer.

Roelfsema, C., Thurstan, R., Beger, M., Dudgeon, C., Loder, J., Kovacs, E., Gallo, M., Flower, J., Cabrera, K., Ortiz, J., Lea, A., and Kleine, D. (2016). A citizen science approach: A detailed ecological assessment of subtropical reefs at Point Lookout, Australia. *PLOS One*, 11(10), e0163407. https://doi.org/10.1371/journal.pone.0163407.

Shirk, J.L., Ballard, H.L., Wilderman, C.C., Phillips, T., Wiggins, A., Jordan, R., McCallie, E., Minarchek, M., Lewenstein, B.V., Krasny, M.E., and Bonney, R. (2012). Public participation in scientific research: A framework for deliberate design. *Ecology and Society*, 17(2), 29.

Short, F.T., Matso, K., Hoven, H.M.,Whitten, J., Burdick, D.M., and Short, C.A. (2001). Lobster use of eelgrass habitat in the Piscataqua River on the New Hampshire/Maine Border, USA. *Estuaries and Coasts*, 24(2), 277–284.

Short, F.T., Short, C.A., and Burdick-Whitney, C.L. (2002). *A manual for community-based eelgrass restoration*. Report to the NOAA Restoration Center, Jackson Estuarine Laboratory, University of New Hampshire, Durham, 1–54.

Thelen, B., and Thiet, R. (2009). Molluscan community recovery following partial tidal restoration of a New England estuary, USA. *Restoration Ecology*, 17(5), 695–703.

Wiggins, A., and Crowston, K. (2011). From conservation to crowdsourcing: A typology of citizen science. Paper presented at the *Hawaii International Conference on System Sciences* (HICSS), Kauai, HI, January 4–7.

# 9

# CITIZEN SCIENCE AND MARINE POLICY

*Bryony L. Townhill and Kieran Hyder*

## Introduction

Citizen science is one of the many terms used to describe the collaboration of professional scientists with amateurs for scientific projects, often involving conservation or environmental objectives (Miller-Rushing et al., 2012). Citizen scientists have been recording scientific information for centuries (Silvertown, 2009), and more formally participating in research and monitoring programs since at least the 1950s, with bird surveys, such as the Wetland Bird Survey, the Beached Bird Survey, and the Waders and Wildfowl Surveys (Stowe, 1981 in Evans et al., 2000; Prater, 1981; Miller-Rushing et al., 2012), in particular, being popular with citizen scientists. Indeed, in the UK, much of the country's biodiversity indicators rely on data provided by citizen scientists and volunteers (Bain, 2016).

There are many different types of environmental citizen science projects, from those which collect data, increase communication to the public, and include political influencing and social networking, to those that collect and analyze huge quantities of data, and those which go on to influence government policy (Shirk et al., 2012, Cigliano et al., 2015). However, there are currently far fewer organizations and citizen scientists carrying out monitoring of the marine environment, when compared with terrestrial or freshwater (Teleki, 2012, Roy et al., 2012, Thiel et al., 2014). Therefore, a significant opportunity exists for marine scientists to make further use of citizen science (Cigliano et al., 2015). The United Nations Environment Programme has stated that citizen science is an essential part of sustainability (Au et al., 2000), indicating how important it is that such opportunities are explored within marine science.

One area where coastal and marine citizen science especially holds promise is in support of policy and legislation. Marine legislation is increasing in complexity, and large data sets and evidence base are generally required to support decisions about marine policy and management (Hyder et al., 2015) because the questions that need addressing are at large spatial and temporal scales (e.g. impacts of climate change). This is set against the reduction in the funding available for evidence gathering. Yet it is still important to maintain the quality and breadth of evidence collected. This often impacts long-term research and monitoring first, so innovative ways of collecting and analyzing data are required. As a result, data collection methods can no longer simply rely on trained scientists using expensive scientific vessels and equipment. Making use of citizen scientists is one way in which professional scientists can continue research programs while reducing costs (Danielsen et al., 2009). However, it is very important to realize that while the time of volunteers may be free, there are often significant costs involved in such programs (Blaney et al., 2016), and they need to be adequately resourced.

This chapter aims to provide a broad overview of the value and challenges of scientists and the public contributing to marine policy development and implementation. The current state of marine citizen science and the link with policy is discussed, along with specific examples of projects that directly contribute to decision-making and monitoring. Some of the barriers to policy uptake are described, along with how these can be overcome by following best practice guidelines, and then the future of citizen science and policy is discussed, including guidance, data quality, and new technologies.

## The policy challenge

Science is necessary to inform policy (Fletcher, 2007), and there are many current gaps in our understanding of the marine environment that must be filled to fully reach evidence-based policy development (Cigliano et al., 2015). The extent to which citizen science research can influence policy is thought to have been underestimated (Evans et al., 2000), and there are evidence gaps that citizen science may be helpful in filling, particularly to cover larger areas with a larger workforce. However, since the findings of peer-reviewed scientific papers often do not reach the media or the public, the coverage that community and volunteer-based studies often receive gives projects greater potential to reach the political agenda and influence policy (Evans et al., 2000). The are several ways that citizen science projects can influence policy and therefore promote conservation and sustainability (Figure 9.1). Scientific and public interests help to develop questions to be answered by citizen science projects. These answers can then be used to produce outcomes including legislative actions, building skills and knowledge of citizen scientists, and producing data. This process illustrates that a project should be designed with the end in mind to ensure that it produces suitable outputs to inform policy (Shirk et al., 2012) and that there must be good communication links to ensure that the desired impact is achieved (Cigliano et al., 2015). However, attention must be paid to the public interests of a project to attract sufficient numbers of volunteers and ensure their maintained interest and development.

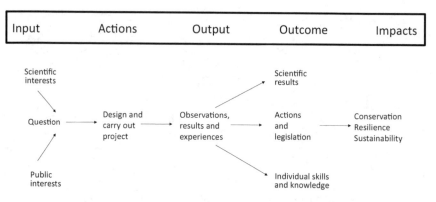

**FIGURE 9.1** The framework for volunteer participation in citizen science. Each project includes input from either scientific or public interests, and must use these to produce scientific, socio-economic, or individual outcomes. Adapted from Shirk et al. (2012).

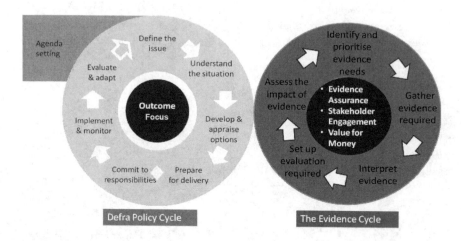

**FIGURE 9.2** The policy and evidence cycles and how they can work alongside to inform policy decisions. Adapted from Defra (2010).

National legislation and international agreements often require relatively detailed knowledge of ecological trends to make informed policy and management decisions (Danielsen et al., 2009). There are a number of steps in the cycles of policy making and evidence gathering which take time and which must be robustly carried out before policy can be set. The policy cycle focuses on the outcomes of the process, while evidence gathering focuses on assurance, engagement, and cost-effectiveness. These cycles can work side by side to ensure that evidence helps policy makers understand the situation and develop and appraise policy options (Figure 9.2).

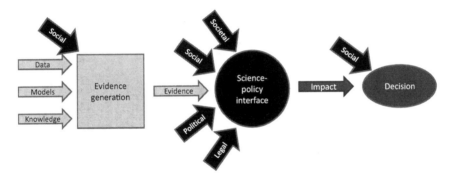

**FIGURE 9.3**  The external factors affecting evidence generation, the science-policy interface, and decisions.

Evidence is not the only influence on policy, however, with society and politics also playing a part at the science-policy interface (Figure 9.3). This can make it difficult to demonstrate the benefits of citizen science in underpinning marine decision-making; in many cases there is not a simple causal link between individual parts of the evidence base and decision-making (Hyder et al., 2015). Instead, the contribution of citizen science to the evidence base that underpins decision-making needs to be better established.

## Policy impact

There is a range of citizen science projects that already influence marine policy around the world, particularly for biodiversity, environment, management, and pollution (Hyder et al., 2015). Most projects contribute to biodiversity and to pollution research, with fewer projects directly contributing to environment and management (Table 9.1). A survey to determine motivations of citizen scientists found that policy relevance of projects was not necessarily the main driver for participation, and that citizen scientists prefer to associate with specific species or groups of organisms (Geoghegan et al., 2016), perhaps leading to a high participation in biodiversity projects.

Citizen science is becoming embedded in some public bodies and agencies, and governments are recognizing that citizen science is a way to involve the public in evidence gathering (POST, 2014, see also Chapter 7). In the UK, a survey of those public bodies responsible for environment monitoring found that most of them were beginning to support the use of citizen science (Blaney et al., 2016). In a small number of cases, citizen science support was embedded in the organization, at least for certain areas including the mission, priorities, and at senior leadership level. There is, however, less embedding of citizen science into strategic planning and project evaluation. A quarter of respondents from the public bodies stated that the organization was either developing its approach to citizen science, or it was already

**TABLE 9.1** The range of areas of marine policy that are influenced by citizen science and their frequency. Adapted from Hyder et al. (2015).

| Policy Area | Topic | Frequency* |
| --- | --- | --- |
| Biodiversity | Number, distribution, rare, invasive, protected areas | High |
| Environment | Habitat, seafloor, hydrodynamics, environmental change | Low-Med |
| Management | Resource, exploitation, marine spatial planning, food | Low-Med |
| Pollution | Pollutants, nutrients, litter, noise, light, emergency response | Low-High |

* Relates to ease of carrying out and interest to volunteers (e.g. charismatic species, amateur enthusiasts).

embedded. Blaney et al. (2016) concluded that there is potential within these bodies to support citizen science. The environmental areas in which citizen science was most embedded were non-marine biodiversity, with embeddedness in marine biodiversity much lower. Citizen science was considered to be quite highly embedded for invasive species (see Chapter 4), climate (see Chapter 3), and protected sites (see Chapter 7), all of which have marine components. However, there is clearly the need for more dialogue between scientists and decision-makers to ensure that citizen science is embedded in higher level documents and utilized alongside more traditional approaches.

There are several benefits of citizen science that are recognized by government bodies (POST, 2014). In terms of collection of evidence, citizen science projects can contribute novel data and can produce continuous sampling and long time series that would not be feasible without large numbers of volunteers. The Scottish Environment Protection Agency (SEPA, 2013) is encouraging the use of citizen science and engagement in projects to increase the number of long-term datasets across Scotland. If organizations can match their science needs with citizen science projects and vice versa, then they are much better able to benefit from citizen science (McKinley et al., 2015). A project with many citizen scientists can also produce a large amount of data in a relatively small amount of time and with a large geographic coverage (Silvertown, 2009; Finn et al., 2010). The scientific value of a project can be increased enormously by increasing the quantity or spread of data collected, which in some cases can only be achieved with the aid of volunteers (Foster-Smith and Evans, 2003, McKinley et al., 2015). As well as collecting data, citizen science projects can also make use of the volunteer hours available to analyze large datasets and help to leverage the benefits of historical data, for example in Zooniverse projects, which may be too big to analyze otherwise (Dickinson et al., 2012). Some of the data produced or analyzed in this way may not be available to policy makers without citizen science programs. Through citizen science data, organizations may be able to set their future priorities as they can see knowledge and data gaps (McKinley et al., 2017). The resources required to conduct the study can be lower, at least in the long term, and the reputation of a project and the dataset can be increased because local communities are engaged in the data collection process and are educated about the need for such data (McKinley et al., 2017). The impact on policy can then be greater, as the citizens involved have some buy-in to the process and may understand the need for any management actions that are put in place (Cigliano et al., 2015). Policy makers acknowledge the role of local amateur experts as well as the importance of citizen science in engaging volunteers around issues (Geoghegan et al., 2016). However, it is important to recognize that this does not mean that governments should lead citizen science projects; rather they should work alongside scientists with expertise in citizen science to leverage the maximum benefit from these programs (Cigliano et al., 2015).

---

### BOX 9.1 LONG-TERM CITIZEN SCIENCE MONITORING OF WATERBIRDS INFORMS INTERNATIONAL POLICY: THE WEBS PROJECT

An example of how long-term citizen science is used in international policy is the WeBS project (www.bto.org/volunteers-surveys/webs). This is a UK partnership between the British Trust for Ornithology, the Royal Society for the Protection of Birds, and the Joint Nature Conservation Committee in association with the Wildfowl and Wetlands Trust. The scheme uses volunteers to monitor waterbirds with the aim of identifying population sizes, trends, and distributions. The WeBS project fulfills the UK's agreement within the international Bonn Convention on the Conservation of Migratory Species of Wild Animals, to provide adequate monitoring programs to ensure that habitats for migratory waterbirds are identified, protected, and managed appropriately. The data are used to satisfy obligations under the Bonn Convention. The results are also used in decision-making by government, such as by providing evidence in designating protected areas and in environmental impact assessments. The data are combined with records from other countries in the International Waterbirds Census. The project began in 1947 with 3,000 volunteers carrying out monthly counts of birds at wetland sites, and now has volunteers counting monthly at 2,000 sites each winter. Volunteers do not require any specific training, but must be able to identify wetland bird species, with training provided if required. Their counts can be submitted either through the WeBS website or on paper recording forms, and so citizen scientists who do not have access to or knowledge of the internet are able to contribute. Volunteers receive a newsletter from WeBS and an annual report of the survey results, helping to keep them engaged and to see how their work contributes to conservation. Volunteers can stay involved in the project for years, showing the commitment that can be achieved in such projects.

---

Often the impact of science is measured by the number of peer-reviewed publications, but, in fact, projects can have much more impact by linking with policy. Citizen science projects can be perceived as being of lower value than "professional" science, when in fact they can affect management and policy directly and they are able to be picked up by environment managers more easily because they are part of the grey literature (Theobald et al., 2015; see Chapters 2, 7, and 8). A review of publication rates of citizen science projects by Theobald et al. (2015) found that projects led by governmental bodies had lower publication rates than those led by academic institutions. This is perhaps not surprising given the push by academic institutes to increase their publication rates, but it may also mean that those projects run by government bodies create their impact by the data feeding directly into government policy.

## Policy outlook: guidance and best practices

The growth in citizen science research in recent years may be a great opportunity for governments and scientists wanting to determine the effects of global change on the world's environment. Simple, long-term datasets can be valuable indicators of change in ecosystems caused by human activities such as pollution or climate change, or indeed improvements in an ecosystem when pollution has been cleared up or a reserve put in place (McKinley et al., 2015). Local observers are well-placed to provide data on the changes taking place at the local scale (Theobald et al., 2015), and citizen science is thought to be the only practical way of answering ecological questions on a global scale (Dickinson et al., 2012).

### Project planning

Any project that collects and manages large amounts of data needs careful planning (Hochachka et al., 2012) and a strong design (Bain, 2016), particularly if it is to be robust enough to be used in policy decisions. Information on cost and benefits is required early in the project to ensure its success (Blaney et al., 2016). Blaney et al. (2016) describe four different approaches to be used to evaluate environmental monitoring methods: (1) Return on Investment (ROI) approach, which considers only financial aspects of a project; (2) Cost-Benefit Analysis (CBA), which considers monetary and non-monetary costs and benefits to society as a whole; (3) Cost-Effectiveness Analysis (CEA), which makes a comparison between different options; and (4) Multi-Criteria Analysis (MCA), which evaluates relative preference for different options. These different evaluation methods can be used at the start of a project to determine the most appropriate approach to data collection and to ensure that the benefits and effectiveness of a project is appropriately balanced with the costs. Once an approach has been decided, there is a lot of guidance available on designing and implementing successful citizen science projects (for example Dickinson et al., 2010; Sharpe and Conrad, 2006; Dickinson et al., 2012; Hochachka et al., 2012; Shirk et al., 2012; Tweddle et al., 2012; Cigliano et al., 2015, and this book). As well as published articles, there are many websites which provide detailed information and recommendations on project development, such

as Citizen Science Central (www.citizenscience.org) and CitSci.org (www.citsci.
org) (Dickinson et al., 2012).

Another consideration is that some policy decisions require more targeted or
specific data than others. Dickinson et al. (2010) make the distinction between
targeted monitoring and surveillance monitoring, with targeted monitoring being
based on a hypothesis or designed to answer a specific question, whereas surveillance monitoring collects larger amounts of data to see environmental changes in
the longer term. These two types of monitoring should be approached differently
from the outset in designing the projects and deciding the type of data required,
the geographic scope, and the technology, to ensure that the objectives can be
met. The level of citizen scientist involvement required and the type of volunteers
are also important to decide at an early stage so that the project can be designed
appropriately (Danielsen et al., 2009; Cigliano et al., 2015). Regardless of the type
of project, there are five basic principles of any successful citizen science project
including those that influence policy (Silvertown, 2009):

- Use standardized data collection methods.
- Make explicit assumptions.
- Have a hypothesis.
- Validate the data.
- Give volunteer feedback.

Bonney et al. (2009) and Shirk et al. (2012) present a nine-step model for developing a citizen science project, which can be applied to projects that have a policy
goal:

1   *Choose a scientific question*: large scale questions that participants can relate to
    and that involve only simple data-collection methods.
2   *Form a team*: multidisciplinary teams are important and need to include scien-
    tists, educators, technologists, and evaluators to ensure that the questions are
    framed correctly and meet their objectives. Policy makers can be included at
    this early stage.
3   *Develop, test, and refine protocols and supporting materials*: good data will only
    be obtained if there are clear protocols, simple forms, and good support
    materials.
4   *Recruit participants*: employ as many types of media as possible that are aimed at
    your target group.
5   *Train participants*: provide simple training materials that are can be accessed via
    the internet.
6   *Accept, edit, and display data*: data must be made available to the public for
    review.
7   *Analyze and interpret data*: this can be challenging if the project is not designed
    well from the outset.

8    *Disseminate results*: use a variety of media to pass information to your target groups (scientific publications, reports, internet, magazines, etc.).

9    *Measure outcomes*: this should include the scientific, policy, and educational outputs.

These steps are particularly applicable to monitoring and surveillance programs that are aimed at supporting policy decisions because the programs need to be well-planned from the start to ensure that the data gathered are fit for the program's purpose.

Surveillance projects also do not necessarily use trained volunteers, but scientists can provide very basic training in the form of guidance on a website or within a mobile phone app to standardize the data they receive. Recruitment of participants may also be less formal than in targeted programs, with word of mouth or social media determining the number of participants (see Chapter 13). Some groups are often willing to be citizen scientists, such as divers who are generally keen to collect data (Wright et al., 2016; see Chapter 12).

The skill level of citizen scientists also needs consideration when designing the project as some monitoring schemes may require skilled taxonomists, for example using the expertise of amateur or retired volunteers (Mackechnie et al., 2011). Some projects require volunteers to attend a training course (e.g. Seagrass-Watch[1] and Seasearch[2]), whereas other projects may require no prior knowledge and using identification charts or web-based materials is sufficient training (e.g. The Great Eggcase Hunt[3]). Statisticians can be used within projects to ensure that volunteer data is reliable and interpreted correctly (Bain, 2016).

By deeply involving volunteers in the data collection and analysis, they can become engaged in the whole project, including the policy process (Cigliano et al., 2015). Cigliano et al. (2015) designed a series of toolkits in which to engage citizens in science projects, including a specific policy change toolkit which includes steps to ensure that participants feel involved in the policy and advocacy process. They concluded that this could increase the chances of policy change, as more people are seen to be concerned.

Another constraint which should be considered early in the project design is cost, because dedicated project staff are required in an effective citizen science program (Bonney et al., 2009). Training volunteers involves only a relatively small cost in comparison to using professional scientists (Finn et al., 2010). Some projects also charge volunteers to take part in their projects (e.g. FeederWatch[4] and BirdSleuth[5] at Cornell Lab of Ornithology), bringing in income but potentially reducing the number of volunteers. Some projects charge organizations or individuals to get access to their data (e.g. Victorian Department of Sustainability and Environment and Seagrass Watch), although participants may object to paying for data that they have themselves collected (Keenan et al., 2012). Other projects are sponsored by commercial companies, for example the UK Marine Conservation Society's Big Beach Clean-Up.[6] Long-term funding is an important factor in the sustainability of projects (Sharpe and Conrad, 2006), which is particularly important in surveillance projects.

## Access and communication

Marine citizen science projects have some constraints that are not experienced to the same extent in terrestrial or freshwater systems. For example, there can be access difficulties since not everyone lives by the coast, perceived ownership issues of working further from home, and safety concerns when working in or near water (Cigliano et al., 2015). Once marine data are collected there are barriers to the uptake within policy. There can be challenges with communication between citizen scientists and policy makers (see Chapter 13 for a fuller discussion), which needs strong project leaders and scientists to facilitate, and there can be differences in understanding of an issue between policy makers and communities (Cigliano et al., 2015).

## Motivation

To ensure that citizen science projects result in data that can be used to benefit society or the environment, understanding the initial and continuing motivations of citizen scientists is important, so that the volunteers complete the project and submit the data that they have collected (Geoghegan et al., 2016). Motivations for data submission and involvement in environmental citizen science projects include altruism, pleasing someone else, sharing knowledge, personal development, contributing to projects with national importance, and policy making (Hyder et al., 2015; West et al., 2015; Geoghegan et al., 2016). Projects that involve some sort of initial commitment from volunteers, such as time spent training or investment in equipment, are more likely to maintain their volunteers than those which require only a simple way to sign-up (West et al., 2015). Later in a project, project leaders should engage with citizen scientists to maintain their motivations to encourage final data submission (Rotman et al., 2012). Furthermore, West et al. (2015) found that in projects where three types of submission methods were available, 100% of participants submitted their data, showing the importance of flexibility in projects when dealing with volunteers (Geoghegan et al., 2016). Lastly, acknowledging contributions and giving feedback to volunteers once a project has ended may keep them engaged and more likely to participate in other projects in the future (West et al., 2015, see also Chapter 13).

## Data quality control

One potential problem with citizen science projects is the quality of the data produced. As with any research, if data quality procedures are inadequate from the start, the data itself is not likely to be of good quality (Crall et al., 2010). Designing the project from the start to collect simple, repeatable, verifiable, calibrated, and reliable data will help ensure that the project produces high quality data (Crall et al., 2010; Mackechnie et al., 2011, Cigliano et al., 2015). Providing citizen scientists with training, in the form of workshops, clear and simple instructions on websites, or field lessons, will greatly improve data accuracy. If professional scientists create the methodologies and design the protocols and then field test them on a small scale, the data collected during the project is more likely to be robust (Delaney et al., 2008).

In projects that involve species identification, volunteers may inaccurately identify species, especially those that lack obvious distinguishing features. This can be overcome by providing sufficient training, including providing photographs and other training materials, or only using the most experienced volunteers for specific tasks (Crall et al., 2010). This would improve the overall data quality of the project and hence the usability of the data in policy terms. Crall et al. (2010) also suggest that continuously carrying out assessments of error rates would improve data quality and provide those using the data with information on potential pitfalls. Carrying out quality control of data as they are collected is essential, as it allows for timely back-correction of previously analyzed samples and it ensures that all data collected are usable (Mackechnie et al., 2011). It is important to standardize protocols and record sampling effort (see also Chapter 4), especially when analyzing volunteer or amateur data, to accurately understand datasets (Bonardi et al., 2011). This ensures that projects can continue, and that the data is used and interpreted in the correct way by other users and by managers and policy makers, and critics of such policy.

## Data quality confidence

Policy makers must have assurances from scientists that their research is robust and their data accurate if they are to make decisions based on that research. Monitoring data over large areas need to be consistent and of sufficiently high quality and extent to be used in policy, and so projects could be integrated into regional and national frameworks and data shared among organizations (Crall et al., 2010). Some citizen science projects only use records that have been verified by an expert or trained volunteer, while some carry out checks on a sample of the data to ensure data quality (Bain, 2016). Galaxy Zoo[7] and the Zooniverse[8] portals use citizen scientists to scour thousands of online datasets and images using the power of numbers to increase accuracy. For example, when more and more people classify the same galaxies within an image, they can get a measure of confidence by the agreement of all those people (Bain, 2016). Citizen science–generated data may be expected to contain some error and bias, but valuable information can still be extracted if this is taken into account (Bain, 2016).

As data are often used by those who did not design the survey, it is incredibly important that metadata is included when publishing data (Bain, 2016). This ensures that the dataset is not misunderstood or analyzed incorrectly, and that policy decisions are not made based on a misinterpretation of the data collected. An example of a data storage portal is the Marine Environmental Data and Information Network (MEDIN)[9] that has been set up to provide marine data to users globally. It has strict metadata standards and guidelines that must be followed by those uploading data. Storing data in this type of portal with appropriate metadata allows scientists and non-scientists to carry out the correct statistical analyses (Bain, 2016).

## *Technology*

Citizen science can make use of many different types of technologies, and as new technologies become available, the application of citizen science will continue to change and adapt (Newman et al., 2012).Volunteer surveys can be carried out using paper and pen, or data can be entered directly into an app on a smartphone or tablet making use of GPS or sensors on portable devices. Data analysis can be carried out remotely through intermediary websites, allowing volunteers with little background knowledge to become involved. Organizations can also exploit the social aspects of citizen science and use it as a form of social media, which helps to keep volunteers engaged (see Chapter 13). Environmental projects may be able to make use of new technologies as they develop and become more widely available, which can save time and allow for more complex data to be recorded easily. Indeed, the increased use of such technologies will streamline data collection and improve data management and quality control and may also increase participation rates (Newman et al., 2012). Data quality can be improved by using GPS facilities to record locations, and photographs can be uploaded to aid data validation.

Smartphone apps are rapidly becoming widely used in collecting citizen science data. They provide the opportunity to collect real time data (Venturelli et al., 2017), reducing recall or transcribing error found in more traditional methods. They can also be linked to GPS and so provide very accurate location information. They can save time in waiting for records to be logged or returned, and they can be easy to use, fun, and informative for the volunteer. There are so many apps out there now that there needs to be consistency across apps to make the most of the data. For example, there are many apps used in different countries and globally to record recreational fish catches, but the data that they collect are not necessarily comparable (Venturelli et al., 2017). Data entered by recreational fishers can be used in mandatory monitoring schemes for fisheries regulations, such as the European Union multi-annual plans, and in making management decisions. It is therefore essential that as apps such as this are developed, consistent standards are used to make the most of the data that is collected, and that developers see beyond their narrow view of the questions that they want answering from their app, to a broader view of the extra value that could be gained if they collected data in a standardized and comparable way and made the data available to wider users. Venturelli et al. (2017) suggest some standards for recreational fishing apps, which could also be applied to other types of technology or citizen science apps. In this way, the impact of a project can be increased (Hyder et al., 2015), and the data could be used to inform international rather than only regional or national policy.

## Conclusions

While it is very unlikely that citizen science will totally replace traditional monitoring approaches to surveys (Hyder et al., 2015), citizen science has a large role to play in providing future evidence, science, and monitoring (Mackechnie et al., 2011). Citizen science has been underrepresented in the scientific literature in the past (Theobald et al., 2015) because it is often perceived as not conforming to the usual rigorous, structured, and scientifically designed methods of projects conducted by professional scientists. However, it is a powerful technique that, if used correctly, can add value to the evidence base used to support marine policy through the collection, entry, synthesis, and analysis of large data sets that are difficult by any other means. Good quality citizen science data can be used by managers, conservationists, and policy makers to coordinate national and international conservation efforts (Hochachka et al., 2012). In fact there are numerous examples of this in coastal and marine contexts: citizen science surveys of habitat use by manta rays in the Great Barrier Reef in Australia are used to inform management and can be used in conjunction with surveys around the world to improve international management of the species (Jaine et al., 2012). This is only possible if data from different projects are compatible. Citizen science data may also be used to monitor changes in the environment caused by climate change (see Chapter 3), by providing information to which policy makers can respond. Monitoring datasets provided by citizen scientists have also been used to inform policy within the UK's Marine Conservation Zone designation process (see also Chapters 2, 7, and 8); Seasearch dive survey results were used as evidence to inform the designation of certain areas, as were The Wildlife Trust's Shoresearch survey results.[10] The UK's Marine Litter Action Network collects data on marine litter around the coasts which influenced policy making on the use of disposable plastic bags, and provided data for the EU Marine Strategy Framework Directive (MSFD).[11] Guidelines have been produced by the OSPAR Commission[12] (Convention for the Protection of the Marine Environment of the North-East Atlantic) to standardize the collection of marine litter data, enabling that data to be used within the MSFD. There is great potential for similar existing and future records to be analyzed to show changes in the marine environment caused by pollution (see Hyder et al., 2017 and Chapter 6) or climate change (see Chapter 3).

Informing and influencing coastal and marine conservation policy through citizen science requires careful planning and can yield benefits beyond policy. It is essential to design a project in detail before starting to collect data, defining the policy question to be answered from the start. Carrying out a trial of the methodologies and protocols will help to identify any areas that may be difficult for unskilled volunteers, such as identification of certain taxa. Careful choice of technology can help to enhance the project and make the project appeal to certain groups of potential citizen scientists. Technology can enhance the project in certain cases, and can reduce data errors by using integrated filter software. Marine scientists and policy makers should carefully consider where citizen science may be used in order to direct funding and effort to the correct areas, and more engagement with citizen scientists is necessary to fulfill the potential benefits of linking coastal and marine citizen science and policy (Hyder et al., 2015). The educational aspects of citizen science projects should also not be overlooked because as well as benefiting individual volunteers, it can also enhance community involvement in conservation and stewardship of the marine environment. To accomplish conservation outcomes for policy like those previously mentioned, collaboration between scientists and non-scientists is needed, especially to address global-scale changes (Theobald et al., 2015). Citizen science also has the direct benefit of engaging the public in science and conservation, and so increasing public understanding and stewardship of the marine environment.

## Web resources

1  www.seagrasswatch.org/.
2  www.seasearch.org.uk/.
3  www.sharktrust.org/en/great_eggcase_hunt.
4  http://feederwatch.org/.
5  www.birdsleuth.org/.
6  www.mcsuk.org.
7  www.galaxyzoo.org/.
8  www.zooniverse.org/.
9  www.oceannet.org/.
10  www.hiwwt.org.uk/.
11  www.mcsuk.org/what_we_do/Clean+seas+and+beaches/Campaigns+and+policy/Marine+Litter+Action+Network.
12  www.ospar.org/documents?v=7260.

## Literature cited

Au, J., Bagchi, P., Chen, B., Martinez, R., Dudley, S., and Sorger, G. (2000). Methodology for public monitoring of total coliforms, *Escherichia coli* and toxicity in waterways by Canadian high school students. *Journal of Environmental Management*, 58(3), 213–230.

Bain, R. (2016). Citizen science and statistics: Playing a part. *Significance*, 13, 16–21.

Blaney, R.J., Philippe, A.C., and Pocock, M.J.O., and Jones, G. (2016). *Citizen science and environmental monitoring: Towards a methodology for evaluating opportunities, costs and benefits*. Final report on behalf of UKEOF WRc, Fera Science, Centre for Ecology and Hydrology.

Bonardi, A., Manenti, R., Corbetta, A., Ferri, V., Fiacchini, D., Giovine, G., Macchi, S., Romanazzi, E., Soccini, C., Bottoni, L., Padoa-Schioppa, E., and Ficetola, G. (2011). Usefulness of volunteer data to measure the large scale decline of "common" toad populations. *Biological Conservation*, 144(9), 2328–2334.

Bonney, R., Cooper, C., Dickinson, J., Kelling, S., Phillips, T., Rosenberg, K., and Shirk, J. (2009). Citizen science: A developing tool for expanding science knowledge and scientific literacy. *BioScience*, 59(11), 977–984.

Cigliano, J., Meyer, R., Ballard, H., Freitag, A., Phillips, T., and Wasser, A. (2015). Making marine and coastal citizen science matter. *Ocean & Coastal Management*, 115, 77–87.

Crall, A., Newman, G., Jarnevich, C., Stohlgren, T., Waller, D., and Graham, J. (2010). Improving and integrating data on invasive species collected by citizen scientists. *Biological Invasions*, 12(10), 3419–3428.

Danielsen, F., Burgess, N., Balmford, A., Donald, P., Funder, M., Jones, J., Alviola, P., Balete, D., Blomley, T., Brashares, J., Child, B., Enghoff, M., Fjeldså, J., Holt, S., Hübertz, H., Jensen, A., Jensen, P., Massao, J., Mendoza, M., Ngaga, Y., Poulsen, M., Rueda, R., Sam, M., Skielboe, T., Stuart-Hill, G., Topp-Jørgensen, E., and Yonten, D. (2009). Local participation in natural resource monitoring: A characterization of approaches. *Conservation Biology*, 23(1), 31–42.

Defra. (2010). *Defra's Evidence Investment Strategy 2010–2013 and Beyond*. London, UK: Department of Environment and Rural Affairs. [Online] www.gov.uk/government/

uploads/system/uploads/attachment_data/file/69292/pb13346-eis-100126.pdf [Accessed February 10, 2017].

Delaney, D., Sperling, C., Adams, C., and Leung, B. (2008). Marine invasive species: Validation of citizen science and implications for national monitoring networks. *Biological Invasions*, 10(1), 117–128.

Dickinson, J., Shirk, J., Bonter, D., Bonney, R., Crain, R., Martin, J., Phillips, T., and Purcell, K. (2012). The current state of citizen science as a tool for ecological research and public engagement. *Frontiers in Ecology and the Environment*, 10(6), 291–297.

Dickinson, J., Zuckerberg, B., and Bonter, D. (2010). Citizen science as an ecological research tool: Challenges and benefits. *Annual Review of Ecology, Evolution, and Systematics*, 41(1), 149–172.

Evans, S., Birchenough, A., and Fletcher, H. (2000). The value and validity of community-based research: TBT contamination of the North Sea. *Marine Pollution Bulletin*, 40(3), 220–225.

Finn, P., Udy, N., Baltais, S., Price, K., and Coles, L. (2010). Assessing the quality of seagrass data collected by community volunteers in Moreton Bay Marine Park, Australia. *Environmental Conservation*, 37(1), 83–89.

Fletcher, S. (2007). Converting science to policy through stakeholder involvement: An analysis of the European Marine Strategy Directive. *Marine Pollution Bulletin*, 54(12), 1881–1886.

Foster-Smith, J., and Evans, S. (2003). The value of marine ecological data collected by volunteers. *Biological Conservation*, 113(2), 199–213.

Geoghegan, H., Dyke, A., Pateman, R., West, S., and Everett, G., 2016. *Understanding motivations for citizen science*. Final report on behalf of UKEOF, University of Reading, Stockholm Environment Institute (University of York) and University of the West of England.

Hochachka, W., Fink, D., Hutchinson, R., Sheldon, D., Wong, W., and Kelling, S. (2012). Data-intensive science applied to broad-scale citizen science. *Trends in Ecology & Evolution*, 27(2), 130–137.

Hyder, K., Townhill, B., Anderson, L., Delany, J., and Pinnegar, J. (2015). Can citizen science contribute to the evidence-base that underpins marine policy? *Marine Policy*, 59, 112–120.

Hyder, K., Wright, S., Kirby, M., and Brant, J. (2017). The role of citizen science in monitoring small scale pollution events. *Marine Pollution Bulletin*, 120, 51–57.

Jaine, F., Couturier, L., Weeks, S., Townsend, K., Bennett, M., Fiora, K., and Richardson, A. (2012). When giants turn up: Sighting trends, environmental influences and habitat use of the manta ray *Manta alfredi* at a coral reef. *PLoS One*, 7(10), e46170.

Kennan, M., Williamson, K., and Johanson, G. (2012). Wild data: Collaborative e-research and university libraries. *Australian Academic & Research Libraries*, 43(1), 56–79.

Mackechnie, C., Maskell, L., Norton, L., and Roy, D. (2011). The role of "Big Society" in monitoring the state of the natural environment. *Journal of Environmental Monitoring*, 13(10), 2687–2691.

McKinley, D.C., Miller-Rushing, A.J., Ballard, H.L., Bonney, R., Brown, H., Evans, D.M., French, R.A., Parrish, J.K., Phillips, T.B., Ryan, S.F., and Shanley, L.A. (2015). Investing in citizen science can improve natural resource management and environmental protection. *Issues in Ecology*, 19, 1–27.

Miller-Rushing, A., Primack, R., and Bonney, R. (2012). The history of public participation in ecological research. *Frontiers in Ecology and the Environment*, 10(6), 285–290.

Newman, G., Wiggins, A., Crall, A., Graham, E., Newman, S., and Crowston, K. (2012). The future of citizen science: Emerging technologies and shifting paradigms. *Frontiers in Ecology and the Environment*, 10(6), 298–304.

POST. 2014. Environmental citizen science. *POSTNote, number 476, Houses of Parliament.* London, UK, Parliamentary Office of Science and Technology. [Online] http://research briefings.parliament.uk/ResearchBriefing/Summary/POST-PN-476 [Accessed February 22, 2017].

Prater, A.J. (1981). *Estuary Birds of Britain and Ireland.* Carlton: Poyser.

Rotman, D., Preece, J., Hammock, J., Procita, K., Hansen, D., Parr, C., Lewis, D., and Jacobs, D. (2012, February). Dynamic changes in motivation in collaborative citizen-science projects. In *Proceedings of the ACM 2012 Conference on Computer Supported Cooperative Work,* 217–226. ACM. [Online] http://dl.acm.org/citation.cfm?id=2145238 [Accessed February 22, 2017].

Roy, H.E., Pocock, M.J., Preston, C.D., Roy, D.B., Savage, J., Tweddle, J.C., and Robinson, L.D. (2012). Understanding citizen science and environmental monitoring: final report on behalf of UK Environmental Observation Framework. NERC Center for Ecology & Hydrology and the Natural History Museum, 179 pp.

SEPA. (2013). *Performance Measure: Citizen Science.* Edinburgh, Scotland: Scottish Environment Protection Agency. [Online] www.sepa.org.uk/about_us/sepa_performs/quarterly_performance/citizen_science.aspx [Accessed August 23, 2013].

Sharpe, A., and Conrad, C. (2006). Community based ecological monitoring in Nova Scotia: Challenges and opportunities. *Environmental Monitoring and Assessment,* 113(1–3), 395–409.

Shirk, J., Ballard, H., Wilderman, C., Phillips, T., Wiggins, A., Jordan, R., McCallie, E., Minarchek, M., Lewenstein, B., Krasny, M., and Bonney, R. (2012). Public participation in scientific research: A framework for deliberate design. *Ecology and Society,* 17(2).

Silvertown, J. (2009). A new dawn for citizen science. *Trends in Ecology and Evolution,* 24(9), 467–471.

Teleki, K.A. (2012). Power of the people? *Aquatic Conservation: Marine and Freshwater Ecosystems,* 22, 1–6.

Thiel, M., Penna-Díaz, M.A., Luna-Jorquera, G., Salas, S., Sellanes, J., and Stotz, W. (2014). Citizen scientists and marine research: Volunteer participants, their contributions, and projection for the future. *Oceanography and Marine Biology: An Annual Review,* 52, 257–314.

Theobald, E., Ettinger, A., Burgess, H., DeBey, L., Schmidt, N., Froehlich, H., Wagner, C., HilleRisLambers, J., Tewksbury, J., Harsch, M., and Parrish, J. (2015). Global change and local solutions: Tapping the unrealized potential of citizen science for biodiversity research. *Biological Conservation,* 181, 236–244.

Tweddle, J.C., Robinson, L.D., Pocock, M.J.O., and Roy, H.E. (2012). *Guide to citizen science: Developing, implementing and evaluating citizen science to study biodiversity and the environment in the UK.* Lancaster, UK: NERC/Centre for Ecology & Hydrology.

Venturelli, P., Hyder, K., and Skov, C. (2017). Angler apps as a source of recreational fisheries data: opportunities, challenges and proposed standards. *Fish and Fisheries* 18(3), 578–595.

West, S.E., Pateman, R.M., and Dyke, A.J. (2015). *Motivations and data submissions in citizen science.* Report to Department of Environment and Rural Affairs. London, UK.

Wright, S., Hull, T., Sivyer, D., Pearce, D., Pinnegar, J., Sayer, M., Mogg, A., Azzopardi, E., Gontarek, S., and Hyder, K. (2016). SCUBA divers as oceanographic samplers: The potential of dive computers to augment aquatic temperature monitoring. *Scientific Reports,* 6(1), 30164.

# PART III

The people and
perspectives of coastal
and marine citizen science:
diverse interests, needs,
and benefits

# 10

# COLLABORATING WITH INDIGENOUS CITIZEN SCIENTISTS TOWARDS SUSTAINABLE CORAL REEF MANAGEMENT IN A CHANGING WORLD

The *One People One Reef* program

*Nicole L. Crane, John B. Rulmal Jr., Peter A. Nelson, Michelle J. Paddack, and Giacomo Bernardi*

## Introduction

Citizen scientists have gathered data and informed lines of inquiry for the scientific community for at least the last century (Cohn, 2008; Silvertown, 2009; Miller-Rushing et al., 2012), but acceptance and increasing application of this approach by professional scientists have accelerated dramatically in the last 10 years (Couvet et al., 2008; Follett and Strezov, 2015). Museums such as the Field Museum in Chicago,[1] the California Academy of Sciences,[2] and the Smithsonian Institution[3] have involved citizens in their scientific endeavors, including the use of photographs, notes, and even specimens. More recently, organizations such as the Oceanic Society,[4] Earthwatch,[5] Reef Check,[6] and others have successfully involved citizen scientists directly in data collection to support scientific endeavors.

Long before the term *citizen science* became well-known, there was a long history of professional, "Western," or conventional scientists[7] working with indigenous peoples, utilizing local knowledge to support their science, for example by ethnobotanists to understand healing practices and uses for local plants (Heckler, 2009; Ugulu, 2011). This is also true in the marine sciences and fisheries management (Johannes, 1981; Berkes et al., 2000; Drew, 2005; Thurstan et al., 2015). The concept of traditional ecological knowledge (TEK) has become more widely recognized and accepted by the scientific community, including the coastal and marine scientific communities, particularly in instances where indigenous people are seeking to reconnect with their traditional management (Pitcher, 2001; Williams et al., 2008; Kittinger et al., 2012, 2015; Friedlander et al., 2014; Crane et al., 2017). But an often less recognized relationship is that between indigenous people and professional scientists as true collaborators.

In our experience, the recovery and re-application of TEK for management and conservation, combined with citizen science, can be a powerful approach. It has particular relevance to communities that are often marginalized economically, socially, and governmentally. Combining citizen science with TEK offers an effective and meaningful way for conventional science to engage with these communities and assist with implementing lasting and effective conservation and management programs. These efforts, however, require a two-way exchange of knowledge to develop research agendas and management plans for the best chance for success. Despite increasing recognition of TEK as a valuable resource for conventional science, and its relevance to conservation and management, indigenous people are often asked for information but are not included in either the research agenda or management planning. Not surprisingly, this incomplete form of collaboration can lead to skepticism and even resentment by local communities (Berkes et al., 2000; Christie, 2004; see also Chapter 13).

While many global conservation and management strategies are producing good results (e.g. Marine Protected Areas; Abelson et al., 2016; Chapter 7), some are leading to social challenges and cultural clashes (Christie, 2004), suggesting that locally driven approaches, especially in autonomously governed regions, may be the most effective strategy (McClanahan et al., 2006; Wamukota et al., 2012; Crane et al., 2017). Involving local people directly in the entire spectrum of the scientific-management process, from data collection to planning and implementation, not only empowers individuals and communities, but it also enhances local capacity and reduces the need for external resources (Drew, 2005; Hilborn, 2007; Braschler, 2009; Kittinger et al., 2012, 2015; Wamukota et al., 2012). Indigenous people can benefit in significant ways from conventional science, especially during this time of rapid environmental change where their familiar ecological context may be shifting. Conventional science, similarly, is greatly enhanced by data collected by local science teams (citizen scientists) who hold valuable TEK and can help inform the science process, especially in regions that are hard to access on a regular basis. (Braschler, 2009; Bourgoin, et al., 2013; Friedlander et al., 2014; Crane et al., 2017). Finally, if a shared goal of the professional science team and the local communities is conservation and management, then local communities need to be leading the efforts, and view them as endemic to their needs rather than an outside idea, for the best chances of long-term success (Christie, 2004; Berkes et al., 2006; see also Chapter 13).

Collaborative approaches to conservation planning and program implementation are now the standard among many agencies and organizations facilitating ecosystem and resource protection and management (Hilborn, 2007; Couvet et al., 2008; Wendt and Starr, 2009; Wilson et al., 2010; Goring et al., 2014). Collaboration can take many forms, however, and there has not yet been a standard applied to the process of involving stakeholders (Berkes et al., 2000; Couvet et al., 2008; Dickinson et al., 2012). In addition, many conservation efforts are focused on the "protection" and "conservation" of sensitive ecosystems such as coral reefs. These are words that have important connotations, and often have the effect of leaving out

**FIGURE 10.1**    Clockwise from upper left: researcher Nicole Crane collecting benthic data, a local catch, a young woman from the island of Ifaluk.

the key stakeholders themselves – namely the people who rely on the areas being conserved for their livelihoods, and their need to extract resources.

Indigenous people, despite their pivotal roles in linking knowledge with contemporary needs and economies, have not always been acknowledged for their input. Professionally trained scientists and conservationists, rather than working with local people as key collaborators and data collectors, often attempt to enlist the support of local people to implement plans the scientists have already developed – not always a successful or sustainable approach (Berkes et al., 2000; Christie, 2004; Cinner et al., 2009; Wamukota et al., 2012; Chapter 13; see also Chapter 3 for an example of a successful citizen science project that includes indigenous communities). With the rapid onset of climate change and the associated perturbations to ecological systems, it is a critical time to develop authentic collaborations and incorporate historical data to understand and manage marine systems in a culturally and ecologically sustainable way (Kittinger et al., 2012; 2015; Thurstan et al., 2015).

Here, we present the *One People One Reef* program, which operates in the Federated States of Micronesia and is aimed at strengthening community capacity to manage their marine resources using adaptive frameworks and input from both conventional and local (citizen) science teams (Figure 10.1).

## Case study: *One People One Reef*

Authors Crane (Cabrillo College) and Nelson (H.T. Harvey & Associates) partner with colleagues Giacomo Bernardi (University of California, Santa Cruz), Michelle Paddack (Santa Barbara City College), and author Rulmal (Ulithi Falalop Community Action Program) and local science teams from the Yap outer islands.

Together they comprise *One People One Reef* – a collaborative approach to reef management.

The *One People One Reef* program was initiated by the people of Falalop Island, Ulithi Atoll, Federated States of Micronesia, and a team of scientists from Santa Cruz, California, USA, and has now expanded to the communities of all four inhabited islands of the atoll: Falalop, Asor, Mog Mog, and Federai (Figure 10.2) and more recently to outer island communities across Yap state waters. The communities recognized that their subsistence fisheries were declining and some of their reefs were degraded, causing concern. In 2009, our professional science team was contacted to help address these declines. Scientists met with local chiefs, leaders, and fishers to assess the scope of the problems. The professional science team asked the Falalop community to identify the major problems, describe historical trends in reef degradation and changes in resource management, fishing methods, and other potentially contributory factors. Collectively, the professional science team and the local community representatives began to understand the nature of the problem, and recognized the need for a local science team to help collect data. The Falalop community was to lead the development of a management plan, based on the science produced by the local and professional science teams, and rooted in traditional management frameworks – *a true collaboration*. The professional science team did not present the plans, rather they worked with the local teams to support locally derived plans.

## Regional geography and the geo-political context

The Federated States of Micronesia (FSM) is an island nation of four states (Yap, Chuuk, Pohnpei, Kosrae) in the Western Pacific with autonomous governance by individual island communities, and is a part of the US Compact of Free Association. This agreement provides for US economic assistance, defense of the FSM, and other benefits in exchange for operating rights in the FSM (and other agreements). The geopolitical context is important as it recognizes autonomous governance – built into the constitution. The autonomous nature of governance and traditional land and ocean tenure rights make this a region particularly well suited for locally driven management and conservation. Decisions can be made quickly, and communities can adopt unique approaches and take a leadership role, with professional scientists taking a supportive role.

Yap State consists of 138 islands and atolls, 22 of which are populated, extending approximately 800 km (500 miles) eastward into the tropical western Pacific Ocean (Figure 10.2). Although the Yap outer islands encompass over 259,000 km² of ocean, the state consists of only 117 km² of land, much of which barely rises above sea level (the main island of Yap is a "high" island). The 2010 census estimated a population of 11,376 people in Yap State.

Although Yap State is a collection of islands, "outer islanders" (people from islands other than the largest main islands of Yap proper) often have a strong sense of cultural identity, and in many cases, they differ significantly from communities on the main islands, including their language and leadership structure. Ulithi is the largest atoll in the Yap outer islands, and by some records the fourth largest atoll in the world (Figure 10.2). Communities on Ulithi often serve in a leadership role for the outer islands. If collaborative management can work here, it sets the stage for a management framework that can extend across a vast area of understudied and critical coral reef habitat in the Western Pacific.

Ulithi Atoll is approximately 161 km east of the main island of Yap. The lagoon measures $36 \times 24$ km and encompasses over 550 km$^2$ (212 square miles), making it one of the largest on Earth. Ulithi consists of 40 islets and four inhabited islands, collectively making up only 4.5 km$^2$ of land, most barely more than a meter above sea level (Figure 10.2). The total population of Ulithi is about 1,000, depending on the time of year (it has one of the two high schools in the outer islands, to which youth come during the school year from the neighboring islands). The four inhabited islands are Falalop (which has the high school and lies just outside the main atoll), with a population of between 500–700 people; Mog Mog, the governance and spiritual center of the outer islands, with a population of approximately 150; Asor, with a population of approximately 70; and Federai to the southeast, with a population of approximately 150.

## Hofagie Laamle – *One People One Reef: a collaboration*

In the following project description, we refer to the professional science teams (of which the co-authors Crane and Nelson are members), and to the local science

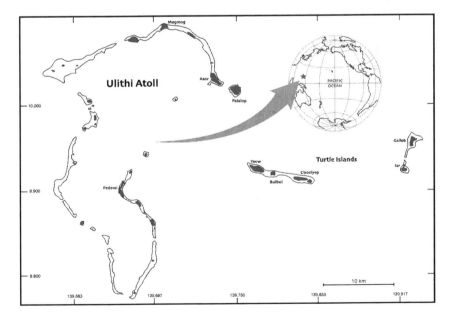

**FIGURE 10.2**  Case study location. Ulithi Atoll and associated islands are located in the Western Pacific Ocean.

teams (of which co-author Rulmal is a member) to explain roles throughout the project. Though co-author Rulmal is also a member of the local community, we refer to the local community in the third person for clarity. Although referred to separately for the purposes of clarification, the teams work collaboratively.

*Hofagie Laamle* (translated loosely to "unite this Atoll/group of islands connected by reefs") is the name the people of Ulithi gave to this program to emphasize the importance of the reefs to their community as a whole. People of Ulithi depend on their reefs, and the reefs depend on the people for stewardship. The goal of the program is to build capacity within communities to manage their reefs through an understanding of the changing ecology of the system, including both their own and external impacts. With a better understanding of the system and drivers of decline, communities can plan for modifications to fishing methods and other management strategies, especially those derived from traditional practices. Local capacity to manage is enhanced by fostering collaborations between professional scientists and local citizen scientists that combine traditional knowledge with modern science.

The *One People One Reef* collaborative has three main goals:

1   Collect sound fishery and environmental data to better understand the ecosystems and to support management. The data are collected by both professional science teams and local science teams.
2   Support the development of reef management plans that address ecological issues, meet community needs, and are sensitive to traditional frameworks. An important part of this goal is to collectively interpret and discuss the results and analyses of the data, and *how* they can support planning.
3   Enhance sustainable and adaptive management planning throughout the outer islands of Micronesia.

The program approach relies on a two-way exchange of knowledge. The professional science team needs information from the community to inform their research approach, such as what the main resource issues are, what approaches have been tried, which are failing, what the major barriers are, past and current fishing practices, and what the community sees as some of the key ecological changes on their reefs. This information helps to frame questions and develop science objectives. The community also benefits from specialized knowledge, skills, and technology from the professional science team to inform their management. For example, connectivity between reefs, fish biomass, and benthic characteristics can help inform management priorities. We facilitate knowledge transfer at community meetings, informal gatherings, cultural exchanges, and interviews and focus groups with as many different demographics as possible including leaders, men, women, elderly people, youth, and fishermen. We use a combination of informal storytelling and discussion, and more structured interview questions.

Data collection is a collaborative effort. The professional science teams collect data from the reefs including fish diversity and abundance, fish biomass, benthic composition, reef complexity, genetics, and other attributes, with a keen appreciation for information requested specifically by the local people. We were alerted, for example, to the presence of a "weedy" coral in Ulithi observed by local people, and so began monitoring its distribution and abundance at their request. This coral, a species of *Montipora* (Crane et al., 2016), has begun to grow abundantly, forming large areas of mono-specific coral coverage on otherwise diverse reefs. Local science teams are now collecting data on the spread of *Montipora*. In addition to monitoring this *Montipora* sp., local science teams collect data on landed fish, including species, length, sex, reproductive status, location where caught, and gear used. They send these data to the professional science teams for analysis, and we share results with the community. This allows the community to assess the impact of certain gear, and the status of specific fisheries, among other things.

Our premise is that the management plans themselves and the implementation of those plans will come from the community, and our teams of professional and local scientists can facilitate this by providing information and advice as needed. We analyze the ecological and fisheries data, and inform fishers and leaders about key patterns we see that suggest overfishing, for example, or other human impacts such as eutrophication. Together we discuss these needs with the community leaders, and support the development of an effective management plan. We note that chiefs and community leaders often identify traditional methods as the best means to address management concerns, and incorporate these where possible.

### The scientists: you train us, we train you

Our collaborative team of scientists includes a core team of four to six professionally trained scientists and about eight locally trained scientists from Ulithi Atoll (Figure 10.3). Our US-based scientists, usually with undergraduate and graduate students, initially survey the reefs and provide access to technologies such as genetic tools and underwater video equipment, as well as statistical analyses to determine patterns in the data. These data, and the emerging results, are shared with the local science teams and local leaders.

On Ulithi, a local project coordinator helps assemble the local science teams, and meets regularly with them. They discuss issues specific to their island, and common issues among the islands. The professional science team trains the local science teams in several data collection techniques (see later), and data are transferred to one island where they are entered into a database. That database is transported to the main Yap island, and uploaded to a shared drive where our professional science team can analyze it and send results back to the community. We also discuss the findings directly with the community when we are on-site.

The local science teams consist of two to four individuals per community, selected by the communities. These individuals are introduced as the "local scientists," and take on the important role of bridging science with management at the local level. They are self motivated, hard working, and respected by their communities. They work closely with fishers (and are often fishers themselves) to collect data

**FIGURE 10.3**  Clockwise from top left: *One People One Reef* local scientists (with Nicole Crane), "professional" science team, scientist Giacomo Bernardi working with fishermen and local teams to sort a catch, local scientist collecting data.

on landed fish. Their challenging job includes recording the catches on formal data sheets, identifying and measuring fish, determining sex and reproductive condition, and recording details of the fishing effort (e.g. habitat, gear, conditions) – all before the fishers become anxious to get their catch distributed and cooked (there is limited refrigeration). The fishers are also sometimes reluctant to talk about fishing location and even gear in some cases (necessary data), and the local scientists need to find ways to build trust. The most important drivers of success for this part of the citizen science are mutual trust, buy-in, and leadership on the part of the fishermen (see Chapter 13 on the importance of communication and building trust). The local science teams are responsible for this, and without that communication and collaboration at the local level, these data would not be available. To date, the people, leaders, and fishers of Ulithi Atoll have developed the largest database of landed fish in the entire region – over 90,000 fish as of January 2017.

This model of a two-way exchange of information has been transformative to the professional scientists and to the local communities. We have been able to see the critical role that cultural changes and social patterns have on resources, and how an understanding of that can inform the scientific questions we ask. On a local level, *One People One Reef* has facilitated a change in social dynamics, and a stronger, more informed connection to the ecological systems that have sustained these communities for centuries, and probably millennia.

## Data: telling a story

Because the local communities' main concerns were declines in the size and availability of fish, and because information from landed fish can elucidate the impacts of fishing and inform future management directions, we initiated a dialogue with the community on the current status of their fisheries, fishing methods, how methods differed from the recent past, and details about fish processing, storage, and distribution. We specifically sought data needed to inform local management and to compare Ulithi fisheries to other regional and national databases.

We compiled data from interviews, semi-structured interviews, and focus group meetings, and analyzed them using a coded grounded theory approach for patterns (Corbin and Strauss, 1990), as well as analysis methods similar to those used by Huntington and Cinner (Cinner et al., 2009; Huntington, 1998; Huntington, 2000). We coded these interviews and focus group comments to identify the main issues and themes that the communities articulated as most important with respect to their reefs and found that concerns about management, community issues, loss of tradition, and resource depletion were most frequently cited (Figure 10.4).

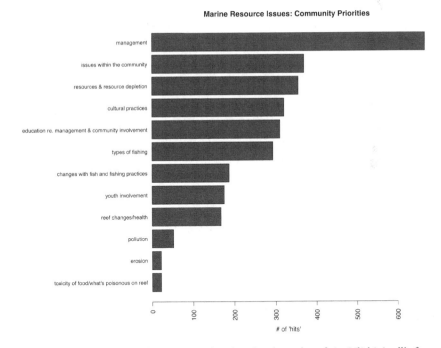

FIGURE 10.4    Priorities and concerns related to local coral reefs in Ulithi Atoll's four communities, determined by frequency of references in interviews and focus groups.

*Note: Management* theme included current types of fishing utilized, resource depletion, and management problems. *Community* theme included youth engagement, education about the reef, and management, leadership problems, and health. *Cultural/traditions* theme included historical fishing, historical management, community taboos, and changes in traditions. *Ecosystem* theme included reef changes, toxicity in fish, erosion, pollution on reefs, new corals, and algal abundance.

We used these priorities identified by the communities to develop ideas and questions to investigate further. For example, within "types of fishing," under the management theme, we could identify the primary types of current versus historical fishing methods. Fewer fishing methods are in common use currently (Table 10.1), likely resulting in fewer trophic guilds being caught, which we believe is having an impact on the reefs (see later and Crane et al., 2017). Local leaders and fishers have incorporated this information into management plans, some of which include restricting or banning night spearfishing (which targets parrotfish), and shallow cast nets that also target herbivorous fish, primarily surgeonfish (Figure 10.4).

We also worked with local families to implement a seafood consumption calendar in 2015. Local science teams went to households in the community and explained to each family how to complete the calendars with information on which meals included seafood for each day, the source of that seafood (e.g. reef fish caught by spear), and how many fish were shared. These data enabled us to tie fisheries data to consumption data, allowing us to better understand patterns in food and fishing preference, and how they could contribute to changes on the reefs. For example, the island of Mog Mog has some of the most degraded reefs, and they are among the reefs with the lowest biomass of fish (Crane et al., 2017). Families on Mog Mog tracked their seafood consumption for one month in July 2015

**TABLE 10.1** Fishing methods. Note that fish traps are being "revived" and some communities are starting to use them again today.

| Fishing method | Historical use (pre-WW2) | Current use |
| --- | --- | --- |
| Fish traps on the sand | X | |
| Fish traps on drift logs | X | |
| Fish traps on reefs | X | * limited |
| Trolling with hand and line and lure | X | X |
| Flying fish – long line with coconut buoy | X | |
| Bottom fishing (hook and line) | X | X |
| Hook and line (reef) | X | X |
| Kite fishing | X | |
| Pole or hand line (from shore) | X | X |
| Pole spear (day) | X | |
| Torch fishing for the flying fish – open water | X | |
| Torch fishing – reef flat | X | |
| Speargun/Hawaiian sling | | X |
| Gillnet | | X |
| Throw net | | X |
| Community net | X | X |
| Fish drive on the reef flat | X | X |
| Reef net | X | X |
| Hukilau | X | |
| Reef gleaning | X | X |
| Purse seiners (occasional commercial fishermen, not from FSM) | | X |

(approximately 85% of the island inhabitants participated). Fifty-two percent of all their meals consisted of fresh seafood, with the remaining meals either consisting of no meat or canned fish. Of the fresh fish, 95% were from nearby reefs. This compares with Falalop, which is outside the Atoll, and had comparatively higher biomass of fish on their reefs (Crane et al., 2017). Falalop (with approximately 30% of inhabitants participating in the seafood consumption study) reported 53% of the meals with fresh seafood, and the remaining meals consisting of canned fish, canned meat, and no meat (Falalop has the only airport on the Atoll, and residents have access to more imported meats). Seventy-six percent of their fresh fish came from reefs while 24% were caught in the open water, including the use of a local FAD (fish attracting device). The people in each community have used these data to manage their reefs differently: Mog Mog has limited or restricted some types of fishing so as not to target key fish on degraded reefs, while Falalop has closed some reefs to fishing (since they can rely on the pelagic fishes more) to recover local reefs through rotating closures.

The inconsistencies in fish naming poses one of our greatest challenges with the data on landed and consumed fish. In Ulithian, there are often several names for the same fish species, depending on color phase, sex, size, and other attributes. This allows fishers to distinguish between phases in life history that help them better understand who should eat it (certain fish are set aside for individuals of specific status), what time of year it is best caught, and so forth. For professional scientists accustomed to using a single taxonomically based scientific name for a species and who do not speak the local language, this represents a challenge. In addition, each island can have a different naming system. So, one of the first things we did was match our scientific names with local names, using books, pictures, names, and a wide representation of fishers. This continues to be a challenge today. A local scientist, Mario Dohmai, is developing a translation document with local fish names, scientific names, and pictures to document them. This document will be critical for making the link between local knowledge and conventional science moving forward. We are also currently developing a DNA barcoding library to positively identify fish associated with local names and corresponding photographs.

To ensure high data quality, the local project coordinator works with the local science teams to go over the data and any challenges they have encountered. The local scientist responsible for data entry goes through each record and flags any inconsistencies so s/he can check with the individual data collector or fisher. Finally, the professional science team checks the database, notes inconsistencies, and seeks clarification from the local teams and fishers. This process can be lengthy, and can delay analysis, but it is critical to making sure we have confidence in the data and the story they tell. When data are thoroughly analyzed, they are a powerful indicator of what is happening on the reef and can help the communities better understand the impact of certain fishing methods, which fish are being caught undersized or close to maturity, and which fish are spawning at what times of the year, among other patterns. One example of data being collected are the main types of fish (names in Ulithian) caught with different fishing methods (Figure 10.5). These data can be used to assess impact on trophic guilds.

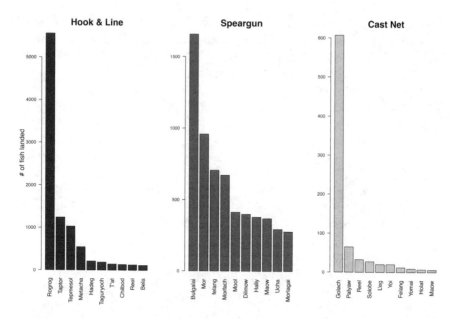

**FIGURE 10.5** The most commonly reported fish (Ulithian names) from three gear types (6/27/14–19/13/15).

*Note: Rogrog* and *Taptor* are emperors, *Bulgalai, Mor, Felang. Morfach* and *Golach* are acanthurids (surgeon-fish). Speargun and castnet are therefore mostly targeting herbivorous fishes.

Landings data (from 2014–2015) showed that spearfishing accounted for almost 50% of the total recorded catch from Ulithi, and 61% of the catch was composed of a few species of herbivorous fish: surgeonfish including *Ctenochaetus striatus, Acanthurus lineatus, Naso lituratus, Acanthurus olivaceus,* parrotfish including *Chlorurus spilurus* and chub (*Kyphosus cinerascens*). The second most common method (just under 40% of landings) was hook and line, which targets primarily higher trophic level fish (predators) such as emperors, grouper, and snapper (Figure 10.5). Cast nets again targeted herbivorous fish *Acanthurus triostegus,* especially on Mog Mog island.

These data show that large numbers of herbivorous fish were caught, especially by speargun. Fishermen were particularly targeting large male parrotfish (often at night). This was likely having an impact on the reproductive capacity of the population (since parrotfish are sequential hermaphrodites – and the larger, more colorful ones are mostly male). In addition, the depletion of herbivorous fish, which have a role in keeping algae from dominating coral reefs, could have an impact on coral recruitment and survivorship of corals (Dulvy et al., 2004; Graham et al., 2006; Heenan and Williams, 2013; Crane et al., 2017). By sharing these ecological stories and interpreting data *with* community leaders, those managers and leaders have reported that they better understand the impacts of their fishing, and the connection between fishing and stressed reefs (such as the impacts of the removal of too many herbivorous fishes). They have utilized these data in their management, which includes gear restrictions to minimize impacts on herbivorous fishes, utilizing more hook and line to take pressure off the herbivorous guild, and rotating closures in some areas. Our professional science team was also able to better understand potential drivers of reef change using these data (Crane et al., 2017).

## Management successes

The *One People One Reef* project has resulted in substantial local change to the management of fisheries and reef resources. Management includes areas closed to fishing, bans on the take of some fish, phasing out the use of gillnets and some cast nets, and bans on night spearfishing for parrotfish. Falalop, Asor, Mog Mog, and Federai communities have each closed portions of the reef under their respective jurisdictions. While this is not a new practice, it is being revisited and re-implemented across the Atoll. More than half of the island of Falalop (Figure 10.6, marked in upper part of photo) has been temporarily closed to fishing. The ban on gillnets was initiated in 2013 and is in effect across much of the atoll. Some of the night spearfishing targeting parrotfish – especially large terminal males, asleep in the reef – was disallowed first in Falalop, then Asor, followed by Mog Mog and finally, in 2015, Federai. Mog Mog restricts cast nets and limits spearfishing. All four islands of Ulithi Atoll have now developed or strengthened management plans. The management plans are adaptive, and change in response to a variety of factors, including natural disaster, celebrations, and decisions by community leaders.

Fishing restrictions come at a cost, such as not being able to access needed protein, yet the communities report a general acceptance and recognition that the changes will recover fish populations and ensure long-term food security. Unsolicited reports from the community of Falalop claim rapid, positive effects from their management, including (per interviews) species they have not seen in many years, increased abundance, and spillover effects into the fished areas. We interpret these reports and the communities' acceptance as evidence of substantial conservation success. Nonetheless, it will only be through the data, and especially the landings data collected by local scientists, that we – the professional science team and the communities – will be able to determine if these management measures have had the desired effect. We attribute this success in part to the autonomous nature of governance and the ability of communities to make rapid decisions, and in part to the collaborative science approach that relies on training local scientists and the partnership between these communities and professional scientists. We are currently analyzing data to determine the effects of management on biomass of fishes on reefs.

## Being a part of One People One Reef: from the local perspective

Like anywhere in the world, trust and credibility are key to a successful partnership (see Chapter 13), and the outer islands of Yap are no exception. Bringing

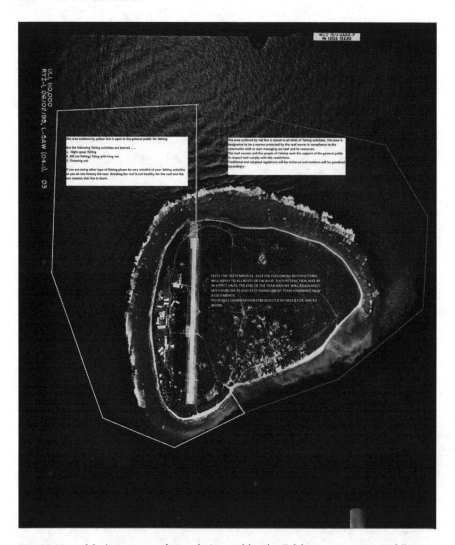

**FIGURE 10.6** Marine protected area designated by the Falalop community in fall 2012. The area marked in the upper part of the photo is a no-fishing zone (except for shore fishing and community fishing), and the area marked in the lower part of the photo restricts some fishing, while allowing some fishing.

professional science teams into these communities may be met with mistrust and opposition; clear goals, consistent with local needs and interests, and a real partnership likely offer the best way towards a successful long-term effort. Recognition of the body of traditional knowledge and its relevance to conservation validates the important role that local communities play in these efforts. Without that recognition, however, local knowledge may not be readily shared unless the use and value of that knowledge is understood. For example, people may be reluctant to share information with professional teams about reefs, management, jurisdiction, and traditions because they question the value of sharing, and may not fully trust what will be done with the information.

Obtaining accurate local information and data from local participants depends not only on how it is collected, but also who is asking for it, and how the community is approached. In small, tight-knit communities like those of the outer islands, people are clearly capable of working together to achieve common goals effectively, but may be reluctant to expend energy on an endeavor whose outcome might have little apparent local benefit. It is critical that the outcomes be clear, and that they be articulated by the communities themselves. "People will often hear what you have to say, but more importantly they will remember and respect what you *do*" (John Rulmal, Jr.).

The *One People One Reef* professional science team came to the outer islands by invitation, and listened to what the people had to say. We were clear from the beginning that management would be difficult, that it would depend on the active participation of local science teams, and that plan development and implementation were up to the local community. We provided modern scientific knowledge and data analyses to help outer islanders understand the nature and extent of the problems, and made ourselves available for questions. We shared all the data collected, returned regularly, and worked closely with the local people. This helped build trust, and most importantly empowered communities on Ulithi to be leaders in management. These reefs are their reefs. Citizen scientists in this context need to be more than data collectors; they need to be co-leaders in the program, helping to determine goals and objectives (e.g. co-created projects [Shirk et al., 2012] or extreme citizen science [Haklay, 2013]).

Navigating local social networks can be difficult, and "outside" teams are best served by being open, honest, and transparent. Decisions about local science team composition and who should be involved are best left up to a process decided by the community leaders. There are examples of conservation and management projects that come into a community and suggest teams (an "outreach and education" committee, an "enforcement" committee, etc.). These constructs can lead to tensions in communities. Governance and oversight, transfer of knowledge, and even training programs should be implemented by local leaders who understand social and political protocols.

## Building capacity for future citizen science-based management

In addition to the management and conservation successes, there have been significant positive ancillary benefits for the Ulithi communities from the *One People One Reef* program. The effort to discuss management among the islands (an issue they all have in common) has led to increased dialogue among leaders, and a revival of open communication channels. During this time of rapid environmental and cultural change, improved communication is critical to maintain consistent policies and to make the most effective use of a growing database to refine management and conservation. Although the exact management plans are difficult to document, all four inhabited islands of the atoll now have established policies in place – a testament to their dedication. In theory, a reef manager or owner may choose to close (or not) an area or parts of an area for whatever reason they choose, but the reality is that they need community support. Scientific data gathered by the local science teams since 2012 have helped local leaders re-establish their roles and responsibilities. There has been a renewed interest in traditions and cultural history around fishing and management. The community is coming together around the conservation and improved management of a critically important ecosystem, and a shared understanding of its interconnectivity.

Another spin-off, articulated by many in the community, is the interest shown by the youth, many of whom have become disconnected from their communities. Some of the youth have expressed interest in reconnecting with traditional ways and better understanding how these traditions fit with the modern world. There is a growing interest among the youth around marine work, conservation, and the merging of science and tradition. The *One People One Reef* program involved youth from all four islands in 2015, 2016, and 2017, with strong community support. Because people from all the islands are measuring fish for a common database, they are talking about and remembering traditional names – bringing them back. Traditional boundaries and fishing jurisdictions, which are often neglected by the youth, are being talked about and enforced again.

Youth are motivated by seeing local leadership with the program, and particularly the active participation of their peers. This experience encourages them to come back and do more in their own communities. In one youth's words, "We are not doomed to destruction after all."

### Reviving and understanding traditional practices

*One People One Reef* is leading to a rediscovery of traditions, and understanding how modern science can complement traditional practices. It is providing a venue to talk about these traditions and management.

### Examples

- *Mol igil bong*: The first fish caught. Fishing rights belong to certain clans. They can open and close a fishing area. *Mol igil bong* is when someone from the clan (manager or owner) fishes, gets a good first catch of the season, and decides to open the area to fishing by the rest of his clan. When someone from outside of that clan is granted permission to fish there, they practice *Fa'ad elbong* ("string from the *ibong*") – two fish strung with bellies together are given to the clan that owns the area (an elder of the clan). This practice had become increasingly rare, but our interviews indicate a resurgence, apparently stimulated by the communities' increased involvement in data collection and management decisions. The practice ensures tenure over fishing grounds.

- People are paying renewed attention to where their fish are caught. "We used to know this, [but] don't so much anymore. We are beginning to talk about it more" (Fisherman). Community members said that some elders could identify the source reef for emperors (*rogrog*), based on their coloration. This used to help reef owners know where people were fishing, and served as a check to ensure that fishers were not fishing in a closed area.
- Local scientists measuring others' fish was not welcomed initially. Now it is acceptable. Historically, catches were checked by chiefs as the canoes came to shore. That practice was largely lost, but people are paying attention now that the local science teams are checking – similar in many ways to the traditional practice.
- Certain fish species were reserved for chiefs. Larger grouper, for example, were taboo for others. Men eat certain fish away from the main island – in the boat, on an island, or at beach canoe house – such as barracuda and groupers. These taboos provide an additional means of conservation, as well as protecting the greater community from potential toxins such as ciguatera.
- Turtle harvesting seasons. Historically, people didn't harvest turtles in the water (they do sometimes now). They used to take all turtles to Mog Mog for approval and blessing before slaughtering and distributing. This limits the take as it requires a long trip to the island. People are talking about this again, and why it is they used to do those things (it was *management!*).

## Best practices

Some reasons the *One People One Reef* program has met with great local support and participation in the Yap outer islands, and specifically on Ulithi Atoll, include:

- The program recognizes the importance and sensitivity of the local community perspective and needs first, before the professional science team's goals.
- Reports (including scientific results) are written, presented, and *discussed* in a way that local people can understand them and apply the results to their management needs.
- Communities are respected. *One People One Reef* makes locals true partners in the conservation effort.
- There are no documents, agreements, or contracts, such as commitments to no-take reserves or spatial closures required by the professional scientists. The community decides what it wants to contribute in terms of written commitments.
- The professional science team follows through on commitments, maintains effective communications with the community (to the extent that technology allows), and provides analytical support and advice on request.

## The future

Ulithi has been the trendsetter for the outer island chain in the recent past (since the building of landing strip in World War II, and the establishment of the high school in 1964) and these trends often make their way to the rest of the neighboring (outer) island chain. The *One People One Reef* collaborative program is a model that is beginning to expand through these islands, with the initial leadership of Ulithi. Its success will depend on the collaboration, mutual understanding, and commitment of all involved.

> To me, we have a moral responsibility here to set positive trends for the rest of our neighbors. I have seen divisions arise between islands, and it is time to unify around the management of a system that unites us all. *Hofagie Laamle* (*One People One Reef*).
>
> (John Rulmal, Jr.)

The combination of shared knowledge to understand and manage a complex human-natural coupled system leads to planning that is woven into the cultural and governance structure of the communities. That integration is the framework for sustainable management and conservation, led by local communities, and supported, rather than driven, by conventional science. This has the greatest potential for success in the long-term.

> We need to have a common understanding around management, so that everyone agrees and supports it. Understanding the old ways, and the impacts of the new ways, can help us protect the ocean for our children, and their children.
>
> (Isaac "Ike" Chief, Asor Island, Ulithi Atoll)

## Web resources

1 www.fieldmuseum.org/science/citizen-science.
2 www.calacademy.org/citizen-science.
3 www.si.edu/volunteer/citizenscience.
4 www.oceanicsociety.org/.
5 www.earthwatch.org/.
6 www.reefcheck.org.
7 We use the term "professional scientist" throughout this chapter to refer to university-trained people who practice science as their full-time professional job, and "conventional science" to refer to ways of generating knowledge using the classic Newtonian "scientific method" (Ballard and Huntsinger, 2006; Berkes and Turnaer, 2006). We prefer these terms instead of "Western science and scientists" because there are many ways of knowing in the "Western world," and professional scientists conduct conventional science globally beyond the Western world.

## Literature cited

Abelson, A., Nelson, P., Edgar, G., Shashar, N., Reed, D., Belmaker, J., Krause, G., Beck, M., Brokovich, E., France, R., and Gaines, S. (2016). Expanding marine protected areas to include degraded coral reefs. *Conservation Biology*, 30(6), 1182–1191.

Ballard, H.L., and Huntsinger, L. (2006). Salal harvester local ecological knowledge, harvest practices and understory management on the Olympic Peninsula, Washington. *Human Ecology*, 34, 529–547.

Berkes, F., Colding, J., and Folke, C. (2000). Rediscovery of traditional ecological knowledge as adaptive management. *Ecological Applications*, 10(5), 1251.

Berkes, F., and Turner, N. (2006). Knowledge, learning and the evolution of conservation practice for social-ecological system resilience. *Human Ecology*, 34(4), 479–494.

Bourgoin, J., Castella, J., Hett, C., Lestrelin, G., and Heinimann, A. (2013). Engaging local communities in low emissions land-use planning: A case study from Laos. *Ecology and Society*, 18.

Braschler, B. (2009). Successfully implementing a citizen-scientist approach to insect monitoring in a resource-poor country. *BioScience*, 59(2), 103–104.

Christie, P. (2004). Marine protected areas as biological successes and social failures in Southeast Asia. *American Fisheries Society*, 42, 155–164.

Cinner, J., McClanahan, T., Daw, T., Graham, N., Maina, J., Wilson, S., and Hughes, T. (2009). Linking social and ecological systems to sustain coral reef fisheries. *Current Biology*, 19(3), 206–212.

Cohn, J. (2008). Citizen science: Can volunteers do real research? *BioScience*, 58(3), 192.

Corbin, J., and Strauss, A. (1990). Grounded theory research: Procedures, canons and evaluative criteria. *Zeitschrift für Soziologie*, 19, 418–427.

Couvet, D., Jiguet, F., Julliard, R., Levrel, H., and Teyssedre, A. (2008). Enhancing citizen contributions to biodiversity science and public policy. *Interdisciplinary Science Reviews*, 33(1), 95–103.

Crane, N.L., Paddack, M.J., Nelson, P.A., Abelson, A., Rulmal, J., and Bernardi, G. (2016). Corallimorph and Montipora Reefs in Ulithi Atoll, Micronesia: documenting unusual reefs. *Journal of the Ocean Science Foundation*, 21, 10–17.

Crane, N., Paddack, M., Nelson, P., et al. (2017). Atoll-scale patterns in coral reef community structure: Human signatures on Ulithi Atoll, Micronesia. *PLoS One*.

Dickinson, J., Shirk, J., Bonter, D., Bonney, R., Crain, R., Martin, J., Phillips, T., and Purcell, K. (2012). The current state of citizen science as a tool for ecological research and public engagement. *Frontiers in Ecology and the Environment*, 10(6), 291–297.

Drazen, J.C., and Tissot, B.N. (2014). Understanding the scale of marine protection in Hawai'i: From community-based management to the remote Northwestern Hawaiian Islands. *Mar. Manag. Areas Fish*, 69, 153.

Drew, J.A. (2005). Use of traditional ecological knowledge in marine conservation. *Conservation Biology*, 19, 1286–1293.

Dulvy, N., Polunin, N., Mill, A., and Graham, N. (2004). Size structural change in lightly exploited coral reef fish communities: Evidence for weak indirect effects. *Canadian Journal of Fisheries and Aquatic Sciences*, 61(3), 466–475.

Follett, R., and Strezov, V. (2015). An analysis of citizen science based research: Usage and publication patterns. *PLoS One*, 10, 1–14.

Goring, S.J., Weathers, K.C., Dodds, W.K., Soranno, P.A., Sweet, L.C., Cheruvelil, K.S., Kominoski, J.S., Rüegg, J., Thorn, A.M., and Utz, R.M. (2014). Improving the culture of interdisciplinary collaboration in ecology by expanding measures of success. *Frontiers in Ecology and the Environment*, 12(1), 39–47.

Graham, N.A., Wilson, S.K., Jennings, S., Polunin, N.V., Bijoux, J.P., and Robinson, J. (2006). Dynamic fragility of oceanic coral reef ecosystems. *Proceedings of the National Academy of Sciences*, 103(22), 8425–8429.

Haklay, M. (2013). Citizen science and volunteered geographic information: Overview and typology of participation. In *Crowdsourcing Geographic Knowledge: Volunteered Geographic Information (VGI) in Theory and Practice*, 105–122. Berlin: Springer.

Heckler, S. (2012). *Landscape, Process and Power*. New York: Berghahn Books.

Heenan, A., and Williams, I.D. (2013). Monitoring herbivorous fishes as indicators of coral reef resilience in American Samoa. *PLoS One*, 8, e79604.

Hilborn, R. (2007). Moving to sustainability by learning from successful fisheries. *Ambio*, 36, 296–303.

Huntington, H.P. (1998). Observations on the utility of the semi-directive interview for documenting traditional ecological knowledge. *Arctic*, 51, 237–242.

Huntington, H.P. (2000). Using traditional ecological knowledge in science: Methods and applications. *Ecological Applications*, 10(5), 1270.

Johannes, R. (1981). *Words of the Lagoon: Fishing and marine lore in the Palau district of Micronesia.* Berkeley, CA: University of California Press.

Kittinger, J., Finkbeiner, E., Glazier, E., and Crowder, L. (2012). Human dimensions of coral reef social-ecological systems. *Ecology and Society*, 17(4).

Kittinger, J.N., McClenachan, L., Gedan, K.B., and Blight, L.K. (Eds.). (2015). *Marine Historical Ecology in Conservation: Applying the Past to Manage for the Future.* Berkeley: University of California Press. McClanahan, T.R., Marnane, M.J., Cinner, J.E., and Kiene, W.E. (2006). A comparison of marine protected areas and alternative approaches to coral-reef management. *Current Biology*, 16, 1408–1413.

Miller-Rushing, A., Primack, R., and Bonney, R. (2012). The history of public participation in ecological research. *Frontiers in Ecology and the Environment*, 10, 285–290.

Pitcher, T.J. (2001). Fisheries managed to rebuild ecosystems? Reconstructing the past to salvage the future. *Ecological Applications*, 11, 601–617.

Silvertown, J. (2009). A new dawn for citizen science. *Trends in Ecology & Evolution*, 24, 467–471.

Thurstan, R., McClenachan, L., Crowder, L., Drew, J., Kittinger, J., Levin, P., Roberts, C., and Pandolfi, J. (2015). Filling historical data gaps to foster solutions in marine conservation. *Ocean & Coastal Management*, 115, 31–40.

Ugulu, I. (2011). Traditional ethnobotanical knowledge about medicinal plants used for external therapies in Alasehir, Turkey. *International Journal of Medicinal and Aromatic Plants*, 1, 101–106.

Wamukota, A.W., Cinner, J.E., and McClanahan, T.R. (2012). Co-management of coral reef fisheries: A critical evaluation of the literature. *Marine Policy*, 36, 481–488.

Wendt, D.E., and Starr, R.M. (2009). Collaborative research: An effective way to collect data for stock assessments and evaluate marine protected areas in California. *Marine and Coastal Fisheries*, 1, 315–324.

Williams, I., Walsh, W., Schroeder, R., Friedlander, A., Richards, B., and Stamoulis, K. (2008). Assessing the importance of fishing impacts on Hawaiian coral reef fish assemblages along regional-scale human population gradients. *Environmental Conservation*, 35(3), 261.

Wilson, J.R., Prince, J.D., and Lenihan, H.S. (2010). A management strategy for sedentary nearshore species that uses marine protected areas as a reference. *Marine and Coastal Fisheries*, 2, 14–27.

# 11

# ENGAGING YOUTH AND SCHOOLS IN COASTAL CITIZEN SCIENCE

## Balancing both education and science goals

*Ann Wasser*

## Introduction

Engaging youth in citizen science can be a unique and rewarding experience for both youth and the scientists and resource managers that benefit from their data collection, and those benefits, are both scientific and educational. Citizen science has been undertaken by adults for decades through activities like the Audubon Society's Christmas Bird Count, but focusing on youth is a relatively new venture (Ballard et al., 2016). Programs like the Cornell Lab of Ornithology's Celebrate Urban Birds[1] in the United States, and several water quality monitoring programs, like the Wasser Schafft program[2] in Austria, have developed monitoring protocols focused on youth. In Austria, the Federal Ministry of Science, Research and Economy and the Center for the Cooperation of Science and School have even developed a program called Young Science, that connects schools, universities and research institutions to facilitate working on a wide range of citizen science projects across the country.[3] Programs designed specifically for youth participation like these have the potential to help further the citizen science movement and increase public science literacy. These positive educational outcomes are only recently under research and evaluation, and more evidence is needed on how youth-focused citizen science programs can be designed to balance the need for rigorous scientific data collection and science learning. In this chapter, I describe one program, LiMPETS, that may provide lessons for effective design of youth-focused citizen science programs for coastal and marine conservation.

Youth-based coastal and marine citizen science programs are much less common than programs focused on adult citizen scientists.[4] Examples in this short list of youth-based marine citizen science programs are the Seattle Aquarium's Citizen Science program that monitors the rocky and muddy shores of Puget Sound;[5] the Summer on the Marsh program developed by New England Ocean

Science Education Collaborative (NEOSEC),[6] which is utilized by marine science summer programs throughout New England; and, in California, the Long-term Monitoring Program and Experiential Training for Students (LiMPETS)[7] program has been engaging youth and adults in monitoring the rocky intertidal and sandy beach habitats since 2002. The common goals of these youth-based programs are to increase ocean and science literacy of the next generation, develop a long-term dataset that is of use to researchers and resource managers, and encourage students to be environmental leaders and develop pro-environmental personal behaviors (Bursky, 2014).

The convergence of science and education goals in youth-based programs can present challenges when trying to balance the scientific integrity of the data with the educational needs of students and teachers (see section "Unique Aspects of Using Youth in Coastal and Marine Citizen Science"). While this balance between educational/outreach goals and conservation-science/management goals is common among citizen science programs in general, it can be particularly tricky for youth-based programs because of the challenges in working within the constraints of formal school institutions (Ballard et al., 2016) and the skepticism many scientists have about youth-collected data (Burgess et al., 2016). But working with youth also offers exciting opportunities for citizen science.

From the perspective of teachers and schools, citizen science offers a chance for science learning through participation in authentic science and inquiry practices, like those promoted by the Next Generation Science Standards in the United States (NGSS, 2013). As these national standards for science education are implemented across the United States, citizen science programs are a being touted as prime opportunities for teachers to engage their students in hands-on, inquiry-based, real-world science consistent with established science education research (National Research Council, 2007). For citizen science programs, students and teachers can be an ideal audience to work with because of the structure that already exists within the school system. A school-focused citizen science program can recruit, train and support teachers and their students, with numbers ranging from one class of 25 students to four or five classes of 30 students or more. To effectively recruit and train this many participants in depth outside of a school setting is incredibly difficult. Being able to leverage the infrastructure of schools can create a win-win situation, if the science and education goals are balanced appropriately to ensure high quality data collection that is useful to resource managers while also meeting the educational needs and academic abilities of the students participating.

## LiMPETS as a case study for youth-based coastal and marine citizen science

LiMPETS is an environmental monitoring and education program for students, educators and volunteer groups. The LiMPETS Rocky Intertidal program was started in 1971 to monitor sites in and around Santa Cruz, California, in response to the 1969 oil spill off the coast of Santa Barbara, to develop a long-term intertidal monitoring program for the Santa Cruz coast. The protocols were originally developed for use with undergraduate students, but it became apparent that trained high school students could do similar data collection with small shifts in protocols. This hands-on program now monitors the coastal ecosystems of California's National Marine Sanctuaries to increase awareness, scientific understanding and stewardship of these ecologically important areas (see Chapter 7). There are three organizations that currently coordinate LiMPETS across California: the Greater Farallones Association, the Pacific Grove Museum of Natural History and the Channel Islands National Marine Sanctuary.

Two distinct monitoring programs make up the core of LiMPETS: the Rocky Intertidal Monitoring Program and the Sandy Beach Monitoring Program. The Sandy Beach program was developed in 2000 to engage students in hands-on science with a coastal indicator species, the Pacific mole crab (*Emerita anaologa*). Both programs are designed to provide students with the opportunity to participate in the scientific process while contributing to the statewide LiMPETS rocky intertidal and sandy beach datasets. Through research-based monitoring and standardized protocols, students develop their ability to ask and answer scientific questions while gaining experience using tools and methods employed by field scientists, and learn to analyze and interpret data. The online data entry system allows participants to archive their data electronically and to view and analyze long-term trends in the data.

## Education

### Teacher training workshops

The LiMPETS program is based on a teacher training model that has been developed and fine-tuned over 10 years. To begin their participation in LiMPETS, teachers must first attend a full-day teacher training workshop that covers all aspects of the LiMPETS program. Each of the two monitoring programs has its own associated workshop.

The workshops begin with an introduction to LiMPETS and the National Marine Sanctuary system and then continue with a training presentation that teachers will use with their students. After the training presentation, teachers participate in a few of the hands-on training elements that are provided in a five-unit curriculum (Table 11.1) that has been developed for the range of monitoring protocols within the rocky intertidal and sandy beach programs. Once teachers have been through the identical training their students will receive, they head out into the field with the LiMPETS Program Coordinator, who will accompany them on all trips. At the beach or in the tide pools (Figure 11.1), teachers engage in the full suite of monitoring protocols covering many of the common mistakes made by students, safety concerns and commonly asked questions. Common mistakes made by students include misidentification of algae species, misreading calipers and recording data incorrectly on their datasheets. This field trip provides teachers

**TABLE 11.1** LiMPETS curriculum. The LiMPETS curriculum is a guide for teachers to participate with their students in LiMPETS. Each unit provides teachers with the information necessary to complete a different piece of LiMPETS.

| Curriculum Unit | Topics Covered |
| --- | --- |
| Unit 1: Getting Started – Background Information for Teachers | Basics of Intertidal Ecology, Field Monitoring Techniques and Marine Conservation Efforts |
| Unit 2: Engage and Prepare – In-class Introductory Activities for Monitoring | Preparation activities for students – Notes pages for training presentation, Claymation field ID game, crossword puzzle to learn terms, photo ID and measuring activities |
| Unit 3: Investigate and Archive – Monitoring in the Field and Data Entry | Pre-trip Planning, Monitoring Equipment Checklist and Data Entry Directions |
| Unit 4: Analyze and Interpret – Data Analysis Activities for the Classroom | Graphing Data, Data Analysis Lessons, Comparing Data to previously published scientific data |
| Unit 5: Communicate – Effectively Communicating Science and Taking Action in Your Community | Creating a Scientific Poster, Preparing a Scientific Talk, Effective Science Communication through Blogs and Videos |

**FIGURE 11.1** Teachers participate in the practice rocky intertidal monitoring photo activity.

an opportunity to fully experience what their students will experience in the field. After returning from the field, teachers work in small groups to enter their data into the LiMPETS online and publicly accessible database. The final activities are data analysis and science communication, where teachers walk through the final two units of the curriculum and close the loop on the full scientific process. Data analysis lessons range from simple graphing to data comparison to data reported in scientific journals. The science communication lessons address everything from creating a scientific poster, developing a scientific talk, to blogging effectively, and creating engaging videos that convey a scientific message. Teachers walk away with a full understanding of the LiMPETS program and how to successfully implement the program with their students, and many have scheduled their field programs.

All lessons in the LiMPETS curriculum are aligned to the Next Generation Science Standards (NGSS Lead States, 2013), Common Core Math and Language Arts Standards (National Governors Association, 2010) and the National Oceanographic and Atmospheric Administration's Ocean Literacy Principles (NOAA, 2013). The curriculum alignment is a major selling point for teachers to prove to their school administrators exactly how the LiMPETS field trip(s) address the standards required by the State of California.

## Student preparation

After teachers are trained, they work with the LiMPETS Coordinator in their region to schedule their field monitoring day(s). Depending on the classroom schedule and transportation availability, students monitor their field site from 1 to 10 times over the course of a school year. Once field days are scheduled, the in-class training is scheduled with their LiMPETS Program Coordinator.

On the day of the training, the LiMPETS Program Coordinator will present 45–60 minutes of training and then engage the students in a practice monitoring activity. For the Rocky Intertidal program, students use a large photo of a tide pool and a quadrat to do a simulated monitoring session. For the Sandy Beach program, students utilize calipers and photocards of sand crabs (*Emeria analoga*) to practice measuring and sexing the crabs to understand the process before they are in the field (Figure 11.2).

In addition to the LiMPETS Program Coordinator's pre-field trip training, teachers are asked to have their students read and review the Student Factsheets that provide more information about the habitat they will be monitoring and the field methods being used to monitor. Students are also required to take online quizzes before they monitor. These results are then emailed to the students. These results are used for two reasons by the teacher: (1) to see where their students are having challenges and (2) to have a graded activity related to their monitoring experience. These scores are used by the LiMPETS Coordinators, in concert with other indicators, to score the student data as part of the QA/QC based on a clearly developed

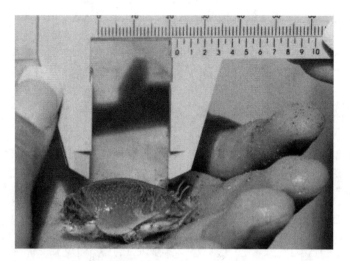

**FIGURE 11.2**   Measuring a sand crab carapace.

*Source:* Amy Dean, Greater Farallones Association.

rubric. Other training resources teachers and students can utilize include online species identification quizzes, online practice monitoring, and a Claymation identification game. Each of the student resources aims to address the different learning styles of students: auditory, visual and kinesthetic.

## Students in the field

Getting students into the field is the most rewarding part of the process and can also be the most challenging. For LiMPETS, we have to schedule monitoring times around the tides, which can be difficult based on the limited number of hours students are in school and the infrequency of low tides that occur during the school day. The other challenge in getting school groups out is dealing with school bus availability and cost. Depending on the region, there are varying amounts of bus scholarship money to help offset the cost to schools to participate.

Once students are in the field, the LiMPETS Coordinator reviews the protocols to ensure that students have a clear understanding of their methods. The class is then divided up into small groups of three to five students to begin their monitoring. Each group is provided with all the equipment and datasheets necessary to complete their monitoring. The teacher(s) and LiMPETS Coordinator roam between field groups to answer questions and ensure that the data are being collected accurately and species are being identified correctly. Monitoring tends to last between one and three hours, based on the number of students, their efficiency and the number of animals that they find. When scheduling, we plan for at least a two-hour block to allow for review and adequate monitoring time.

## Conservation and monitoring projects

### Sandy Beach

The Sandy Beach Monitoring Program monitors population of the Pacific mole crab (*Emerita analoga*) along the California coast. The science and resource management goals of this program are to (1) assess the abundance and fecundity of the sand crab population, because it is the base of the sand beach food web and sand crabs can be an indicator of beach health (Ferdin et al., 2002; Dugan et al., 2005); (2) assess the sand crab population density; and (3) assess the rate of acanthocephalan parasite infection in sand crabs, because the parasites affect birds and mammals up the food chain.

To monitor the sand crabs, students work in small groups on transects, taking sand cores at regular intervals. The length of the transect and the spacing between cores samples varies based on the width of the swash zone. The sand cores are taken using a clam gun and cores depths vary by monitoring site, either 10 cm or 20 cm deep. Students use a set of mesh bags to separate the crabs from the sand by pouring water over the sand and the crabs. Once the crabs have been separated, each crab is measured and sexed (Figure 11.2) and the data are recorded on the pre-prepared datasheet. The crabs are then released back into the ocean away from the transect line, except for the schools that participate in the optional dissection that sample crabs for parasites. At the end of the monitoring event, the LiMPETS Coordinator checks all data sheets to make sure they are filled out and instructs students to fill out any missing information.

### Rocky Intertidal

The Rocky Intertidal Monitoring Program assesses the invertebrate and algae populations along the California coast. The science and resource management goals of this program are to (1) develop a baseline dataset of species composition and distribution in case of a natural or manmade disaster; (2) assess changes in the intertidal community structure due to sea level rise, water temprature increases and/or ocean acidification; and (3) help assess the impacts of the California State Marine Protected Areas (MPAs). The last goal happened serendipitously: the state MPAs were put into place in Central California in 2005. Some LiMPETS monitoring sites fall inside MPAs and other are outside, making for ideal reference sites.

To monitor the rocky intertidal, students work in small groups using 0.25 m² quadrats to determine the abundances of 20 species of algae and invertebrates (Figure 11.3). These quadrats are laid along a transect from low to high intertidal zones at regular intervals to determine diversity, seasonality, and species shifts in the intertidal. Transect length and quadrat interval spacing varies by monitoring site, from 14 m to 65 m based on the width of the intertidal zone at low tide. The topography of the monitoring sites varies from wide flat sedimentary rocky intertidal benches to short, steep, granitic outcrops; this dictates the length of the transect. Intervals vary by site, as well, to accurately capture the variance of the

FIGURE 11.3   Pacific Grove High School students monitoring at Point Pinos, Pacific
Grove, California.

*Source:* Ann Wasser, Pacific Grove Museum of Natural History.

monitoring site. For shorter, steeper monitoring sites, the transects are shorter as
is the quadrat spacing to capture zonation. With longer, flatter intertidal sites, the
transects are longer as is the spacing between sampling quadrats. With the exception
of two sites, all monitoring sites include a mussel bed, as they are good indicators
of the zero-tide height (mean low water). Total area counts monitor limpet (*Lottia giangantea*), sea star (*Pisaster ochraceus*), anemone (*Anthopleura xanthogrammica and
Anthopleura sola*) and black abalone (*Haliotis cracherodii*) populations within a defined
area. This protocol allows larger, solitary species that are harder to capture using
vertical transect methods to be accounted for.

## Data quality/control

The outside perception of LiMPETS data quality has been an ongoing challenge
because the scientific community has had a difficult time believing that high school

students can accurately collect data on intertidal algae and invertebrates. A comparison study between trained intertidal field technicians and LiMPETS-trained high school students found that there was no statistical difference between the two sampling groups (Pearse et al., 2000). Even so, LiMPETS has been continually improving the data quality assurance processes in training, in the field and through the back end of the online database. This has been an interesting process because of the organic nature in which LiMPETS was developed. The rocky intertidal and sandy beach monitoring programs were developed separately and each had a different end-use focus. The rocky intertidal data set was developed to be used with undergraduate students and to act as a baseline to assess future environmental impacts. As such a quality assurance and quality control (QA/QC) plan was not originally developed. The Sandy Beach Program was developed to be primarily a science education program for the Greater Farallones National Marine Sanctuary, so there was not a defined end use for the data. However, data quality has become a focus of the program because of the role LiMPETS now plays in monitoring the coastal ecosystems of California's National Marine Sanctuaries and California State Marine Protected Areas.

## QA/QC in the field and back in the classroom

The LiMPETS Coordinator and the trained teacher(s) work with the student groups to ensure the highest data quality by making sure that the groups are performing sampling methods and data entry correctly and accurately. If there are any deficiencies, corrective action is taken on the spot and errors are fixed when possible. Depending on the teacher, either the students themselves or the teacher will enter the data from the field sheets. LiMPETS coordinators encourage students to do it, and argue that entering data makes the experience real for the student who feels like s/he has contributed to a larger scientific goal.

The LiMPETS network partners, including resource managers from the MPAs and scientists, have developed a rigorous QA/QC plan that clearly outlines a series of rubrics to qualify the data for inclusion in the database and remove individual judgement by teacher or student in assessing data quality. This plan includes a system of training requirements, and data quality checks in the field as well as in the data entry process. Metadata is collected for all trips and the online database allows end users to filter the data by its quality to exclude any data they don't want to utilize. So, while students are always encouraged to enter their data, teachers and program coordinators know that some data quality might be low. In that case, the monitoring event is given a QA/QC score and will ultimately be voided after the end of the school year and the student has completed her/his LiMPETS experience.

Several components of the program that happen after data collection aren't necessary for ensuring data quality, but are crucial for the science education goals of the program. An important aspect of LiMPETS is that students have access to their own data and all the data collected previously for the whole program, so they can look at their monitoring site over time, and/or compare across sites up and down the California coast. This inquiry activity allows for development of science reasoning practices and puts the data in context for the students; in a SciStarter survey, 84%

**FIGURE 11.4** Branson School (Marin County, California) students presenting their LiMPETS monitoring research at the American Geophysical Union conference in San Francisco in 2015.

*Source:* Amy Dean, Greater Farallones Association.

of citizen scientists want to see their data after submission (Ceccaroni and Jaume, 2017). Similarly, teachers are encouraged to facilitate students presenting to outside audiences in their community or to scientists. The act of creating messaging for their communication project, whether it is a poster, blog or video, requires students to have a clear enough understanding of a phenomenon to be able to articulate it to an outside audience, and research conducted on the program found disseminating to outside audiences can increase youth identity with science (Ballard et al., 2016).

## LiMPETS data use

Data collected by the LiMPETS program have many uses beyond science education. Student-collected data over the last 45 years, now incorporated into LiMPETS, have been used in several ways.

## California State Marine Protected Area (MPA) monitoring

In 1999, the California State Legislature recognized the need to protect the long-term health of the state's marine ecosystems with the passage of the Marine Life Protection Act. As part of this process to develop the MPAs, the non-profit Ocean Science Trust was established to design and implement a monitoring plan for the MPAs across the state (see Chapter 7). LiMPETS was a part of this effort for both the North Central Coast and South Coast MPA areas (California Marine Protected Areas, 2017). As the Ocean Science Trust moves forward in establishing long-term monitoring plans for MPAs, LiMPETS will be included because it lies at the intersection of data collection and public education that the State of California needs to successfully implement the MPAs in the long term. For students participating in LiMPETS, it is a motivator and point of pride that they are contributing to a long-term data set that can be used by the State of California to assess the health of the beaches and rocky shores.

Professional monitoring of the MPAs in California is currently being carried out by the Partnership for Interdisciplinary Studies of Coastal Oceans (PISCO)[8] and its partner organizations. This monitoring, while extensive, is also expensive. By utilizing youth citizen scientists in monitoring the state can cut costs, engage a public audience in the scientific process and increase awareness of the role of MPAs in broader conservation efforts. The *State of the California North Central Coast 2010–2015* report outlines species recovery as a result of the implementation of MPAs (California Ocean Science Trust, 2016). This report is a valuable tool in informing LiMPETS teachers and students about the impact of their work and helps the cycle of education, monitoring and conservation continue.

## National Marine Sanctuary Condition Reports

The Office of National Marine Sanctuary Condition Reports (ONMS, 2015) provide summaries of resources in each sanctuary, pressures on those resources, the current condition and trends, and management responses to the pressures that threaten the integrity of the marine environment. Specifically, the Condition Reports include information on the status and trends of water quality, habitat, living resources and maritime archaeological resources and the human activities that affect them. The Condition Reports document the condition of sanctuary resources based on sanctuary staff judgments after consultation with selected partners and best available information. The reports serve as a tool to determine if the sanctuaries are achieving their resource protection and improvement goals as reflected in National Marine Sanctuaries Report performance measures. The Condition Reports also serve as a reporting tool to be used by policy makers and act as a supporting document during the Management Plan Review Process that happens at each sanctuary every 10 years.

For the 2015 Monterey Bay National Marine Sanctuary's Condition Report, LiMPETS mussel (*Mytilus californianus*) data (Figure 11.5) were utilized to determine the long-term stability of the mussel population in northern Monterey Bay,

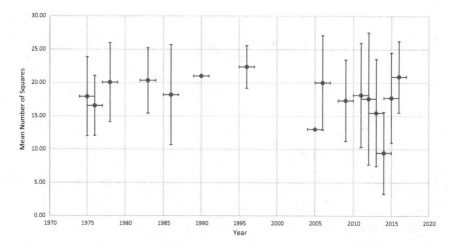

**FIGURE 11.5** Estimates of abundance of mussels (*Mytilus californianus*) from counts made in 0.25m² quadrats randomly placed within plots on mussel-dominated, mid-zone, intertidal platforms at Almar Ave, Santa Cruz, California. LiMPETS quadrat counts are done by number of squares (presence/absence) instead of the point contact method.

with the exception of rocky intertidal sites that are popular for harvesting (ONMS, 2015). With this information and future monitoring data, the Sanctuary staff can assess the health of mussel populations and work with the California Department of Fish and Wildlife to regulate their collection as needed. As the data collection in the Monterey Bay area by LiMPETS continues to increase, the dataset will only serve to be a greater asset to the National Marine Sanctuary in its mission to serve as the trustee of a system of underwater parks.

## National Marine Sanctuary Conservation Series

The *National Marine Sanctuary Conservation Series* is a peer-reviewed online journal that provides a forum to publish results that focus on the complex issues facing the National Marine Sanctuary System. In 2015, LiMPETS published a paper in the *Conservation Series* looking at the recovery and stability of surfgrass meadows in northern Monterey Bay after the termination of a domestic sewage discharge (Pearse et al., 2015). Using citizen science–collected data, this study found that surfgrass communities are remarkably resilient, even after chronic disturbance (in this case by domestic sewage) removes the foundation species (surfgrasses). Although recovery of the surfgrasses took decades, most taxa in the community returned to abundances similar to those recorded in the comparison plot within a few years, and the overall community structure displayed persistent stability. This paper highlights the importance of looking at species recovery because of past conservation efforts and is valuable to continuing conversations around public action and conservation.

As the first peer-reviewed published paper for LiMPETS, it serves as an example that data collected by citizen scientists, even young citizen scientists, can be of publishable quality.

## Scientific conferences

Students and LiMPETS staff have developed and presented posters and talks at a range of conferences on the West Coast. Conferences have included the American Geophysical Union, Monterey Bay National Marine Sanctuary's Currents Symposium, State of the Central California Marine Protected Areas Symposium and the Multi-Agency Rocky Intertidal Network (MARINe). The opportunity to present at these conferences provides students with the opportunity to be experts, provides the scientific community with information from a unique long-term data set, and highlights the power of citizen science to produce credible information. As these presentations continue and the credibility of citizen science increases within the broader scientific community, it is the goal to have LiMPETS data included with professionally collected data in the publication of peer-reviewed papers.

## Lessons learned

### LiMPETS: a model for youth-based citizen science

After more than a decade of program evolution and fine-tuning, LiMPETS has developed a successful model for youth-based citizen science, and so can provide several best practices:

### 1 Decide on your target audiences

Citizen science projects have multiple audiences, and it is important that program managers address each of those audiences effectively. The two most direct audiences are the data end user(s) and the data collectors. Each of these audiences are involved in the project for very different reasons, and it is important that you acknowledge what they expect to get out of their involvement and what they need to be successful.

The first step in developing a youth-based citizen science project is deciding what age group your project can effectively engage without compromising data quality. Be realistic from the beginning on this, because it will help avoid issues in the future. With youth-based programs, your data collectors may not be participating by choice; it may be a teacher or another adult that brought them to the program. Trying to engage groups that are too young just to try to engage them in hands-on science does not serve your data needs, nor does it provide an experience where students feel they can be successful at science.

The data end users (i.e. researchers and resource managers) that are involved with youth-based citizen science tend to be a unique group that sees the additional value of education and outreach involved in targeting a younger audience. But because they cannot use data that doesn't meet high quality standards, it is important to provide them an opportunity to provide input on protocol development and data quality assurance and quality control measures. Be very clear and honest with your data end users about the ability of what your data collectors (i.e. students) can and cannot collect, and the quality of the data.

If it is decided that the program will work with organized youth groups, be it school groups or other organized youth groups, it is important that the teacher or group leader is fully trained in the protocols; understands the science, conservation and education goals; and has clear expectations of their students. Be as specific as possible about who the potential data end users are, what their requirements are for the data and how they intend to use the data, so the teacher or group leader can impress the importance of it on their students.

## 2 Design and test protocols

Working with your end data user(s), design a set of protocols that will get them the information they need, keeping in mind the ability of the data collectors and the required educational component of the project.

It is important that you test your protocols with multiple groups within your target age group. We have found that a class of high school juniors from one school can be very different from juniors from another high school in their abilities, maturity and level of engagement. You want to be sure that you are designing protocols that serve all abilities within the age range you are trying to serve.

## 3 Design and test your quality assurance and quality control plan

The design and implementation of a solid quality assurance and quality control (QA/QC) plan is invaluable. The end data client(s) should be a part of the development of this plan (Cigliano et al., 2015) and it should be used as a tool to communicate the power and limitations of your data. Based on our experience, having this detailed plan developed up front can help you plan other elements of your program and minimize possible future issues. Your QA/QC can help you with everything from what your trained adult to student ratio will be in the field, to designing your data entry and database systems, and developing a process to assess the quality of the data and whether this happens before or after data entry.

If you know of an organization that is conducting similar research or monitoring programs with professional scientists, it can be helpful to set up replicate sampling between your student groups and the scientists to determine what the error rate is, if any, between the professional scientists and students. LiMPETS was able to do this, and it has been an invaluable tool for communicating with end data clients about the quality of youth-collected data. The scientific community is still coming around to the value and power of citizen science data (Theobald et al., 2015;

Burgess et al., 2016), and the more ways you can demonstrate the accuracy, the greater the use of your data will be.

Because of the organic nature in which LiMPETS was developed, the QA/QC has come years later and was much more difficult to complete than it would have been had it been developed in the beginning. It will be invaluable to the development of the program and the usability of the data collected to have a QA/QC plan designed and vetted by scientists and data clients before large scale monitoring begins (Cigliano et al., 2015).

## 4 Design a training that is effective for the target age group you are working with

Effective training is an important piece for any citizen science project, but even more so for youth audiences. In our experience working with school groups, there are a few elements that are a must. First, developing a training that addresses multiple learning styles. For many students sitting through a slideshow presentation will provide most of the information they need to be successful during their field experience. However, many students (and adults) need to access the information through a variety of modalities. The LiMPETS in-class training provides students with visual, auditory and hands-on practice. Additionally, there are practice monitoring tools, quizzes and additional readings on the website that students can access after the in-class training to be better prepared for the field.[9]

Second, the training and the citizen science program itself should address current education standards in the geographic area that will be monitored. Examples include the Foundations-10 and Senior Secondary Curriculum in Australia (ACARA, 2017) and the Key Stages of the National Curriculum in the United Kingdom (Department for Education, UK, 2017). Check the national and regional standards for the area you will be monitoring for how the program can best align for school involvement and provide the data the program is looking for. This is important if you intend to utilize school groups. The current standards for most states in the United States are the Common Core and Next Generation Science Standards, both of which align well with the principles of citizen science. These connections are particularly strong for citizen science programs that provide opportunities for students to analyze data and communicate the results of their analysis.

The last essential element to training youth to participate in citizen science is utilizing technology. It has been our experience that most students are more engaged when we use more technology. This has been seen with even our small switch from using PowerPoint for presentations to using Prezi. Unfortunately, to keep students' attention in this age of technology, we have to engage in small acts of "edu-tainment" in training to make sure they are getting the information in a way that they are able to retain and recall once they are in the field. Edu-tainment provides pieces of entertainment with an educational component. Examples of edu-tainment could be a funny video or game that engages the trainees and makes a concept funny and more memorable. The use of technology to assist students in accessing and engaging with the information needed to be successful in their participation has proven to be helpful in increasing student engagement.

## 5 The field experience

Depending on the audience you choose to work with, the planning of the field experience can be complicated. The experience needs to be long enough to collect adequate data, but short enough to keep the attention of students and fit into their school schedule. It helps to have all the gear set up for each of the monitoring groups before the students get there, so when they arrive you can jump into a quick protocol review before starting the data collection.

During the monitoring event, the LiMPETS Coordinator, the teacher(s) and chaperones make sure the students are safe, on-task, collecting data accurately and being responsible for the equipment they have borrowed.

## 6 Data entry

The data entry process should be user-friendly and look as much like the datasheet(s) as possible so there is no confusion when entering the data. After entering the data, having an intermediate step for students to review their data before it is submitted helps catch any typing errors. Once submitted the data should be reviewed by a program staff person before the data is permanently added to the database. Many of the student groups and their teachers need reminders to enter the data. They can get busy after their field experience, and it can become an out-of-sight, out-of-mind situation.

## 7 Staff requirements

Engaging youth in citizen science endeavors requires a unique skill set of the staff managing and delivering the program. There needs to be a balance of in-depth knowledge of the scientific content area, experience with educational principles and practices, statistical ability and program management skills. Having a group that has members that are stronger in some areas than others helps to balance out the program overall. That has been a contributing factor to the success of the LiMPETS network. There are coordinating partners that come from a pure science background, science education background and conservation background, and each of those strengths helps to continually improve the program. Keeping the different elements needed for program success in mind and staffing accordingly will be an asset over the long term for any program.

## Unique aspects of using youth in coastal and marine citizen science

Youth-based citizen science programs have very distinct positive aspects and challenges, including (1) a highly transient student population, (2) risk management and (3) perceived data quality.

## 1 Transient population

Because students eventually move on in their education, they are a transient population, which means being willing to put in the effort and time to train them knowing that you may only have one or two monitoring days with them. The payoffs are the experience for the students to fully participate in the scientific process in a meaningful way, the education they receive about the importance of the research, and an understanding and appreciation of the ocean because of their participation. When using youth to collect data, education and outreach must almost be a primary goal because otherwise your return on investment would be negligible.

## 2 Risk management

Risk management for youth-based audiences is also very different from working with adults. Depending on the structure of your program and your insurance, you may or may not have to have liability waivers signed by a parent or guardian. For LiMPETS, the risk management lies with the schools that are participating. They are required by their districts to have permission slips and waivers, and the LiMPETS staff is just providing the content for the trip; the teachers are ultimately responsible. Working with youth in or near the ocean brings its own challenges because of the dynamics of the environment and the increased safety concern. Many organizations have elected to require a certified lifeguard be present with students in the ocean. This varies widely by program and insurance provider. Be sure to check with your insurance carrier before deciding what you need to have to work with youth in or near the water. It is the responsibility of the LiMPETS Coordinator to make sure that the conditions at site are safe enough for students. If the conditions are not safe (e.g. high surf advisories), sampling is cancelled until conditions improve.

## 3 Perceived data quality

There is a lot of skepticism of the quality of student-collected data (Blanchette et al., 2016). However, these concerns can be addressed with a well-developed QA/QC plan as described earlier. A similar QA/AC plan has been developed and successfully used by Reef Check California for its adult participants who monitor the rocky reefs and kelp forests of coastal California.[10] The Environmental Protection Agency has developed a template for quality assurance plans for citizen science programs that clearly outlines and defines the components of a strong quality assurance plan (US EPA, 2017).

## Conclusion

Youth-based citizen science, when planned and executed well, can meet both scientific and educational needs. It does take more intentional planning and additional participant support, but the potential impact can also be greater for both long-term conservation goals and the public understanding of the scientific process. If your program can collect meaningful, accurate data that is of direct use to resource managers, you can further their ability to conserve the resource, especially in a climate of reduced funding for data collection.

Student participants, hopefully, walk away with a greater understanding of the scientific process, including data analysis and interpretation and an appreciation for the information needed to begin to make conservation decisions. With this information and experience, optimistically, students will be able to look at data and statistics presented to them and have a basic understanding of what it took for researchers to get to those numbers. These skills could be transferable to many aspects of their lives including being informed citizens and consumers. And, on the most basic level, students will have gained an understanding, appreciation and deeper connection to the coast environment, which may lead to increased conservation attitudes and actions (Packer, 2004).

---

**BOX 11.1  CITIZEN SCIENCE HIGHLIGHT – SCIENCE COMMUNICATION**

In addition to providing students with an opportunity to participate in hands-on field science, LiMPETS provides multiple avenues for students to communicate the results of their data collection and analysis. For students to truly understand their findings, they need to be able to effectively communicate them to the public, whether that public is their classmates, attendees at a scientific conference or an online audience. To help support this very important final step in the scientific process, LiMPETS provides teachers support through the curriculum and access to a LiMPETS Coordinator to help facilitate students designing an effective communication piece that makes sense for their target audience. The four forms of science communication that LiMPETS focuses on are (1) scientific posters, (2) scientific talks, (3) blogging and 4) video projects. This range of styles allows teachers and students to choose a format that best suits them and their audience.

LiMPETS Field Blog – http://limpets.org/field-blog/

---

**BOX 11.2  CITIZEN SCIENCE HIGHLIGHT – JANE ORBUCH**

Jane Orbuch is a high school teacher at San Lorenzo Valley High School and has been working with the LiMPETS program for more than 10 years. Mrs. Orbuch's students work in small groups as part of the Watershed Academy to complete independent research projects that they work on for three years, usually beginning in their sophomore year of high school. These student teams collect data at their rocky intertidal monitoring site 5 to 10 times per year. During their first semester, students hone in on their research question and collect data accordingly. Students work with Mrs. Orbuch and the LiMPETS Program Coordinator to analyze their results and develop their conclusions. Student groups then present their work at the local science fair and some groups even present at the Monterey Bay National Marine Sanctuary's Currents Symposium, which is a venue for presenting current research happenings in the Sanctuary. Many student groups have won first prize at the Santa Cruz County Science Fair and gone on to the California State Science Fair. One group moved on to an international science fair with their LiMPETS-based science project.

## Web resources

1 www.celebrateurbanbirds.org.
2 www.citizen-science.at/projekte/wasser-schafft.
3 www.youngscience.at/ueber-uns-ys/.
4 www.scistarter.com.
5 www.seattleaquarium.org/citizen-science.
6 www.neosec.dreamhosters.com/summer-on-the-marsh.
7 www.limpets.org.
8 www.piscoweb.org.
9 www.piscoweb.org.
10 www.piscoweb.org.

## Literature cited

ACARA (2017). *Overview – Introduction – The Australian Curriculum v8.3.* [Online] www.australiancurriculum.edu.au/seniorsecondary/overview.

Ballard, H., Dixon, C., and Harris, E. (2016). Youth-focused citizen science: Examining the role of environmental science learning and agency for conservation. *Biological Conservation*, 208, 65–75. http://dx.doi.org/10.1016/j.biocon.2016.05.024.

Blanchette, C.A., Raimondi, P., Gaddam, R., Burnaford, J., Smith, J., Hubbard, D.M., Dugan, J.E., Altstatt, J., and Bursek, J. (2016). *South Coast Baseline Program Final Report: Rocky Intertidal Ecosystems.* California Sea Grant, National Oceanographic and Atmospheric Administration: San Diego, CA. [Online] https://caseagrant.ucsd.edu/sites/default/files/SCMPA-22-Final-Report_wAppendices.pdf [Accessed March 23, 2017].

Burgess, H., DeBey, L., Froehlich, H., Schmidt, N., Theobald, E., Ettinger, A., HilleRisLambers, J., Tewksbury, J., and Parrish, J. (2016). The science of citizen science: Exploring barriers to use as a primary research tool. *Biological Conservation, 208, 113–120.* doi:10.1016/j.biocon.2016.05.014.

Bursky, S. (2014). Summer Science in New England: Ocean Education through Informal Science Centers. Boston, MA. *New England Ocean Science Education Collaborative.* [Online]. www.neosec.dreamhosters.com/wp-content/uploads/2015/02/Summer-Science-final-report-2-21-2014.pdf [Accessed March 23, 2017].

California Marine Protected Areas (MPAs). (2017). *California Marine Protected Areas (MPAs).* [Online] www.wildlife.ca.gov/Conservation/Marine/MPAs [Accessed May 5, 2016].

California Ocean Science Trust. (2016). *State of the California North Central Coast: A summary of the marine protected area monitoring program 2010–2015.* [Online] http://oceanspaces. org/sites/default/files/u1173/ncc_sotr_linked_updated_2016.pdf.

Ceccaroni, L., and Piera, J. (2017). *Analyzing the Role of Citizen Science in Modern Research.* Hershey, PA: Information Science Reference.

Cigliano, J., Meyer, R., Ballard, H., Freitag, A., Phillips, T., and Wasser, A. (2015). Making marine and coastal citizen science matter. *Ocean & Coastal Management,* 115, 77–87.

Department for Education, United Kingdom. (2017). *National curriculum in England: Science programmes of study – GOV.UK.* [Online] www.gov.uk/government/publications/ national-curriculum-in-england-science-programmes-of-study/national-curriculum-in-england-science-programmes-of-study [Accessed March 23, 2017].

Dugan, J.E., Ichikawa, G., Stephenson, M., Crane, D.B., McCall, J., and Regalado, K. (2005). *Monitoring of coastal contaminants using sand crabs.* Central Coast Regional Water Quality Control Board: San Luis Obispo, CA. [Online] www.swrcb.ca.gov/water_issues/pro-grams/swamp/docs/sandcrab.pdf [Accessed March 23, 2017].

Ferdin, M., Kvitek, R., Bretz, C., Powell, C., Doucette, G., Lefebvre, K., Coale, S., and Silver, M. (2002). *Emerita analoga* (Stimpson) – possible new indicator species for the phycotoxin domoic acid in California coastal waters. *Toxicon,* 40(9), 1259–1265.

National Governors Association. (2010). *Common Core State Standards.* Washington, DC: National Governors Association Center for Best Practices, Council of Chief State School Officers.

National Research Council. (2007). *Taking Science to School: Learning and Teaching Science in Grades K-8.* Washington, DC: National Academies Press.

NGSS Lead States. (2013). *Next Generation Science Standards: For States, by States.* Washington, DC: National Academies Press.

NOAA. (2013). *Ocean literacy: The essential principles and fundamental concepts of ocean sciences for learners of all ages.* Version 2. [Online] www.coexploration.org/ oceanliteracy/documents/ OceanLitGuide_LettersizeV2.pdf [Accessed March 23, 2017].

ONMS. (2015). *Monterey Bay National Marine Sanctuary Condition Report Partial Update: A New Assessment of the State of Sanctuary Resources 2015.* Silver Spring, MD: US Department of Commerce, National Oceanic and Atmospheric Administration (Office of National Marine Sanctuaries).

Packer, J.M. (2004). *Motivational factors and the experience of learning in educational leisure settings.* Doctoral dissertation, Queensland University of Technology.

Pearse, J.S., Doyle, W.T., Pearse, V.B., Gowing, M.M., Pennington, J.T., Danner, E., and Wasser, A. (2015). *Long-term monitoring of surfgrass meadows in the Monterey Bay National Marine Sanctuary: Recovery followed by stability after the termination of a domestic sewage discharge.* Marine Sanctuaries Conservation Series ONMS-15–10. Silver Spring, MD: US Department of Commerce, National Oceanic and Atmospheric Administration, Office of National Marine Sanctuaries.

Pearse, J.S., Osborn, D., and Roe, C. (2017). *Assessing sanctuary shorelines: A role for volunteers, particularly highschool students, in resource management.* [Online] http://escholarship.org/uc/ item/2d97c5wk [Accessed March 23, 2017].

Theobald, E., Ettinger, A., Burgess, H., DeBey, L., Schmidt, N., Froehlich, H., Wagner, C., Hille Ris Lambers, J., Tewksbury, J., Harsch, M., and Parrish, J. (2015). Global change and local solutions: Tapping the unrealized potential of citizen science for biodiversity research. *Biological Conservation,* 181, 236–244.

US EPA. (2017). *Quality assurance project plan for citizen science projects, citizen science for environmental protection, US EPA.* [Online] www.epa.gov/citizen-science/quality-assurance-project-plan-citizen-science-projects [Accessed March 24, 2017].

# 12

# UNIQUELY MARINE

## Snorkelers and divers as citizen scientists

*John A. Cigliano and April D. Ridlon*

## Introduction

The rapid successful expansion of coastal and marine citizen science (Thiel et al., 2014; Cigliano and Ballard, Chapter 1), as with terrestrial citizen science, is undoubtedly due to the significant advantages of collaborating with the public. For example, relying on professional scientists alone might increase precision and accuracy of data collection but, because of the resources required, often cannot provide the coverage needed to study and monitor coastal and marine systems at the appropriate temporal or spatial scale, given the scale of the stressors affecting coastal and marine systems (Beeden et al., 2014). Collaborating with citizen scientists can also expand the spatial and temporal scale at which a study is conducted, as well as increase the likelihood of collecting finer-grained information, such as detecting environmental perturbations and changes, and increase the effectiveness of, or allow for, long-term monitoring of species and habitats (Miller-Rushing et al., 2012, McKinley et al., 2015). Because marine research in particular requires extensive resources, citizen scientists are often critical, and necessary, to the ongoing life of marine monitoring projects, which would otherwise not be financially sustainable.

For marine conservation, these advantages are particularly evident with divers and snorkelers. Divers and snorkelers can be a passionate, committed, and effective group of citizen scientists due to their connection to and familiarity with coastal and marine ecosystems (Martin et al., 2016). Projects that engage divers and snorkelers as citizen scientists have conducted a variety of conservation-related projects, including biodiversity assessments (Stuart-Smith et al., 2017), long-term community-level monitoring (Sweatman et al., 2011), population assessment and monitoring (Cigliano and Kliman, 2016), benthic habitat mapping and human impact assessment (Roelfsema et al., 2016), species threat assessment (Edgar et al., 2017), and assessment of community-level responses to fishing pressure (Stuart-Smith et al., 2017).

Divers and snorkelers engage in coastal and marine citizen science in two general ways: (1) indirectly (i.e. opportunistically), when divers collect data while recreationally diving and snorkeling, and without direct oversight by project staff (similar to citizen scientists acting as sentinels in invasive species projects, see Chapter 4); and (2) directly, when divers enter the water specifically to engage in the project, after receiving some training from and oversight by the project leaders. While many projects engage divers and snorkelers in one of these ways, some projects allow for citizen scientists to become engaged in either way.

There are quite a few programs that engage divers and snorkelers indirectly. For example, Dive Into Science[1] relies on SCUBA divers to submit ocean temperature data that are logged during their recreational dives on their dive computers. Divers use a standard template to enter data, which is then submitted through their website. Earthdive[2] collaborates with divers and snorkelers around the world to monitor indicator species, such as sharks, snappers, and lobsters, during their recreational dive or snorkeling trips. CoralWatch[3] collects data on coral bleaching; citizen scientists are provided a color chart to assess bleaching and a pre-printed waterproof data form (dive slate) to record data. As with Dive Into Science, divers and snorkelers enter their data through the website for both Earthdive and CoralWatch.

The challenges and opportunities of indirectly engaging divers and snorkelers as citizen scientists are similar to those that face any project indirectly engaging citizen scientists, whether they are divers, beachwalkers, or birders. These are discussed at length in this book (Chapters 4, 6, 13, and 14) and in several other publications (e.g. Bonney et al., 2009; Geoghegan et al., 2016; Hyder et al., 2015; Rotman et al., 2012; Shirk et al., 2012; West et al., 2015). Therefore, we focus our discussion on the unique challenges and opportunities of working directly with divers and snorkelers as citizen scientists.

Projects that engage divers and snorkelers directly generally require more investment in time and resources than projects that indirectly engage citizen scientists (Beeden et al., 2014). This investment is often in the form of training and direct oversight of data collection by project staff (e.g. Roelfsema et al., 2016) or by Divemasters and SCUBA Instructors, who are trained by project scientists and staff (e.g. Branchini et al., 2015). This increased investment in training and oversight allows for more complex tasks to be performed by the citizen scientists and higher confidence in data quality (Kosmala et al., 2016; Stuart-Smith et al., 2017).

In this chapter, we profile two successful marine citizen science programs that directly engage divers and snorkelers. We also present as a case study a project led by the chapter authors. Our goal is to provide lessons learned and best practices for coastal and marine citizen science project that directly engage divers and snorkelers as citizen scientists.

## Profiles of coastal and marine citizen science programs involving divers and snorkelers

### Reef Check Foundation[4]

One of the most well-known and widespread citizen science efforts is the Reef Check Foundation. Founded in 1996, Reef Check now operates with volunteer teams in 90 countries worldwide. Reef Check focuses on rocky reefs in California, USA (Reef Check California), and tropical reefs worldwide (EcoDiver Program). Citizen scientists have the option of forming their own Reef Check Teams or joining established EcoExpeditions.

Reef Check has made significant contributions to marine conservation. For example, using a long-term data set (2007–2011) collected on permanent transects, Chavanich et al. (2012) were able to determine the effect of mass bleaching on corals and reef organisms in the Gulf of Thailand and in the Andaman Sea; Marks et al. (2015) documented the spread of the non-native brown algae *Sargassum horneri* along the southern Pacific coast of North America; Cerrano et al. (2016) documented the distribution and abundance of protected species in the Portofino Marine Protected Area (northwest Mediterranean Sea); and Micheli et al. (2012) found that the resilience of the pink abalone *Haliotis corrugata* to climate-driven hypoxia is increased in marine reserves.

*Data Collection Methods*: Reef Check has established simple and scientifically robust methods for surveying coral reefs based on standardized transect methods and indicator species (Hodgson et al., 2006). Indicator species are chosen based on ecological and economic value, sensitivity to anthropogenic impact, and ease of identification. Transects consist of four sequentially placed 20 m segments, separated by 5 m to ensure the independence of each segment, at two depth contours (2–6 m and > 6–12 m), if possible. Fish are surveyed by divers swimming slowly along the transect and stopping every 5 m, waiting one minute for indicator fish to emerge before proceeding to the next 5 m stopping point. The fish are counted and size (total length) is recorded while swimming and while stopped (Hodgson et al., 2006). For the EcoDiver Program, the transect is 5 m wide with a 5 m maximum height (Hodgson et al., 2006). For Reef Check California, the transect is 2 m wide and 2 m high (Freiwald et al., 2015). To search for invertebrates, divers swim slowly within the transect in a "S" pattern, looking for invertebrates on the substrate and in crevices (Hodgson et al., 2006). Benthic cover is estimated using a standardized Point-Intercept method (Hodgson et al., 2006; Done et al., 2017). Methods can be adjusted to meet the needs of the organization/volunteer team using them (e.g. more taxonomic specificity can be added, provided training is done). Citizen scientists are provided with prepared field sheets and data sheets for recording and submitting data, respectively (Excel spreadsheets that are specific to their region, e.g. Atlantic/Caribbean, Indo-Pacific). Prepared dive slates are available for purchase. Data sheets are submitted by email or online.

*Training*: Teams are composed of a Team Scientist, a Team Leader, and the volunteer survey team. The Team Scientist is generally a marine biologist or someone who is experienced in marine natural history, and the Team Leader is generally an experienced diver, such as a Divemaster or Instructor, who is responsible for dive safety. The Team Leader and Scientist are required to be trained by a Reef Check Trainer and all team members must be certified as Reef Check EcoDivers. Training consists of a two- to three-day course that teaches the Reef Check methodology, and how to identify indicator fish and invertebrate species, and substrates. To become certified, participants are given a photographic identification exam (85% pass rate) and in-situ identification skills (95% pass rate) (Done et al., 2017).

*Data QA/QC:* The intensive nature of the training and rigorous certification requirements, along with oversight by a Team Scientist, increases the chance that the data collected are of high quality. Team Scientists are responsible for data checking, analysis, and data submission. Dive slates and data are immediately reviewed after the dive to determine if any errors have been made (i.e. data not matching the Team Scientist's observations). If possible, these are corrected while the team is still on site and the transect is in place. The Team Scientist also makes sure that data sheets are filled out correctly and compares the data as entered on the Excel spreadsheet with the original data to make sure that there are no transcription errors. Reef Check does a third check for errors and inconsistencies in the submitted spreadsheets (Hodgson et al., 2006). Original data sheets are sent to Reef Check California Regional Managers, who then check whether data were entered correctly (Freiwald et al., 2015). Done et al. (2017) report that data collected by citizen scientists using the point intercept technique are highly accurate when estimating benthic cover of coral reefs, in the range of estimates from 1% to 50%, and Gillett et al. (2012) found that the Reef Check California protocol (which is based on the Reef Check protocol) produced estimates of fish density that were comparable to surveys conducted by professional scientists.

### Reef Environmental Education Foundation (REEF)[5]

Founded in 1990, REEF conducts fish surveys (REEF Fish Survey Project) in five regions throughout the world (Tropical Western Atlantic, Northeast United States and Canada, West Coast of North America, Tropical Eastern Pacific, and Hawaiian Islands). REEF engages divers both indirectly and directly; surveys are done by any interested diver, in organized groups, or through organized trips (REEF Field Surveys) in which volunteer divers collect data under the direction of a REEF scientist or staff member (much like the Earthwatch model; see later). REEF also has "Advanced Assessment Teams" of highly trained volunteers that participate in special regional monitoring and assessment efforts, such as monitoring contracts with National Marine Sanctuaries. In addition to the fish surveys, REEF also has an exotic species sighting program (e.g. Lionfish Project), and the Grouper Moon Project, in collaboration with the Cayman Islands Department of the Environment.[6]

REEF data have been used, for example, to estimate the amount of nitrogen and phosphorus supplied by aggregating Nassau grouper (*Epinephelus striatus*) (Archer et al., 2014); model demographic trends, habitat associations, and interannual variability in recruitment in two managed fish species, the Goliath grouper (*E. itajara*) and the mutton snapper (*Lutjanus analis*) (Thorson et al, 2014); and to estimate variation in relative density over 15 years for 18 fish species (Wolfe and Pattengill-Semmens, 2013a).

*Data Collection Methods:* REEF fish survey methods employ the roving diver technique (RDT) (Pattengill-Semmens and Semmens, 2003). Divers do not survey transects but swim freely throughout a dive site and record every observed fish species. Citizen scientists record species abundance in binned categories: few (2–10);

many (11–100); and abundant (>100). Divers also record survey time, depth, temperature, and other environmental information. Data are submitted electronically through REEF's website. REEF provides (for purchase) survey check-sheets that are pre-printed on underwater paper and waterproof identification guides specific to the regions they survey.

*Training*: REEF provides fish and invertebrate identification training through webinars ("Fishinars"), self-teaching materials, and classroom sessions at REEF Field Stations. REEF characterizes citizen scientists based on five experience levels, and volunteers advance by a combination of comprehensive identification exams and number of surveys completed (Wolfe and Pattengill-Semmens, 2013a).

*Data QA/QC*: The RDT used by REEF has been shown to be comparable and, in one regard, preferable to the standard transect techniques used by professional marine scientists. Holt et al. (2013) found that alpha diversity measures provided by the RDT are consistent with data collected using belt transect methods when comparing alpha diversity among three sites that differed in fish diversity; however, greater species richness within sites was recorded when using the RDT, which suggests that this method is preferable if the goal is to record as many species as possible.

The quality of the collected data is ensured primarily through training and the simple, straightforward methodology. Pattengill-Semmens and Semmens (1998) found that data recorded on species composition and structure by inexperienced REEF divers were comparable to experienced REEF divers, though experienced REEF divers consistently recorded slightly greater species richness. However, the accuracy of inexperienced divers increased rapidly with experience. Furthermore, divers only report species they can positively identify, and REEF staff review submitted data and remove or correct obvious errors. Reef staff will also contact divers if anomalous or unusual sightings are reported (Wolfe and Pattengill-Semmens, 2013a).

## Case study: assessing queen conch (*Strombus gigas*) populations in Belize

The queen conch (*Strombus gigas*) is a large marine gastropod found throughout the Caribbean and is a major fishery in the region (Theile, 2001). In Belize, management of the queen conch fishery consists of size limits (at least 17.75 cm in length with a minimum weight of 86 g for cleaned meat), a closed season corresponding to peak reproduction (July 1–September 30), and a prohibition on the use of SCUBA (Pérez, 1997). Additionally, the government of Belize established a network of 13 Marine Protected Areas (MPA) to protect queen conch, as well as other important fisheries (Cho, 2005).

One such reserve is the Sapodilla Cayes Marine Reserve (SCMR). The SCMR is located at the southern end of the Mesoamerican barrier reef in the Sapodilla range (Figure 12.1) and is divided up into zones of varying levels of protection: a General Use Zone (GUZ), where commercial extractive activities are allowed but managed; two Conservation Zones (CZ), where no commercial extractive activities

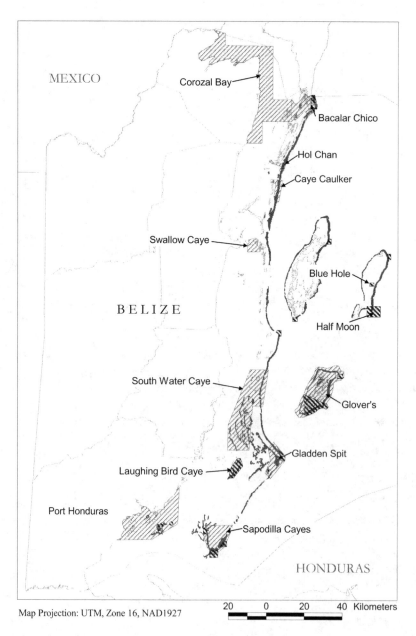

MEXICO

Corozal Bay

Bacalar Chico

Hol Chan

Caye Caulker

Swallow Caye

Blue Hole

BELIZE

Half Moon

South Water Caye

Glover's

Gladden Spit

Laughing Bird Caye

Port Honduras

Sapodilla Cayes

HONDURAS

Map Projection: UTM, Zone 16, NAD1927

20    0    20    40  Kilometers

**FIGURE 12.1**   The Sapodilla Cayes Marine Reserve. The location of the reserve in relation to other reserves in Belize (indicated by cross hatching). Modified
from The Belize Coastal Threat Atlas, World Resources Institute. From
Cigliano and Kliman (2014).

are allowed (subsistence fishing is allowed in one of the CZs), but other non-extractive activities such as SCUBA and snorkeling are allowed; and a Preservation Zone (PZ), where entry is prohibited except with a special permit for research (Figure 12.2). The reserve was declared in 1996 but was not signed into law until April 2009, and, thus, the zoning had not been enforced until 2009. However, on-site management began in 2001, which consisted of enforcing current harvesting regulations throughout the reserve (J. Finch, pers. comm.).

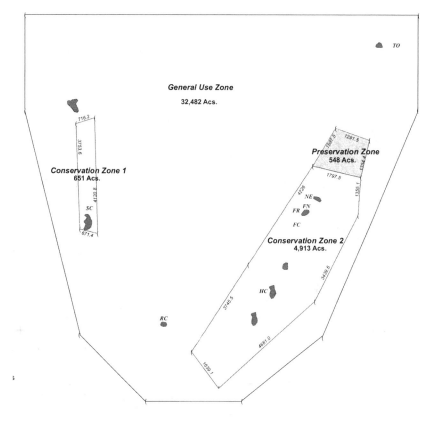

**FIGURE 12.2**   The Sapodilla Cayes Marine Reserve. The zones of the SCMR: General Use Zone – designated for recreational use, research and fishing in accordance to the rules and regulations for the Marine Reserve; Conservation Zone 1 – designated for recreational use only: SCUBA diving and snorkeling and non-extractive sports fishing; Conservation Zone 2 – designated for recreational use, catch and release and subsistence fishing with restricted gear types for traditional fishermen are allowed; Preservation Zone (PZ) – no activities allowed, research allowed with permission. Sampling sites: *FC* – Frank's Cut, *FR* – Frank's Caye, *FN* – Frank's North, *HC* – Hunting Caye, *NE* – Northeast Caye, *RC* – Ragged Caye, *SC* – Seal Caye, *TO* – Tom Owen's Caye. From Cigliano and Kliman (2014).

The purpose of this study was to assess the pre-enforcement status of queen conch populations in the SCMR and to conduct a *Before-After-Control-Impact* (BACI) study on the effectiveness of the reserve in maintaining and replenishing queen conch populations. Because the reserve was mapped but not immediately enforced, we were able to sample each zone of the reserve before and after enforcement.

This study represents a co-created project (Bonney et al., 2009; Shirk et al., 2012). It was developed during a community workshop convened in May 2005 by the Toledo Association for Sustainable Tourism and Empowerment (TASTE; now SEA Belize), the non-governmental organization (NGO) responsible with co-managing the reserve, and Earthwatch Institute. This workshop brought together key stakeholders, scientists, and research organizations to prioritize issues relevant to the sustainability of the SCMR and to formulate research questions to address these issues. Thirty-five individuals representing 19 organizations participated in the workshop. The queen conch survey project was an outcome of this workshop.

Funding and assistance in recruiting citizen scientists was provided by Earthwatch Institute.[7] Earthwatch, which began in 1971, recruits and places citizen scientists on research projects around the world. Thus, unlike REEF and Reef Check, Earthwatch itself does not directly engage citizen scientists, but rather the project scientist(s) directly works with the volunteers who are recruited through Earthwatch. Citizen scientists pay a fee to join Earthwatch expeditions and part of this fee provides funding for the project (see also Chapters 3 and 5). Annual grants range between US$20,000 and US$80,000. The funds primarily cover volunteer expenses (principal investigator salaries are not covered, for example) and it is a per-capita model of funding (i.e. based on the number of citizen scientists engaged in the project). Grant duration is three years and is renewable. All projects must incorporate field research and focus on global environmental change.

*Data Collection Methods*: With the assistance of Earthwatch citizen scientists, including international and local citizen scientists (fishers, fisheries officers, TASTE; local citizen scientists were supported by a grant provided to Earthwatch), we conducted surveys of queen conch in the SCMR from 2006 to 2012. Conch aggregations were surveyed both inside and outside each reserve zone at historical conch fishing areas, at known spawning sites, and at random sites throughout the reserve to locate any unknown aggregations. Citizen scientists sampled shallow-water (mean = 1.64 ± 0.01 m) belt transects on snorkel and deep-water (mean = 6.19 ± 0.31 m) belt transects on SCUBA. We recorded size (total length) and lip thickness (a proxy for age), and tagged conch with unique alphanumeric tags (Floy Tag Inc.). Data were used to determine age structure and density of aggregations (Cigliano and Kliman, 2014).

*Training and Safety*: All expeditions began with discussions on marine conservation and the function of MPAs, conch biology, and the research goals of the project. We also discussed the methodology, which was first practiced on land until we determined that the citizen scientists could accurately measure length using a fish measuring board and lip thickness with dial calipers (Figure 12.4). We then held in-water practice sessions before heading out to the study sites. During these in-water

**FIGURE 12.3**   Diver citizen scientist measuring and tagging queen conch.

*Photo credit:* John A. Cigliano.

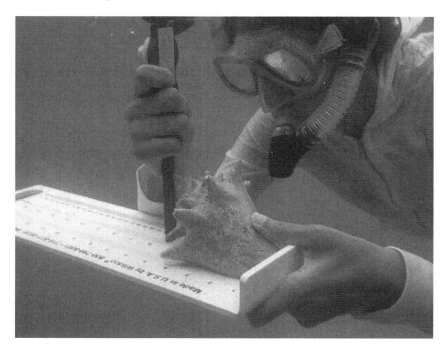

**FIGURE 12.4**   Snorkeler citizen scientist measuring the siphonal (total) length of a
queen conch.

*Photo credit:* John A. Cigliano.

sessions, we practiced data collection and data recording, as well as best practices for in-water behavior.

Safety was, of course, a top concern. For dive teams, we had a dive safety officer (DSO) on every dive. The DSO was not the PI or co-PI so that he could concentrate on diver safety (and the PIs could concentrate on the science). For the snorkeling teams, the PIs acted as safety officers. As an additional safety procedure, our boat was always manned by the boat captain, who also kept watch over all snorkelers so that he could immediately respond to anyone in distress.

*Data QA/QC*: Citizen scientists were divided up into teams, and each team was supervised by one of the co-PIs to ensure that the methodology was being followed correctly. Team members were able to choose the task they were most comfortable with: conch collection (included freediving for snorkelers), conch measurements and tagging, or data recording. All data were recorded on pre-printed, waterproof data sheets. Data were entered by the team members at the end of the research day into spreadsheets on *two* laptop computers. This allowed us to compare the spreadsheets for any differences, which were then checked against the data recorded on the data sheets.

*Project Outcomes*: Approximately 80 citizen scientists participated in the study over seven years, allowing us to survey over 5,000 conch, and tag approximately 4,200 conch, in 11 aggregations throughout all four zones of the reserve, as well as in three deep-water breeding aggregations in or adjacent to the reserve, and 24 additional randomly chosen sites (Cigliano and Kliman, unpubl. data). We would not have been able to achieve this spatial coverage without the citizen scientists. The SCMR appears to be an important nursery area for queen conch (Cigliano and Kliman, 2014), and the reserve appears to be effective in protecting and restoring queen conch populations, though additional sampling is required to determine if this is a long-term effect (Cigliano and Kliman, unpubl. data).

## Lessons learned

Directly engaging divers and snorkelers raises challenges and considerations that are unique to collaborating with citizen scientists in these contexts. Next we summarize some of these considerations and suggest some best practices to address them based on our own experiences, our profiles of REEF and Reef Check, and from our review of the literature.

### Comfort level of divers and snorkelers

Comfort in the water is key to being able to collect any type of data underwater, not only accurately but safely. We have observed snorkelers and divers having difficulty conducting simple sampling techniques because of a lack of comfort in the water. All SCUBA diving activities include risks and require a level of vigilance and attention to safety on the part of the diver, thus the recreational certification level and amount of experience appropriate for the type of diving (e.g. in strong currents, deep water) should be considered a minimum requirement for any volunteer engaged in underwater research. It is also advisable to have a member of the project team act as a dive/snorkel safety officer, as is done with Reef Check and our queen conch project.

In addition to diver safety and accurate data collection, comfort level in the water can affect the citizen scientist's effect on the habitat. Avoiding inadvertent damage to habitats can also be more difficult when collecting data while diving and snorkeling because these citizen scientists are now conducting activities that are not part of the recreational training. Damage often comes in the form of breaking fragile structures (e.g. coral colonies) when divers and snorkelers come in physical contact with these structures, and from kicking up sediment (Cigliano, pers. obs.; Krieger and Chadwick, 2013; Plathong et al., 2000; Zainal Abidin and Mohamed, 2014).

We have also found that the level of comfort that volunteers have in the water may also be affected by their familiarity with carrying the type of gear that is required to collect the data. Even the simplest tools such as collection bags, meter tapes, or large dive slates will require divers and snorkelers to make adjustments to maintain their safety and comfort, and will require some period of acclimation. Carrying gear could also increase the likelihood of contact with (and damage to) substrates, especially for those who are not accustomed to it.

## Communication underwater

Compared to citizen science projects that can be done on land or from a boat, the fact that communication is limited while underwater poses a unique challenge to underwater research, and one that should be explicitly considered due to its potential effect on the quality of the data and the safety of the citizen scientists. Communication between recreational divers and snorkelers is typically done via hand signals, but when engaged in data collection, the divers' hands are often not free, and communications may be much more complicated than what can be conferred with hand gestures anyway (Cigliano and Ridlon, pers. obs.). Buddy pairs will often be working closely with one another to collect data and should be able and willing to keep in close contact with one another throughout a dive, much more so than is necessary during a typical recreational dive.

## Time limitation

The time available to collect data underwater is also considerably limited in comparison to intertidal or terrestrial projects. The length of a given dive is limited by a diver's air consumption, depth, and prior time spent underwater (nitrogen accumulation), all of which are unique considerations for underwater data collection. Air limitation can be more severe with inexperienced divers, but even experienced divers may find themselves using air up more quickly when engaged in a research project due to the additional rigors of data collection, carrying gear, and so forth. In any case, since divers must stay in pairs, the amount of time the volunteers have to collect data will always be constrained by the individual with the least amount of air left or greatest accumulation of bottom time. Overall, the time limitations on underwater research result in a comparative increase in effort to produce a given unit of data, which underscores the need for thorough training in the methods of a project prior to data collection, efficient data collection techniques for volunteer divers, and for data quality control both in and out of the water.

## Effects on behavior of organisms

The presence and swimming behavior of recreational divers and snorkelers have been shown to have various effects on the behaviors of many marine species (e.g. attraction, aversion), in some cases eliciting anti-predator behaviors and altering other key activities, including feeding (e.g. Ridlon et al., in prep). Knowing whether, how, or how closely to approach marine species to observe them or take other forms of data is therefore likely to impact the quality and even the accuracy of the data collected (Dearden et al., 2010). Even experienced scientific divers can elicit unintended behavioral reactions, and this further underscores the importance of training citizen scientists in collecting accurate data with minimal disturbance to the behaviors of organisms that they are observing.

## Cost and resource limitations

Certainly, there are many successful models for conducting both remote and local underwater research with volunteer divers (see REEF and Reef Check descriptions), and yet using citizen scientists to collect data underwater can compound some of the challenges of, and present some unique limitations to, a marine research project.

Recreational SCUBA certification and much of the equipment associated with diving is expensive, which necessarily limits the volunteer pool to those who can afford the expense of the training and gear. Thus, unlike most terrestrial research projects that can recruit any interested volunteer from a local community and provide data collection training, projects that utilize diving are constrained to engaging citizens who already have a very specific and expensive type of training. This can pose unique challenges in recruiting and maintaining a sufficient pool of volunteers, and the equity of access for people who can't afford expensive gear or trips, especially for longer term projects. It also often requires bringing volunteers in from outside the local community where the research is being conducted because the pool of potential citizen scientists could be limited, especially when it is located at a remote site; this can limit or even undermine local investment in the project and its goals.

Additionally, the relatively complicated equipment required for diving adds logistical complexity to projects that employ citizen scientists. For example, researchers using volunteer divers are limited to conducting studies at field sites with reasonable access to rental equipment, or to using volunteers that can provide their own equipment, and in any case, must plan to be nearby an air compressor capable of filling SCUBA tanks. Of course, professional scientists also face these logistical challenges while conducting underwater research, but providing for the comfort and safety of volunteers who are diving requires more planning, and more abundant and easily accessible resources.

## Underwater data collection methods

Given the added complexity of skills that divers and snorkelers need to engage in underwater research projects, the simpler the type of data being collected and the method of data collection employed, the more successful citizen scientists are likely to be in producing accurate data (see the profiles on REEF and Reef Check). Inherent variability between scientific observers' data collection abilities is recognized as a potential source of bias in underwater datasets. However, training and experience can reduce variability in precision and accuracy of volunteers as compared to professional scientists, sometimes in a short amount of time (Darwall and Dulvy, 1996; Harding et al., 2000; Mumby et al., 1995; Williams et al., 2008).

## Recommendations for best practices

Based on the REEF and Reef Check profiles, the preceding discussion on the challenges of working with divers and snorkelers, and our own experiences in the queen conch project, we have the following specific recommendations to ensure safe, accurate, and useful citizen science projects with divers and snorkelers:

1   *Training*: Volunteers should be trained in species identification and data collection methods prior to the first sampling. It is ideal for the volunteers to be well-versed in species identification before data collection begins. Testing volunteers on their knowledge before data collection and/or requiring a minimum accuracy in identification to collect data will increase the confidence in the quality of the data. Underwater species keys and guides can be useful (e.g. REEF uses these) but may be distracting for volunteers to use while also collecting data, especially for new divers or snorkelers who need to focus on their buoyancy control and body position in the water as well as data collection and recording methods.

   In addition, the data collection methods should be first taught and practiced on land whenever possible. The skills that are required to collect data along a transect line, by point-count method, and particularly within a belt transect, or using quadrats to calculate abundance data and estimate percent cover are not complicated, but become more difficult when done underwater. As we have found, training citizen scientists in sampling techniques on land before they get in the water and during pre-sampling training dives/snorkels is an effective way of ensuring that sampling is safe (due to familiarity with the technique), effective (see case study), and efficient (especially important for divers given the time limitation discussed earlier). Pre-dive/snorkel briefings on proper in-water behavior can also significantly reduce the damage to habitat by snorkelers and divers (Krieger and Chadwick, 2013; Webler and Jakubowski, 2016). Practicing methods on land will also provide the research staff the opportunity to better observe the volunteers and resolve training issues as needed.

Planning the dive before getting in the water and having the appropriate amount of above-water training on data collection methods can also go a long way towards eliminating the need for "conversations" underwater.

2   *In-water quality control checks*: It is also advisable to conduct in-water training before data collection begins. This will allow project staff to assess the abilities of the citizen scientists. Deficiencies can then be corrected or appropriate tasks for a given skill and comfort level can be assigned (see later). It will also provide an opportunity to train divers and snorkelers in proper in-water behaviors as needed to ensure their safety, reduce diver or snorkeler-related damage to the habitat, and minimize affecting the behavior of organisms. Project leaders should explicitly train volunteers in techniques for diving with gear attached, for example, showing them how to minimize dragging gear or adjust their buoyancy to account for heavier gear, before sampling begins.

Some collection techniques will require in-water training or at least quality control. For example, measuring the length/body size of species underwater can present a unique challenge to new volunteers (magnification effect), particularly with mobile species such as fish. This can be remedied by practicing length/size estimates prior to data collection with objects of known length and width, or by simply measuring stationary objects underwater (e.g. coral heads) after guessing their length and then checking with a buddy/professional scientist (Darwall and Dulvy, 1996, Freiwald et al., 2015).

3   *Dividing up tasks by skill level*: As with any project that uses citizen scientists, it is helpful to have a variety of tasks that can be assigned to individuals with the appropriate skills (see queen conch case study). Divers that are "better on air" can take the deeper part of a transect or do tasks at slightly deeper depths and snorkelers who are better at freediving can collect specimens, for example. Those more comfortable in the water can carry gear and perform more complex underwater tasks (e.g. securing objects with zip ties, measuring and sexing animals, searching for cryptic species), while less experienced divers can record data. And buddy pairs can be arranged such that an experienced volunteer can provide in-water QC for a less experienced one. We have found that allowing citizen scientists to choose their task not only increases data accuracy but also increases volunteer enjoyment and satisfaction (Cigliano, pers. obs.).

4   *Data sheets*: Volunteers should be provided with pre-made data sheets, preferably that they have used in a mock data collection on land prior to beginning data collection so that they are familiar with their use once in water (this also provides a permanent record of the data, which is not possible if volunteers used their own dive slates). Data sheets that use abbreviations should include a key to define them whenever possible. Using size class and abundance class

"bins" instead of exact values can increase ease of data collection for volunteers and ensure accuracy. Listing target species, clearly labeling data categories (e.g. lip thickness), and including pre-printed values to be circled on data sheets will also increase the efficiency and accuracy of data collection and recording. Data sheets should be rinsed and hung to dry immediately after data collection to preserve the original data/prevent smudging.

5    *Data QA/QC*: Because communication is limited underwater, checking the data sheets with a buddy immediately after the dive or at the end of the research day can greatly increase accuracy and maintain quality of the data. We have found that efficiency and accuracy increases when the volunteer who originally recorded the data reads from the data sheets to one of her team members, who enters the data into the spreadsheet. It can also be beneficial to have all members of the research group engaged in data entry, to facilitate discussion and address questions about data entry (we broke into groups of three or four volunteers and a project staff member in our queen conch project). The professional scientist(s) should then check the data entry for errors, as is done by Reef Check Team Scientists. To further assist the detection of data entry errors, we maintain two separate spreadsheets that volunteers enter data into so that staff can compare the spreadsheets for any differences due to incorrect entry, which is then checked against the data sheets. It is always important to get the data entered immediately (ideally at the end of each day, definitely before the group disbands), but this is especially important when working with a group of volunteers in a short-term, intensive effort to collect data (as is almost always the case with projects done in remote locations), since lag times between data collection and entry greatly increase the likelihood of errors and, thus, unusable data, as volunteers may not remember the data collection or be available to consult.

6    *Snorkel instead of SCUBA*: Given the cost and logistical requirements of diving at remote sites, using snorkel as the primary mode of collecting data where possible, by using local volunteers whenever possible, and by limiting field sites to those within easy access of a SCUBA rental equipment shop, can minimize or eliminate some of these logistical challenges.

## Conclusion

Generally, volunteer diver and snorkeler data compares favorably with data collected by professional scientists, and are most reliably accurate for numerically dominant, conspicuous, and slow-moving or sessile species (Bernard et al., 2013; Gillett et al., 2012; Done et al., 2017; Mumby et al., 1995; Uychiaoco et al., 2005; Williams et al., 2008). However, care must still be taken with training and study design. For example, in one validation study, Reef Check volunteer data agreed with data collected by scientists in percent estimations of coral cover, but not fish densities, and volunteer data also failed to show the long-term trends captured by scientists' data in widespread changes (increases and decreases) in the abundance of a number of highly mobile but very recognizable fish species (parrotfish and snappers; Forrester et al., 2015). Additionally, when conspicuous or well-known taxa are included in a community survey, volunteers may overestimate their abundance/density as compared to data taken by scientists, perhaps due to the ease of identification or familiarity with the species (e.g. urchins in kelp forest surveys; Gillett et al., 2012). Conversely, when focal species are rare, cryptic or hard to identify, the detectability of those species decreases for all observers, and volunteers are not likely to be successful at capturing accurate data, even when those species are included in volunteer training (Bell, 2007; Bernard et al., 2013; Branchini et al., 2015). Thus, surveys designed to compare biodiversity via species richness are less likely to be executed with a high degree of accuracy using volunteer divers, although increased experience of the volunteer via participation in multiple surveys may increase the accuracy of species richness estimates (Williams et al., 2008)

However, surveys of the type run by Reef Check and REEF have been successful in gathering accurate data (Pattengill-Semmens and Semmens, 2003; Gillett et al., 2012; see earlier profiles), and similar projects can likewise be successful when the proper amount of training, in-water oversight (by professional scientists) and/or quality control measures are in place (see our recommendations for best practices). Additionally, multiple surveys by dive teams in the same place may increase the accuracy of volunteer data on community assemblages (Schmitt et al., 2002), potentially mitigating the tendency to misrepresent the abundances of mobile species and/or presence of less common species. And the use of standardized survey methods within (i.e. over years) and across projects, as is done by REEF and Reef Check, allows for the detection of long-term trends because any biases in data collection due to methodology will likely be consistent across years and projects (Wolfe and Pattengill-Semmens, 2013b). Collaborating with citizen scientists also allows for the collection of large data sets (e.g. queen conch project), which can further increase the detection of long-term trends (e.g. Ward-Paige et al., 2010).

Despite the unique challenges inherent in conducting underwater research with citizen scientists, divers and snorkelers are often passionate and dedicated volunteers. Certified SCUBA divers, in particular, have demonstrated an investment in exploring underwater habitats by undergoing rigorous and lengthy training, and many feel deeply connected to the marine ecosystems that they have spent time diving in. This sense of place, coupled with their enjoyment of marine realms normally hidden to non-divers and snorkelers, can engender a unique level of commitment to volunteering as citizen scientists, and a fierce dedication to research projects, particularly those that are focused on marine conservation. In addition, many divers and snorkelers are already skilled in species identifications, and generally inclined towards closely observing the marine world, which makes them natural citizen scientists. Of course, as with all citizen science programs, care must be taken to ensure that the data collected by volunteer divers and snorkelers are accurate and useful, and that the well-being and safety of citizen scientists are cared for. We have found that following the guidelines discussed here will help achieve both, while hopefully also engaging volunteers in such a way that increases their appreciation for, and dedication to, marine ecosystems.

The conservation issues facing the ocean are complex and occur over large spatial and temporal scales (Parsons et al., 2014; Cigliano et al., 2016). Engaging divers and snorkelers as citizen scientists is an effective way to collect data to address these issues at the local, regional, and global scale. Indeed, in some cases it is the only way to collect data of the geographic breadth and/or length of time necessary. Here, we focused on population and community surveys, but divers and snorkelers can also contribute to scientific knowledge and management of marine ecosystems in other ways, and are often uniquely positioned to do so. For example, divers and snorkelers can serve as the "front line" of observers who first recognize invasive species and alert the scientific community to their location and spread (i.e. acting as "sentinels"; Chapter 4), or conversely, the first to notice the population decline or absence of formerly common native species. They can also serve as "watchdogs" for human impacts to marine systems via changes in familiar recreational diving sites that may otherwise be under monitored. Finally, these passionate citizen scientists can assist in mobilizing wider community involvement of the type that is essential in adaptive management (Aceves-Bueno et al., 2015).

In conclusion, when marine researchers employ training, quality control, and data management techniques that have proven to be successful in engaging divers and snorkelers in projects that match their strengths as a volunteer population, citizen science can be a critical tool for the advancement of coastal and marine research and conservation.

## Web resources

1  www.diveintoscience.org.
2  www.earthdive.com.
3  www.coralwatch.org.
4  www.reefcheck.org.
5  www.REEF.org.
6  www.reef.org/programs/monitoring.
7  www.earthwatch.org.

## Literature cited

Aceves-Bueno, E., Adeleye, A., Bradley, D., Tyler Brandt, W., Callery, P., Feraud, M., Garner, K., Gentry, R., Huang, Y., McCullough, I., Pearlman, I., Sutherland, S., Wilkinson, W., Yang, Y., Zink, T., Anderson, S., and Tague, C. (2015). Citizen science as an approach for overcoming insufficient monitoring and inadequate stakeholder buy-in in adaptive management: Criteria and evidence. *Ecosystems*, 18(3), 493–506.

Archer, S., Allgeier, J., Semmens, B., Heppell, S., Pattengill-Semmens, C., Rosemond, A., Bush, P., McCoy, C., Johnson, B., and Layman, C. (2014). Hot moments in spawning aggregations: Implications for ecosystem-scale nutrient cycling. *Coral Reefs*, 34(1), 19–23.

Beeden, R., Turner, M., Dryden, J., Merida, F., Goudkamp, K., Malone, C., Marshall, P., Birtles, A., and Maynard, J. (2014). Rapid survey protocol that provides dynamic information on reef condition to managers of the Great Barrier Reef. *Environmental Monitoring and Assessment*, 186(12), 8527–8540.

Bell, J. (2007). The use of volunteers for conducting sponge biodiversity assessments and monitoring using a morphological approach on Indo-Pacific coral reefs. *Aquatic Conservation: Marine and Freshwater Ecosystems*, 17(2), 133–145.

Bernard, A., Götz, A., Kerwath, S., and Wilke, C. (2013). Observer bias and detection probability in underwater visual census of fish assemblages measured with independent double-observers. *Journal of Experimental Marine Biology and Ecology*, 443, 75–84.

Bonney, R., Cooper, C., Dickinson, J., Kelling, S., Phillips, T., Rosenberg, K., and Shirk, J. (2009). Citizen science: A developing tool for expanding science knowledge and scientific literacy. *BioScience*, 59(11), 977–984.

Branchini, S., Pensa, F., Neri, P., Tonucci, B., Mattielli, L., Collavo, A., Sillingardi, M., Piccinetti, C., Zaccanti, F., and Goffredo, S. (2015). Using a citizen science program to monitor coral reef biodiversity through space and time. *Biodiversity and Conservation*, 24(2), 319–336.

Cerrano, C., Milanese, M., and Ponti, M. (2016). Diving for science – science for diving: volunteer SCUBA divers support science and conservation in the Mediterranean Sea. *Aquatic Conservation: Marine and Freshwater Ecosystems*, 27(2), 303–323.

Chavanich, S., Viyakarn, V., Adams, P., Klammer, J., and Cook, N. (2012). Reef communities after the 2010 mass coral bleaching at Racha Yai Island in the Andaman Sea and Koh Tao in the Gulf of Thailand. *Phuket Marine Biological Center Research Bulletin*, 71, 103–110.

Cho, L. (2005). Marine protected areas: A tool for integrated coastal management in Belize. *Ocean and Coastal Management*, 48, 932–947.

Cigliano, J., Bauer, A., Draheim, M., Foley, M., Lundquist, C., McCarthy, J., Patterson, K., Wright, A., and Parsons, E. (2016). The Kraken in the aquarium: Questions that urgently need to be addressed in order to advance marine conservation. *Frontiers in Marine Science*, 3, 174.

Cigliano, J., and Kliman, R. (2014). Density, age structure, and length of Queen Conch (*Strombus gigas*) in Shallow-Water aggregations in the Sapodilla Cayes Marine reserve, Belize. *Caribbean Journal of Science*, 48(1), 18–30.

Darwall, W.R., and Dulvy, N.K. (1996). An evaluation of the suitability of non-specialist volunteer researchers for coral reef fish surveys. Mafia Island, Tanzania – a case study. *Biological Conservation*, 78(3), 223–231.

Dearden, P., Theberge, M., and Yasué, M. (2010). Using underwater cameras to assess the effects of snorkeler and SCUBA diver presence on coral reef fish abundance, family richness, and species composition. *Environmental Monitoring and Assessment*, 163(1), 531–538.

Done, T., Roelfsema, C., Harvey, A., Schuller, L., Hill, J., Schläppy, M., Lea, A., Bauer-Civiello, A., and Loder, J. (2017). Reliability and utility of citizen science reef monitoring data collected by Reef Check Australia, 2002–2015. *Marine Pollution Bulletin*, 117(1–2), 148–155.

Edgar, G., and Stuart-Smith, R. (2009). Ecological effects of marine protected areas on rocky reef communities – a continental-scale analysis. *Marine Ecology Progress Series*, 388, 51–62.

Edgar, G.J., Stuart-Smith, R.D., Cooper, A., Jacques, M. and Valentine, J., (2017). New opportunities for conservation of handfishes (Family Brachionichthyidae) and other inconspicuous and threatened marine species through citizen science. *Biological Conservation*, 208, 174–182.

Forrester, G., Baily, P., Conetta, D., Forrester, L., Kintzing, E., and Jarecki, L. (2015). Comparing monitoring data collected by volunteers and professionals shows that citizen scientists can detect long-term change on coral reefs. *Journal for Nature Conservation*, 24, 1–9.

Freiwald, J., Wisniewski, C., Wehrenberg, M., Shuman, C., and Dawson, C. (2015). *Reef Check California Instruction Manual: A Guide to Rocky Reef Monitoring* (8th ed.). Pacific Palisades, CA: Reef Check Foundation.

Geoghegan, H., Dyke, A., Pateman, R., West, S., and Everett, G. (2016). *Understanding motivations for citizen science*. Final report on behalf of UKEOF, University of Reading, Stockholm Environment Institute (University of York) and University of the West of England.

Gillett, D., Pondella, D., Freiwald, J., Schiff, K., Caselle, J., Shuman, C., and Weisberg, S. (2012). Comparing volunteer and professionally collected monitoring data from the rocky subtidal reefs of Southern California, USA. *Environmental Monitoring and Assessment*, 184(5), 3239–3257.

Harding, S., Lowery, C., and Oakley, S. (2000). Comparison between complex and simple reef survey techniques using volunteers: Is the effort justified. In *Proceedings of the 9th International Coral Reef Symposium. International Coral Reef Society, Bali*, 883–889.

Hodgson, G., Hill, J., Kiene, W., Maun, L., Mihaly, J., Liebeler, J., Shuman, C., and Torres, R. (2006). *Reef Check Instruction Manual: A Guide to Reef Check Coral Reef Monitoring*. Pacific Palisades, CA: Reef Check Foundation.

Holt, B., Rioja-Nieto, R., Aaron MacNeil, M., Lupton, J., and Rahbek, C. (2013). Comparing diversity data collected using a protocol designed for volunteers with results from a professional alternative. *Methods in Ecology and Evolution*, 4(4), 383–392.

Hyder, K., Townhill, B., Anderson, L., Delany, J., and Pinnegar, J. (2015). Can citizen science contribute to the evidence-base that underpins marine policy? *Marine Policy*, 59, 112–120.

Kosmala, M., Wiggins, A., Swanson, A., and Simmons, B. (2016). Assessing data quality in citizen science. *Frontiers in Ecology and the Environment*, 14(10), 551–560.

Krieger, J., and Chadwick, N. (2013). Recreational diving impacts and the use of pre-dive briefings as a management strategy on Florida coral reefs. *Journal of Coastal Conservation*, 17(1), 179–189.

Marks, L., Salinas-Ruiz, P., Reed, D., Holbrook, S., Culver, C., Engle, J., Kushner, D., Caselle, J., Freiwald, J., Williams, J., Smith, J., Aguilar-Rosas, L., and Kaplanis, N. (2015). Range expansion of a non-native, invasive macroalga *Sargassum horneri* (Turner) C. Agardh, 1820 in the eastern Pacific. *BioInvasions Records*, 4(4), 243–248.

Martin, V.Y., Christidis, L., and Pecl, G.T. (2016). Public interest in marine citizen science: Is there potential for growth? *BioScience*, 66(8), 683–692.

McKinley, D.C., Miller-Rushing, A.J., Ballard, H.L., Bonney, R., Brown, H., Evans, D.M., French, R.A., Parrish, J.K., Phillips, T.B., Ryan, S.F., and Shanley, L.A. (2015). Investing in citizen science can improve natural resource management and environmental protection. *Issues in Ecology*, 19, 1–27.

Micheli, F., Saenz-Arroyo, A., Greenley, A., Vazquez, L., Espinoza Montes, J., Rossetto, M., and De Leo, G. (2012). Evidence that marine reserves enhance resilience to climatic impacts. *PLoS One*, 7(7), e40832.

Miller-Rushing, A., Primack, R., and Bonney, R. (2012). The history of public participation in ecological research. *Frontiers in Ecology and the Environment*, 10(6), pp. 285–290. http://doi.org/10.1890/110278.

Mumby, P.J., Harborne, A.R., Raines, P.S., and Ridley, J.M. (1995). A critical assessment of data derived from Coral Cay Conservation volunteers. *Bulletin of Marine Science*, 56(3), 737–751.

Parsons, E.C.M., Favaro, B., Aguirre, A.A., Bauer, A.L., Blight, L.K., Cigliano, J.A., . . . Foley, M.M. (2014). Seventy-one important questions for the conservation of marine biodiversity. *Conservation Biology*, 28(5), 1206–1214.

Pattengill-Semmens, C.V., and Semmens, B.X. (1998). Fish census data generated by non-experts in the Flower Garden Banks National Marine Sanctuary. *Journal of Gulf of Mexico Science*, 2, 196–207.

Pattengill-Semmens, C.V., and Semmens, B.X. (2003). Conservation and management applications of the reef volunteer fish monitoring program. In *Coastal Monitoring Through Partnerships*, pp. 43–50. Dordrecht, the Netherlands: Springer.

Pérez, J. (1997). Status of queen conch, *Strombus gigas*, in Belize. In *International Queen Conch Conference*, ed. J.M. Posada and G. Garcia-Moliner, 84–85. Caribbean Fishery Management Council, San Juan, Puerto Rico.

Plathong, S., Inglis, G.J., and Huber, M.E. (2000). Effects of self-guided snorkeling trails on corals in a Tropical Marine Park. *Conservation Biology*, 14(6), 1821–1830.

Ridlon, A.D., Warner, R.R., and Gaines, S.D. (in prep). Partial habituation to chronic recreational SCUBA diving by a coral reef fish.

Roelfsema, C., Thurstan, R., Beger, M., Dudgeon, C., Loder, J., Kovacs, E., Gallo, M., Flower, J., Gomez Cabrera, K., Ortiz, J., Lea, A., and Kleine, D. (2016). A citizen science approach: A detailed ecological assessment of subtropical reefs at point lookout, Australia. *PLOS One*, 11(10), e0163407.

Rotman, D., Preece, J., Hammock, J., Procita, K., Hansen, D., Parr, C., Lewis, D., and Jacobs, D. (2012). Dynamic changes in motivation in collaborative citizen-science projects. In *Proceedings of the ACM 2012 Conference on Computer Supported Cooperative Work*, 217–226. ACM. [Online] http://dl.acm.org/citation.cfm?id=2145238 [Accessed April 22, 2017].

Schmitt, E., Sluka, R., and Sullivan-Sealey, K. (2002). Evaluating the use of roving diver and transect surveys to assess the coral reef fish assemblage off southeastern Hispaniola. *Coral Reefs*, 21(2), 216–223.

Shirk, J., Ballard, H., Wilderman, C., Phillips, T., Wiggins, A., Jordan, R., McCallie, E., Minarchek, M., Lewenstein, B., Krasny, M., and Bonney, R. (2012). Public participation in scientific research: A framework for deliberate design. *Ecology and Society*, 17(2).

Stuart-Smith, R., Edgar, G., Barrett, N., Bates, A., Baker, S., Bax, N., Becerro, M., Berkhout, J., Blanchard, J., Brock, D., Clark, G., Cooper, A., Davis, T., Day, P., Duffy, J., Holmes, T., Howe, S., Jordan, A., Kininmonth, S., Knott, N., Lefcheck, J., Ling, S., Parr, A., Strain, E., Sweatman, H., and Thomson, R. (2017). Assessing national biodiversity trends for rocky and coral reefs through the integration of citizen science and scientific monitoring programs. *BioScience*, 67(2), 134–146.

Sweatman, H., Delean, S. and Syms, C. (2011). Assessing loss of coral cover on Australia's Great Barrier Reef over two decades, with implications for longer-term trends. *Coral Reefs*, 30(2), 521–531.

Thiel, M., Penna-Díaz, M.A., Luna-Jorquera, G., Salas, S., Sellanes, J., and Stotz, W. (2014). Citizen scientists and marine research: Volunteer participants, their contributions, and projection for the future. *Oceanography and Marine Biology: An Annual Review*, 52, 257–314.

Theile, S. (2001). *Queen Conch Fisheries and Their Management in the Caribbean*. Brussels, Belgium: TRAFFIC Europe.

Thorson, J., Scheuerell, M., Semmens, B., and Pattengill-Semmens, C. (2014). Demographic modeling of citizen science data informs habitat preferences and population dynamics of recovering fishes. *Ecology*, 95(12), 3251–3258.

Uychiaoco, A., Arceo, H., Green, S., Cruz, M., Gaite, P., and Aliño, P. (2005). Monitoring and evaluation of Reef protected areas by local fishers in the Philippines: Tightening the adaptive management cycle. *Biodiversity and Conservation*, 14(11), 2775–2794.

Ward-Paige, C., Pattengill-Semmens, C., Myers, R., and Lotze, H. (2010). Spatial and temporal trends in yellow stingray abundance: Evidence from diver surveys. *Environmental Biology of Fishes*, 90(3), 263–276.

Webler, T., and Jakubowski, K. (2016). Mitigating damaging behaviors of snorkelers to coral reefs in Puerto Rico through a pre-trip media-based intervention. *Biological Conservation*, 197, 223–228.

West, S.E., Pateman, R.M., and Dyke, A.J. (2015). *Motivations and data submissions in citizen science*. Report to Department of Environment and Rural Affairs. London, UK.

Williams, I.D., Walsh, W.J., Schroeder, R.E., Friedlander, A.M., Richards, B.L., and Stamoulis, K.A. (2008). Assessing the importance of fishing impacts on Hawaiian coral reef fish assemblages along regional-scale human population gradients. *Environmental Conservation*, 35(3), 261–272.

Wolfe, J.R., and Pattengill-Semmens, C.V. (2013a). Fish population fluctuation estimates based on fifteen years of reef volunteer diver data for the Monterey Peninsula, California. *California Cooperative Oceanic Fisheries Investigations Reports*, 54, 141–154.

Wolfe, J.R., and Pattengill-Semmens, C.V. (2013b). Estimating fish populations from REEF citizen science volunteer diver order-of-magnitude surveys. *California Cooperative Oceanic Fisheries Investigations Reports*, 54, 127–140.

Zainal Abidin, S., and Mohamed, B. (2014). A review of SCUBA diving impacts and implication for coral reefs conservation and tourism management. *SHS Web of Conferences*, 12, 01093.

# PART IV

# Conclusions – lessons learned and best practices for coastal and marine conservation citizen science

# 13

# COMMUNICATION AND TRUST-BUILDING WITH THE BROADER PUBLIC THROUGH COASTAL AND MARINE CITIZEN SCIENCE

*Edward J. Hind-Ozan, Gretta T. Pecl,
and Christine A. Ward-Paige*

## Introduction

The quality of communication between marine scientists and those whose lives and livelihoods are entwined with our seas and oceans can be the making or breaking of a marine research or conservation initiative. When scientists' communication with the project participants is slow to arrive or poorly crafted, or where project communications infrastructure such as websites and apps are clunky or broken, citizen scientists have been found to consistently drop out of projects (Rotman et al., 2014). Likewise, if scientists transmit information to the public in a manner that is vague, misleading, or inappropriate (e.g. jargon heavy), confidence and trust in those experts can be quickly lost, resulting in societal inaction or non-compliance. The history of oceans research is littered with examples of well-intentioned efforts undermined by misinformation, poor correspondence, and broken trust (Wilson, 2003; Christie, 2004; van Densen and McCay, 2007; Wilcox, 2012).

Contrastingly, when scientists and marine stakeholders work to develop close professional relationships and trust, research goals have a greater potential of being realized. For instance, the 1990s infamous collapses of cod populations on Canada's Grand Banks and in Europe's North Sea would likely never have happened if scientists, politicians, managers, and fishers had been on the same page and trusted each other. In both locations, scientists had access to the knowledge to help manage fish stocks sustainably. Yet, their inability to disseminate their own knowledge to fishers and politicians (Europe) or for some to properly consider the knowledge of fishers (Canada) meant the potentially species-saving knowledge was not communicated to those who needed to receive it. The results were near (Europe) and actual (Canada) marine catastrophes (Neis, 1992; Hutchings et al., 1997; Daw and Gray, 2005).

At Apo Island in the Philippines, however, greater consideration was given to the quality of communication as part of another marine research initiative. In the early

1980s, off-island scientists approached the island's local community with a plan for setting up a marine reserve to protect local coral reefs. Their default interaction was not to instruct fishers in a top-down manner to fish less, but to respectfully inform islanders that they could make a better livelihood through fishing more sustainably (Alcala and Russ, 2006). It was reported by Apo Island residents to one of the chapter authors (Hind-Ozan) that these marine scientists were welcomed to Apo Island because they did not come across as elitist or superior. The scientists communicated their plan in deliberately open workshops where all local fishers and residents were encouraged to ask questions and voice opinions on the potential setting up of the reserve. Fully informed, and having gained confidence and trust in the scientists and their plans during the conversations, the community agreed to set up the marine reserve (Alcala and Russ, 2006).

It should not be surprising that the likelihood of a successful outcome for scientific research results from making an effort to communicate well and to build trust. Terrestrial-based citizen science projects offer several examples. For instance, the scientists leading the Chicago Area Pollinator Study openly admitted that the citizen scientists they recruited lost interest in their study as a result of infrequent and unclear scientist-citizen communication (Druschke and Seltzer, 2012). eBird, contrastingly, has achieved great success in sustaining the enrollment of a large following of amateur birdwatchers through its carefully designed communications strategy (Sullivan et al., 2009), including a highly accessible online hub where individuals and institutional partners can easily share and disseminate information. Its website ensures that the goals and procedures of the research project are immediately clear. Project leaders have also taken measures to ensure the citizen scientists enjoy their participation (e.g. running bird photography contests via social media) and feel valued as co-investigators (e.g. by naming an "eBirder of the Month"). Email newsletters sent to "eBirders" show how the bird sightings they contribute are integrated into real-world scientific research, as well as how they inform conservation policy. Such steps have helped the citizen scientists feel a degree of ownership over the eBird project and the ownership feeling has contributed to participants' considerable trust in the citizen science process in which they are participating (Dickinson et al., 2012).

Like much successful coastal and marine research, coastal and marine citizen science needs to be consistently constructed on the sturdy foundations of high quality scientist-citizen communication. In fact, the need for effective communication is likely higher in the case of citizen science. When cod stocks collapsed in Europe's North Sea, fisheries scientists were still able to amass the scientific data they believed requisite for making their biological assessments. A period of poor communication for them with politicians and fishers did not stop their data collection activities. When their communications with politicians and fishers eventually improved, they were then able to pass on their collected data from the fallow period of communication to these two groups, both of whom engaged with it in a manner that has allowed cod stocks to slowly rebuild (Kraak et al., 2013). However, if a citizen science project suffered a similar communications failure, it would not have a chance of this ultimately positive outcome because there would be no data to pass on if good communication was re-established. As the example of the Chicago Area Pollinator Study shows, when citizen scientists do disengage as a result of poor communication, the career scientists organizing the citizen science project cannot continue data collection activities.

One might think, in our ever more connected world, that addressing project communications is as simple as implementing a social media strategy. This, however, is a common error for new citizen science projects. While social media in coastal and marine citizen science projects can play a role in communication, we will show in this chapter that it is face-to-face and email contact with career scientists that grab citizen scientists' attention. It is not only we, as career scientists ourselves, who are making this assertion. Participants who contributed to the Plastics Project, a citizen science project involving volunteers sorting sand samples from beaches for marine debris, have stated that opportunities to interact with experts at public events and through other forms of direct communication are most engaging (Wehner, 2011). Only 1%–2% preferred to receive project information via social media, while nearly 50% preferred to receive information through lectures, training seminars, and email. A great project website or app is likely to stand unused unless the citizen scientists using it also have a personal relationship with project scientists and coordinators, even if virtual.

In this chapter we document two case studies of our own work, describing steps taken in regard to trust-building and communication, as well as for data collection. Each of the case studies illustrates how good communication has been the key to the success of the project. Among the professional scientists working on the projects, we have built close and collaborative relationships with our citizen scientists or with project staff who then interacted with citizen scientists. We then discuss how to overcome barriers to effective communication within a marine or coastal citizen science project. And we conclude the chapter with a call for increased focus on project communication strategies within coastal and marine citizen science. We hope our chapter will facilitate research and inform conservation professionals on how to confidently devise a communications strategy for any marine or coastal citizen science project in which they become involved.

## Building trust: stories of communications success through citizen science

The two case studies presented here provide examples of how requirements for scientist-citizen communication need to be adapted for each coastal and marine citizen science project. Redmap is an online web portal and smartphone app where Australia-based fishers, boaters, and SCUBA divers can submit photographic observations of marine species they believe to be unusual for the given area. eOceans also uses an online reporting system and invites data contributions from ocean users; it asks SCUBA divers, fishers, surfers, stand-up paddleboarders, and boaters, among others, to report sightings of sharks, rays, seahorses, turtles, whales, seals, jellyfish, and even garbage.

We present the two projects via project narratives, where special attention is given to the communications strategy used by each. The stories of planning and delivery for the projects provide important pointers on how to communicate and build trust with citizen scientists. You will see that engagement with different stakeholders requires different communication strategies and that differing project backgrounds and data-collection goals must be acknowledged and accounted for. What you are unlikely to find in this chapter, therefore, is a "copy and paste" approach to scientist-citizen communication. Hopefully, however, you will be able to adopt parts of the approaches illustrated here in your own project.

## Redmap

### Study and conservation goals

Large-scale climate-driven shifts in species distribution are being observed in every system and region of the globe (Poloczanska et al., 2013; Pecl et al., 2017). Documenting and responding to these changes, across vast scales, is a challenge for ecologists, natural resource managers, and communities. In particular, countries like Australia, with around 60,000 km of coastline and a very large marine territory, face considerable challenges when it comes to monitoring, especially because the waters around Australia are warming at approximately two to four times the global average (Hobday and Pecl, 2014), leading to range shifts of many marine species (Sunday et al., 2015).

Redmap (Range Extension Database and Mapping project)[1] invites recreational and commercial fishers, SCUBA divers, snorkelers, boaters, beachcombers, and others to report marine species that are uncommon to a particular location. Redmap is essentially a framework for efficiently collecting, collating, verifying, sharing, and using geo-referenced species observational data. We (chapter author Gretta Pecl and the Redmap management team colleagues) designed the project with two overarching and equally weighted aims: (1) ecological monitoring to provide an early indication of potential range shifts, and (2) actively engaging the broader community on issues of marine climate change, largely using their own data. The second aim requires effective communication. Although awareness of climate change is reasonably high across the Australian population (Lee et al., 2015), the marine environment for many is "out-of-mind and out-of-sight." For instance, research that some of the Redmap team has been involved with indicates that awareness of climate change is apparently low in some of the country's fisheries sector (Nursey-Bray et al., 2012). Redmap provides a unique and previously untapped data source for the scientific community, and has a goal of actively engaging the marine and broader community in constructive dialogue on marine climate change. Importantly, fishers, divers, and boaters can contribute to marine science and learn about the impacts of ocean warming on marine life while they undertake recreational activities.

## The scientists and citizen scientists of Redmap

Redmap is hosted nationally by the Institute for Marine and Antarctic Studies in Hobart, Tasmania, and operates via a small part-time national team (within which chapter co-author Gretta Pecl is Chief Investigator) in collaboration with regionally led and state-based teams. The national team includes a dedicated Communications Officer. Scientists within each regional team consult with local fishers and divers, as well as other local marine science experts, on suitable species to track in each region. Ocean users, such as recreational and commercial fishers, SCUBA divers, snorkelers, boaters, beachcombers, and others are the citizen scientists. They send in photographs of the "listed" or pre-identified species when they observe them in the regions of interest, as well as of any other species they know or think are unusual for that location. Approximately 80 volunteers, marine experts from around Australia, form a nationwide verification panel responsible for reviewing the accuracy of each citizen scientist submission. Their expert taxonomic review of each sighting adds rigor to the data collection process while allowing for participation to be opportunistic and not require specialized training. This combination of volunteer and professional experts helps to ensure a high quality of data.

The scientists on the Redmap team also help produce educational resources relating to the listed species explaining why they are of research interest, and regularly draft resource articles for the project Web page and newsletter, and/or for the media. They regularly contact our citizen scientists via email or Facebook to ask them to provide feedback or input on various aspects of the project, whether large (e.g. grant applications and new ideas) or small (e.g. which book to have as a competition prize). Furthermore, the project scientists have become involved in promoting the project and disseminating results via a "Redmap Champions" program (described later). Like the project scientists, some of the citizen scientists have written resource articles for the Redmap website and newsletter.

## Project outcomes

Redmap started as a smaller pilot project in the island state of Tasmania in 2009, after consultation with the local fishing and diving community on what species they felt were likely to experience changing distributions, what information they were comfortable reporting, and at what scale. In late 2012, the project extended nationally and has, as of 2016, had almost one million visitors to the website, attracted over 245 media reports, and been awarded five major awards for community engagement and scientific excellence (e.g. the University of Tasmania's Award for Outstanding Community Engagement).[2] The resulting data have contributed to over 20 peer-reviewed scientific publications on the probable range extension of several species, such as manta rays, argonauts, and various bony fish (Grove and Finn, 2014; Couturier et al., 2015; Stuart-Smith et al., 2016). As a testament to the positive engagement with participants by Redmap, national expansion of the project was initiated after fishers and divers from other states heard about the project from Tasmanian citizen scientists and requested capacity to report unusual observations in their own regions.

Communication and trust between scientists and citizen scientists within the project can uniquely impact communication *outside* the project. In 2015, the team used Facebook to ask the project's citizen scientists what they thought about spending AUS$5,000 on making a scientific paper open access. Our strong preference was to make the results open access, but the Redmap volunteers told us that they would prefer for the money to be kept for conducting new research, as long as they were provided with a free-to-access lay summary, which was provided.[3]

In terms of conservation outcomes, data submitted to Redmap have been used in peer-reviewed papers showing the systematic evaluation of range shifts for marine species (e.g. Robinson et al., 2015). The many fisher and diver citizen scientists who submitted observations to Redmap have also been consulted in the drafting and publishing of these range shift assessments as a "report card" designed to disseminate project results to the general public.[4] People that contributed data to the report card, and other project citizen scientists via Facebook, were asked to provide feedback on the design, text, and format of the report card. The project team revised the report card based on these suggestions, altering the text, symbols, and adding more information on the background to the project.

Redmap has also made small but influential data contributions to a number of larger peer-reviewed studies (e.g. Johnson et al., 2011; Last et al., 2011). These works, together with Robinson et al. (2015), have been instrumental in the development of a strong understanding of species and ecosystem changes occurring in one of the fastest warming regions of the Southern Hemisphere (Hobday and Pecl, 2014). Redmap observations have triggered focused studies on particular species, providing an indication of where limited resources for research could be constructively directed (e.g. Ramos et al., 2014; 2015). Some novel or unusual observations have revealed useful/interesting biological phenomena and are worthy of detailed examination/reporting in the literature (e.g. Couturier et al., 2015; Grove and Finn, 2014). Other observations have been used to inform an examination of the ecosystem impacts of multi-species shifts (Marzloff et al., 2016), or to provide the basis for the discussing of the socio-economic impacts of range shifts (Madin et al., 2012). Lastly, many of the sightings submitted to Redmap that are not designated as technically "out-of-range" have been valuable for improving knowledge of the distribution of poorly known or rare species. These have contributed species distribution data to the Australian Faunal Directory.[5]

## Project communications

The outcomes described would unlikely have become reality if it were not for our attention to communication.[6] Engagement is one of Redmap's two major goals; our management team has committed considerable thought and time to developing a thorough and formal engagement strategy. On an annual basis, we also draft a shorter communication plan for implementation, taking into account available resources, upcoming events, current marine climate change issues, and immediate requirements of the project. Our engagement plan specifies measurable engagement goals, identifies and prioritizes key target audiences (e.g. fishers and divers are the management team's primary concern) and highlights key messages of interest to communicate to each target group. A key step in planning a project is to consider what information sources are trusted by our audience (see Martin et al., 2016 for details). Moreover, our management team is careful to ensure project engagement is structured as a two-way process, with feedback, input, and dialogue from citizen scientists included as a matter of critical importance. One way this has been ensured is by asking focus groups of volunteers to provide feedback on website design, app functionality, and content of the final report card.

We believe Redmap's primary and most important form of communication with our citizen scientists is one-to-one communication via email after they submit sightings. Immediately after submission, they receive a thank-you email that explains the next part of the process. After a verifying scientist has examined the sighting, another email is drafted based on the check boxes that the scientist selects in the project database (e.g. is correct species, is not correct species). The scientist either sends an auto-populated email, or alternatively, many of our scientists elect to personalize the message and add additional information that may be of interest to the observer. Communication also occurs via our website, electronic newsletter, and as with many citizen science projects, via an active Facebook page and Twitter account.

The extended Redmap team regularly delivers presentations and Q&A sessions at various venues (e.g. boat shows, fishing competitions and events, dive clubs, school visits, and marine community festivals) and in a range of formats (e.g. small group meetings and presentations, one-on-one discussions at festival/event stands and stalls, formal public forums, webinars) around the country. Sometimes, members of our project team do more than just attend such forums – for example, entering a local diving or fishing competition – to illustrate to our citizen scientists that we are also passionate divers and fishers who share similar interests and values with them. Recently, we trialed a "Redmap Champions" program, where our project team trains interested members of the public in how to disseminate project information and outcomes. Champions have attended events alongside project scientists or made presentations on the project to their local dive, fishing, or community groups.

Redmap has a significant communication challenge in that within and between its target audience groups of recreational fishers, commercial fishers, and divers, there are considerable differences in values, beliefs, views on conservation, and levels of dissatisfaction with resource management. During planning, the project's management team, therefore, carefully considers phrasing, pitch, tone, and framing of message communication. A formal evaluation of the communication and engagement undertaken by the Redmap team was conducted in 2013, using an online survey. The survey was sent to key marine scientists, fishers, Redmap users, researchers, and government managers. We obtained 52 responses. Results demonstrated success to date, with 80% of participants surveyed indicating that they had learned about marine climate change impacts through the project. Also, 78% of people said they had discussed Redmap with others, and 97% said they trusted the information generated and disseminated by Redmap (Nursey-Bray, unpubl. data).

## eOceans

### Study and conservation goals

eOceans (eoceans.org) is an "umbrella" program that hosts various ocean-focused, citizen science projects (eShark, eManta, Global Marine Conservation Assessment, etc.) for which chapter author C.A. Ward-Paige is science lead. The overarching goal, thus far, of the eOceans projects is to describe marine animal populations and evaluate conservation needs and successes. Projects include both ongoing "event-based" monitoring and "snapshot" hypothesis-driven research questions. For monitoring, eShark collects time-stamped, georeferenced effort and encounter information on sharks, rays, turtles, seahorses, jellyfish, cetaceans, seals, and garbage, including absences, from various marine resource users. These data are used to fill data gaps, establish baselines, describe spatial and temporal patterns in animal populations, and to evaluate management successes and needs. Hypothesis-driven projects, like eManta, and the recent (2016) Global Marine Conservation Assessment, run for short durations (e.g. two to six months depending on how quickly the required number of citizen scientists participate in the survey) and are generally one-off summaries that accumulate the experiences of area-specific experts to improve our understanding of a subject – for example, to understand the global status and human use patterns of manta rays (Ward-Paige et al., 2013) or to evaluate the public's knowledge and potential for success of different marine conservation strategies (Ward-Paige and Worm, in review).

### The scientists and citizen scientists of eOceans

eOceans aims to include the observations of all ocean-going explorers with a range of experiences, encounters, perspectives and skills. There are four main contributors to eOceans: science, outreach, field, and advisory teams (Figure 13.1). A member of our science team (C.A. Ward-Paige), who has in-depth understanding of the value, limitations, and uses of citizen science data, developed the "Diver Survey" portion of the Pew Global Shark Assessment with R.A. Myers (2003–2007).[7] The science team (now C.A. Ward-Paige and occasional students) directs and conducts all aspects of eOceans projects, from conception to analysis and publication. Outreach teams, who are on-the-ground regional partners, facilitate communication between citizen scientists (called "field teams" within the eOceans structure) and the science teams. Our outreach teams play an integral role in recruiting committed field team members and in motivating their ongoing reporting. Members of our outreach teams are typically highly motivated, self-starting individuals or organizations (e.g. non-governmental organizations [NGOs], dive tourism operators) that already have education and outreach missions to provide science-based information about marine conservation. Field teams provide the data, which includes their field experiences (effort and encounters) and detailed observations (e.g. eShark) or summaries of past experiences (e.g. eManta). Each project typically has its own field team members, and members may contribute to multiple projects. To build trust between the science team and field teams, our outreach teams share regular data and publication updates. An external advisory group of professional scientists and conservationists provides general oversight and advice to the science team on the direction or details of projects.

Members of our field teams vary greatly in experience and motivation. About 85% of observations are reported from dive or snorkel events, but they are also contributed from fishing, surfing, paddling, boating, and beach walking events. Some of the field team members also perform outreach and motivation tasks, gathering and entering data for others, validating records, and providing insights on how to interpret results. Training for the field teams differs depending on the project. When organizing eShark dives, for example, novice divers are given tutorials about the species to look for and how to search the area for individuals. A qualified dive leader also assists them.

## Project outcomes

Although other successful fish monitoring citizen science projects had proved their worth (Pattengill-Semmens and Semmens, 2003), when eOceans projects commenced in 2004, there was lukewarm support from the scientific community when describing shark and ray populations using citizen scientist observations made by untrained recreational divers. We heard concerns that recreational divers would be too preoccupied with the act of diving and their underwater safety to search for, and detect or count, sharks or rays. There was also concern that identification of sharks to the species level would be too difficult for non-scientists. This sentiment made it difficult to proceed with describing shark and ray populations using the observations of divers, without first understanding the extent to which their observations could be used. Early projects, therefore, focused on understanding the data generated by citizen scientists, which we did through an evaluation of the merits and limitations of our field teams' observations as a data source (Ward-Paige and Lotze, 2011) when using the protocols of other recreational fish monitoring programs (Ward-Paige et al., 2010, 2011).

This early evaluation of data quality and procedures helped, for example, to define what questions could be reliably collected on survey forms (e.g. presence/absence, number to the species level for many sharks and rays), which could be excluded (e.g. depth, habitat, sex, behavior), and what could be added to increase the quality of data and number of reports, without making it too cumbersome (e.g. presence of other animals and garbage). The lessons learned in the initial years led to the second iteration of the online eShark diver form, and a series of publications about both the effectiveness of volunteer-collected data, as well as of shark and ray populations. These included the findings that some census methodologies overestimate shark presence (Ward-Paige et al., 2010), while others are best suited to counting low-density fishes like sharks and rays (Ward-Paige and Lotze, 2011).

Although eShark was technically launched in 2004 (only the website name changed from "Diver Survey" to eShark in 2008), it was not until the project evaluation and population biology research (described earlier) was published that event-based eShark participation started to gain momentum. Various enthusiastic and key actors in the tourism industry who keenly follow shark research contacted the science lead (C.A. Ward-Paige) to help motivate, organize, launch, and carry out years of concentrated diver censuses in their areas. Their goal was to establish baselines and monitor the populations they see on a regular basis. These groups became valued outreach teams for eOceans, helping to foster communication that kept field teams enrolled over the years (see next section).

Data quality is monitored and assessed in various ways across eOceans projects. eShark, for instance, asks field team members to report their level of diving experience, which is cross-checked with the number of records submitted, and informs on their ability to detect and count sharks (Ward-Paige and Lotze, 2011). They are also provided with drop-down lists and photos of species when reporting and are given the opportunity to state if they were unable to identify the species observed. Citizen scientists can also submit pictures, which the science and outreach teams use to confirm IDs. For eOceans "snapshot" projects, photos, interviews, maps, and detailed dive logs are kept and compared among field team members,[8] or with other data sources to establish validation and reliability levels in reporting (e.g. Food and Agriculture Organization materials (REEF, 2003; Ward-Paige et al., 2010, 2013; Ward-Paige and Lotze, 2011).

Our outcomes to date, therefore, are based on this robust dataset, which includes more than 1.3 million dives across eOceans projects. In addition to scientific papers, our findings have contributed to policy and management decisions. The eManta project, for example, was conducted prior to the 2013 CITES[9] meeting where manta rays were being proposed for listing on Appendix II, but without quantitative information to support their listing. Knowing this, the project aimed to assess if and where manta rays were being caught, and to compare those observations to abundance hotspots, tourism areas, and reported landings. These were then used to describe the driving forces of population change and to understand the extent to which international trade was threatening their survival (Ward-Paige et al., 2013). The projects results were influential in the ultimate listing of manta rays in Appendix II by CITES.

## Project communications

As with Redmap, regular communication between the various actors of eOceans projects has been a key determinant in ensuring the desired data are collected.

Our outreach teams provide an essential link between the science team and field teams in various stages of our work. This is especially true for eShark monitoring, where concentrated censuses are underway (e.g. Thailand, Fiji, Indonesia, Cambodia, South Africa). In these cases, the science team outlines the research goals, data needs, and collection methods to the outreach teams, who in turn communicate this to other outreach team members (if more than one is working on the same project) and/or the field teams. Together, all three teams decide on the temporal and spatial resolution of the data collection (e.g. all months or twice per year).

Both the science and outreach teams solicit questions, comments, concerns, and suggestions from the field teams' citizen scientists before, during, and after launching a project. In the case of eShark, the science team extracts the data and provides summaries of effort and encounters, which are then distributed via the outreach teams to the field teams. Summary updates are also shared in poster format on social media showing, for example, the amount of data that have been gathered and interesting sightings, and reiterating the goals of the collection. These summaries serve to motivate ongoing participation, act as a tool for first-pass validation of the data, and provide an important trust-building link between the science team and field teams by showing that the data are being used, and used responsibly.

Field teams know the sites they visit and their observations best, and therefore the science team also directly reaches out to the field team members for various data validations – such as clarifying an apparent site outlier, confirming a rare species, or to gather additional information about the site itself. Involving the field team members in such a way allows them to be a closer part of the project team, and hopefully increase their fidelity to these projects going forward.

Branding is an important aspect of eOceans communications that has evolved with the inclusion of new projects and outreach teams over the years. eOceans is rooted in just one event-based monitoring project – the "Diver Survey" that was renamed eShark. However, since 2011, various regional concentrated eShark censuses have been launched, now including eShark-Thailand, eShark-Indonesia, eShark–South Africa, and the Great Fiji Shark Count. As well, "snapshot" censuses have been conducted, including eManta and the Global Marine Conservation Assessment. On occasion, when we have reached out to eShark contributors to participate in "snapshot" surveys, a few individuals expressed that they had contributed all their observations to eShark and that Shark Guardian – one of our outreach teams – should be contacted for these data. These individuals did not realize that the eShark team was conducting the "snapshot" survey. This confusion was the impetus for creating "eOceans" and moving all eShark and snapshot projects under this program umbrella. Therefore, although communication is still mainly made by outreach teams that promote strong collaborations between our science team and international teams of interested NGOs and other stakeholders, it also offers consistent messaging between projects, which is an important part of fostering trust and brand loyalty.

## Lessons learned

### Methods for building trust

While coastal and marine citizen science in its current form is a relatively recent pursuit (see Chapter 1), when developing a project, a key best practice in the field should be to build scientist-citizen trust through communication. From our case examples and other projects, we suggest the following steps should be considered when setting up and administering a marine citizen science project.

- *Develop a communications strategy from the start and revisit it—*

    The initial step in both case studies presented in this chapter was to make sure that communications were guided and planned in advance. For eOceans, this meant developing an online presence and providing regular data summaries to show that citizen scientist efforts were not going into a black box, but rather to a scientist who was reviewing and examining the data regularly. For Redmap, project managers set out a founding strategy *and* supplemented it with yearly communications reviews.

- *Test and revise your communications—*

    Part of developing a communications strategy can be experimenting to find out which communications work, and which do not. The preliminary stages for eOceans, which relied on recreational SCUBA divers reporting sightings of sharks and other marine organisms, included discovering which research questions recreational SCUBA divers would answer effectively. As new projects are added to eOceans, they undergo rigorous testing and review to ensure that questions on protocols are not misinterpreted and can be recalled. Redmap recruited its citizen scientists as "beta testers," asking them to give functionality feedback on the website and app used for project communications.

- *Engage locally—*

    Citizen science projects are often national, or even global, but citizen scientists are *always* local. eOceans has had to adapt its communication strategy in several of its locations to account for the different types and preferences of citizen scientist. For instance, where internet availability has been limited, communications have been performed with the assistance of printed documents. Redmap used a similar solution through setting up regional management teams across coastal Australia to locally facilitate the national management team's communications. As another example, the designers of the Marine Debris Tracker app (see Chapter 6) maintain communication with citizen scientists to allow them to request additional items for a checklist of potential sighted debris. This list would have become quickly unwieldy if it was available globally, so local lists were used that included only common items found in all locations and those requested locally (Jambeck and Johnsen, 2015).

- *Employ boundary spanners—*

    A boundary spanner is anybody or any institution that takes a role of skillfully and sensitively bridging interests or organizations, committing people to finding new ways forward, or investing time to translate the reality of others for new audiences (Williams, 2010). Their competencies typically include networking, diplomacy, brokering, listening, and sense-making. eOceans would not have been able to adapt its communication strategy if it were not for the outreach teams of local collaborators translating the communications of the science team for the field teams, so that they fit the local cultural context. Shark Guardian played this role for eShark in Thailand (Figure 13.1) and Indonesia. Boundary spanners in marine citizen science projects not only remove language barriers, they make engaging in communication more desirable for citizen scientists by reducing or mitigating any conflict that might exist between them (e.g. fishers) and career scientists (Johnson, 2009).

- *Listen—*

Citizen scientists develop into experts when scientists allow them to engage in direct communication as equals. When Redmap project leaders allowed citizen scientists to override their own preference for allocating AUS$5,000 to an open access publication, the Redmap management team empowered its participants, albeit ironically blocking communication of the project findings to the broader public (although note the publication is easily available by emailing the team). A recently developed set of guidelines for citizen science collaborations

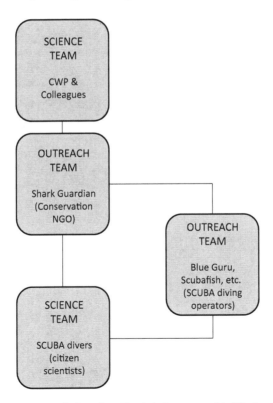

**FIGURE 13.1** Organizational chart for eShark (eOceans.org) in Thailand (with example teams).

and participatory research design in marine-conservation citizen science offers ways to foster trust in these projects (Cigliano et al., 2015). For example, by allowing their earliest enrolled participants to inform design of survey questions, eOceans project leaders fostered such trust.

Listening also involves scientists being available for their project's citizen scientists. Redmap scientists gave their participants this access by taking part in observation activities alongside them, and eOceans outreach teams led training sessions for SCUBA divers in countries, such as Thailand. Both chapter authors involved in these activities have been told by citizen scientists that they enjoyed interacting with professional scientists.

- *Sustain communication—*

Follow-up communications from project leaders can show citizen scientists that the project is dedicated to keeping them informed about the project, even when they are no longer required to collect or contribute data. For eOceans, when sharing peer-reviewed publications resulting from the project, the eOceans project leader (C.A. Ward-Paige) noted the pride in the achievements of the field team members. Citizen scientists who continue to be engaged effectively will continue to trust the project leaders, making them more likely to sign up for future citizen science projects. Redmap's explicit communications strategy has helped participants feel valued when each submission they make is met with an acknowledging email from a scientist verifying their observation (Martin et al., 2016).

- *Be transparent, open, and honest—*

In the initial stages of eOceans, the project leader was careful not to raise the expectations of citizen scientists with respect to contributing to immediate conservation policy. They informed them that they would be helping develop a method, rather than taking part in science that would definitely feed straight into marine policy making. Later, when the project did produce research findings, project leaders reported that participants appreciated the early transparency. With respect to resource users, transparency is especially key to alleviate or avoid conflict; for example, fishers may be unaware that the knowledge they are sharing during citizen science research may be commercially sensitive, or that it could be used by policy makers to inform legislation that may restrict fishing opportunities (Maurstad, 2002). So it is essential for project leaders to be clear at the outset exactly how the data generated by participants will be used, and by whom.

## Conclusion

We chose in this chapter to focus on examples of excellent communications practice in coastal and marine citizen science, with examples from the featured projects and those documented in academic and other literature. This may be evidence that marine and coastal citizen science practitioners are generally taking the requisite care to communicate proactively, openly, and respectfully with the citizen scientists participating in their projects and programs. The scientist-citizen breakdowns in communication and, as a consequence, trust, that have so often undermined research and policy making in other marine fields (e.g. fisheries science), seem little evident for most citizen science. Box 13.1, a testimony solicited for this chapter from citizen scientist participants in coastal and marine citizen science, shows how positive relations currently are in the research field.

However, as we discussed above, there are barriers to trust-building in coastal and marine citizen science, which suggests that there is the potential for the fractious scientist-citizen relationships that have harmed the development of other marine research and conservation initiatives. Cases of such communication failure have been documented in terrestrial citizen science projects, such as Druschke and Seltzer's (2012) Chicago Area Pollinator Study. Given the similar implementation structures to terrestrial citizen science projects, there is no reason to expect that coastal and marine citizen science programs and projects will avoid the same pitfalls if care is not taken to ensure their communications strategies are high quality.

Coastal and marine citizen science practitioners should continue to make efforts to widely document their communication successes and failures so that we can learn from them. Most other marine researchers, like fisheries biologists, can continue to conduct their research even without stakeholder buy-in. But if coastal and marine citizen science practitioners lose the trust of their constituents and their subsequent participation, there is no possibility to conduct research and there is no marine and coastal citizen science. All practitioners reading this share the duty of building and maintaining trust in this research field through striving to communicate to the highest standard possible.

## BOX 13.1

The following are comments from the perspectives of volunteers about communication in coastal and marine citizen science projects.

"In field environments, I have found scientists to be more open to ideas and opinions of citizen scientists than I had expected. My previous interactions had been via marine science Listservs where I noted that scientists were generally submissive of anyone without "proper" scientific credentials." – Philip Karp, citizen scientist on multiple projects, USA

"Feedback is always encouraging. I feel appreciated for my efforts. – Mary Molloy, citizen scientist, Redmap, Australia

"We have been fortunate to have fantastic, honest and prompt communication in all three citizen science projects we are working on. It is so important to have a full understanding of the aims and objectives of the scientists and full trust that the data will be used correctly. We regularly speak to large groups of divers and the general public and need to confidently share the project results to increase participation. Divers are often worried that fishermen will find out shark hot spots and go and fish them, so again we need full trust with the scientists. I really enjoyed seeing our data be put to good use, see it grow and develop and that scientists listen to us and adapt techniques/templates based on our/the divers feedback. To know we are contributing to something so worthwhile is amazing – I never thought citizen science could be so rewarding and effective." – Liz Ward-Sing and Brendon Sing, boundary spanners, Shark Guardian, Thailand

## Web resources

1  www.redmap.org.au.
2  www.redmap.org.au/about/awards-and-recognition/.
3  www.redmap.org.au/news/2013/05/14/tasmanias-road-to-reporting-redmap-report-card/.
4  www.redmap.org.au/article/the-redmap-tasmania-report-card/.
5  www.environment.gov.au/biodiversity/abrs/online-resources/fauna/afd/taxa/PISCES.
6  Redmap's formal engagement strategy document is available on request by emailing enquiries@redmap.org.au.
7  http://oceanconservationscience.org/projects/sharks/pew_global.shtml.
8  http://orientalsea.com/ID-15.htm.
9  Convention on International Trade in Endangered Species of Wild Fauna and Flora.

## Literature cited

Alcala, A., and Russ, G. (2006). No-take marine reserves and reef fisheries management in the Philippines: A new people power revolution. *AMBIO*, 35(5), 245–254.

Christie, P. (2004). MPAs as biological successes and social failures in Southeast Asia. *American Fisheries Society Symposium*, 42, 155–164.

Cigliano, J., Favaro, B., Oester, S., and Parsons, E. (2015). Making marine science matter – a special issue highlighting the third International Marine Conservation Congress. *Ocean & Coastal Management*, 115, 1–3.

Couturier, L., Jaine, F., and Kashiwagi, T. (2015). First photographic records of the giant manta ray *Manta birostris* off eastern Australia. *PeerJ*, 3, e742.

Daw, T., and Gray, T. (2005). Fisheries science and sustainability in international policy: a study of failure in the European Union's Common Fisheries Policy. *Marine Policy*, 29(3), 189–197.

Dickinson, J., Shirk, J., Bonter, D., Bonney, R., Crain, R., Martin, J., Phillips, T., and Purcell, K. (2012). The current state of citizen science as a tool for ecological research and public engagement. *Frontiers in Ecology and the Environment*, 10(6), 291–297.

Druschke, C., and Seltzer, C. (2012). Failures of engagement: Lessons learned from a citizen science pilot study. *Applied Environmental Education & Communication*, 11(3–4), 178–188.

Grove, S.J., and Finn, J.K. (2014). Unusual strandings of greater argonaut *Argonauta argo* in southeast Tasmania, autumn 2014. *Malacological Society of Australasia Newsletter*, 151, 1–3.

Hobday, A., and Pecl, G. (2014). Identification of global marine hotspots: Sentinels for change and vanguards for adaptation action. *Reviews in Fish Biology and Fisheries*, 24(2), 415–425.

Hutchings, J., Walters, C., and Haedrich, R. (1997). Is scientific inquiry incompatible with government information control? *Canadian Journal of Fisheries and Aquatic Sciences*, 54(5), 1198–1210.

Jambeck, J., and Johnsen, K. (2015). Citizen-based litter and marine debris data collection and mapping. *Computing in Science & Engineering*, 17(4), 20–26.

Johnson, C., Banks, S., Barrett, N., Cazassus, F., Dunstan, P., Edgar, G., Frusher, S., Gardner, C., Haddon, M., Helidoniotis, F., Hill, K., Holbrook, N., Hosie, G., Last, P., Ling, S., Melbourne-Thomas, J., Miller, K., Pecl, G., Richardson, A., Ridgway, K., Rintoul, S., Ritz, D., Ross, D., Sanderson, J., Shepherd, S., Slotwinski, A., Swadling, K., and Taw, N. (2011). Climate change cascades: Shifts in oceanography, species' ranges and subtidal marine community dynamics in eastern Tasmania. *Journal of Experimental Marine Biology and Ecology*, 400(1–2), 17–32.

Johnson, T. (2009). Cooperative research and knowledge flow in the marine commons. *International Journal of the Commons*, 4(1), 251.

Kraak, S., Bailey, N., Cardinale, M., Darby, C., De Oliveira, J., Eero, M., Graham, N., Holmes, S., Jakobsen, T., Kempf, A., Kirkegaard, E., Powell, J., Scott, R., Simmonds, E., Ulrich, C., Vanhee, W., and Vinther, M. (2013). Lessons for fisheries management from the EU cod recovery plan. *Marine Policy*, 37, 200–213.

Last, P., White, W., Gledhill, D., Hobday, A., Brown, R., Edgar, G., and Pecl, G. (2011). Long-term shifts in abundance and distribution of a temperate fish fauna: A response to climate change and fishing practices. *Global Ecology and Biogeography*, 20(1), 58–72.

Lee, T., Markowitz, E., Howe, P., Ko, C., and Leiserowitz, A. (2015). Predictors of public climate change awareness and risk perception around the world. *Nature Climate Change*, 5(11), 1014–1020.

Madin, E., Ban, N., Doubleday, Z., Holmes, T., Pecl, G., and Smith, F. (2012). Socio-economic and management implications of range-shifting species in marine systems. *Global Environmental Change*, 22(1), 137–146.

Martin, V., Christidis, L., and Pecl, G. (2016). Public interest in marine citizen science: Is there potential for growth? *BioScience*, 66(8), 683–692.

Marzloff, M., Melbourne-Thomas, J., Hamon, K., Hoshino, E., Jennings, S., van Putten, I., and Pecl, G. (2016). Modelling marine community responses to climate-driven species redistribution to guide monitoring and adaptive ecosystem-based management. *Global Change Biology*, 22(7), 2462–2474.

Maurstad, A. (2002). Fishing in murky waters – ethics and politics of research on fisher knowledge. *Marine Policy*, 26(3), 159–166.

Neis, B. (1992). Fishers' ecological knowledge and stock assessment in Newfoundland. *Newfoundland and Labrador Studies*, 8(2), 155–178.

Nursey-Bray, M., Pecl, G., Frusher, S., Gardner, C., Haward, M., Hobday, A., Jennings, S., Punt, A., Revill, H., and van Putten, I. (2012). Communicating climate change: Climate change risk perceptions and rock lobster fishers, Tasmania. *Marine Policy*, 36(3), 753–759.

Pattengill-Semmens, C.V., and Semmens, B.X. (2003). Conservation and management applications of the reef volunteer fish monitoring program. In *Coastal Monitoring Through Partnerships*, 43–50. Dordrecht, the Netherlands: Springer.

Pecl, G.T., Araujo, M.B., Bell, J.D., Blanchard, J., Bonebrake, T.C., Chen, I.C., Clark, T.D., Colwell, R.K., Danielsen, F., Evengard, B., and Falconi, L. (2017). Biodiversity redistribution under climate change: Impacts on ecosystems and human well-being. *Science*, 655, 6332.

Poloczanska, E., Brown, C., Sydeman, W., Kiessling, W., Schoeman, D., Moore, P., Brander, K., Bruno, J., Buckley, L., Burrows, M., Duarte, C., Halpern, B., Holding, J., Kappel, C., O'Connor, M., Pandolfi, J., Parmesan, C., Schwing, F., Thompson, S., and Richardson, A. (2013). Global imprint of climate change on marine life. *Nature Climate Change*, 3(10), 919–925.

Ramos, J., Pecl, G., Moltschaniwskyj, N., Strugnell, J., León, R., and Semmens, J. (2014). Body size, growth and life span: Implications for the polewards range shift of *Octopus tetricus* in South-Eastern Australia. *PLoS One*, 9(8), e103480.

Ramos, J., Pecl, G., Semmens, J., Strugnell, J., León, R., and Moltschaniwskyj, N. (2015). Reproductive capacity of a marine species (*Octopus tetricus*) within a recent range extension area. *Marine and Freshwater Research*, 66(11), 999.

REEF. (2003). *Reef Environmental Education Foundation Volunteer Survey Project Database*. World Wide Web electronic publication. www.REEF.org.

Robinson, L., Gledhill, D., Moltschaniwskyj, N., Hobday, A., Frusher, S., Barrett, N., Stuart-Smith, J., and Pecl, G. (2015). Rapid assessment of an ocean warming hotspot reveals "high" confidence in potential species' range extensions. *Global Environmental Change*, 31, 28–37.

Rotman, D., Hammock, J., Preece, J., Hansen, D., Boston, C., Bowser, A., and He, Y. (2014). Motivations affecting initial and long-term participation in citizen science projects in three countries. *iConference 2014 Proceedings*.

Stuart-Smith, J., Pecl, G., Pender, A., Tracey, S., Villanueva, C., and Smith-Vaniz, W. (2016). Southernmost records of two *Seriola* species in an Australian ocean-warming hotspot. *Marine Biodiversity*, 1–4.

Sullivan, B., Wood, C., Iliff, M., Bonney, R., Fink, D., and Kelling, S. (2009). eBird: A citizen-based bird observation network in the biological sciences. *Biological Conservation*, 142(10), 2282–2292.

Sunday, J.M., Pecl, G.T., Frusher, S., Hobday, A.J., Hill, N., Holbrook, N.J., Edgar, G.J., Stuart-Smith, R., Barrett, N., Webmerg, T. and Watson, R.A. (2015). Species traits and climate veolocity explain geographic range shifts in an ocean-warming hotspot. *Ecology Letters*, 18(9), 944–953.

van Densen, W., and McCay, B. (2007). Improving communication from managers to fishers in Europe and the US. *ICES Journal of Marine Science*, 64(4), 811–817.

Ward-Paige, C., Davis, B., and Worm, B. (2013). Global population trends and human use patterns of manta and mobula rays. *PLoS One*, 8(9), e74835.

Ward-Paige, C., and Lotze, H. (2011). Assessing the value of recreational divers for censusing elasmobranchs. *PLoS One*, 6(10), e25609.

Ward-Paige, C., Mills Flemming, J., and Lotze, H. (2010). Overestimating fish counts by non-instantaneous visual censuses: Consequences for population and community descriptions. *PLoS One*, 5(7), e11722.

Ward-Paige, C. In review.

Wehner, N. (2011). *Citizen science, communication, and expertise: An examination of the Port Townsend Marine Science Center's plastics project*. Doctoral dissertation, University of Washington.

Wilcox, C. (2012). Guest editorial: It's time to e-Volve: Taking responsibility for science communication in a digital age. *Biological Bulletin*, 222(2), 85–87.

Williams, P. (2010). Special agents: The nature and role of boundary spanners, paper to the ESRC Research Seminar Series: "Collaborative Futures." *University of Birmingham, 10*.

Wilson, D. (2003). Examining the two cultures theory of fisheries knowledge: The case of Bluefish management. *Society & Natural Resources*, 16(6), 491–508.

# 14

# CONCLUSIONS

## Lessons learned and next steps for citizen science in coastal and marine conservation

*Heidi L. Ballard and John A. Cigliano*

## Introduction

The conservation questions and issues we face in coastal and marine systems have arguably never been more pressing. "Wicked problems" like sea-level rise, fisheries declines, and ocean acidification and warming are all occurring simultaneously, creating positive and negative feedback loops depending on where you look and when. There are also significant data gaps that limit both our understanding of these issues and possible solutions (Parsons et al., 2014; Cigliano et al., 2016). Yet the marine conservation field is also equipped with an old but newly powerful tool that may yet help track and address these problems and help fill in these data gaps, in the form of citizen science (Edgar et al., 2016). From crowdsourcing apps that allow beach visitors to track marine litter in Chile, to intensively trained volunteers identifying beached birds, to community science projects co-created by fishers in Micronesia, coastal and marine citizen science as a field is burgeoning in scope, scale, and diversity of projects around the world.

In this book, we have examined a sample of the wide range of coastal and marine citizen science programs, documenting the ways each project contributes scientific information used for conservation research and natural resource management, as well as educational, community development, and policy outcomes. Authors in this book have described the challenges they've faced in developing effective programs, strategies they've used to overcome them, and challenges they still face. They've explained the contexts in which their projects are situated so that we may see when citizen science seems to work well in coastal and marine systems, and when it doesn't. Above all, we hope an overarching lesson from these cases is that citizen science can be a unique and effective approach to addressing conservation science questions, but should be thoughtfully designed and applied to carefully evaluated situations. Citizen science is not a silver bullet, nor is it a one-size-fits-all endeavor.

In this chapter, we aim to synthesize the experiences and lessons from these cases to answer the questions:

- Under what circumstances (e.g, which ecosystems, human communities, conservation needs, kinds of research questions) is citizen science effective for coastal and marine conservation?
- What are key considerations in designing coastal and marine citizen science programs, and what strategies and approaches have been effective in addressing them?
- What can these case studies tell us about the future of coastal and marine conservation, and the role of citizen science?

We discuss citizen science programs that provide data to inform the key conservation issues in the field (coral reef conservation, marine protected area management, ocean health, impacts of climate change, invasive species, ocean litter, anthropogenic effects on marine mammal populations), solutions to conservation issues (seagrass restoration, policy change), and engage important audiences impacting social and ecological systems (youth, fishers, coastal communities, divers, snorkelers, and recreationalists). However, these high-caliber programs have many years of experience and refinement from which we glean lessons that other citizen science programs may apply. Specifically, here we identify strategies for addressing the common challenges faced by conservation-focused citizen science programs, including ensuring data quality, recruiting and retaining participants, institutionalizing mechanisms for informing natural resource management and policy, and maintaining productive partnerships with other non-governmental organizations (NGOs) and government agencies. Finally, we look to the future of coastal and marine conservation and the key role citizen science may play in (1) helping to connect people to their own places and environments in a way that enhances their sense of stewardship for those places, (2) providing concrete approaches to authentically bring important voices and knowledge-holders into conservation science, and (3) offering new ways to partner across sectors as diverse as federal and state agencies, community-based NGOs, schools, fishing associations and industries, and the tourism industry to accomplish coastal and marine conservation goals. We suggest ways that citizen science can be both scaled-up and deepened in the coming years to further enhance its utility for coastal and marine conservation.

## When, where, with whom, and how is citizen science effective for coastal and marine conservation?

Because citizen science as an approach is not a panacea for coastal and marine conservation, it is important to examine under what circumstances it *does* work: which conservation research or management questions seem to lend themselves to including a citizen science component? And what are the main communities and participants engaging in this work, and who is missing or left out? The wide range of case studies in this book affords us the opportunity to look at these questions in turn.

## *Key conservation issues and questions*

Several types of coastal and marine conservation science questions seem to lend themselves to a citizen science approach. For example, several projects in this book illustrate the ways that ongoing citizen science projects provide data over wide spatial and/or temporal scales, sometime in hard-to-reach areas, that enable conservation scientists to answer questions that impact marine ecosystems at these scales. While this is also often true of terrestrial citizen science (Bonney et al., 2014; Theobald et al., 2015), we saw examples unique to coastal and marine systems in this book. Thiel et al. (Chapter 6) and Parrish et al. (Chapter 2) describe how programs collecting data on beach litter and beached birds across hundreds or thousands of kilometers of beach take advantage of the thousands of youth and adults who spend time on the beach anyway. Sewell and Parr (Chapter 4) explain how volunteers collect data on invasive non-native species like mitten crabs in England at scales that allow for tracking invasives in a way they otherwise couldn't. In Chapter 12, Cigliano and Ridlon discuss how divers and snorkelers contribute to long-term biodiversity assessments and community and population monitoring at the regional and global spatial scales. We also saw how citizen science projects can provide data that serve as a baseline to which future anthropomorphic or other perturbations in the system can be compared, often providing an early warning system that managers can use to flag significant changes. Parrish et al. (Chapter 2) explained how COASST data on beached seabirds in the Pacific Northwest of the United States provided crucial baseline information to understand the anomalous mortality rates caused by climate forcing. Cigliano and Ridlon (Chapter 12) described how baseline data on coral reef communities allowed researchers to determine the effect of mass bleaching on corals and reef organisms in the Gulf of Thailand and in the Andaman Sea, and Meyer et al. (Chapter 7) discussed how baseline data collected by multiple projects are used to determine the effectiveness of Marine Protected Areas in California.

We saw several examples of how citizen science can be a useful tool for conservation when it explicitly links science to on-the-ground stewardship and decision-making, by providing scientific information for ecological restoration (Chapter 8), natural resource management (Chapters 7 and 10), and policy decisions (Chapter 9). Disney et al. (Chapter 8) offer a model of the way that volunteers participating in eelgrass restoration in Maine integrate scientific data collection throughout the restoration process; in this way, citizen science and stewardship practices are inextricably intertwined. Meyer et al. (Chapter 7) describe how several citizen science projects involved fishers and divers along the coast of California working closely with agencies to make sure their data inform management of marine protected areas. Crane et al. (Chapter 10) provide an example of a true collaboration between professional and citizen scientists that led to effective fisheries management. Similarly, Townhill and Hyder (Chapter 9) explain that citizen science data collected with reliable technology and methods is particularly well-positioned to inform conservation policy because marine legislation is increasingly reliant on large data sets across wide spatial and temporal scales.

## Key audiences and stakeholders

As with any conservation effort, engaging key stakeholders is crucial; for citizen science in coastal and marine systems, we can see across these cases that engaging key stakeholders and audiences helps to ensure the data collected are acted upon, and participants feel valued, useful, and responsible for conserving coastal and marine systems themselves. We can see that while the participants and partners involved in each project are specific and targeted (or opportunistic), there are some similarities regarding which audiences seem most successfully engaged across cases.

The main set of stakeholders that citizen science significantly engages are recreationists, that is, people with an interest and/or stake in the health of coastal and marine systems, who may not depend on the ocean for their livelihood but are interested, passionate, connected to, or feel responsibility for the oceans and coast near and far from their own homes. Parrish et al. (Chapter 2), Sewell and Parr (Chapter 4), and Thiel et al. (Chapter 6) each describe how their monitoring programs are able to take advantage of local people who live near or visit the coast for pleasure with time and energy to devote to track beached birds, marine litter, or invasive species. Another set of people intimately connected to the oceans for enjoyment is snorkelers and divers; Cigliano et al. (Chapter 12) provides several examples, among many reef monitoring citizen science projects, that rely on snorkelers and/or divers to collecting data on reef species (one of the original programs is REEF,[1] training divers around the globe since 1990; see Chapter 12). Further, ecotourists who pay to experience nature and even volunteer for programs like Earthwatch collect data on marine mammals (Stelle, Chapter 5), mangroves (Cousins et al., Chapter 3), and queen conch (Cigliano and Ridlon, Chapter 12).

For research and monitoring of local fisheries or broad scale management of protected areas, these cases illustrate how fishers and other coastal resource users need to be involved for citizen science projects to be effective: Cousins et al. (Chapter 3) described the ways locals in Kenya collaborated on the mangrove citizen science project that potentially impacts their use of mangrove forests; Crane et al. (Chapter 10) includes co-authors representing multiple local island resource management groups who collectively collect fisheries data; and Meyer et al. (Chapter 7) describe how lobster fishermen in California contribute data to statewide efforts to manage protected areas. Marine resource–dependent communities have a long history of collaborating among themselves and with professional scientists and managers to collect fisheries data (McCay and Acheson, 1990); the cases in this book are just a small sample of the ways in which fishers are crucial partners in coastal and marine citizen science.

Finally, an important and growing constituency of coastal and marine citizen science is youth; with careful training and data quality protocols in place, youth collected intertidal and sand crab data used for coastal management of marine protected areas in California (Wasser et al., Chapter 11), data on marine litter in Chile and globally (Thiel et al., Chapter 6), and multiple kinds of data for eelgrass restoration in Maine (Disney et al., Chapter 8). As teachers, schools, and parents are looking for better ways to increase the scientific literacy of youth globally, citizen science projects can tap into this enthusiastic group of future stakeholders (Ballard et al. 2017).

## What are important considerations for coastal and marine citizen science programs, and what strategies and approaches have been effective in addressing them?

### *Ensuring data quality*

Possibly the most important and oft-debated consideration for citizen science, in terrestrial or coastal and marine systems, is the issue of data quality (Bonney et al., 2014, 2016; Burgess et al., 2017). While numerous publications have offered evidence that many rigorous citizen science programs contribute to peer-reviewed publications (Theobald et al., 2014) and natural resource management and policy (McKinley et al., 2017), many scientists are still concerned about data quality from citizen science (Burgess et al., 2017). In this book, every case study chapter explicitly described the data quality control and quality assurance procedures, such that we can highlight some key strategies for ensuring high quality data in coastal and marine citizen science projects. Unlike many citizen science projects where both training and data entry occurs entirely online, nearly all projects in this book involved some intensive in-person training of participants before they can submit data to the project. For example COASST required an all-day hands-on training with beached bird carcasses (Parrish et al., Chapter 2); Stelle (Chapter 5) trained volunteers on the boat before collecting data on marine mammals; Disney et al.'s (Chapter 8) team trained volunteers in protocols for eelgrass monitoring; and Cigliano and Ridlon (Chapter 12) trained snorkelers and divers on the beach before collecting data on queen conch. Some programs involved a train-the-trainer model, in which local leaders are trained in data collection protocols by project scientists, and then they train those who will collect data on the ground; in Micronesia these were local island project scientists (Crane et al., Chapter 10), and in Chile and California these were teachers (Thiel et al., Chapter 6; Wasser et al., Chapter 11; see also Reef Check in Chapter 12). These in-person trainings can help participants feel accountable, allow them to practice and be certified before collecting data that scientists and managers can actually trust. However, some successful coastal and marine citizen science projects do not include in-person trainings; Sewell and Parr (Chapter 4) explain that participants learn to identify mitten crabs and data entry procedures through online guides and videos, which are key strategies when in-person trainings aren't possible.

Many projects use a variety of quality control measures beyond training. Several projects utilize direct supervision of participants when they are collecting data, so that any questions or anomalous data points can be checked, and data verified, in the field by supervising scientists or staff (for examples, Cousins et al., Chapter 3; Stelle, Chapter 5; Disney, Chapter 8; Cigliano and Ridlon, Chapter 12). COASST includes a data verification procedure post-data submission by participants in which volunteer beach bird identifications are verified against photos and measurements, as does Sewell and Parr's (Chapter 4) Mitten Crab Recording Project; while this level of quality control might not be possible for some projects, Parrish et al. (Chapter 2) argue this is a crucial step in order to provide data for federal agencies and other professional scientists. Cousins et al. (Chapter 3) describe how the Mikoko Pamoja project studying mangrove carbon sequestration includes standardized spreadsheets into which volunteers enter data that automatically check formulas, as well as checking inter-recorder reliability and variability over different data collection sessions. Sewell and Parr (Chapter 4) and Parrish et al. (Chapter 2) both describe providing feedback to volunteers once their records are submitted, which essentially continues to train volunteers and improves their accuracy.

## Recruiting, retaining, and engaging participants

A major challenge for many citizen science projects is garnering enough participation from volunteers to collect high quality data over the space and time windows required to answer the conservation science questions of the project (Hobbs and White, 2012); coastal and marine projects are no different. Participants in citizen science might have very different motives for participating, whether they are to ensure access to natural resources, to recreate in the outdoors, to learn about conservation science or the places they live, to contribute to something they care about, to be social and get together with like-minded people, or to interact with a scientist, among others (Hobbs and White, 2012; West and Pateman, 2016). Projects in this book each engage their participants in ways that address their needs, interests, and goals, and while many authors remark at their constant struggle to recruit and sustain participation, they describe strategies they find effective that may be useful for those designing projects.

With respect to recruiting participants, the more "contributory" citizen science projects conduct outreach and advertise widely within the specific audiences or communities who've shown interest in the topic or focus of the project: COASST advertised through all media channels in specific coastal communities where they see data gaps and will conduct trainings (Parrish et al. Chapter 2; see also Hind et al., Chapter 13), LiMPETS invites teachers in the region to training workshops (Wasser, Chapter 11), and Earthwatch advertises globally through ecotourism media channels (Cousins et al., Chapter 3; Stelle, Chapter 5; Cigliano and Ridlon, Chapter 12). Many citizen science practitioners, in this book and in the field as a whole, acknowledge that some groups of people who could benefit from and contribute to citizen science are largely left out, particularly poor communities of color in developed countries (Soleri et al., 2016). Soleri et al. (2016) suggest deliberate and equitable partnerships between scientists and community-based organizations; in fact, the more collaborative and co-created cases in this book developed deliberate partnerships with groups that have a vested interest in conserving the resource in question, discussed further later (Disney et al., Chapter 8; Crane et al., Chapter 10; Cigliano and Ridlon, Chapter 12). Conservation cannot work if the most marginalized people in society don't have access to the science that contributes to decision-making.

With respect to sustaining participation over time, several cases in this book illustrate how continual, informative, and respectful communication with participants is essential to maintaining a committed volunteer community in citizen science projects, also the focus of Hind et al.'s Chapter 13. Some projects use passive communications, where participants can see new information on project websites, or active communications pushed out to participants, including newsletters, periodic emails, refresher courses, and phone calls. Some projects set up automatic responses to data submissions online, a small gesture that can provide validation to participants. Citizen science participants don't just need contact from projects, but want to know how their contributions make a difference. Specifically, Wasser (Chapter 11), Parrish et al. (Chapter 2), and Disney et al. (Chapter 8) each describe ways that they make sure to return aggregate data and/or findings back to participants in their project so they may see their own data in the context of the whole project, and they are reminded that they are valued contributors to the project's science goals.

Even Stelle (Chapter 5) described how keeping in touch with volunteers has resulted in repeated participation by whale watchers in her program, despite it being typically a one-time excursion. And Townhill and Hyder (Chapter 9) discuss how to motivate citizen scientists to complete the project and submit their data.

### Logistics and safety of participants

One of the particular challenges for coastal and marine citizen science projects, in contrast to most terrestrial projects, is the logistics and safety of involving members of the public in scientific field data collection in, on, or near the water (Cigliano et al., 2015). Several cases in this book present specific logistical or safety challenges and offer strategies for overcoming them. Cousins et al. (Chapter 3) describe higher risk activities for their volunteers like snorkel surveying or sampling from canoes, suggesting that project leaders need to assess and design around the background experience and level of fitness of volunteers. If some work is too dangerous or technical, perhaps it should not be done by volunteers. Thiel et al. (Chapter 6) raised the point that the coastline and beaches also present logistical challenges, with uneven terrain that also might be difficult to access in the first place. They suggest that this may mean the project simply doesn't get data from these areas. This is a fundamental challenge for coastal citizen science when these hard-to-reach areas may, in fact, be precisely where data are needed, as when these areas serve as marine debris catchments. Cigliano and Ridlon (Chapter 12) explain that working with divers and snorkelers in particular can be risky and challenging, and that in addition to the need to ensure the safety of divers and snorkelers, care must be taken to minimize negatively impacting the habitat they are studying while maintaining good sampling techniques. They also discuss the challenges of communication with divers and snorkelers. In the end, because citizen science projects must put the safety of participants above the scientific needs of the project, this may physically limit the types and geographic scope of citizen science for coastal and marine conservation.

## Technology and crowdsourcing

The meteoric increase in the use of apps and smartphones for citizen science is sometimes cited as the reason citizen science as a field has expanded so rapidly in the past two decades (Bonney et al., 2014). That volunteers will enter their data via websites is practically assumed. But additionally, the ability of smartphones to geo-locate and time stamp data collection points, take high quality photos, and send them via internet to project websites, has opened up a new world for members of the public to contribute reliable data, and apps allow complex data to be collected by novices more easily (Newman et al., 2012; Townhill and Hyder, Chapter 9; Hind et al., Chapter 13). This is certainly true for citizen science for coastal and marine conservation, as illustrated by the many examples from cases in this book. Sewell and Parr (Chapter 4) explain that for many projects, the need for scientists to accompany citizen scientists in the field to validate their data has been alleviated by the ubiquity of smartphones that transmit verifiable photos. Stelle (Chapter 5) described the development and use of Whale mAPP so any member of the public can contribute marine mammal sightings via tablet or smartphone. Thiel et al. (Chapter 6) described the Marine Debris Tracker mobile app that allows people to record the location and description of marine debris. Websites allow for not only data submission but also aggregation and creation of projects (like www.citsci.org; Newman et al., 2012); and example for marine environments; Disney et al.'s (Chapter 8) Eelgrass in Maine project led to an online platform for citizen science projects, Anecdata.org, which now has 22 marine citizen science projects involved. The sophistication of data visualizations in coastal and marine citizen science projects, especially mapping platforms, steadily increases participants' ability to see where their data contributes to the overall dataset, as Thiel et al. (Chapter 6) described Marine Data Tracker's interactive map for marine litter data as well as ways to download data to analyze offline.

It's important to note that several projects in this book also describe how they *don't* limit their participants to online or mobile apps for data collection, citing the need to allow access to the project to those without smartphones or the inclination to use computers. Parrish et al. (Chapter 2) provide paper data sheets to volunteers who request them, and many underwater projects in developing country contexts rely on paper or plasticized data sheets that have nothing to do with a smartphone (Cousins et al., Chapter 3; Crane et al., Chapter 10; Cigliano and Ridlon, Chapter 12). However, with much of the developing world "leapfrogging" over landlines for telephone and internet to immediately use cell phones, citizen science projects that use SMS or non-text-based images for data recording are burgeoning in many regions where conservation data is most desperately needed (Ellul et al., 2013).

## Collaboration, communication, and building trust

With the strong history of various forms of collaboration between place-based marine natural resource users and scientists, effective coastal and marine citizen science in its current form (1) reflects the principles of collaboration used for decades, (2) offers new lessons for new contexts and audiences, and (3) raises questions about how new models of citizen science and community science can link or integrate with historical models. Collaborative fisheries management, with indigenous and non-indigenous fishers, has included collaborative monitoring of target species populations, as well as bycatch, by fishers and scientists for many years (Berkes et al., 2007; McCay and Acheson, 1990; Corson, 2004; Obura et al., 2002). The ways that the new models of citizen science and community science do and don't overlap with these historically successful models is an important question for the field of coastal and marine conservation, as commercial fishers are of course a very different stakeholder group than recreational fishers, or indigenous fishers, with which scientists can engage in citizen science. In this book, we have focused on strategies from the new models of primarily contributory and some co-created citizen science projects, and here synthesize the lessons from these projects that might contribute to the larger pool of strategies for collaboration between scientists and non-scientists to inform coastal and marine conservation.

Authors in nearly all chapters provide important communication strategies to consider for the design and implementation of contributory citizen science projects, where participants primarily collect data, and Hind et al.'s entire Chapter 13 is dedicated to this topic, so here we highlight just a few we find particularly important. From the start of a citizen science project, Sewell and Parr (Chapter 4) point out that project scientists and leaders need to "manage expectations" of participants who often come to citizen science projects expecting to see the immediate or large-scale impacts of their work on the conservation issue they care about (in their case, invasive species). Project leaders should discuss with participants early the ways and time frame in which information from the citizen science project will inform conservation management or policy, and then continuing to share scientific information generated by the project along the way. Parrish et al. (Chapter 2) describe not only a variety of ways they provide information to volunteers in the COASST project (newsletters, website updates, phone calls, emails, in-person trainings, and refresher courses), but also the different types of information they provide, including (1) personalized feedback on accuracy of identifications, (2) "data stories" about how COASST data is informing research and management, (3) updates about interesting sightings, and (4) more standard information about project logistics. They emphasize that their responsiveness to questions, as well as the information they "push" out to volunteers, is often highlighted by participants as to why they continue to participate.

We also highlight some important lessons about what authentic collaboration in coastal and marine citizen science looks like, and the trust-building that is required with participants and community-based organizations, from the more collaborative and co-created projects in the book, particularly Cousins et al. (Chapter 3), Disney et al. (Chapter 8), and Crane et al. (Chapter 10). These authors specifically point out the ways that they partnered with participants to (1) build on their traditional ecological knowledge and traditional management practices (Crane et al., Chapter 10),

(2) integrate local resource management into the goals and design of the project (Cousins et al., Chapter 3; Crane et al., Chapter 10), and/or (3) include participants' inquiry and scientific investigation skills in the design of the methods and iterative process of data collection and management (Chapter 10) or restoration (Chapter 8). These strategies are certainly reflective of lessons learned over decades of collaborative natural resource management around the world (e.g. Hulme and Murphree, 2001) and community-based participatory action research (e.g. Israel et al., 2013). They both rely on and help to build trust, a sense of mutual respect, and equitable partnership among participants, scientists, and resource managers. While not all of these strategies are applicable to larger contributory citizen science projects where participants all over the world contribute data online or through apps, some can and are being applied to projects that began as solely data collection, but have evolved to allow for closer contact between participants and project leaders and more collaborative approaches. Disney et al.'s (Chapter 8) project is an example; others include terrestrial projects such as the Monarch Larvae Monitoring Project.[2] This raises yet another lesson from many of the chapters in this book; several authors described ways they continually revise and improve the structures and processes of their citizen science projects to improve communication and participation, whether it meant writing many versions of the identification guide (Parrish et al., Chapter 2); revising protocols to be more aligned with participant constraints and resource managers' data needs (Wasser, Chapter 11); or gradually incorporating and involving participants in designing new methods and new small projects (Disney et al., Chapter 8).

## What can we learn from these case studies about the future of citizen science in coastal and marine conservation?

Looking across cases, we see some lessons about what might make coastal and marine citizen science different from terrestrial citizen science, and what makes citizen science in these coastal and marine systems different from other conservation activities in those systems, such as stewardship, management, fisheries, protection, basic science, tourism, and recreation. From these lessons, we then suggest what cumulative impact citizen science already has or could have in the future on the conservation of the coastal and marine systems.

### The importance of place connection for coastal and marine conservation

The chapters in this book describe citizen science volunteers of a wide variety of ages, cultures, socio-economic classes, and development contexts around the world who all share a common interest: they care about coastal and marine environments. Most live in or near the places they studied through citizen science projects, others were visiting, but in all cases, they were donating their time and energy to help improve the places they care about. When people have a strong connection to the places and landscapes where they live, work, and play, they are more likely to feel responsibility and a sense of stewardship over those places, and are more likely to enact pro-environmental behaviors or conservation actions on behalf of those places (Kudryavtsev et al., 2012). One of the ways that many proponents of citizen science suggest that citizen science can contribute to conservation is by fostering participants' connections to the places under study (Haywood et al., 2014), and some evidence is emerging that this is true; Johnson et al. (2014) found that citizen scientists in India serve as environmental advocates in their local areas, and Newman et al. (2017) found that of 134 citizen science projects analyzed in three databases from around the world, those that engage more dimensions of place are more likely to have their data used for natural resource decision-making. While this study didn't link participants' sense of place with their own conservation behaviors, it begins to show the link between real conservation outcomes and the increased connection to places participants gain, in some cases, when doing citizen science.

This connection to place is certainly true for terrestrial citizen science projects, but we argue, as many before us have, that oceans and beaches and their creatures hold a particular visceral emotional value for many people (Earle, 2009; Nichols, 2014). Therefore, it may be that one of the major contributions to coastal and marine conservation that the cases in this book illustrated, beyond the data and information they provide, is how citizen science bolsters thousands of people's sense of emotional connection to coastal and marine environments. Haywood (2014) found this to be true for participants who walk their beaches monthly for the COASST project (Parrish et al., Chapter 2). Citizen science provides a way for people to connect to place in a way unlike other conservation activities, different from recreation, different from resource use, different from stewardship and restoration activities like cleaning up trash or planting eelgrass; it is inherently about learning more about a vast ocean abyss, or a constantly shifting coast, through collecting data, allowing participants to discover, document, better understand something that is mysterious. Humans are drawn to the ocean while knowing relatively little about it (Nichols, 2014), and citizen science allows people to contribute to our global understanding of this amazing system, interacting with it in a completely unique way. For Earthwatch volunteers visiting a place for the first time to document marine mammals in California (Stelle et al., Chapter 5), queen conch in Belize (Cigliano and Ridlon, Chapter 12), or mangroves in Kenya (Cousins et al., Chapter 3), their sense of place may be about wonder and gaining a new awareness. For indigenous fishers in Micronesia (Crane et al., Chapter 10), who are already intimately familiar with their marine surroundings, the new understanding of their place may come from learning new tools to analyze trends in fish populations or making and using models for sustainable management. In all contexts, citizen science provides a unique way for people to interact with the places they love, and therefore garner more time, resources, skills, energy, and enthusiasm for conservation of coastal and marine systems, beyond the data we already know is powerful.

## Collaboration and partnerships across sectors

Citizen science is, by definition, a collaboration between scientists and members of the public in some form – sometimes this means individuals recruited to help on a scientist-led research project, but in many other cases it can mean partnerships across a wide variety of organizations from many different sectors. This is both a reflection of conservation as a field, and an enhanced version of it, where a single stakeholder simply could not accomplish a conservation goal without help. In the case of citizen science in coastal and marine systems, we saw throughout this book that partnerships were formed to ensure data are useful to specific agencies or scientific research projects, ensure appropriate communities are engaged, and to ensure passionate audiences are recruited and maintained as participants. Concretely, this resulted in partnerships between fishers and scientists (Crane et al., Chapter 10), between teachers and natural resource agencies (Wasser, Chapter 11), between schools and tourism operators and scientists (Stelle, Chapter 5; Thiel et al., Chapter 6), and between local conservation groups and museums (Sewell and Parr, Chapter 4).

The collaborative partnerships in the chapters in this book provide evidence and examples of the key role or functions that need to be played in a successful citizen science project – roles and functions that could be considered essential for most citizen science projects regardless of the ecological and social context:

- Project coordinating body – either one organization, one staff person, or a team of people across organizations;
- Outreach and volunteer recruiting and coordination and communication;
- Education and content to support protocols;
- Scientific data quality assurance and quality control – ensuring rigor, validity, reliability of methods;
- Data management, data repository;
- Data analysis and data visualization on websites or in newsletters;
- Technology development and maintenance;
- "Super" volunteers – participants who become leaders, trainers, participate consistently, become sounding boards for the project leaders/coordinators.

These partnerships are often serendipitous and arise through mutual interests, goals, concerns, and/or overlapping audiences/constituents. However, they don't come to fruition or become sustainable without careful design, relationship-building, support and maintenance, and acknowledging and even celebrating the fact that different sectors and organizations can play different and complementary roles that together make a coastal and marine citizen science project effective.

## Who is learning from whom? Learning and knowledge through coastal and marine citizen science

A key area of scholarship and discussion around citizen science participation is about what the participants or volunteers learn about science (i.e. Bonney et al., 2015) and the environment and the local conservation issue by participating. In this book, several chapters describe the intended or unintended outcomes of the project related to science or environmental education, including youth who learn about marine litter problems (Thiel et al., Chapter 6) or intertidal ecosystems (Wasser, Chapter 11), participants of all ages better understanding invasive non-native species and their spread (Sewell and Parr, Chapter 4), coral reef ecology (Cigliano and Ridlon, Chapter 12), and the science and practice of ecological restoration of eelgrass (Disney et al., Chapter 8). However, many participants already HAVE experience with the place, and knowledge of the conservation issue, in some cases local ecological knowledge, and in other cases traditional knowledge built over generations. For example, local knowledge holders in citizen science include people who walk the beach in their daily lives (Parrish et al., Chapter 2; Thiel et al., Chapter 6) and people who see invasive species on the beach or shoreline (Sewell and Parr, Chapter 4). Traditional knowledge holders include fishers and local communities who use and rely on the natural resources and watch ecosystems change over generations (Crane et al., Chapter 10). Given these considerations, our approach to the learning by participants through coastal and marine citizen science should be considered in a much more subtle, nuanced, bi-directional, and frankly respectful way; not all citizen science participants are blank slates who gain all their knowledge of the system through participation in a project. In fact, citizen science can be most effective when it is a two-way exchange of professional science and traditional or local knowledge; a case in point is when Crane et al. (Chapter 10) cite a key phrase from their local scientist partners: "we train you, you train us."

## The nature and nuance of participation in coastal and marine conservation science

The cases in this book have illustrated another set of questions that continually arises in coastal and marine conservation, and in citizen science, with respect to participation: what does participation actually look like, what should it look like, and who benefits? In Chapter 1 we reviewed a number of ways that authors in the field of citizen science have tried to disaggregate and organize the different types of participation in citizen science (Bonney et al., 2009; Shirk et al., 2012; Haklay et al., 2013; Wiggins and Crowston, 2011). Prior to that, development scholars for decades have debated about the nature of participation in decision-making and governance (e.g. Arnstein, 1969), natural resource management (e.g. Child, 1996; Agrawal and Gibson, 2001), and research and monitoring (e.g. Ashby and Sperling, 1995; Murphree and Hulme, 2001). In the end, much of the discussion might boil down to this: participation is about power, and participatory approaches to science must examine what role that people who traditionally have less power actually take on within the given project, and what kind of say they have in that process. In coastal and marine citizen science, those people might be retirees who are not typically involved in seabird research (Parrish et al., Chapter 2), or locals who normally wouldn't be consulted about scientific eelgrass restoration (Disney et al.,

Chapter 8), or fishers in Micronesia who wouldn't traditionally be involved in the science that determines fishing regulations (Crane et al., Chapter 10).

In each of the cases in this book, we've seen variations for many dimensions of participation: for example, very intensive involvement with the science (living with scientists at their field site for weeks for Earthwatch projects) versus projects that may not require intensive understanding of the conservation science (such as projects that ask app users to submit photos of organisms opportunistically); long duration (years of monitoring the same beach monthly) versus short duration (one day of documenting marine trash on a beach visit). Those are just some of the dimensions of participation; others include frequency of involvement, complexity of the tasks, and others. The variation across successful projects illustrates that "participation" in science can be very nuanced and shouldn't be considered a panacea or one-size-fits-all endeavor in any conservation work.

But participation in citizen science is nuanced not only in what people do, but in what they think, knowledge they contribute, and power they have in the project decision-making. Some coastal and marine citizen science projects involve participants in every stage of the research process; they collaboratively develop protocols, contribute extensive local or traditional ecological knowledge vital to the project, and sometimes apply the findings to management like fisheries regulations (Crane et al., Chapter 10; Meyer et al., Chapter 7) and ecological restoration (Disney et al., Chapter 8). Many other projects are structured so that data collection protocols are set by the professional scientists, participants are trained, and they submit data that project leaders aggregate, analyze, and apply (Parrish et al., Chapter 2; Cousins et al., Chapter 3; Sewell and Parr, Chapter 4; Stelle et al., Chapter 5; Thiel et al., Chapter 6; Meyer et al., Chapter 7; Wasser, Chapter 11; Cigliano and Ridlon, Chapter 12); participants don't typically have any voice or involvement in the way the project is designed or data used (though many project leaders revised protocols based on suggestions from participants). And for the most part, that is exactly what participants expect when they volunteer, and many gain numerous benefits like social engagement with friends, connection to their place, and science skills and knowledge – others don't get these benefits and stop participating, which is feedback for project leaders. Contributory, collaborative, co-created, crowdsourcing, data collection, data processing, extreme citizen science projects *all* have strengths and weaknesses with respect to different dimensions of participation, and like the cases in this book, can be drawn on to design projects that suit the audiences, conservation question, and ecosystem context.

So, the questions about the depth or quality of participation in citizen science (Shirk et al., 2012) shouldn't just be about participant satisfaction or enjoyment, but about whether people have equitable access to the projects in the first place, whether the project would benefit from participants' local ecological knowledge, and whether more involvement in the process and decisions of the research would improve the project in reaching socially just conservation goals. In this way, citizen science for coastal and marine conservation again reflects the same considerations that are evolving in the conservation field more broadly, and will continue into the future.

Overall, the chapters in this book provide diverse evidence that citizen science is and will continue to contribute to coastal and marine conservation, and that these important partnerships between scientists and members of the public are only growing in scope and complexity. Each of the partnerships in this book make it clear that while citizen science is not a one-size-fits-all endeavor, each new effort can learn from the myriad others to improve and evaluate data quality, ability to inform policy and resource management, and the participant experience, learning, and overall community benefits from the project. We hope these pages have provided seeds of new ideas for using a citizen science approach to coastal and marine conservation into the future, as well as critiques that inspire all of us to continually re-evaluate and improve the work we are already doing in this area.

## Acknowledgements

We thank the many contributing authors for sharing their work and writing with us for this book, and the many partners we each work with on our own citizen science research and practice. Particularly we want to acknowledge the many, many hours of time, energy, expertise, and enthusiasm of volunteers, scientists, managers and educators that we have witnessed over years of working in this area, as it is their knowledge and passion that keep us moving forward as a field.

## Web resources

1  www.reef.org.
2  www.monarchlab.org/mlmp.

## Literature cited

Agrawal, A., and Gibson, C.C. (2001). The role of community in natural resource conservation. In *Communities and the Environment: Ethnicity, Gender, and the State in Community-based Conservation*. New Brunswick, NJ: Rutgers University Press.

Arnstein, S.R. (1969). A ladder of citizen participation. Journal of the American Institute of planners, 35(4), 216–224.

Ashby, J.A., and Sperling, L. (1995). Institutionalizing participatory, client-driven research and technology development in agriculture. *Development and Change*, 26(4), 753–770.

Ballard, H., Dixon, C.G. and Harris, E.M. (2017). Youth-focused citizen science: Examining the role of environmental science learning and agency for conservation. *Biological Conservation*, 208, 65–75.

Berkes, F., Berkes, M.K., and Fast, H. (2007). Collaborative integrated management in Canada's north: The role of local and traditional knowledge and community-based monitoring. *Coastal Management*, 35(1), 143–162.

Bonney, R., Ballard, H.L., Jordan, R., McCallie, E., Phillips, T., Shirk, J., and Wilderman, C.C. (2009). Public participation in scientific research: Defining the field and assessing its potential for informal science education. A CAISE Inquiry Group Report.

Bonney, R., Phillips, T.B., Ballard, H.L., and Enck, J.W. (2016). Can citizen science enhance public understanding of science? *Public Understanding of Science*, 25(1), 2–16.

Bonney, R., Cooper, C., and Ballard, H. (2016). The theory and practice of citizen science: Launching a new journal. *Citizen Science: Theory and Practice*, 1(1).

Bonney, R., Shirk, J.L., Phillips, T.B., Wiggins, A., Ballard, H.L., Miller-Rushing, A.J., and Parrish, J.K. (2014). Next steps for citizen science. *Science*, 343(6178), 1436–1437.

Burgess, H., DeBey, L., Froehlich, H., Schmidt, N., Theobald, E., Ettinger, A., HilleRisLambers, J., Tewksbury, J., and Parrish, J. (2017). The science of citizen science: Exploring barriers to use as a primary research tool. *Biological Conservation*, 208, 113–120. doi:10.1016/j. biocon.2016.05.014.

Child, G. (1996). The role of community-based wild resource management in Zimbabwe. *Biodiversity and Conservation*, 5(3), 355–367.

Cigliano, J., Bauer, A., Draheim, M., Foley, M., Lundquist, C., McCarthy, J., Patterson, K., Wright, A., and Parsons, E. (2016). The Kraken in the aquarium: Questions that urgently need to be addressed in order to advance marine conservation. *Frontiers in Marine Science*, 3(174).

Cigliano, J.A., Meyer, R., Ballard, H.L., Freitag, A., Phillips, T.B., and Wasser, A. (2015). Making marine and coastal citizen science matter. *Ocean & Coastal Management*, 115, 77–87.

Corson, T. (2004). *The Secret Life of Lobsters: How Fishermen and Scientists Are Unraveling the Mysteries of Our Favorite Crustacean*. New York: HarperCollins.

Earle, S.A. (2009). *The World is Blue: How our Fate and the Oceans are One*. Washington, D.C.: National Geographic Books.

Edgar, G., Bates, A., Bird, T., Jones, A., Kininmonth, S., Stuart-Smith, R., and Webb, T. (2016). New approaches to marine conservation through the scaling up of ecological data. *Annual Review of Marine Science*, 8(1), 435–461.

Ellul, C., Gupta, S., Haklay, M.M., and Bryson, K. (2013). A platform for location based app development for citizen science and community mapping. In *Progress in Location-Based Services*, pp. 71–90. Berlin: Springer.

Haklay, M. (2013). Citizen science and volunteered geographic information: Overview and typology of participation. In *Crowdsourcing Geographic Knowledge: Volunteered Geographic Information (VGI) in Theory and Practice*, 105–122. Berlin: Springer.

Haywood, B.K. (2014). A "sense of place" in public participation in scientific research. *Science education*, 98(1), 64–83.

Hobbs, S.J., and White, P.C.L. (2012). Motivations and barriers in relation to community participation in biodiversity recording. *Journal of Nature Conservation*, 20(6), 364–373. http:// dx.doi.org/10.1016/j.jnc.2012.08.002.

Hulme, D., and Murphree, M. (2001). *African Wildlife and Livelihoods: The Promise and Performance of Community Conservation*. Oxford, UK: James Currey.

Israel, B.A., Eng, E., Schulz, A.J., and Parker, E.A. (Eds.). (2013). *Methods in Community-Based Participatory Research for Health*. 2nd ed. San Francisco: Jossey-Bass.

Johnson, M.F., Hannah, C., Acton, L., Popovici, R., Karanth, K.K., and Weinthal, E. (2014). Network environmentalism: Citizen scientists as agents for environmental advocacy. *Global Environmental Change*, 29, 235–245.

Kudryavtsev, A., Stedman, R.C., and Krasny, M.E. (2012). Sense of place in environmental education. *Environmental Education Research*, 18(2), 229–250.

McCay, B.J., and Acheson, J.M. (Eds.). (1990). *The Question of the Commons: The Culture and Ecology of Communal Resources*. Tucson, AZ: University of Arizona Press.

McKinley, D., Miller-Rushing, A.J., Ballard, H., Bonney, R., Brown, H., Cook-Pattone, S.C., Evans, D.M., French, R.A., Parrish, J.K., Phillips, T.B., Ryan, S.F., Shanley, L.A., Shirk, J.L.,

Stepenuck, K.F., Weltzink, J.F., Wiggins, A., Boyle, O.D., Briggs, R.D., Chapin, S.F., III, Hewitt, D.A., Preuss, P.A., and Soukup, M.A. (2017). Citizen science can improve conservation science, natural resource management, and environmental protection. *Biological Conservation*, 208, 15–28. http://dx.doi.org/10.1016/j.biocon.2016.05.015.

Newman, G., Chandler, M., Clyde, M., McGreavy, B., Haklay, M., Ballard, H., Gray, S., Scarpino, R., Hauptfeld, R., Mellor, D., and Gallo, J. (2017). Leveraging the power of place in citizen science for effective conservation decision making. *Biological Conservation*, 208, 55–64. http://doi.org/10.1016/j.biocon.2016.07.019.

Newman, G., Wiggins, A., Crall, A., Graham, E., Newman, S., and Crowston, K. (2012). The future of citizen science: Emerging technologies and shifting paradigms. *Frontiers in Ecology and the Environment*, 10(6), 298–304.

Nichols, W.J. (2014). *Blue Mind: The Surprising Science That Shows How Being Near, in, on, or Under Water Can Make You Happier, Healthier, More Connected, and Better at What You Do.* New York: Little, Brown.

Obura, D.O., Wells, S., Church, J., and Horrill, C. (2002). Monitoring of fish and fish catches by local fishermen in Kenya and Tanzania. *Marine and Freshwater Research*, 53(2), 215–222.

Parsons, E., Favaro, B., Aguirre, A., Bauer, A., Blight, L., Cigliano, J., Coleman, M., Côté, I., Draheim, M., Fletcher, S., Foley, M., Jefferson, R., Jones, M., Kelaher, B., Lundquist, C., Mccarthy, J., Nelson, A., Patterson, K., Walsh, L., Wright, A., and Sutherland, W. (2014). Seventy-one important questions for the conservation of marine biodiversity. *Conservation Biology*, 28(5), 1206–1214.

Shirk, J., Ballard, H., Wilderman, C., Phillips, T., Wiggins, A., Jordan, R., McCallie, E., Minarchek, M., Lewenstein, B., Krasny, M., and Bonney, R. (2012). Public participation in scientific research: A framework for deliberate design. *Ecology and Society*, 17(2).

Soleri, D., Long, J., Ramirez-Andreotta, M., Eitemiller, R., and Pandya, R. (2016). Finding pathways to more equitable and meaningful public-scientist partnerships. *Citizen Science: Theory and Practice*, 1(1).

Theobald, E., Ettinger, A., Burgess, H., DeBey, L., Schmidt, N., Froehlich, H., Wagner, C., HilleRisLambers, J., Tewksbury, J., Harsch, M., and Parrish, J. (2015). Global change and local solutions: Tapping the unrealized potential of citizen science for biodiversity research. *Biological Conservation*, 181, 236–244.

West, S., and Pateman, R. (2016). Recruiting and retaining participants in citizen science: What can be learned from the volunteering literature? *Citizen Science: Theory and Practice*, 1(2), 15.

Wiggins, A., and Crowston, K. (2011). From conservation to crowdsourcing: A typology of citizen science. In *Proceedings of the 44th Hawaii International Conference on System Sciences (HICSS), Koloa, Hawaii*, 1–10.

# INDEX